尾田栄一郎

I'm going to sing a mystery song I sang with my friends in middle school. "The pig...is walking...along the road. (Bunchaccha... x2) "There's a car coming head-on. (Bunchaccha x2) "The pig doesn't want to die... "So it avoids the car." (Bunchaccha x2) And now, here's volume 34!

-Eiichiro Oda, 2004

Eiichiro Oda began his manga career at the age of 17, when his one-shot cowboy manga **Wanted!** won second place in the coveted Tezuka manga awards. Oda went on to work as an assistant to some of the biggest manga artists in the industry, including Nobuhiro Watsuki, before winning the Hop Step Award for new artists. His pirate adventure **One Piece**, which debuted in **Weekly Shonen Jump** in 1997, quickly became one of the most popular manga in Japan.

ONE PIECE VOL. 34
WATER SEVEN PART 3

SHONEN JUMP Manga Edition

STORY AND ART BY EIICHIRO ODA

English Adaptation/Megan Bates
Translation/JN Productions
Touch-up Art & Lettering/Susan Daigle-Leach
Design/Sean Lee
Supervising Editor/Yuki Murashige
Editor/Alexis Kirsch

Published by VIZ Media, LLC
P.O. Box 77010
San Francisco, CA 94107

10 9 8 7 6 5 4 3 2
First printing, March 2010
Second printing, June 2010

www.viz.com

THE WORLD'S
MOST POPULAR MANGA
www.shonenjump.com

SHONEN JUMP MANGA

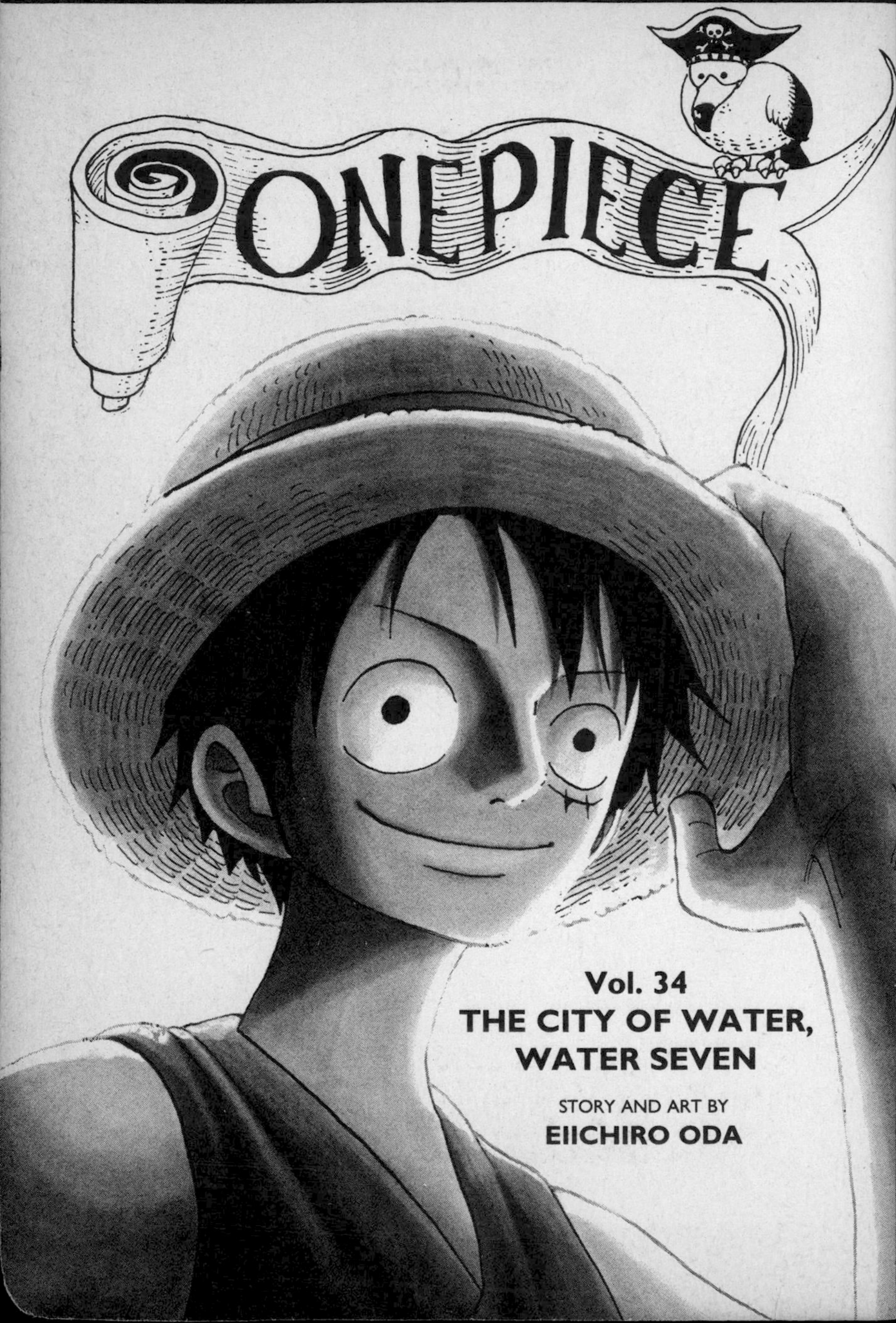
ONE PIECE

Vol. 34
THE CITY OF WATER, WATER SEVEN

STORY AND ART BY
EIICHIRO ODA

Tonjit

Sherry

The Straw Hats

Boundlessly optimistic and able to stretch like rubber, he is determined to become King of the Pirates.

Monkey D. Luffy

A former bounty hunter and master of the "three-sword" style. He aspires to be the world's greatest swordsman.

Roronoa Zolo

A thief who specializes in robbing pirates. Nami hates pirates, but Luffy convinced her to be his navigator.

Nami

A village boy with a talent for telling tall tales. His father, Yasopp, is a member of Shanks's crew.

Usopp

The big-hearted cook (and ladies' man) whose dream is to find the legendary sea, the "All Blue."

Sanji

A blue-nosed man-reindeer and the ship's doctor.

Tony Tony Chopper

A mysterious woman in search of the Ponegliff on which true history is recorded.

Nico Robin

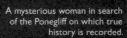

THE STORY OF ONE PIECE

Volume 34

Monkey D. Luffy started out as just a kid with a dream—to become the greatest pirate in history! Stirred by the tales of pirate "Red-Haired" Shanks, Luffy vowed to become a pirate himself. That was before the enchanted Devil Fruit gave Luffy the power to stretch like rubber, at the cost of being unable to swim—a serious handicap for an aspiring sea dog. Undeterred, Luffy set out to sea and recruited some crewmates—master swordsman Zolo; treasure-hunting thief Nami; lying sharpshooter Usopp; the high-kicking chef Sanji; Chopper, the walkin' talkin' reindeer doctor; and Robin, the cool and crafty archaeologist.

Luffy and his crew arrive in the Grand Line and then head on to Skypiea, which they heard about on Jaya. Upon investigating, they discover that the legendary city of El Dorado lies hidden in Skypiea, and they begin to search for the gold. However, they become embroiled in the battle between Kami Eneru, who rules this land, and the indigenous people called the Shandians, and a quest for survival begins! One by one, the warriors fall in the face of Eneru's amazing power. Luffy challenges Eneru, who is after the golden bell. This bell had survived for 400 years and symbolized the friendship between Noland the Liar and the great Shandoran warrior Kalgara. After emerging victorious, Luffy and his crew ring the golden bell triumphantly and depart Skypiea. From the sky, they head back to solid ground and begin looking for a ship's carpenter for the *Merry Go*, which is badly in need of repairs. On an island, they encounter the Foxy Pirates and are challenged to a frightening game called the Davy Back Fight. The three-game contest is tied at one game apiece, and the final match begins. The two captains carry the fate of their crew on their shoulders as they start to fight!! Foxy uses his Slow-Slow Beam and puts Luffy in a precarious position... is it the end for Luffy?!

The Foxy Pirates

This crew's motto is "We take what we want!"

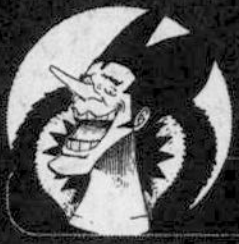

Captain

Foxy the Silver Fox

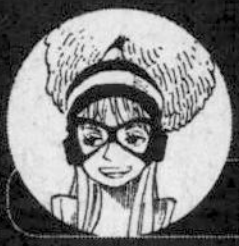

Warrior

Porche

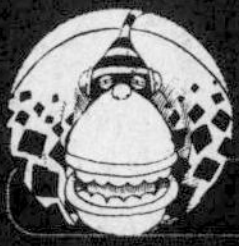

Warrior

Hamburg

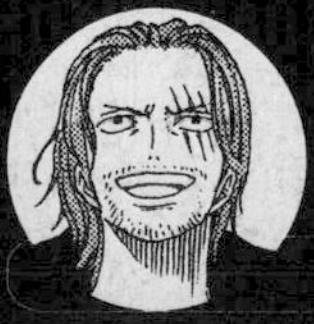

A pirate that Luffy idolizes. Shanks gave Luffy his trademark straw hat.

"Red-Haired" Shanks

Vol. 34
The City of Water, Water Seven

CONTENTS

Chapter 317: K.O.	8
Chapter 318: Closure	31
Chapter 319: Admiral Aokiji of the Navy Headquarters	51
Chapter 320: Ultimate Military Force	71
Chapter 321: One-on-One	91
Chapter 322: Puffing Tom	111
Chapter 323: The City of Water, Water Seven	131
Chapter 324: Adventures in the City on the Water	151
Chapter 325: The Franky Family	171
Chapter 326: Mr. Iceberg	191
Chapter 327: Shipbuilding Island, Repair Dock No. 1	208

Chapter 317: K.O.

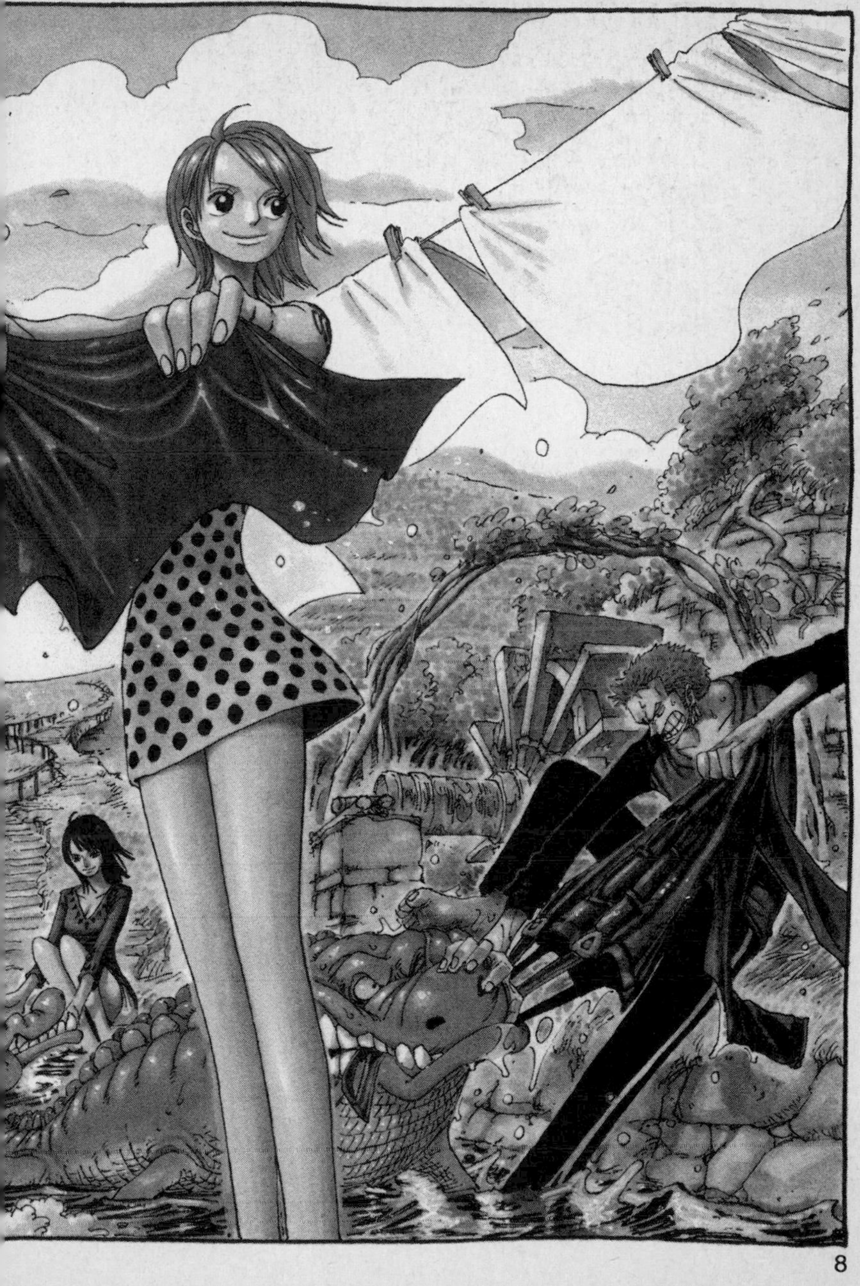

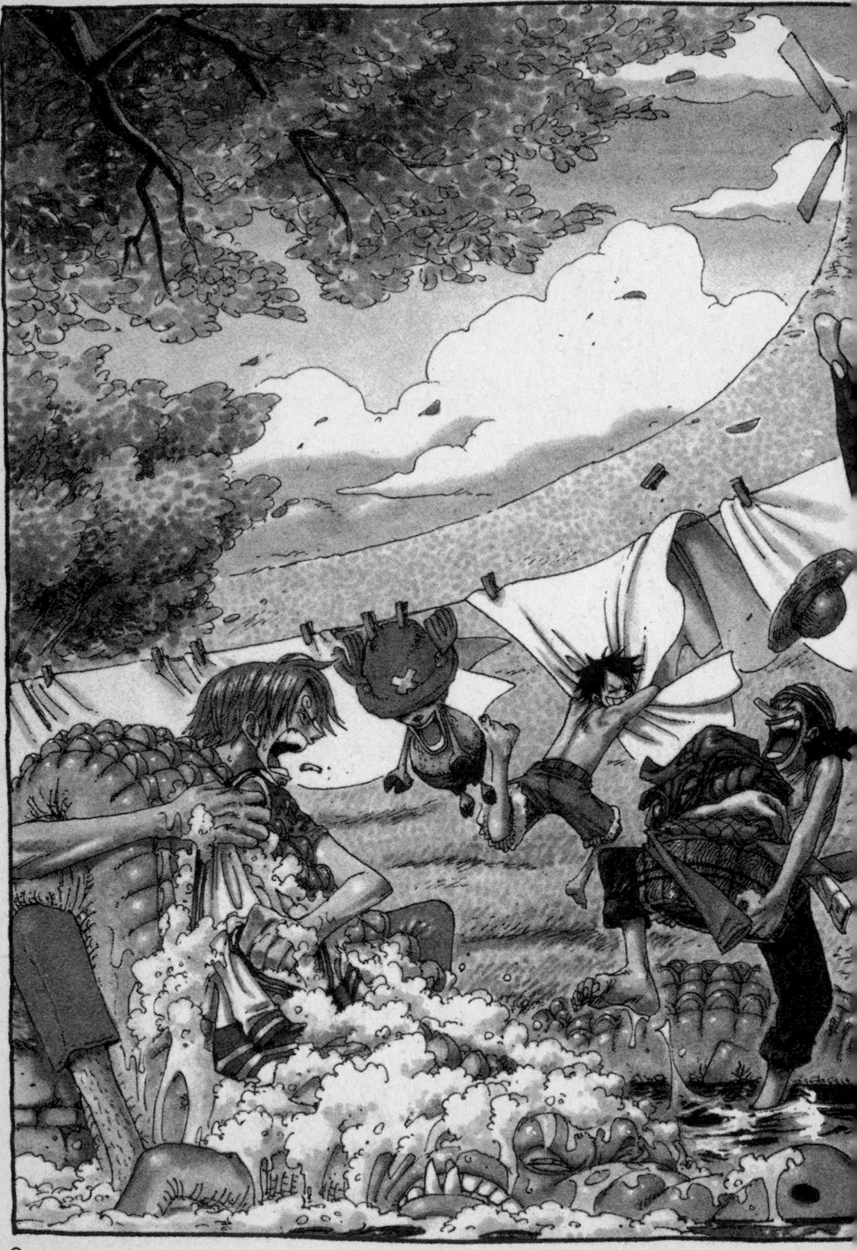

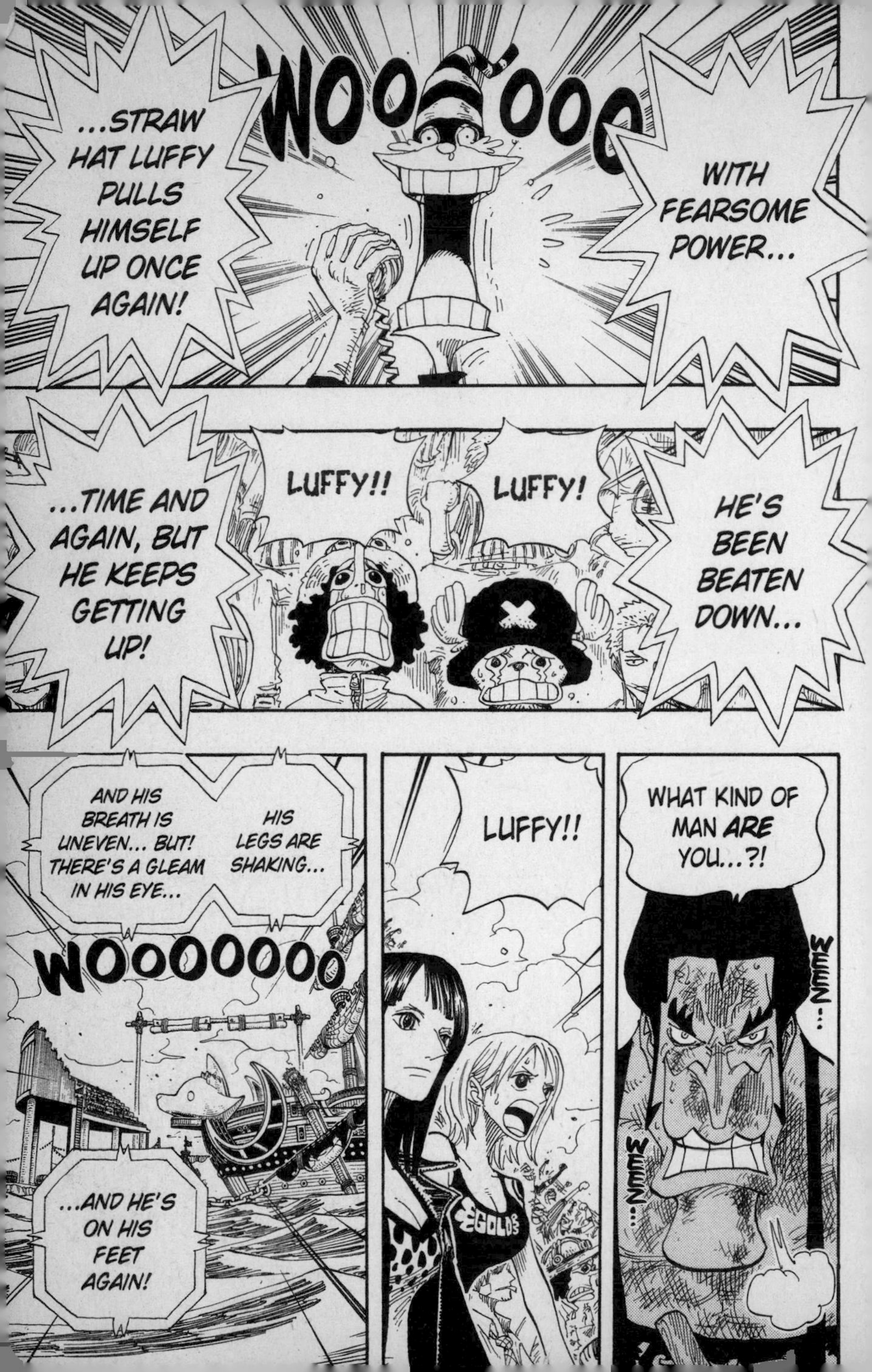
WITH FEARSOME POWER...
WOOOOOO
...STRAW HAT LUFFY PULLS HIMSELF UP ONCE AGAIN!
HE'S BEEN BEATEN DOWN...
LUFFY!
LUFFY!!
...TIME AND AGAIN, BUT HE KEEPS GETTING UP!
WHAT KIND OF MAN ARE YOU...?!
WEEZ...
WEEZ...
LUFFY!!
HIS LEGS ARE SHAKING...
AND HIS BREATH IS UNEVEN... BUT! THERE'S A GLEAM IN HIS EYE...
WOOOOOOO
...AND HE'S ON HIS FEET AGAIN!

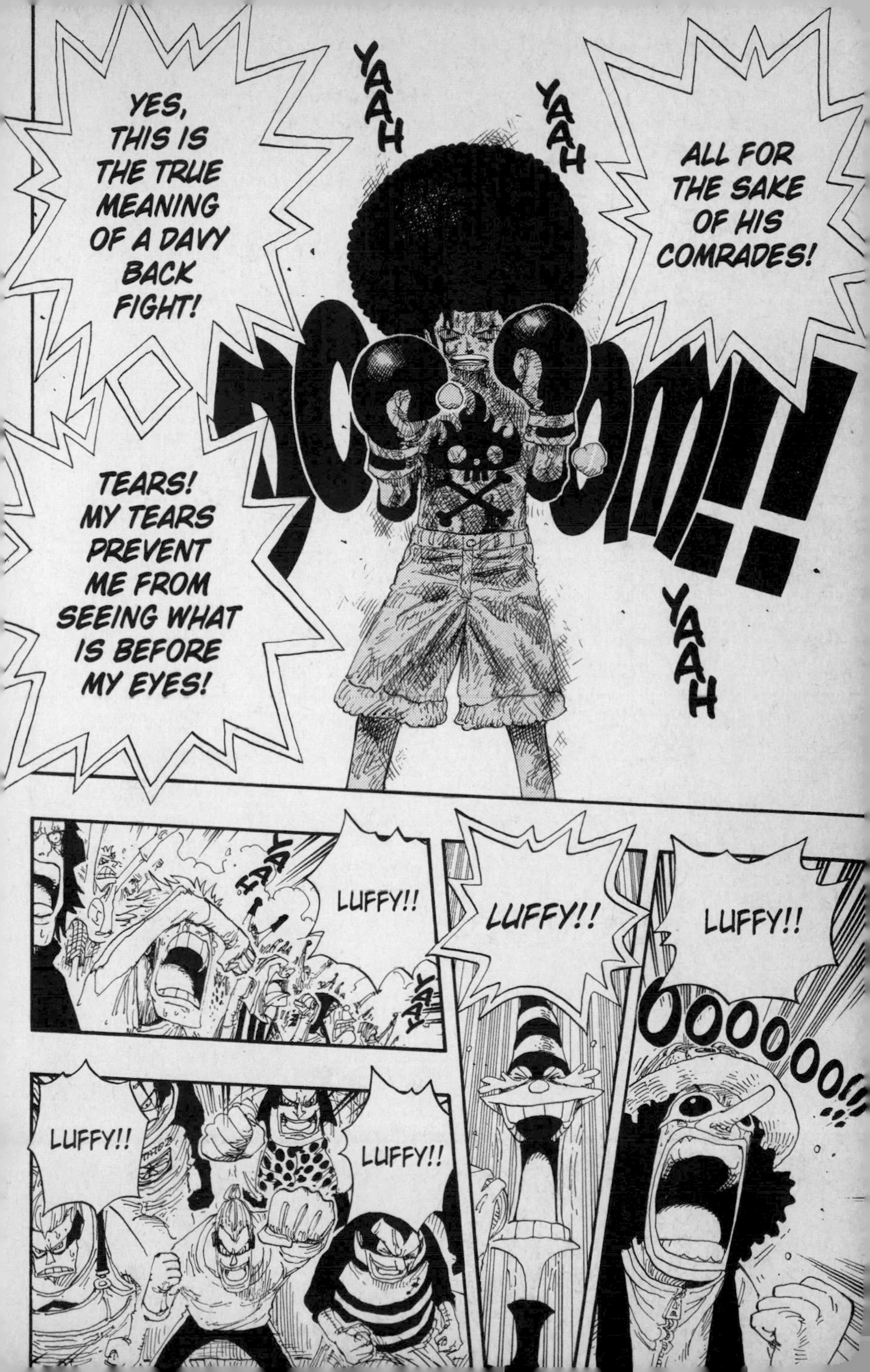
ALL FOR THE SAKE OF HIS COMRADES!
YAAAH
YAAAH
YES, THIS IS THE TRUE MEANING OF A DAVY BACK FIGHT!
DOOOM!!
YAAAH
TEARS! MY TEARS PREVENT ME FROM SEEING WHAT IS BEFORE MY EYES!
LUFFY!!
OOOOOOO!!!
LUFFY!!
LUFFY!!
YAAAH
LUFFY!!
LUFFY!!

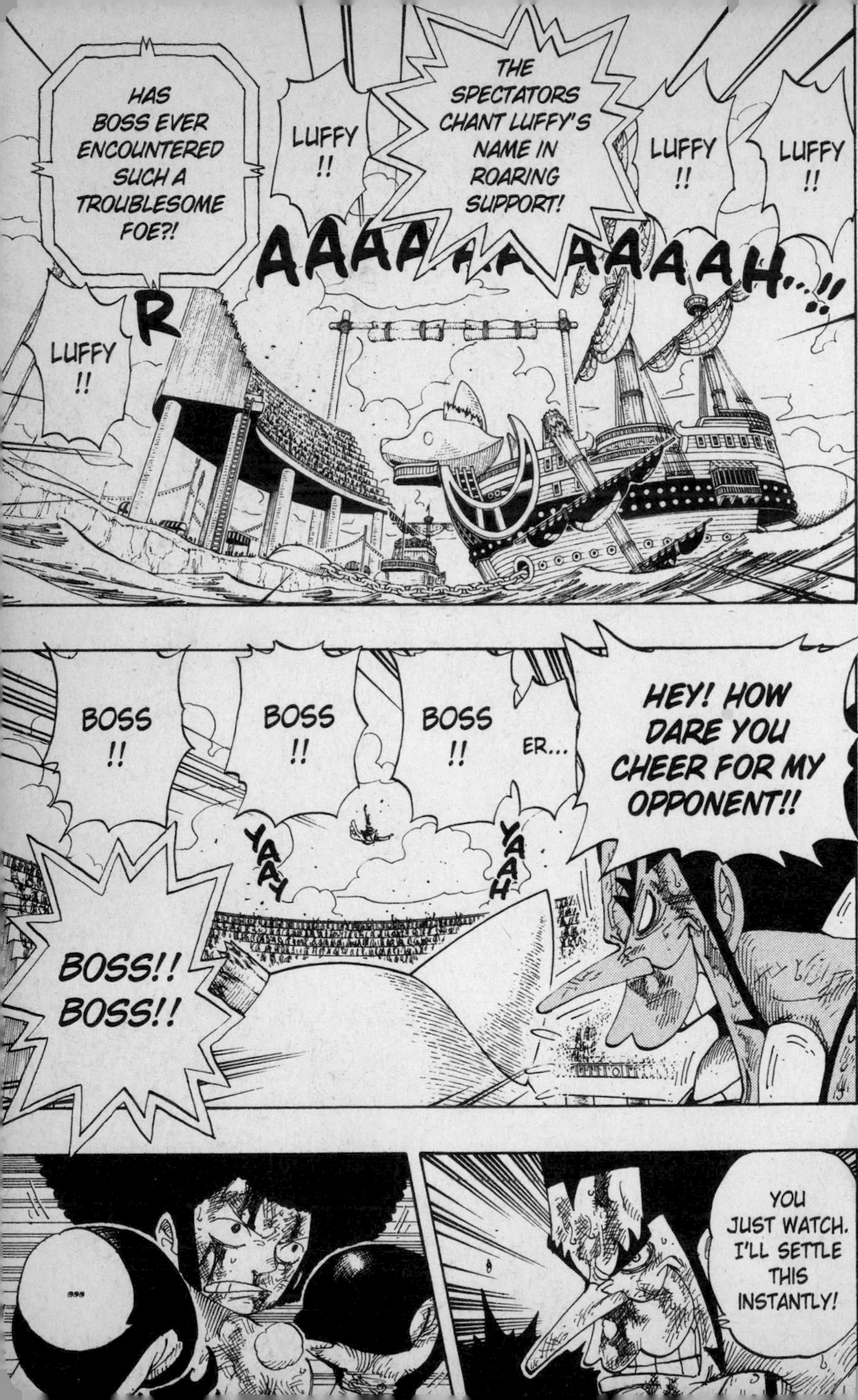
LUFFY!!
LUFFY!!
THE SPECTATORS CHANT LUFFY'S NAME IN ROARING SUPPORT!
LUFFY!!
HAS BOSS EVER ENCOUNTERED SUCH A TROUBLESOME FOE?!
AAAAAAAAAAH...!!
R
LUFFY!!
HEY! HOW DARE YOU CHEER FOR MY OPPONENT!!
ER...
BOSS!!
BOSS!!
BOSS!!
YAAH
YAAH
BOSS!! BOSS!!
YOU JUST WATCH. I'LL SETTLE THIS INSTANTLY!
...

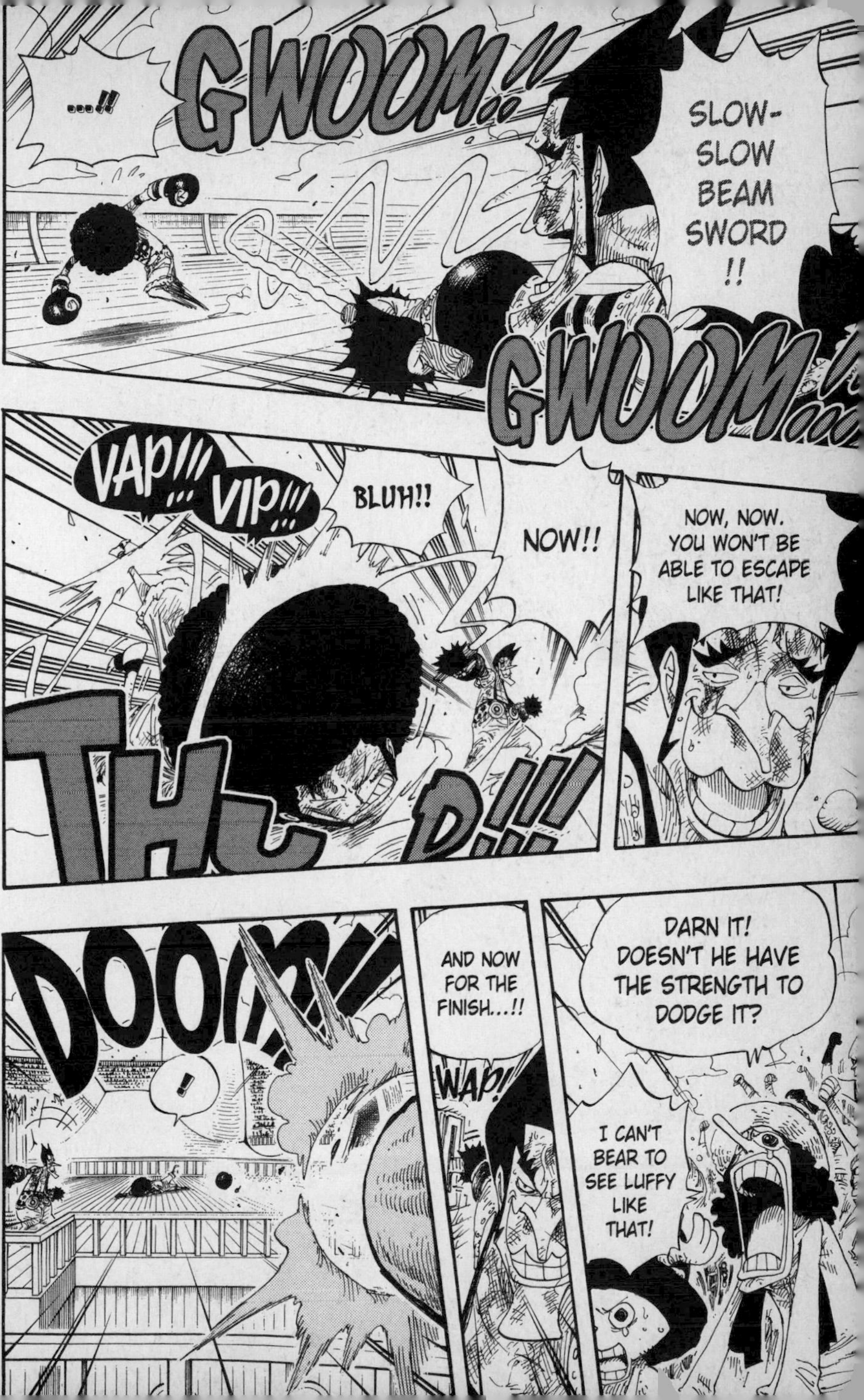
SLOW-SLOW BEAM SWORD!!
GWOOM!!
...!!
GWOOM...!!
NOW, NOW. YOU WON'T BE ABLE TO ESCAPE LIKE THAT!
NOW!!
BLUH!!
VIP!!!
VAP!!!
DARN IT! DOESN'T HE HAVE THE STRENGTH TO DODGE IT?
I CAN'T BEAR TO SEE LUFFY LIKE THAT!
AND NOW FOR THE FINISH...!!
WAP!
!

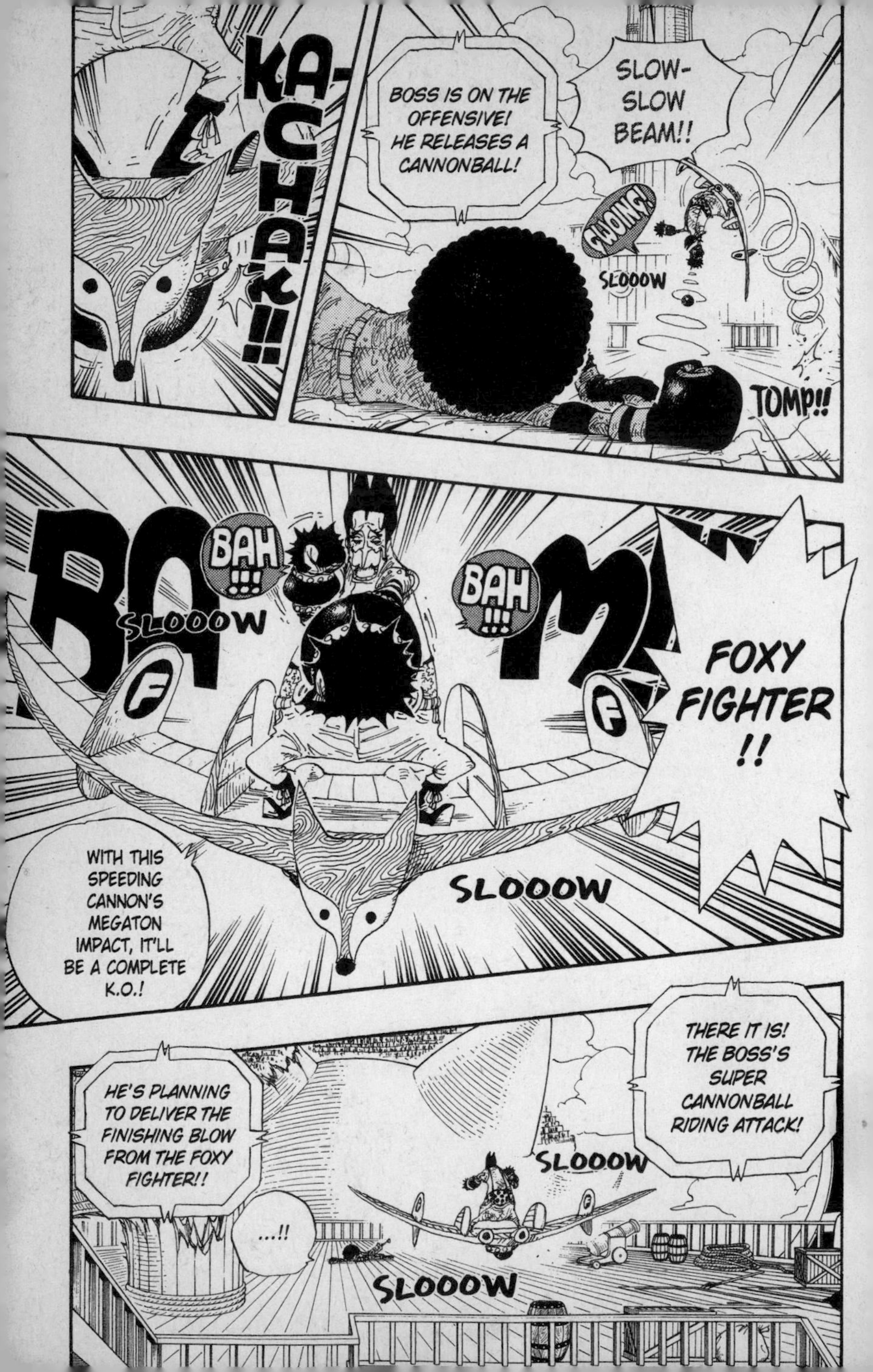
SLOW-SLOW BEAM!!
BOSS IS ON THE OFFENSIVE! HE RELEASES A CANNONBALL!
SWOING!
SLOOOW
TOMP!!
KA-CHAK!!
BAM
BAH!!!
BAH!!!
SLOOOW
FOXY FIGHTER!!
SLOOOW
WITH THIS SPEEDING CANNON'S MEGATON IMPACT, IT'LL BE A COMPLETE K.O.!
THERE IT IS! THE BOSS'S SUPER CANNONBALL RIDING ATTACK!
SLOOOW
HE'S PLANNING TO DELIVER THE FINISHING BLOW FROM THE FOXY FIGHTER!!
...!!
SLOOOW

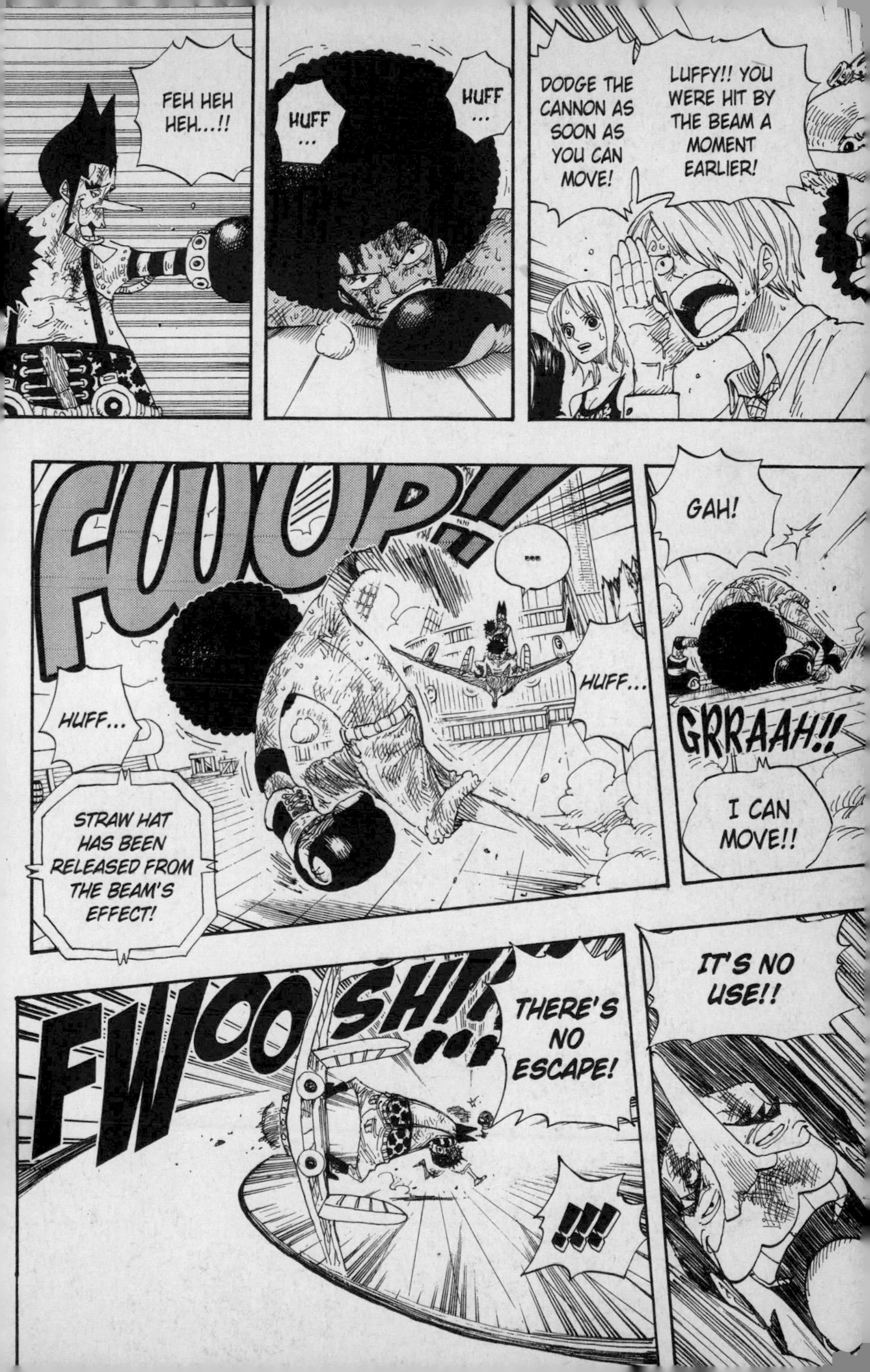
LUFFY!! YOU WERE HIT BY THE BEAM A MOMENT EARLIER!
DODGE THE CANNON AS SOON AS YOU CAN MOVE!
HUFF ...
HUFF ...
FEH HEH HEH...!!
GAH!
GRRAAH!!
I CAN MOVE!!
FUUUP!!
...
HUFF...
HUFF...
STRAW HAT HAS BEEN RELEASED FROM THE BEAM'S EFFECT!
IT'S NO USE!!
FWOOSH!!
THERE'S NO ESCAPE!
!!!

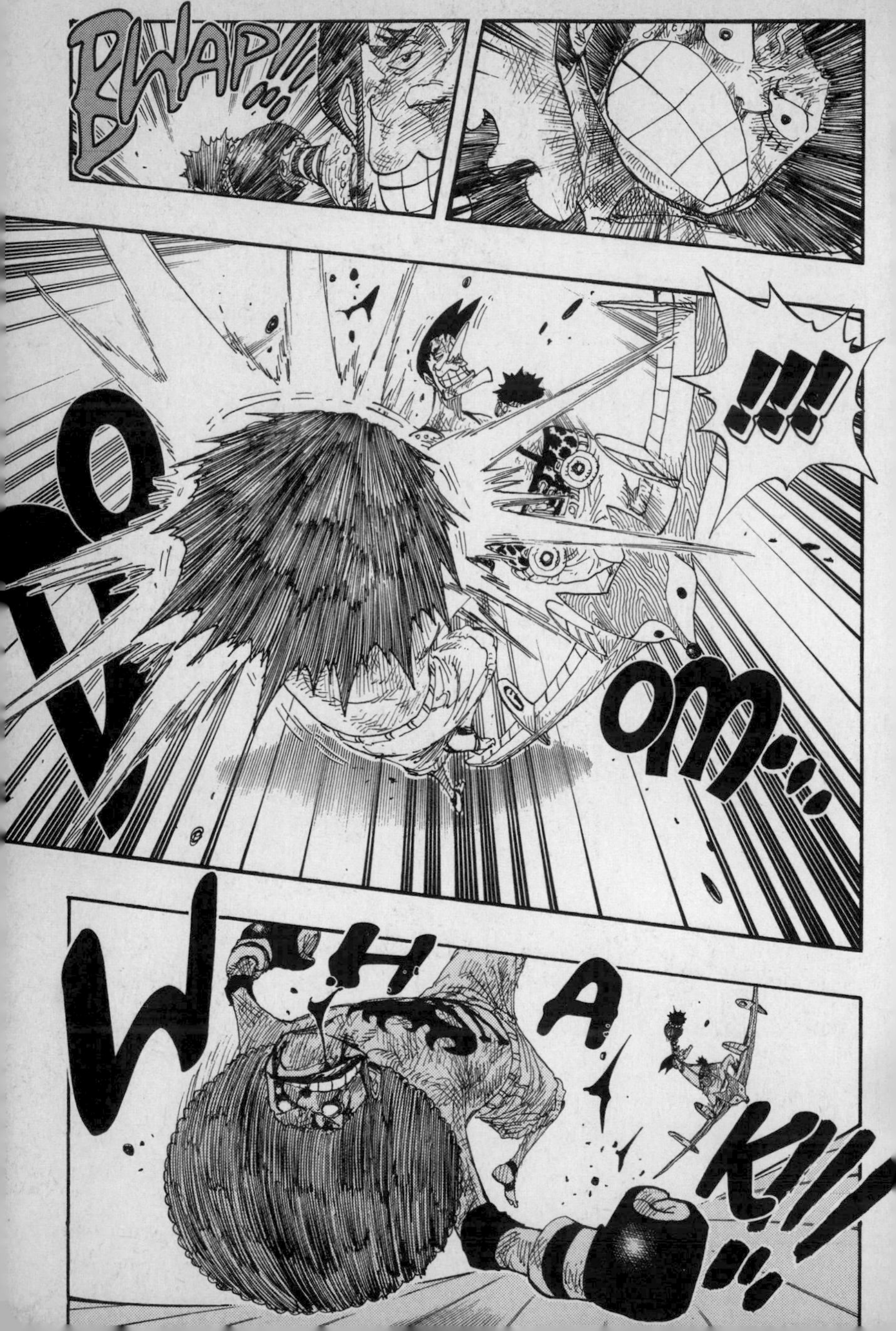
BWAP!!
!!!
DO
OM!!
WHAK!!

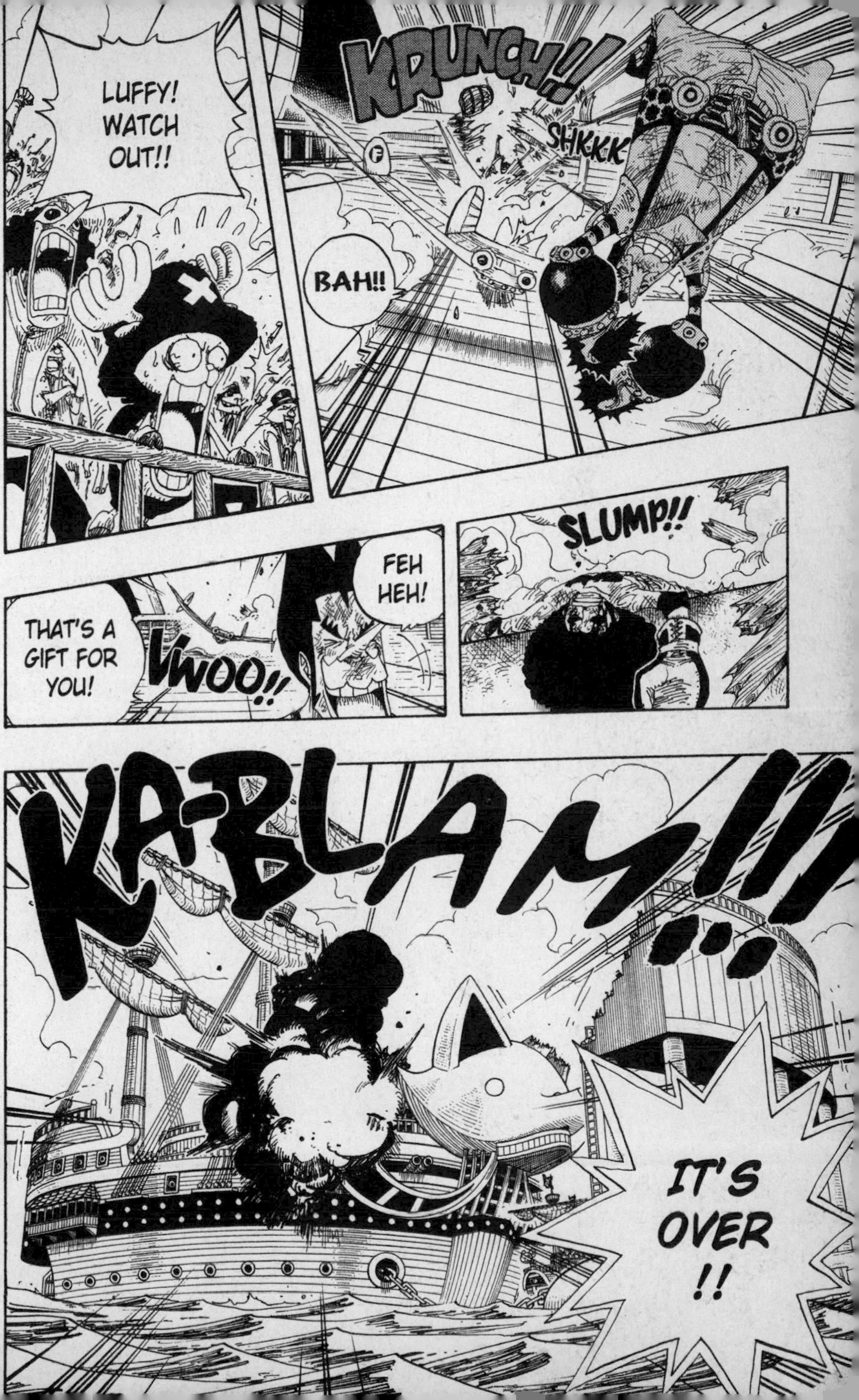
KRUNCH!!
SHKKK
BAH!!
LUFFY! WATCH OUT!!
SLUMP!!
FEH HEH!
THAT'S A GIFT FOR YOU!
VWOO!!
KA-BLAM!!!
IT'S OVER!!

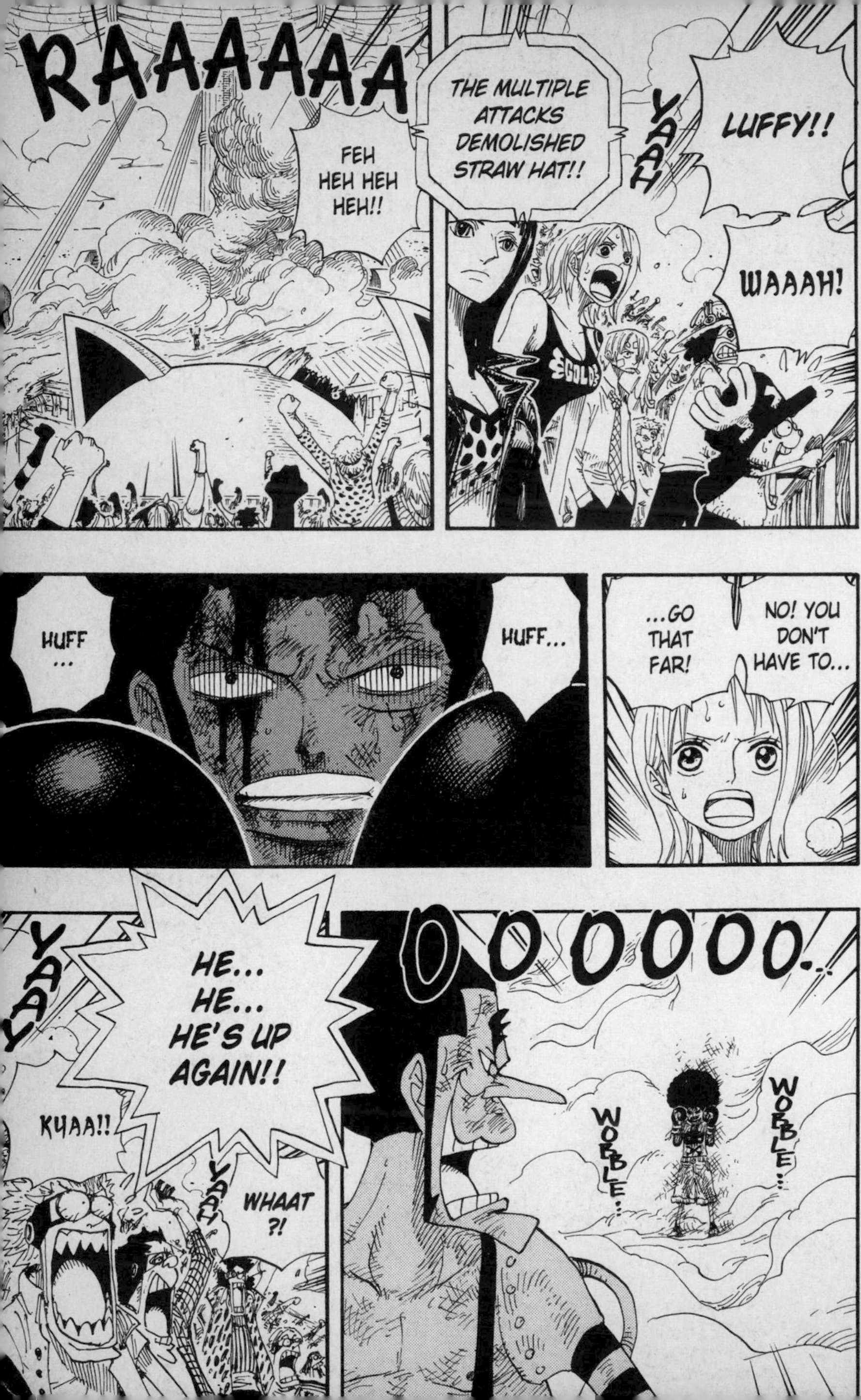
LUFFY!!
YAAAH
THE MULTIPLE ATTACKS DEMOLISHED STRAW HAT!!
WAAAH!
RAAAAAA
FEH HEH HEH HEH!!
NO! YOU DON'T HAVE TO...
...GO THAT FAR!
HUFF...
HUFF...
OOOOOO...
WOBBLE...
WOBBLE...
YAAAY
HE... HE... HE'S UP AGAIN!!
KYAA!!
YAAAH
WHAAT?!

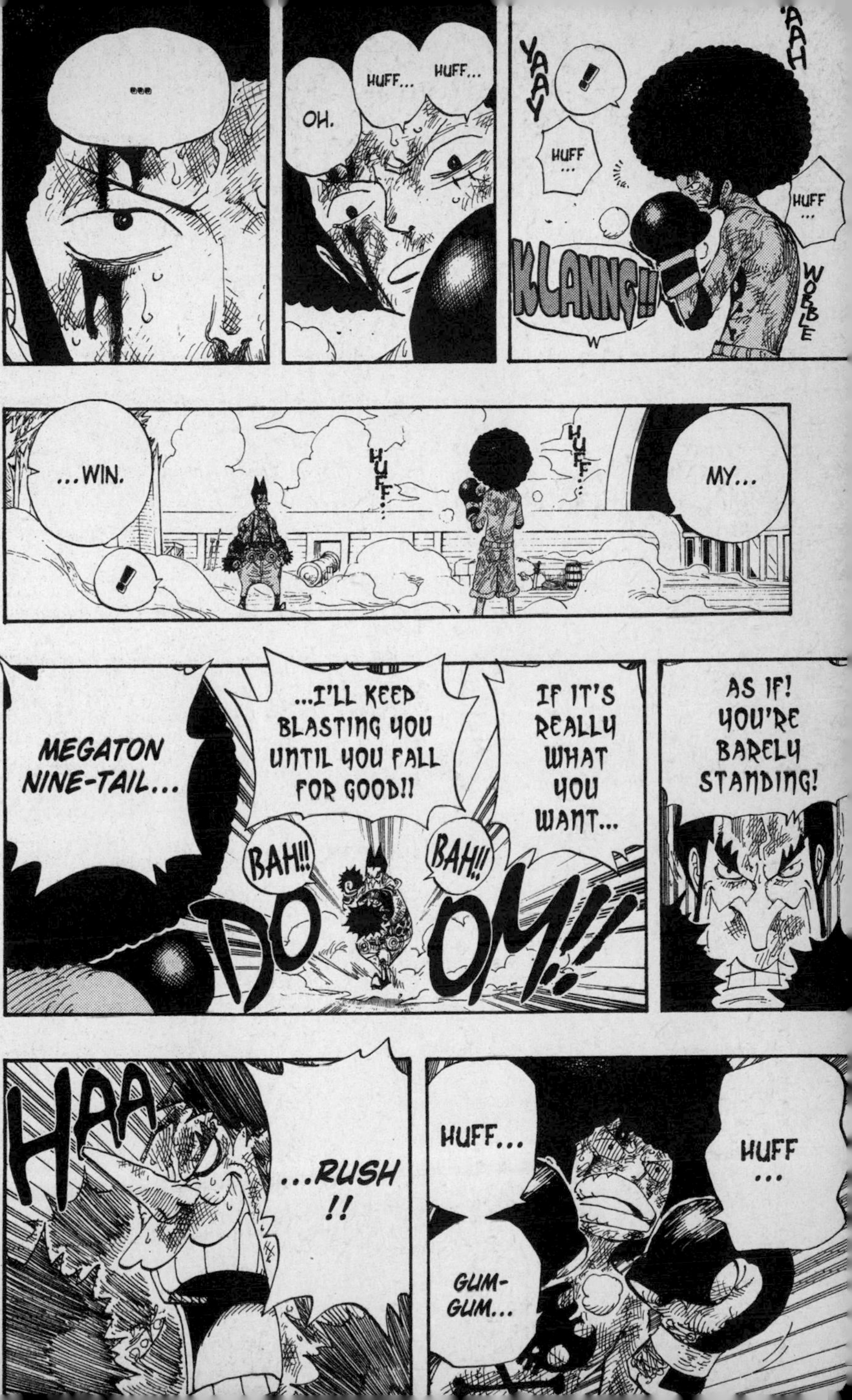
'AAH
YAAAY
!
HUFF ...
HUFF ...
KLANNG!!
WOBBLE
HUFF...
HUFF...
OH.
...
MY...
HUFF...
HUFF...
...WIN.
!
AS IF! YOU'RE BARELY STANDING!
IF IT'S REALLY WHAT YOU WANT...
...I'LL KEEP BLASTING YOU UNTIL YOU FALL FOR GOOD!!
BAH!!
BAH!!
DOOM!!
MEGATON NINE-TAIL...
HUFF ...
HUFF...
GUM-GUM...
...RUSH !!
HAA

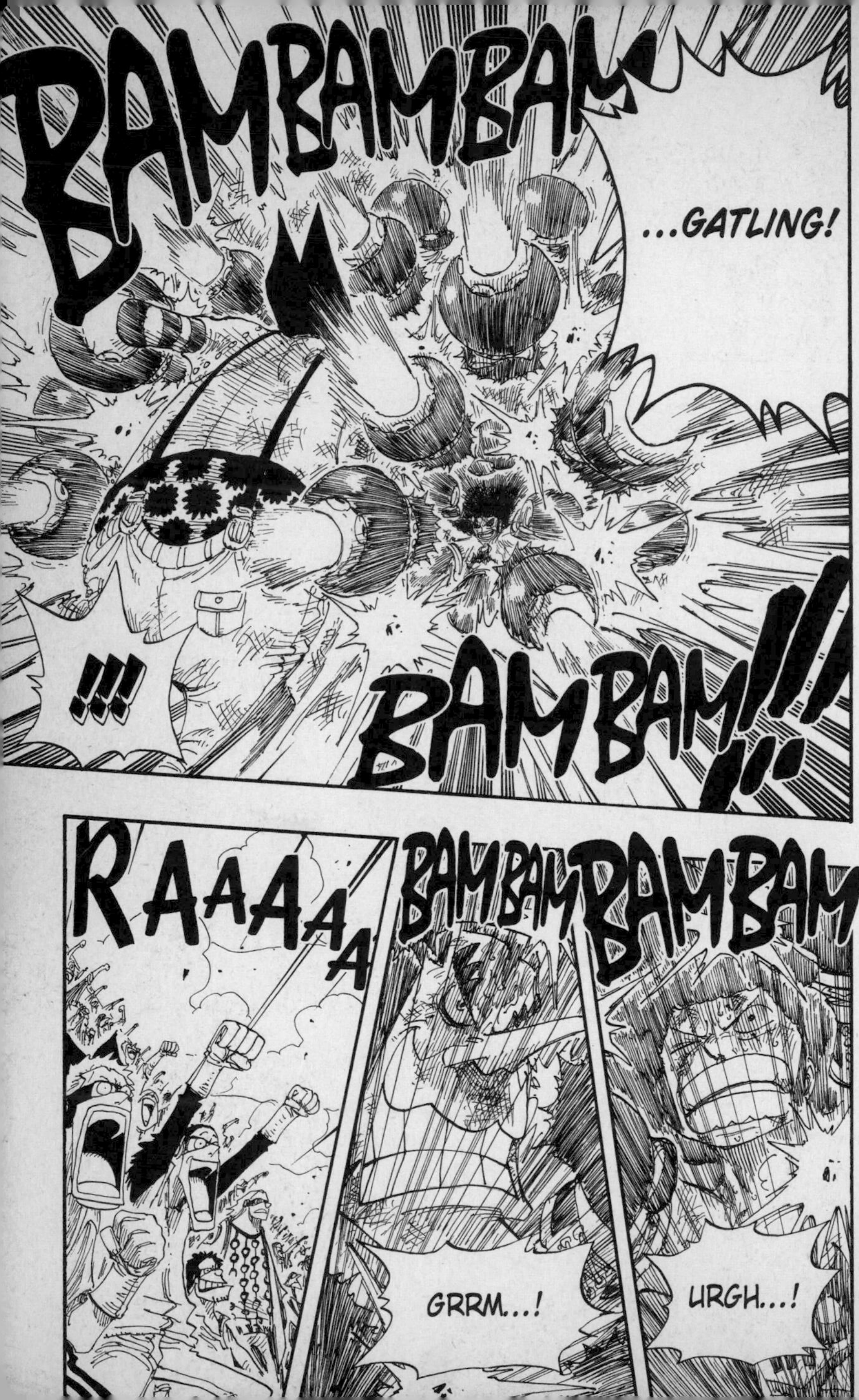

...GATLING!
BAMBAMBAM
BAMBAM!!
!!!
BAMBAM
URGH...!
BAMBAM
GRRM...!
RAAAAA

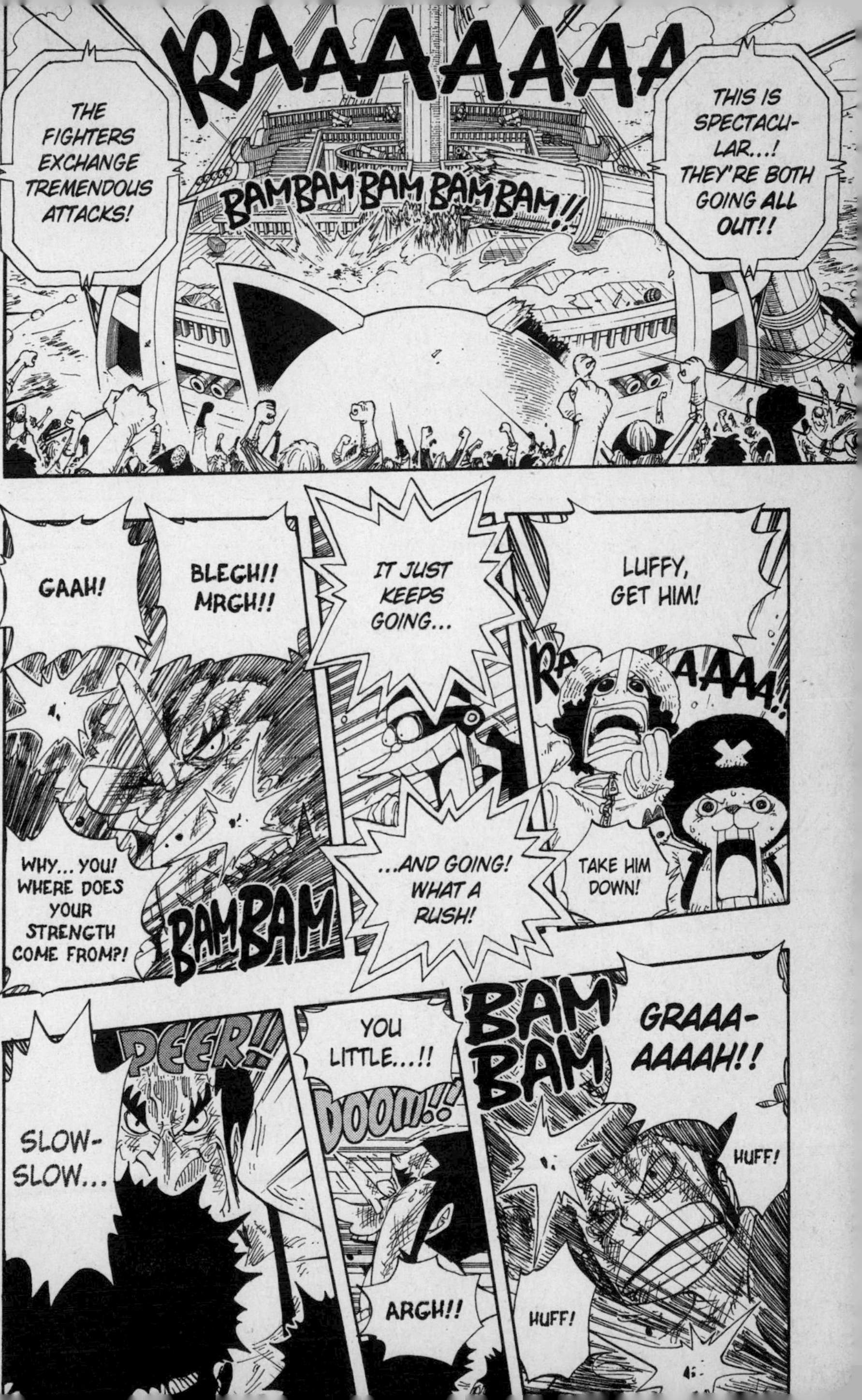
RAAAAAAA
THIS IS SPECTACULAR...! THEY'RE BOTH GOING ALL OUT!!
THE FIGHTERS EXCHANGE TREMENDOUS ATTACKS!
BAMBAM BAM BAMBAM BAM!!
LUFFY, GET HIM!
RAAAAA!!
TAKE HIM DOWN!
IT JUST KEEPS GOING...
...AND GOING! WHAT A RUSH!
BLEGH!! MRGH!!
GAAH!
WHY... YOU! WHERE DOES YOUR STRENGTH COME FROM?!
BAMBAM
GRAAAAAAAH!!
BAM BAM
HUFF!
HUFF!
YOU LITTLE...!!
DOOM!!
ARGH!!
PEER!!
SLOW-SLOW...

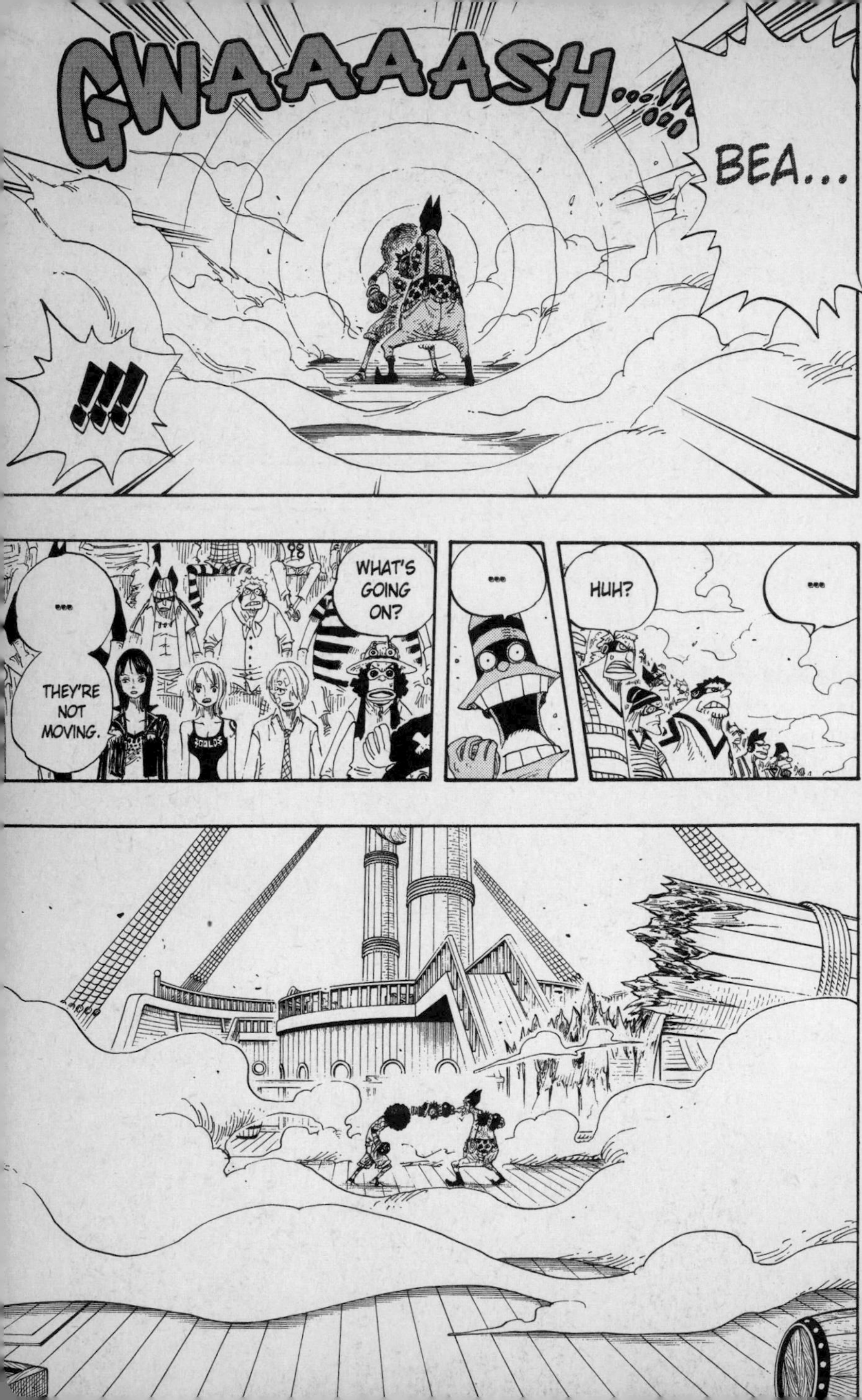
GWAAAASH...
BEA...
!!!
...
HUH?
...
WHAT'S GOING ON?
...
THEY'RE NOT MOVING.

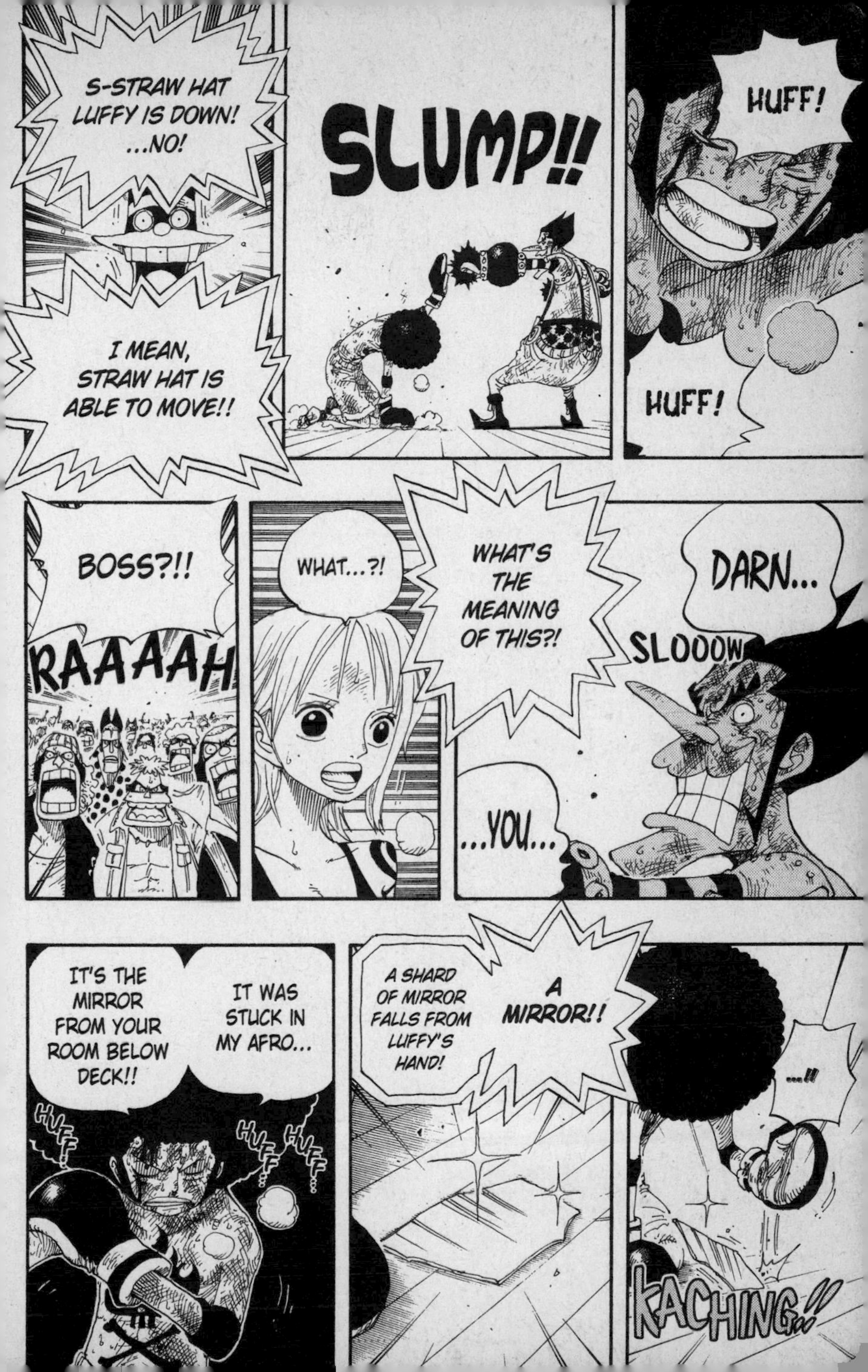
HUFF!
HUFF!
SLUMP!!
S-STRAW HAT LUFFY IS DOWN! ...NO!
I MEAN, STRAW HAT IS ABLE TO MOVE!!
DARN...
SLOOOW
...YOU...
WHAT'S THE MEANING OF THIS?!
WHAT...?!
BOSS?!!
RAAAAH
...!!
KACHING!!
A MIRROR!!
A SHARD OF MIRROR FALLS FROM LUFFY'S HAND!
IT WAS STUCK IN MY AFRO...
IT'S THE MIRROR FROM YOUR ROOM BELOW DECK!!
HUFF
HUFF
HUFF...

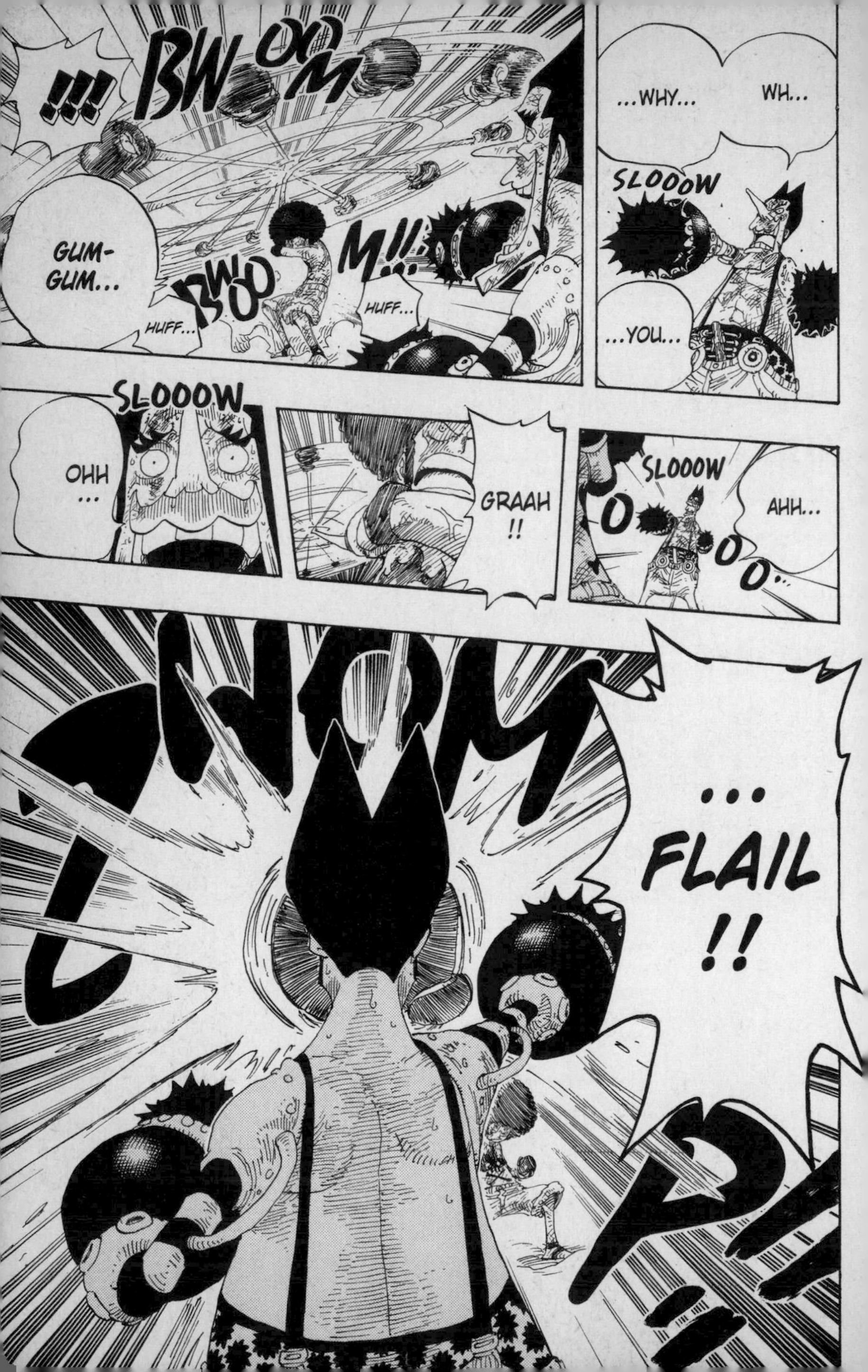
WH...
...WHY...
SLOOOW
...YOU...
!!! BWOOM
BWOOOM!!
HUFF...
GUM-GUM...
HUFF...
SLOOOW
AHH...
OOOO...
GRAAH !!
SLOOOW
OHH ...
... FLAIL !!

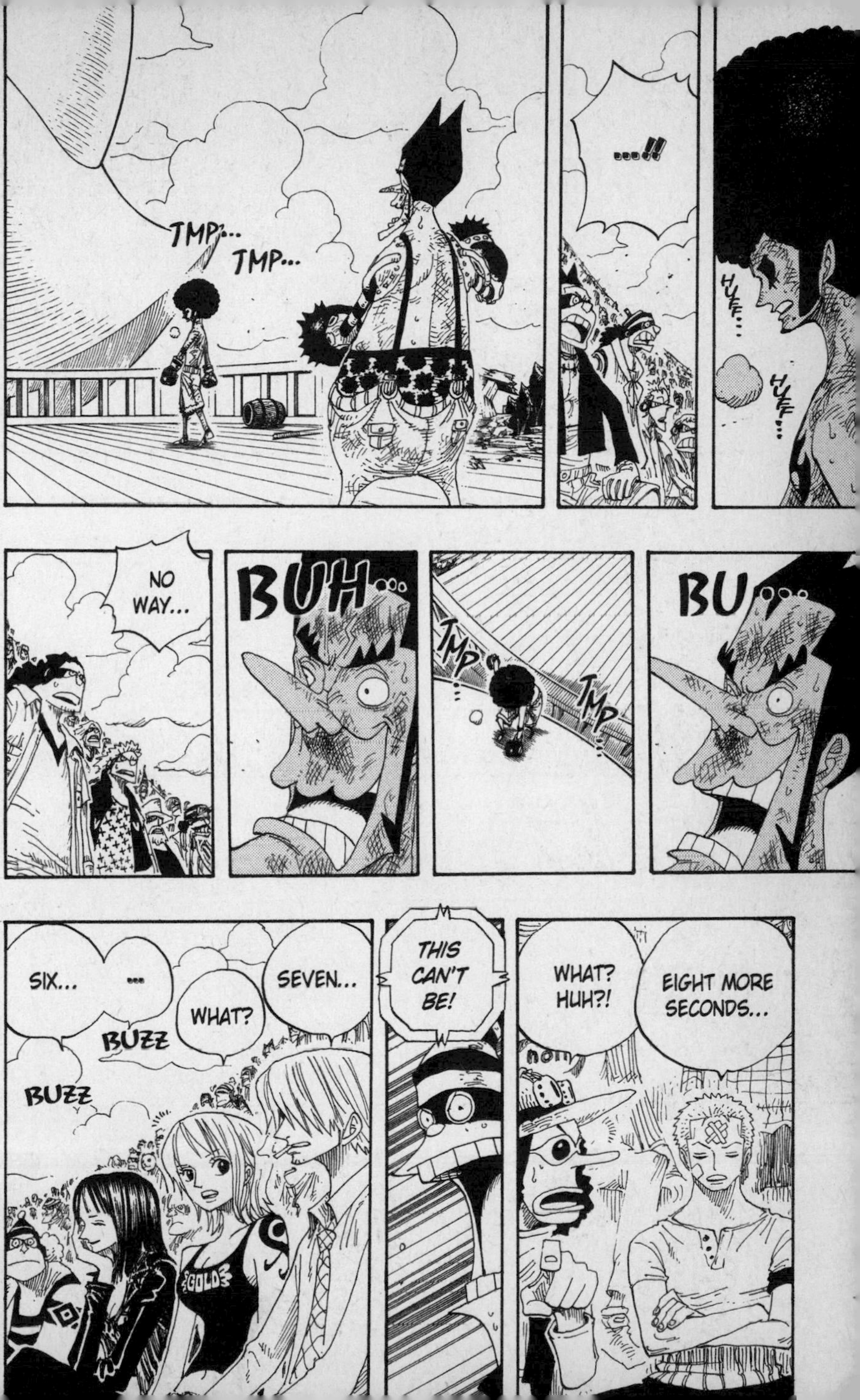
HUFF...
HUFF...
...!!
TMP...
TMP...
BU...
TMP...
TMP...
BUH...
NO WAY...
EIGHT MORE SECONDS...
WHAT? HUH?!
nom
THIS CAN'T BE!
SEVEN...
...
WHAT?
SIX...
BUZZ
BUZZ

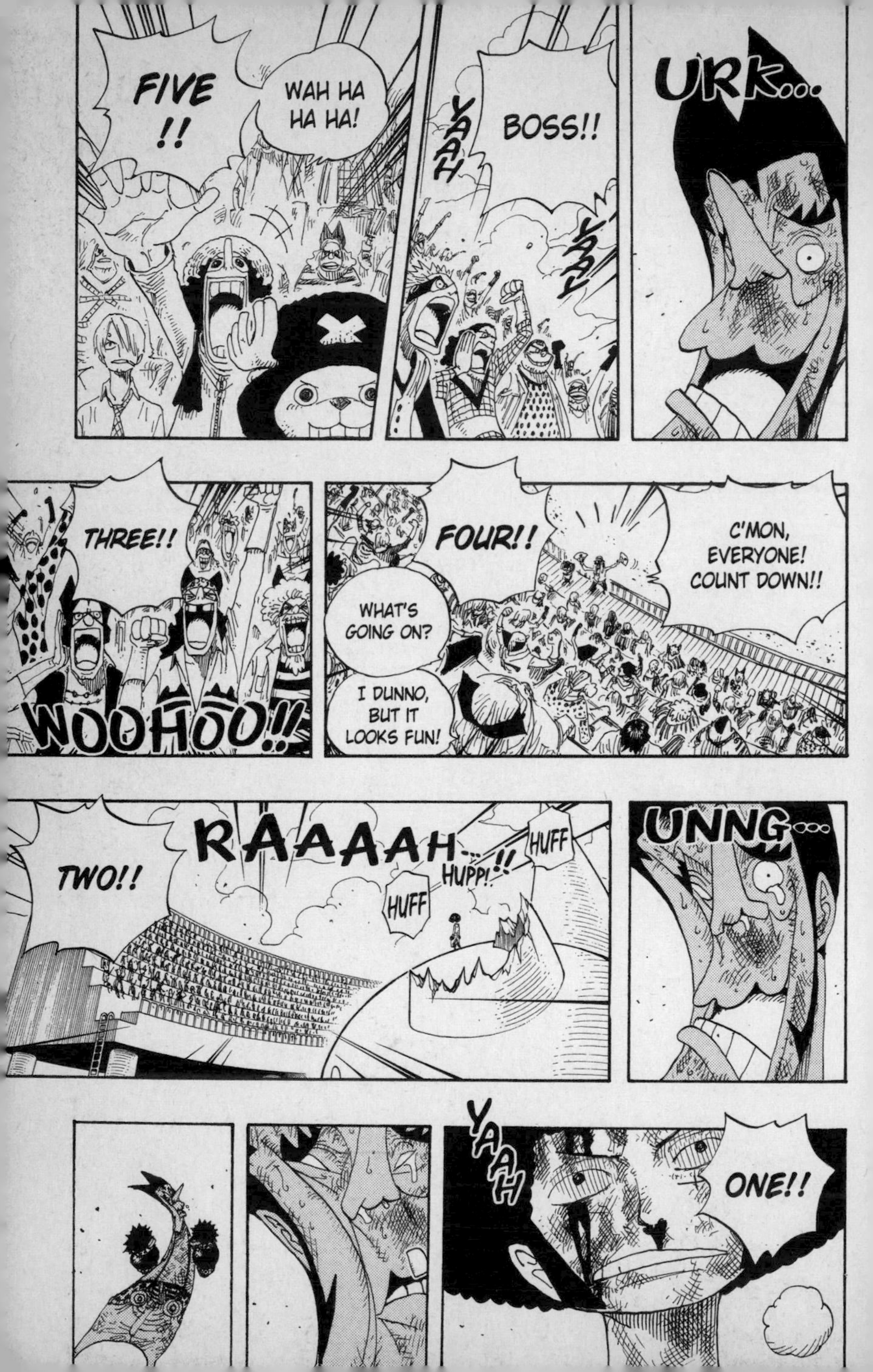
URK...
BOSS!!
YAAAH
FIVE!!
WAH HA HA HA!
C'MON, EVERYONE! COUNT DOWN!!
FOUR!!
WHAT'S GOING ON?
I DUNNO, BUT IT LOOKS FUN!
THREE!!
WOOHOO!!
UNNG...
RAAAAAH...!!
HUFF
HUPP!
HUFF
TWO!!
ONE!!
YAAAH

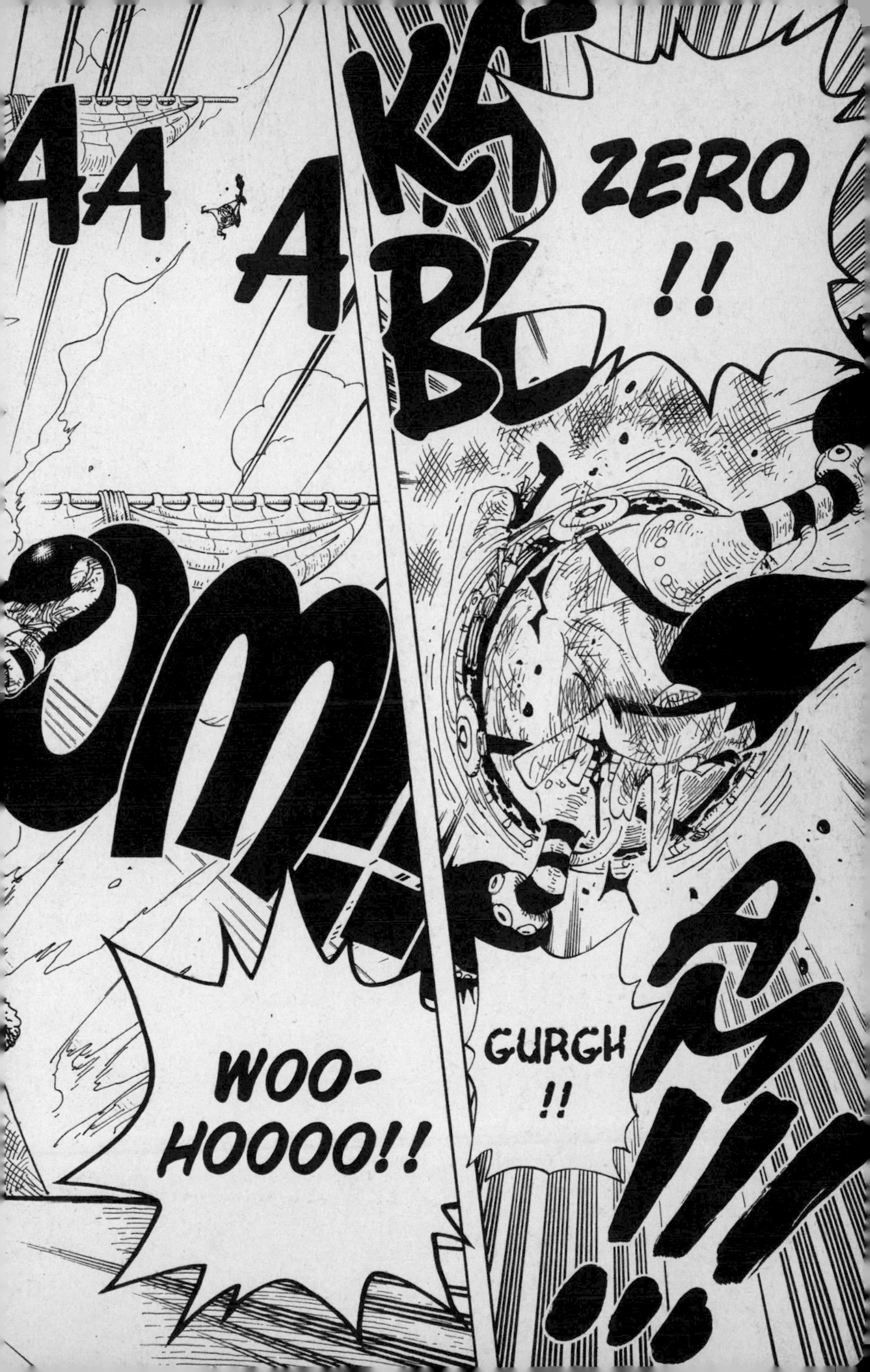

ZERO !!
GURGH !!
WOO-HOOOO!!

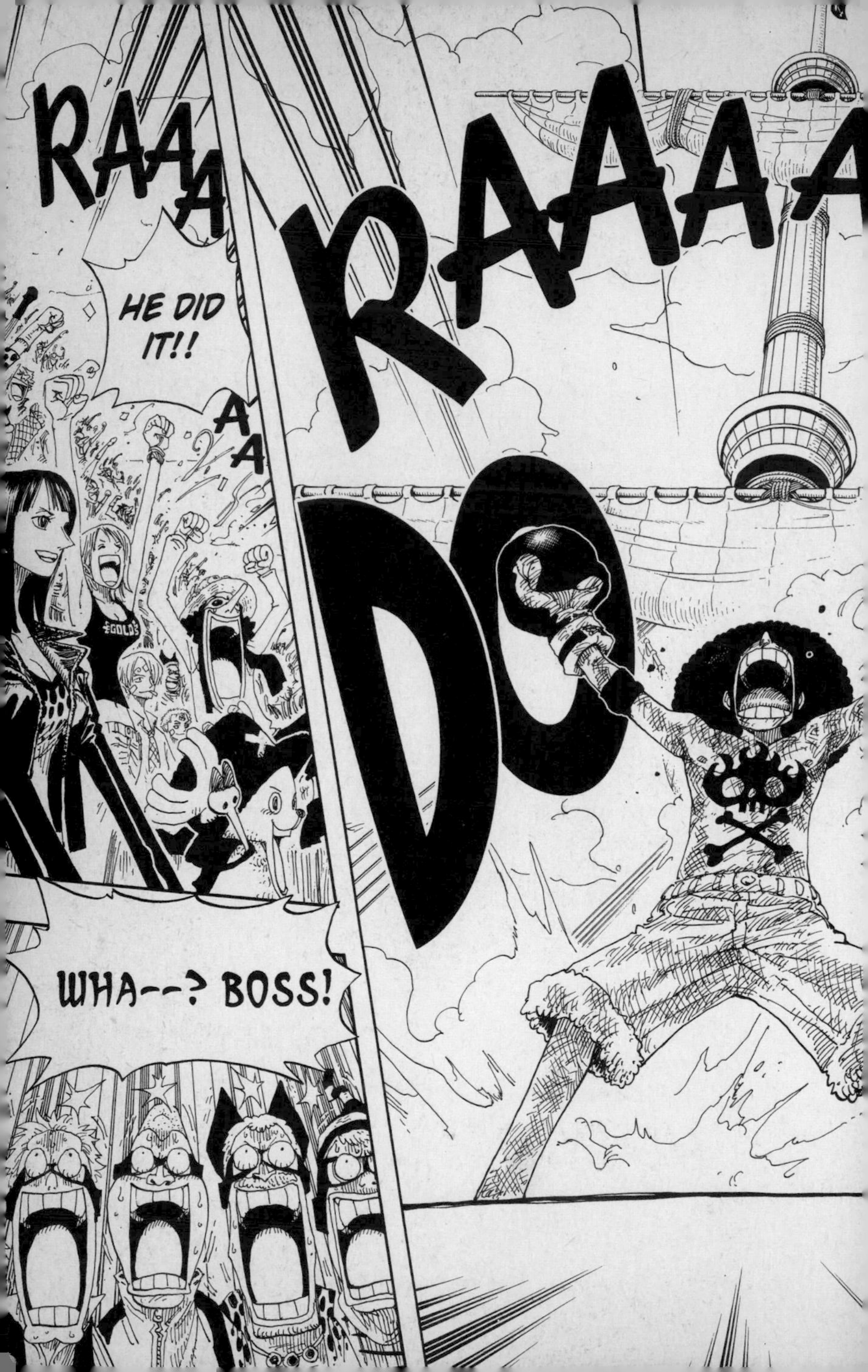

RAAAAA
DO
RAAAA
HE DID IT!!
AA
WHA--? BOSS!

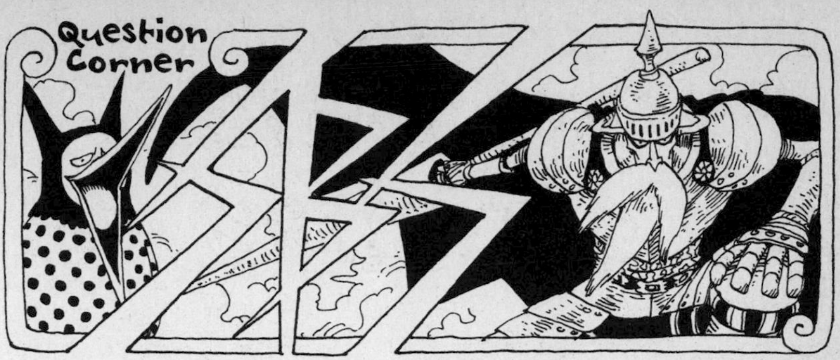
Question Corner

Reader: Robin: "I know you want to start The Question Corner bright and early… But you still haven't made amends for insulting my Cinco Fleurs in volume 32. You're terrible… Bad boy. I won't forgive you. **Seis Fleurs… Clutch!** CRUNCH!! **Cien Fleurs... Delphinium!** SNAP!! TEE HEE… And now, let's begin The Question Corner."
--Anonymous

Oda: Oh...!! Koff...!! I will never say that again...!! Thud.

Q: I was surprised to see Luffy's six-pack abs. Do you have abs like Luffy's too, Oda Sensei?
--Pandaccho

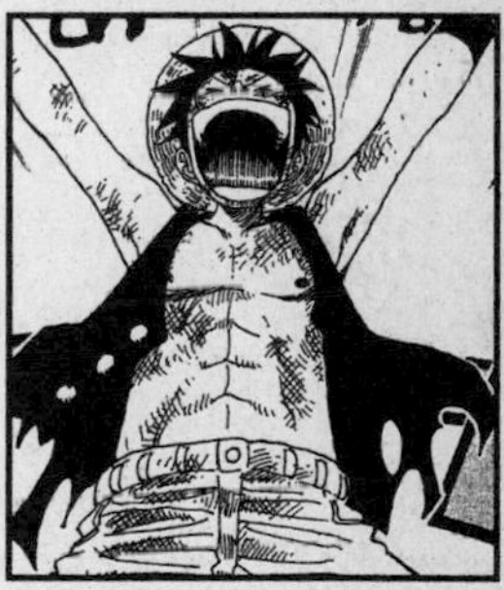

A: Of course. I mean, I look amazing when I take off my shirt. It may not look like it, but when I lean over a little, my belly forms three folds. Call it three-pack abs, if you will. Huh? You don't believe me? Take a look at this belly!! BLUBB See?! BLUBB

Q: Do the Straw Hats ever fall in love? Aren't there any romantic intrigues on the ship?
(Sanji is exempt from this question.)
I'm just a bit curious.
--Naoko

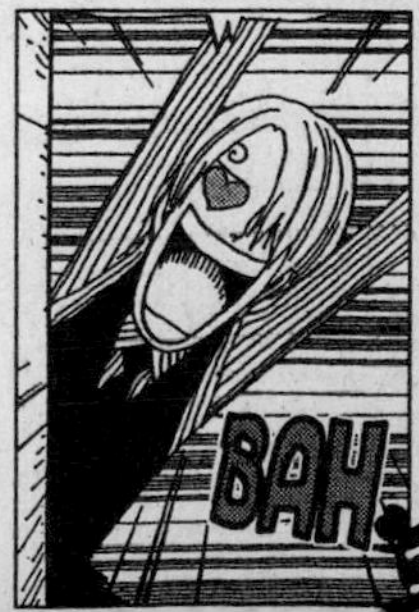
BAH

A: Of course. They're all in love...with their grand adventure...

(↑ so witty)

Chapter 318:
CLOSURE

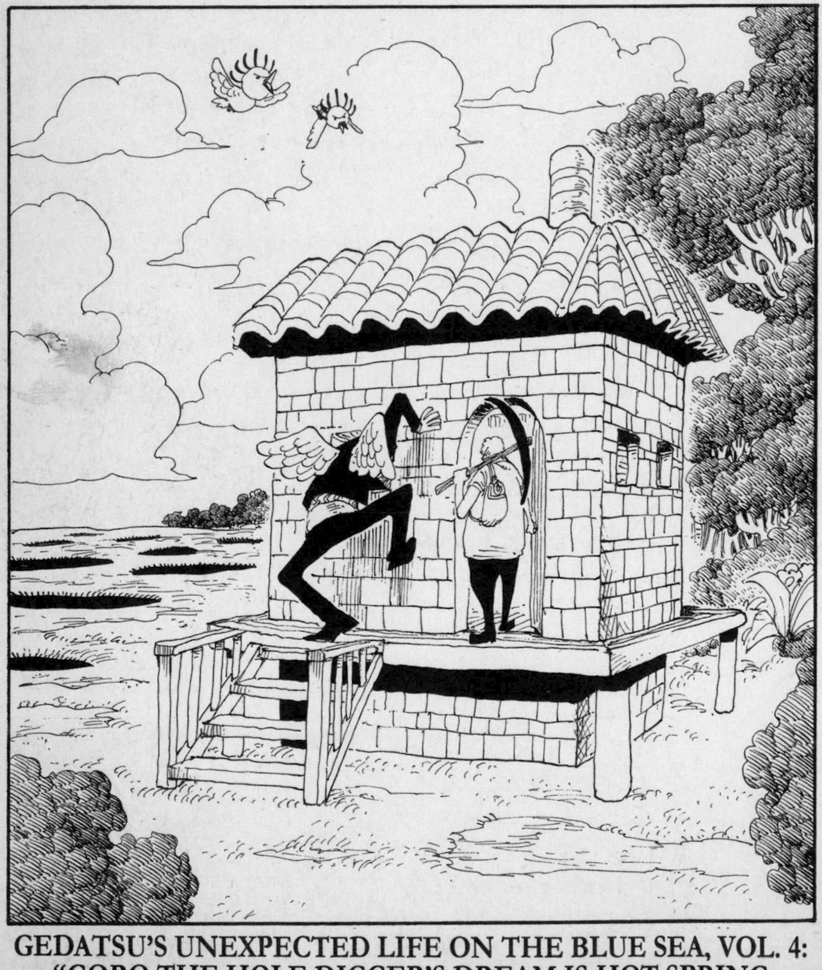

GEDATSU'S UNEXPECTED LIFE ON THE BLUE SEA, VOL. 4:
"GORO THE HOLE DIGGER'S DREAM IS HOT SPRING ISLAND"

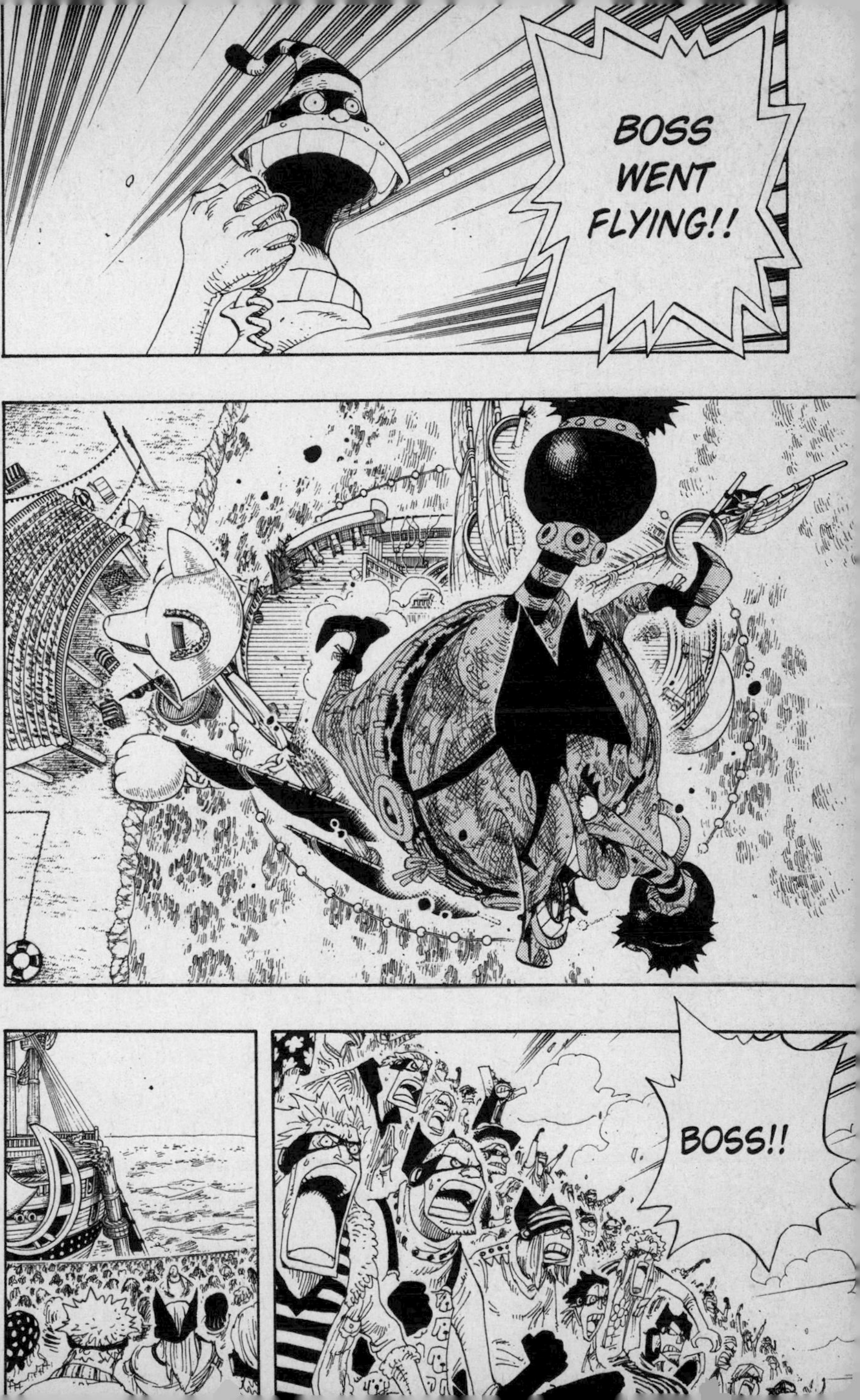
BOSS WENT FLYING!!
BOSS!!

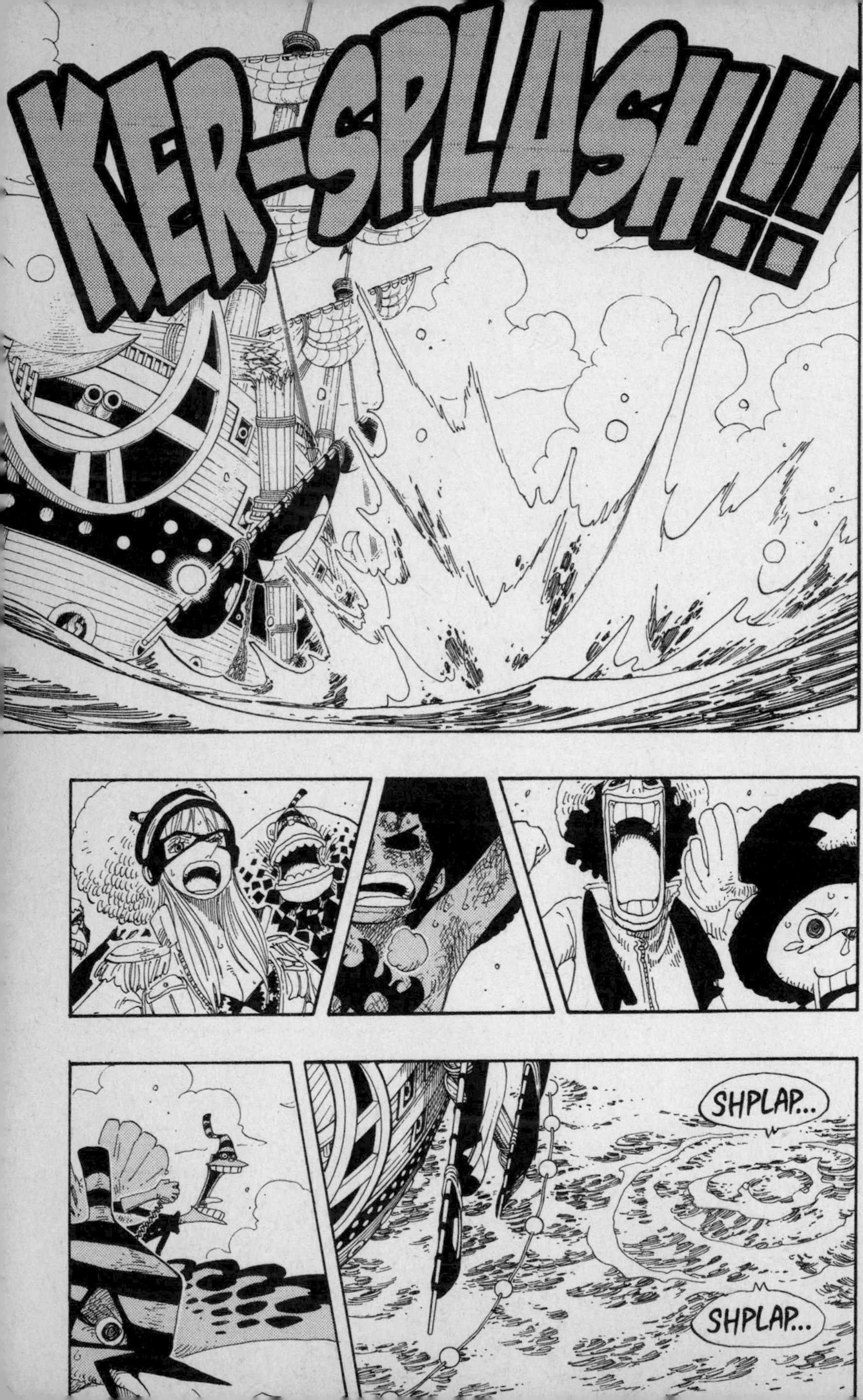
KER-SPLASH!!!
SHPLAP...
SHPLAP...

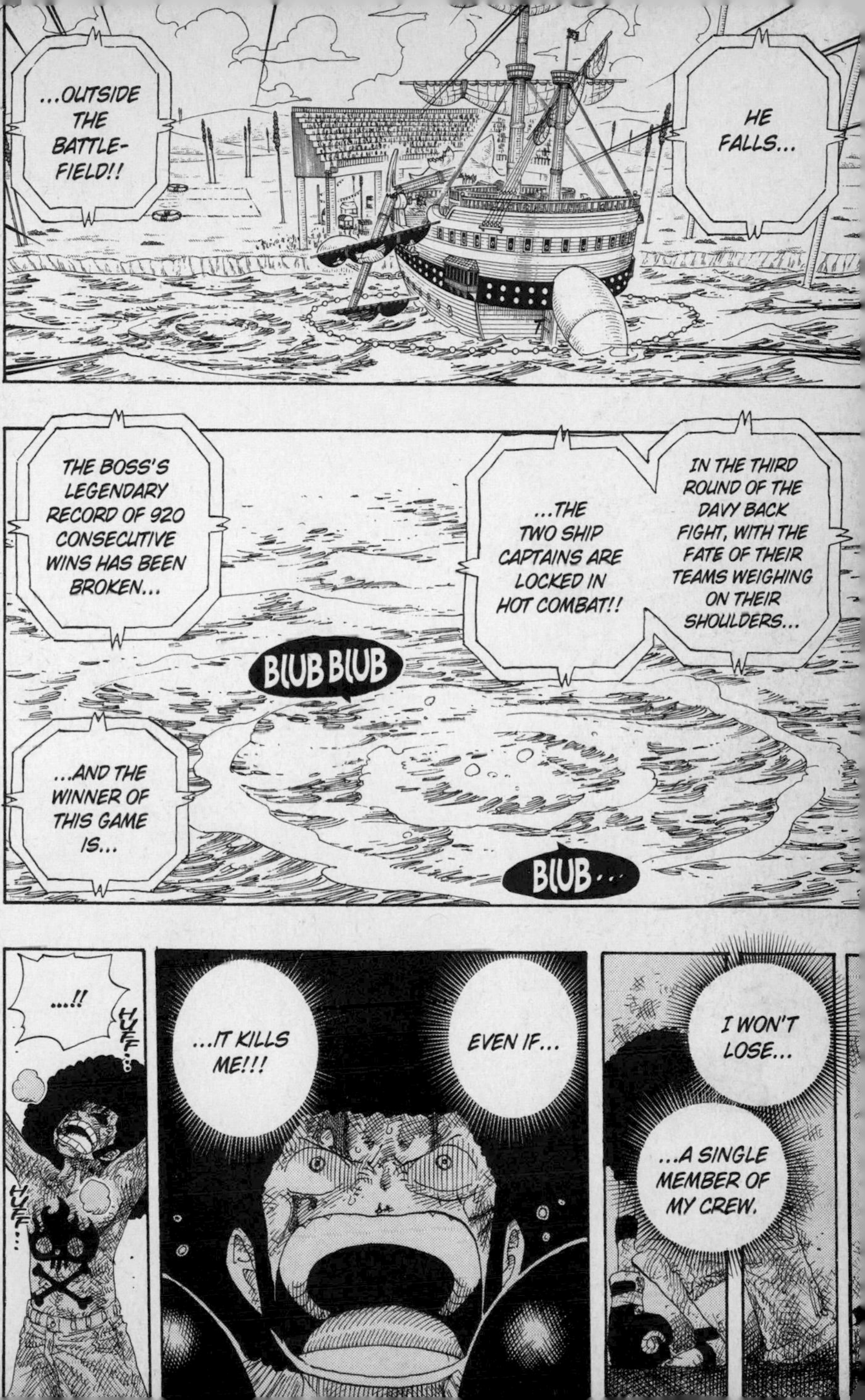
HE FALLS...
...OUTSIDE THE BATTLE-FIELD!!
IN THE THIRD ROUND OF THE DAVY BACK FIGHT, WITH THE FATE OF THEIR TEAMS WEIGHING ON THEIR SHOULDERS...
...THE TWO SHIP CAPTAINS ARE LOCKED IN HOT COMBAT!!
THE BOSS'S LEGENDARY RECORD OF 920 CONSECUTIVE WINS HAS BEEN BROKEN...
BLUB BLUB
...AND THE WINNER OF THIS GAME IS...
BLUB...
I WON'T LOSE...
...A SINGLE MEMBER OF MY CREW.
EVEN IF...
...IT KILLS ME!!!
...!!
HUFF...
HUFF...

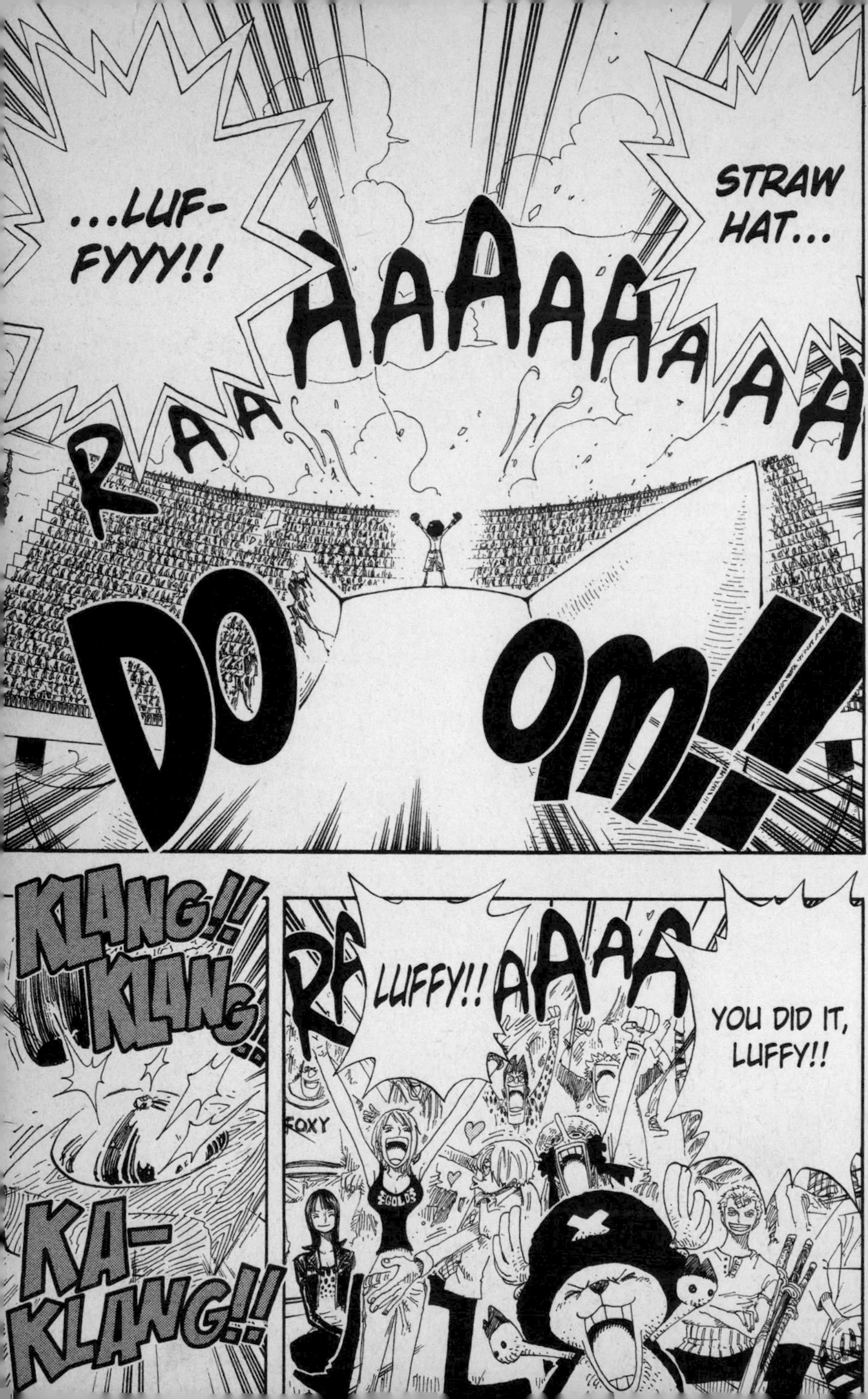
STRAW HAT...
...LUF-FYYY!!
RAAAAAAAAAAA
DOOM!!
YOU DID IT, LUFFY!!
RAAAA
LUFFY!!
FOXY
KLANG!! KLANG...
KA-KLANG!!

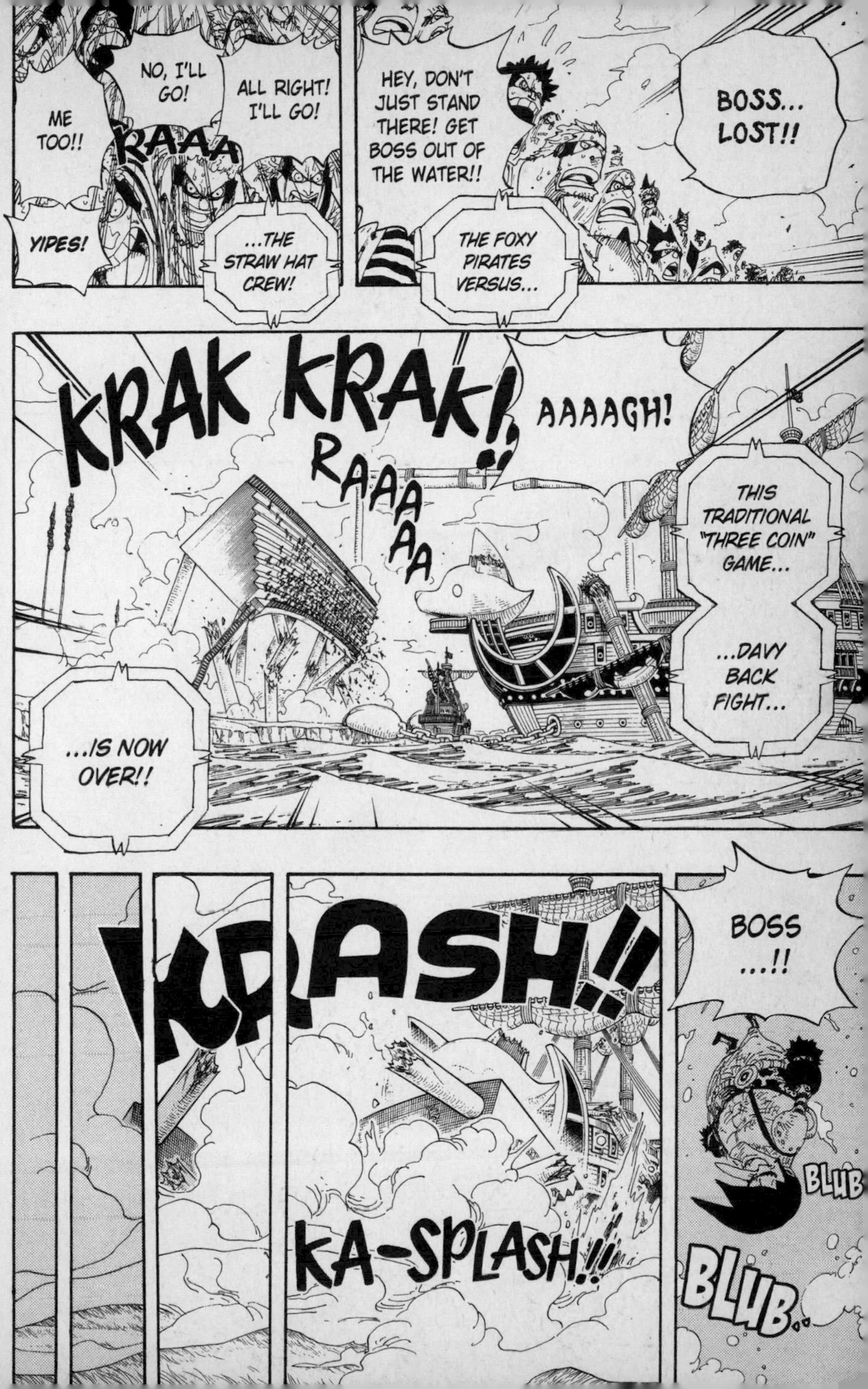
BOSS... LOST!!
HEY, DON'T JUST STAND THERE! GET BOSS OUT OF THE WATER!!
THE FOXY PIRATES VERSUS...
ALL RIGHT! I'LL GO!
NO, I'LL GO!
RAAA
ME TOO!!
YIPES!
...THE STRAW HAT CREW!
THIS TRADITIONAL "THREE COIN" GAME...
...DAVY BACK FIGHT...
AAAAGH!
KRAK KRAK!!
RAAAAA
...IS NOW OVER!!
BOSS ...!!
BLUB
BLUB
KRASH!!
KA-SPLASH!!!

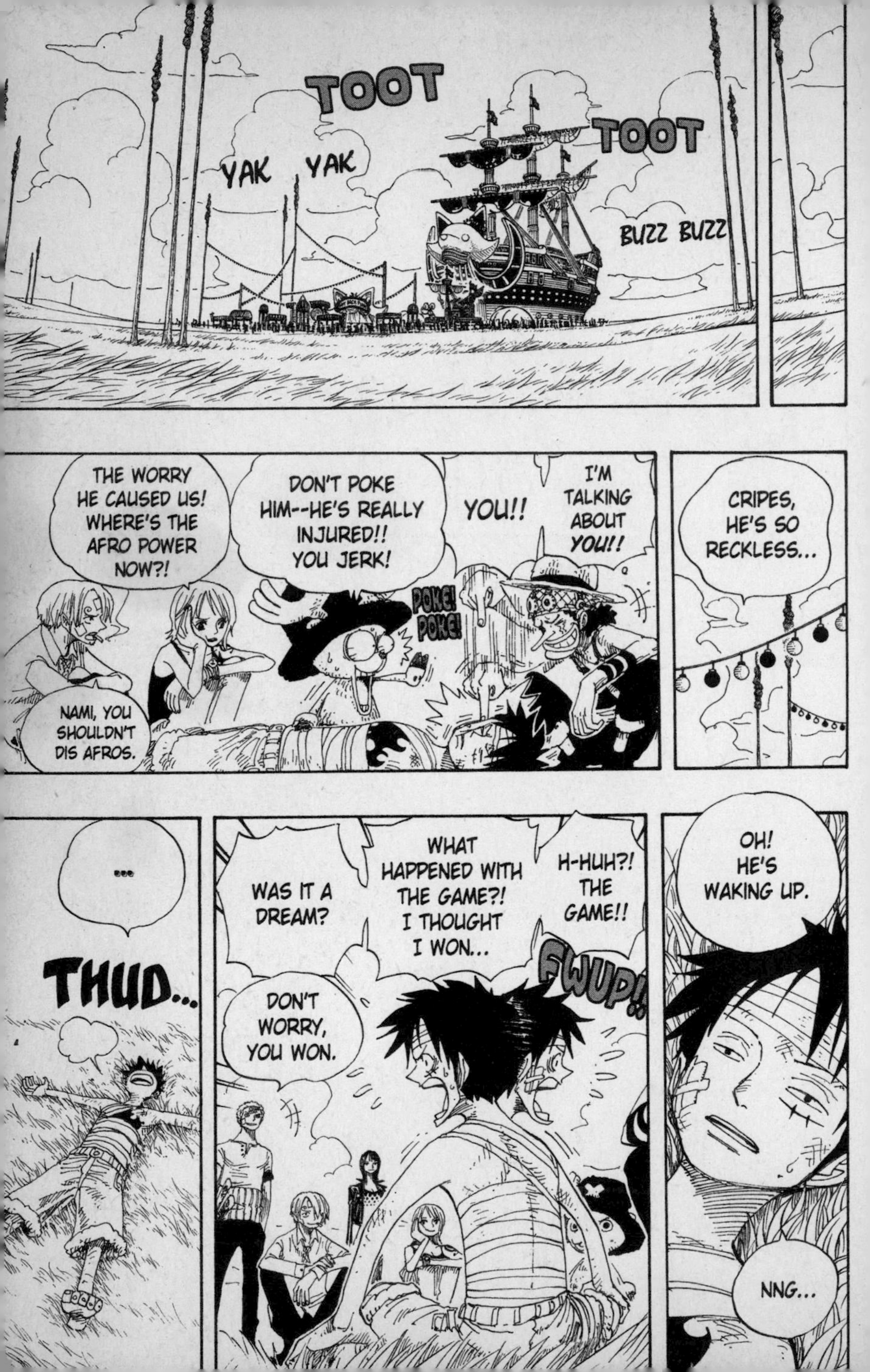
BUZZ BUZZ
TOOT
TOOT
YAK YAK
CRIPES, HE'S SO RECKLESS...
I'M TALKING ABOUT YOU!!
YOU!!
POKE! POKE!
DON'T POKE HIM--HE'S REALLY INJURED!! YOU JERK!
THE WORRY HE CAUSED US! WHERE'S THE AFRO POWER NOW?!
NAMI, YOU SHOULDN'T DIS AFROS.
OH! HE'S WAKING UP.
NNG...
H-HUH?! THE GAME!!
FWUP!!
WHAT HAPPENED WITH THE GAME?! I THOUGHT I WON...
WAS IT A DREAM?
DON'T WORRY, YOU WON.
...
THUD...

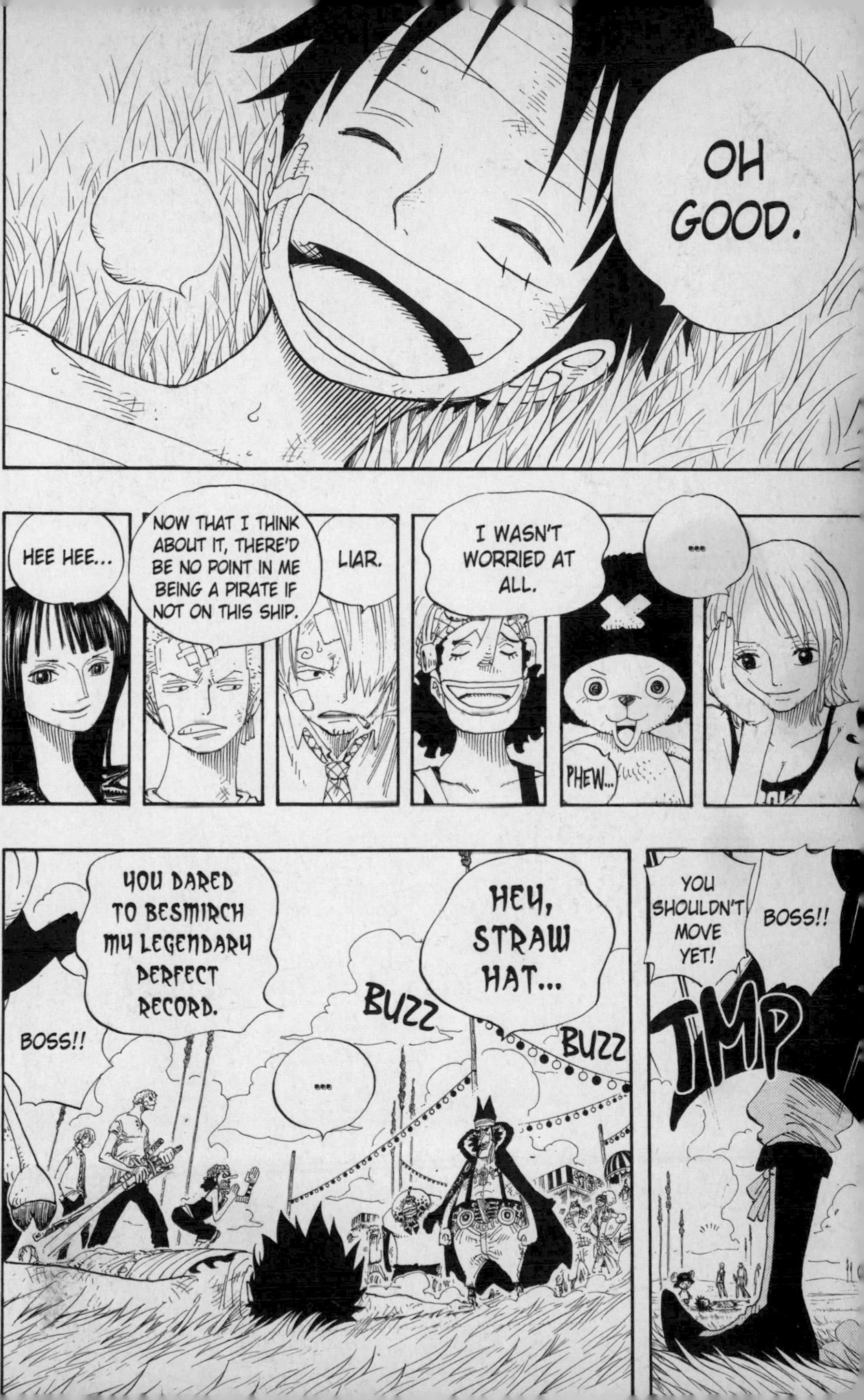

OH GOOD.
...
PHEW...
I WASN'T WORRIED AT ALL.
LIAR.
NOW THAT I THINK ABOUT IT, THERE'D BE NO POINT IN ME BEING A PIRATE IF NOT ON THIS SHIP.
HEE HEE...
BOSS!!
YOU SHOULDN'T MOVE YET!
TMP
HEY, STRAW HAT...
BUZZ
BUZZ
...
YOU DARED TO BESMIRCH MY LEGENDARY PERFECT RECORD.
BOSS!!

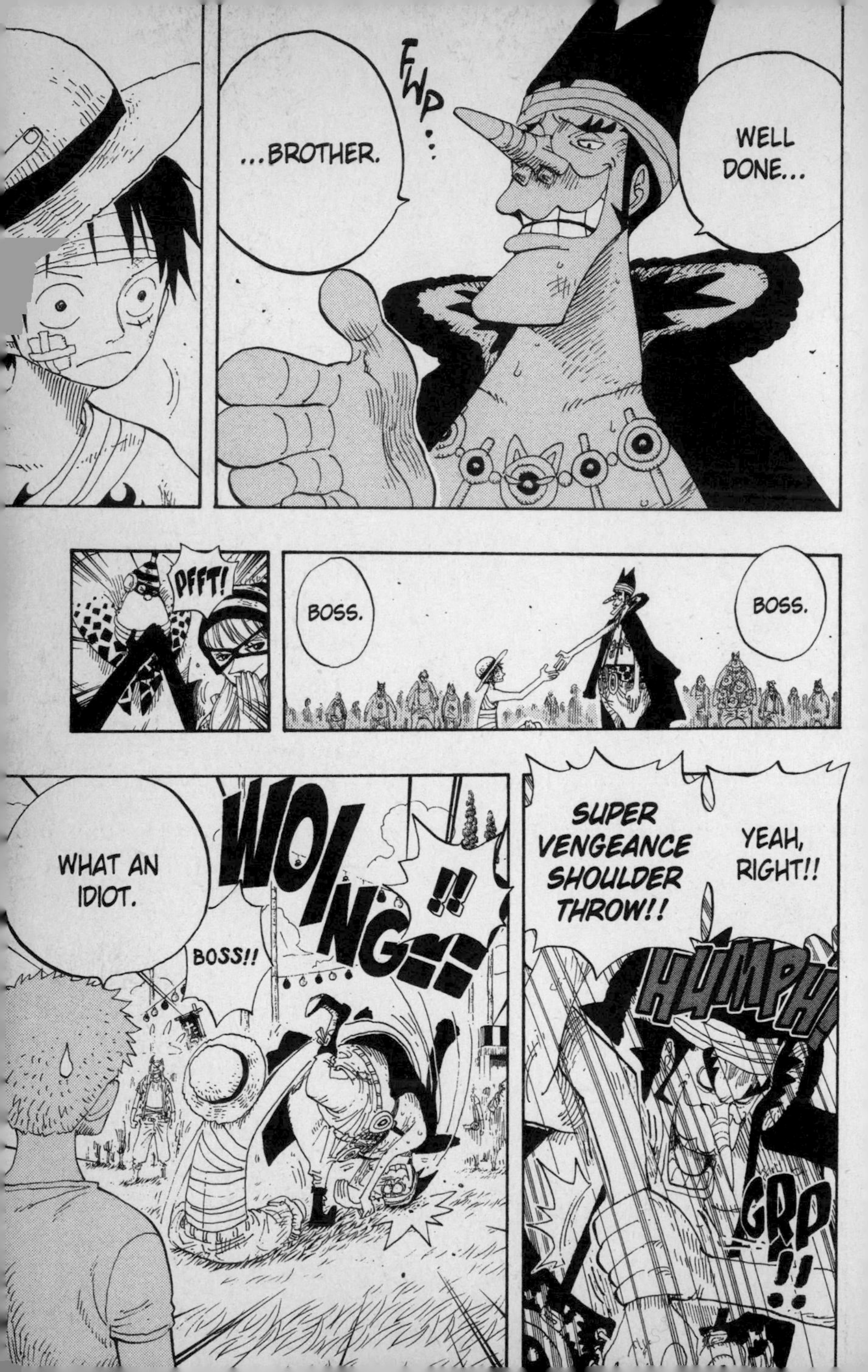
WELL DONE...
FWP...
...BROTHER.
BOSS.
BOSS.
PFFT!
YEAH, RIGHT!!
SUPER VENGEANCE SHOULDER THROW!!
HUMPH!
GRP!!
WOING!!
BOSS!!
WHAT AN IDIOT.

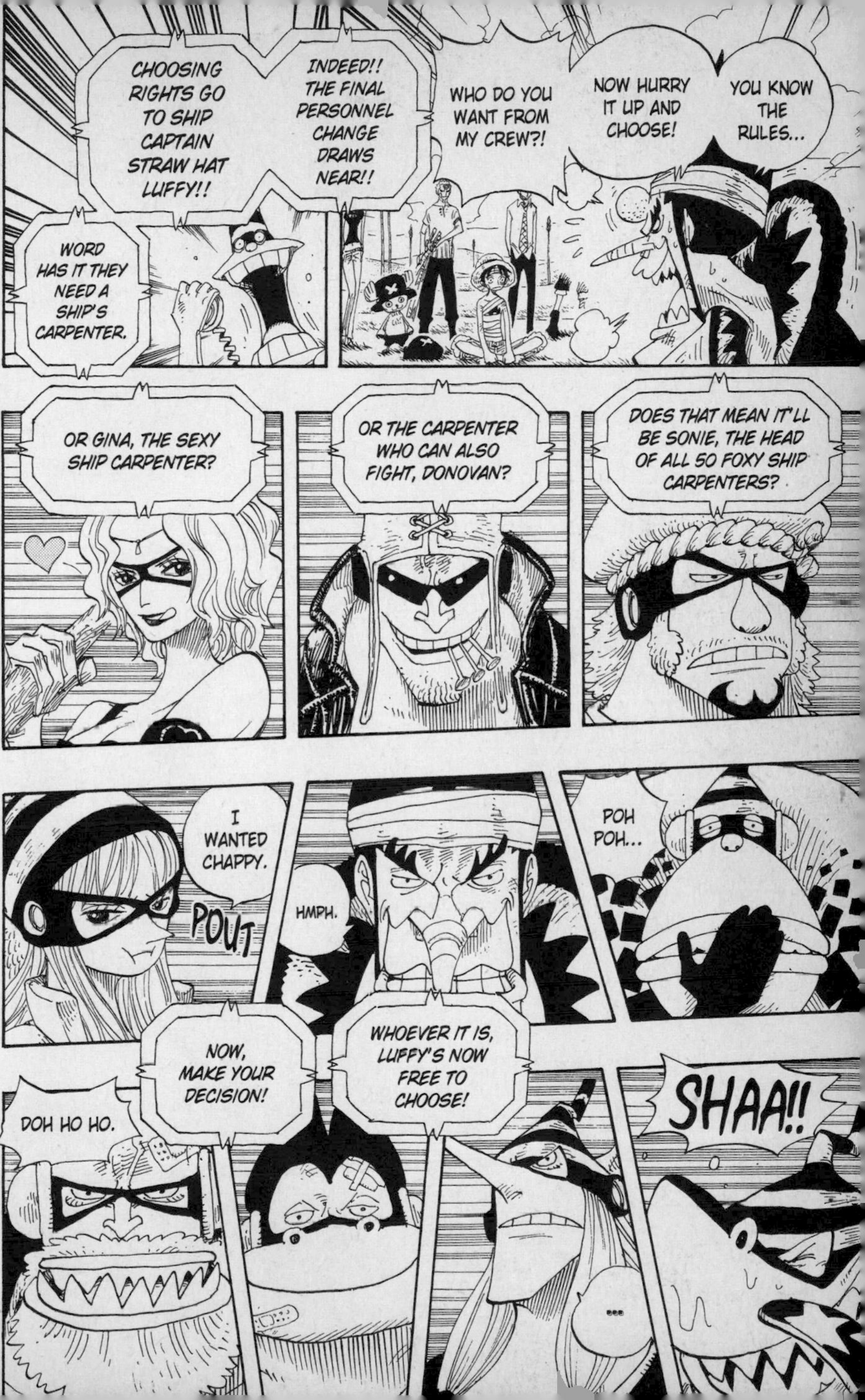

YOU KNOW THE RULES...
NOW HURRY IT UP AND CHOOSE!
WHO DO YOU WANT FROM MY CREW?!
INDEED!! THE FINAL PERSONNEL CHANGE DRAWS NEAR!!
CHOOSING RIGHTS GO TO SHIP CAPTAIN STRAW HAT LUFFY!!
WORD HAS IT THEY NEED A SHIP'S CARPENTER.
DOES THAT MEAN IT'LL BE SONIE, THE HEAD OF ALL 50 FOXY SHIP CARPENTERS?
OR THE CARPENTER WHO CAN ALSO FIGHT, DONOVAN?
OR GINA, THE SEXY SHIP CARPENTER?
POH POH...
HMPH.
I WANTED CHAPPY.
POUT
SHAA!!
...
WHOEVER IT IS, LUFFY'S NOW FREE TO CHOOSE!
NOW, MAKE YOUR DECISION!
DOH HO HO.

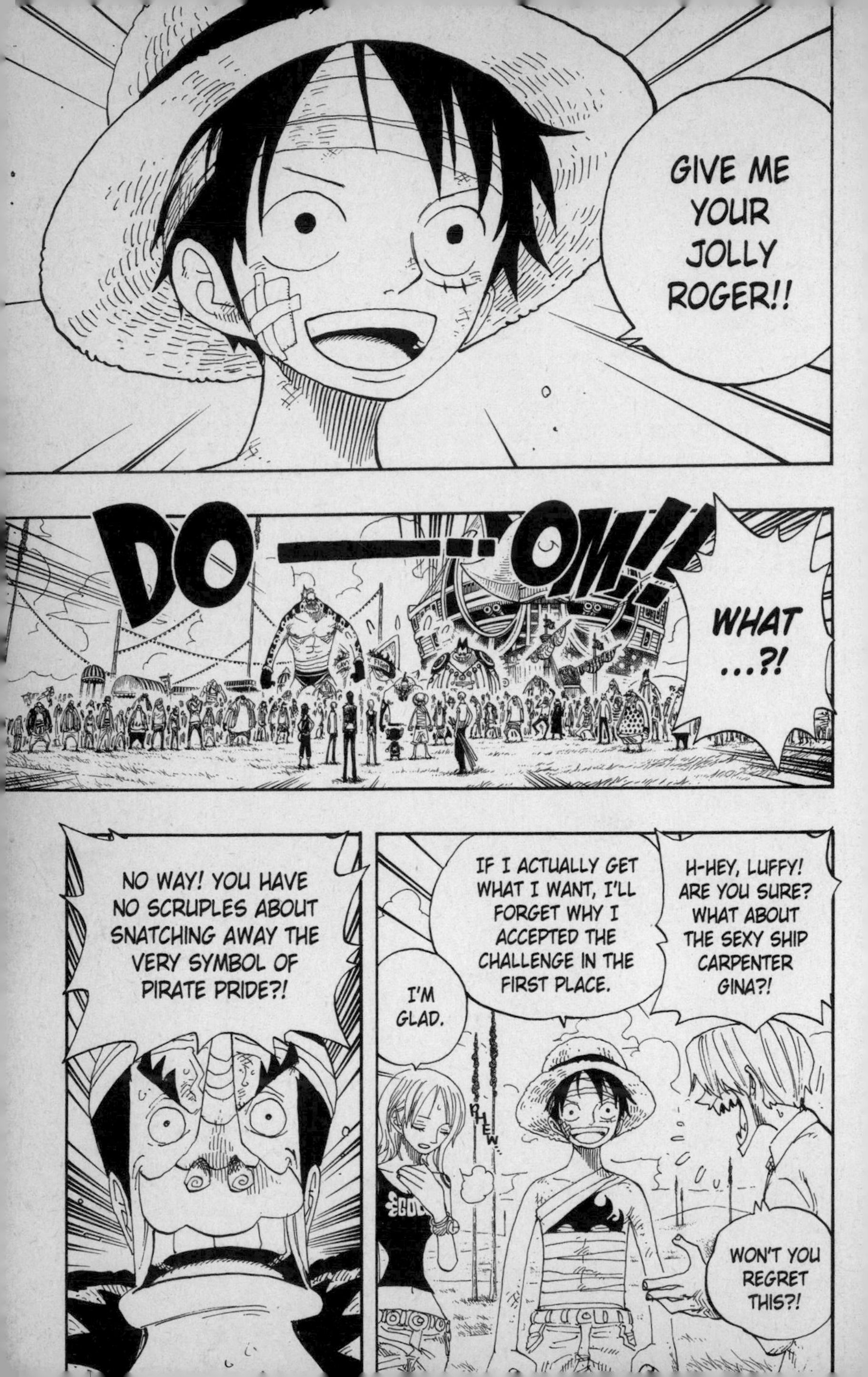
GIVE ME YOUR JOLLY ROGER!!
DO———ON!!
WHAT ...?!
H-HEY, LUFFY! ARE YOU SURE? WHAT ABOUT THE SEXY SHIP CARPENTER GINA?!
WON'T YOU REGRET THIS?!
IF I ACTUALLY GET WHAT I WANT, I'LL FORGET WHY I ACCEPTED THE CHALLENGE IN THE FIRST PLACE.
I'M GLAD.
PHEW..
NO WAY! YOU HAVE NO SCRUPLES ABOUT SNATCHING AWAY THE VERY SYMBOL OF PIRATE PRIDE?!

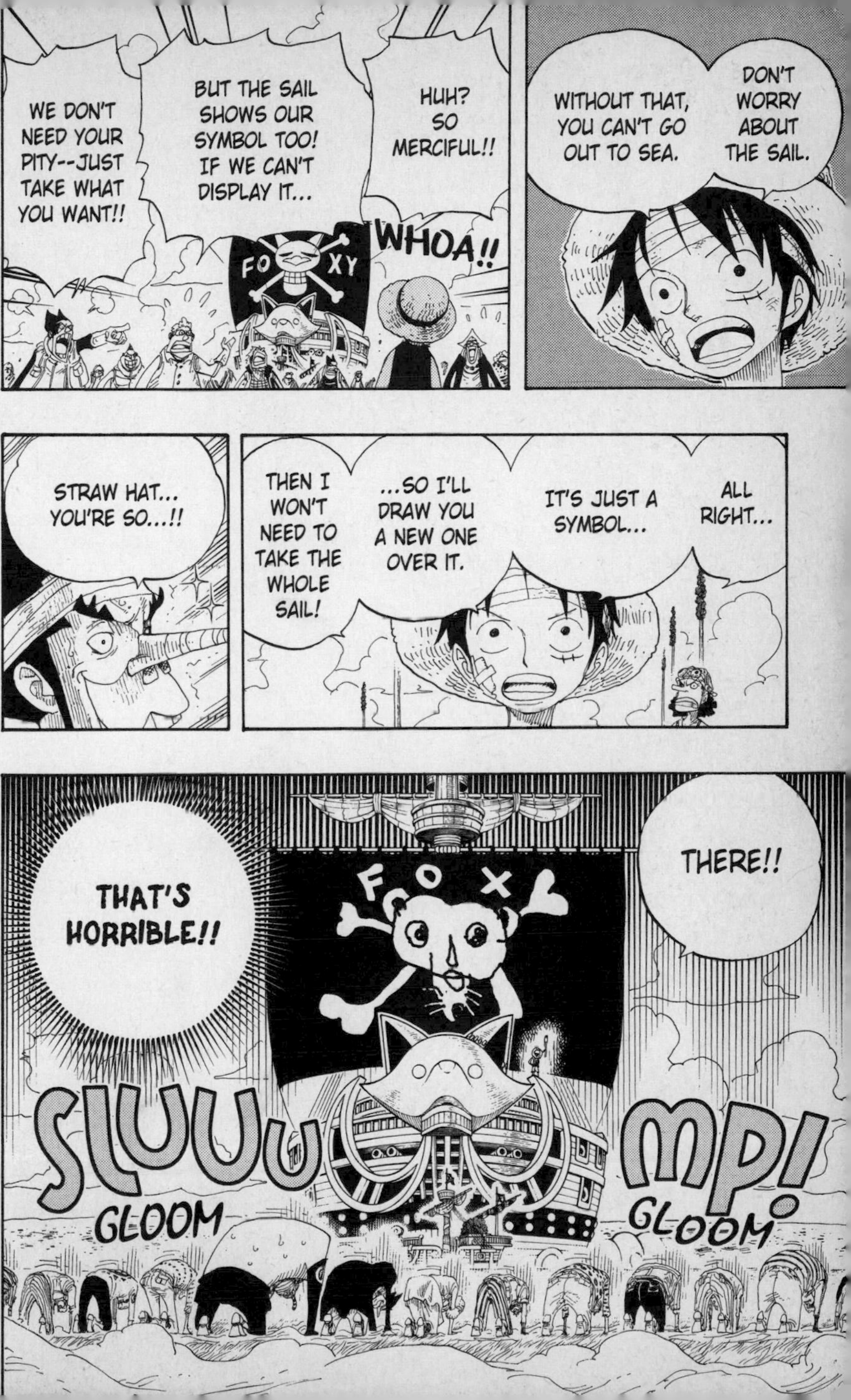
DON'T WORRY ABOUT THE SAIL.
WITHOUT THAT, YOU CAN'T GO OUT TO SEA.
HUH? SO MERCIFUL!!
BUT THE SAIL SHOWS OUR SYMBOL TOO! IF WE CAN'T DISPLAY IT...
WE DON'T NEED YOUR PITY--JUST TAKE WHAT YOU WANT!!
WHOA!!
FO XY
ALL RIGHT...
IT'S JUST A SYMBOL...
...SO I'LL DRAW YOU A NEW ONE OVER IT.
THEN I WON'T NEED TO TAKE THE WHOLE SAIL!
STRAW HAT... YOU'RE SO...!!
THERE!!
THAT'S HORRIBLE!!
FOX
SLUUUMP!
GLOOM
GLOOM

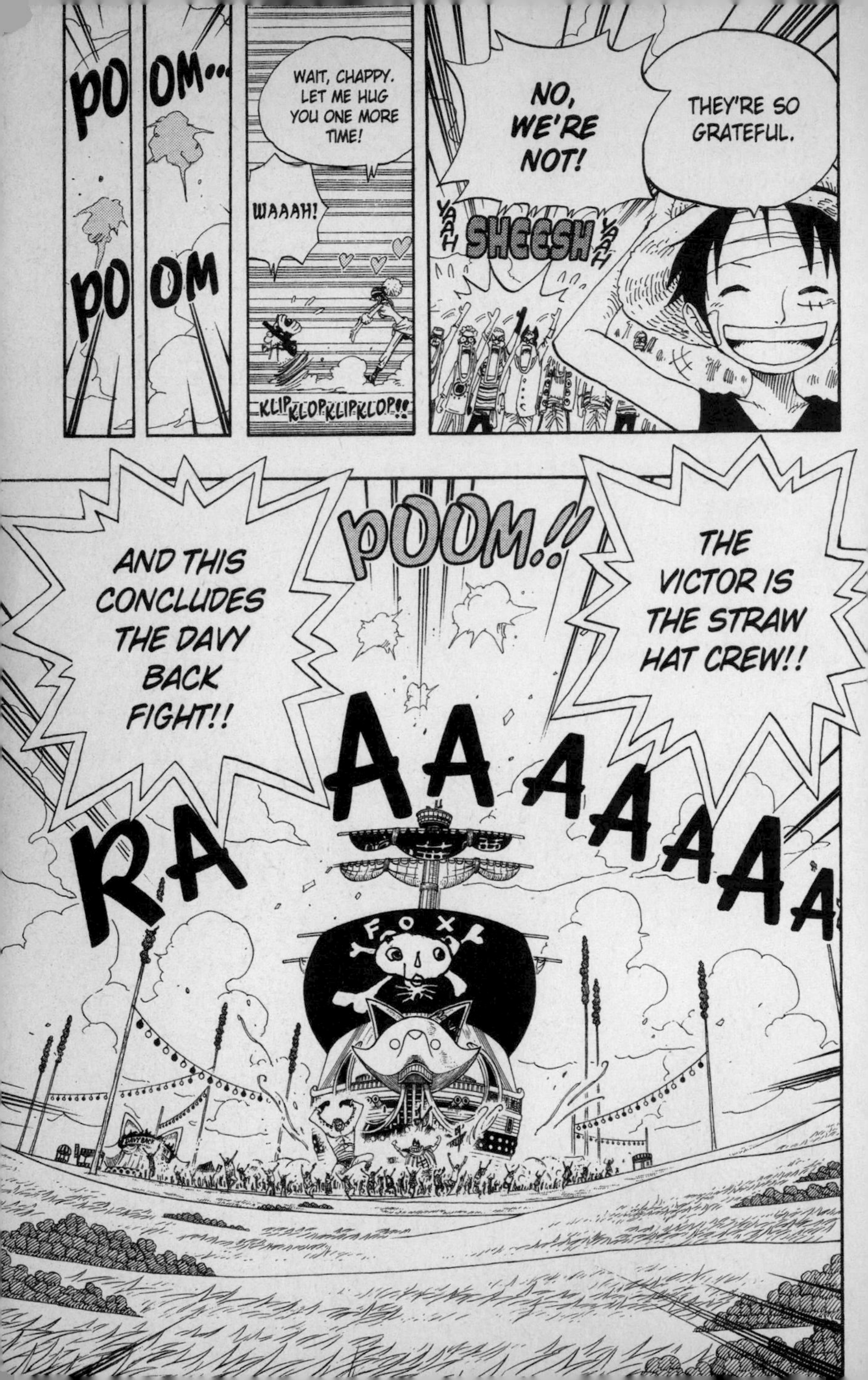

THEY'RE SO GRATEFUL.
NO, WE'RE NOT!
YAAH
SHEESH
YAAH
WAIT, CHAPPY. LET ME HUG YOU ONE MORE TIME!
WAAAH!
KLIP KLOP KLIP KLOP!!
POOM...
POOM
POOM!!
THE VICTOR IS THE STRAW HAT CREW!!
AND THIS CONCLUDES THE DAVY BACK FIGHT!!
RAAAAAAAAA

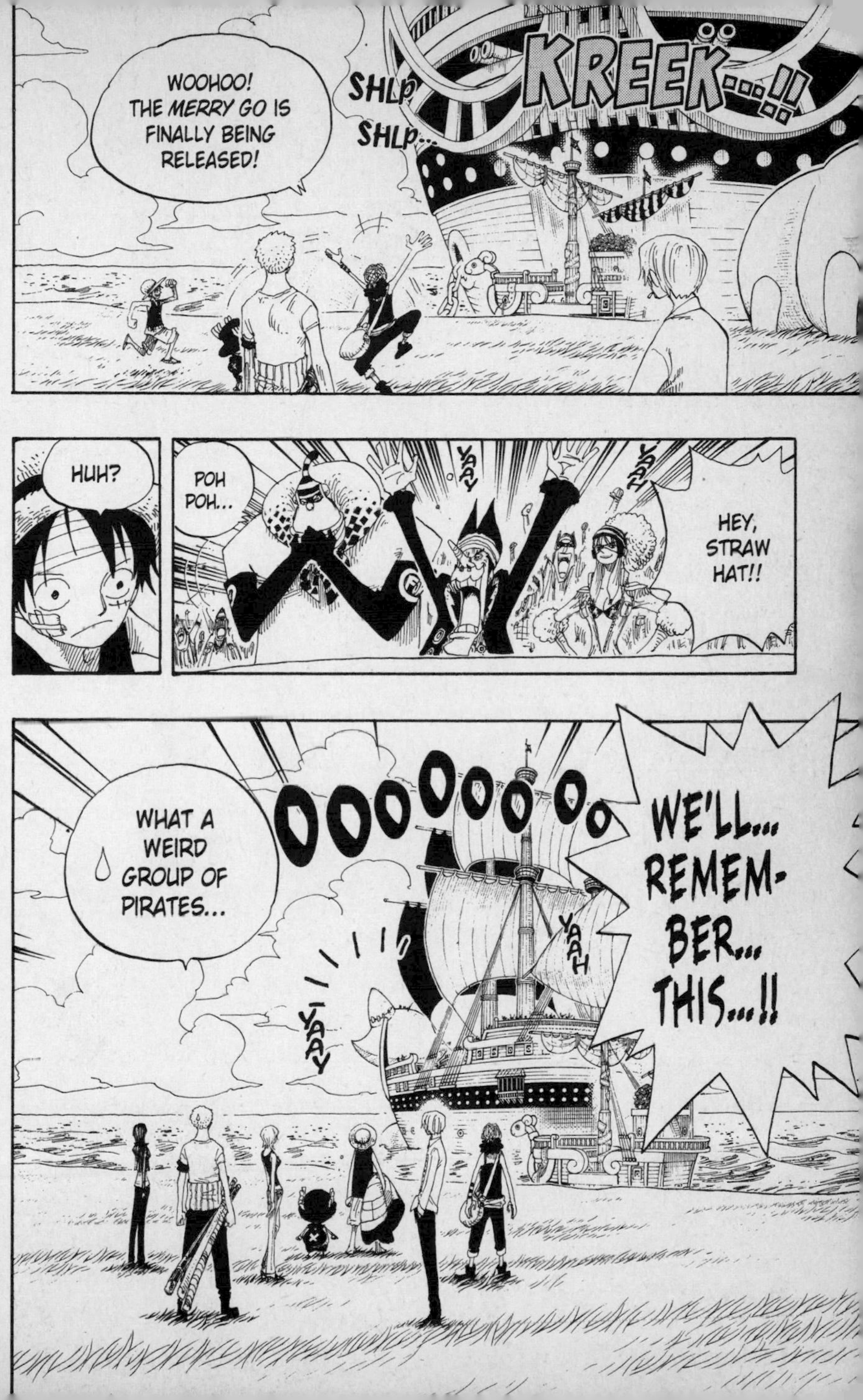
KREEK...!!
SHLP SHLP...
WOOHOO! THE MERRY GO IS FINALLY BEING RELEASED!
HEY, STRAW HAT!!
YAAH
YAAY
POH POH...
HUH?
WE'LL... REMEM-BER... THIS...!!
OOOOOOOO
YAAH
YAAY
WHAT A WEIRD GROUP OF PIRATES...

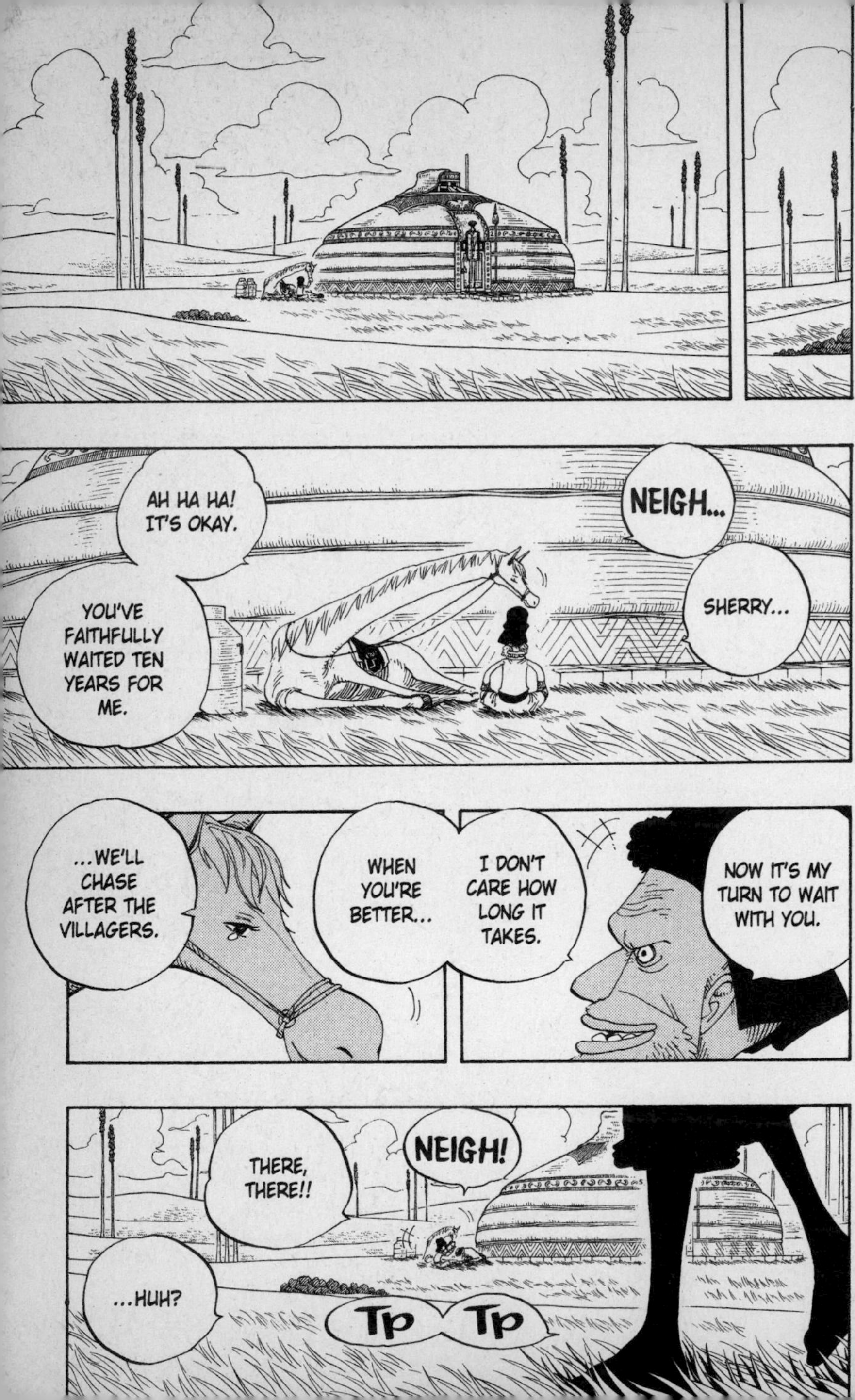
NEIGH...
SHERRY...
AH HA HA! IT'S OKAY.
YOU'VE FAITHFULLY WAITED TEN YEARS FOR ME.
NOW IT'S MY TURN TO WAIT WITH YOU.
I DON'T CARE HOW LONG IT TAKES.
WHEN YOU'RE BETTER...
...WE'LL CHASE AFTER THE VILLAGERS.
NEIGH!
THERE, THERE!!
Tp Tp
...HUH?

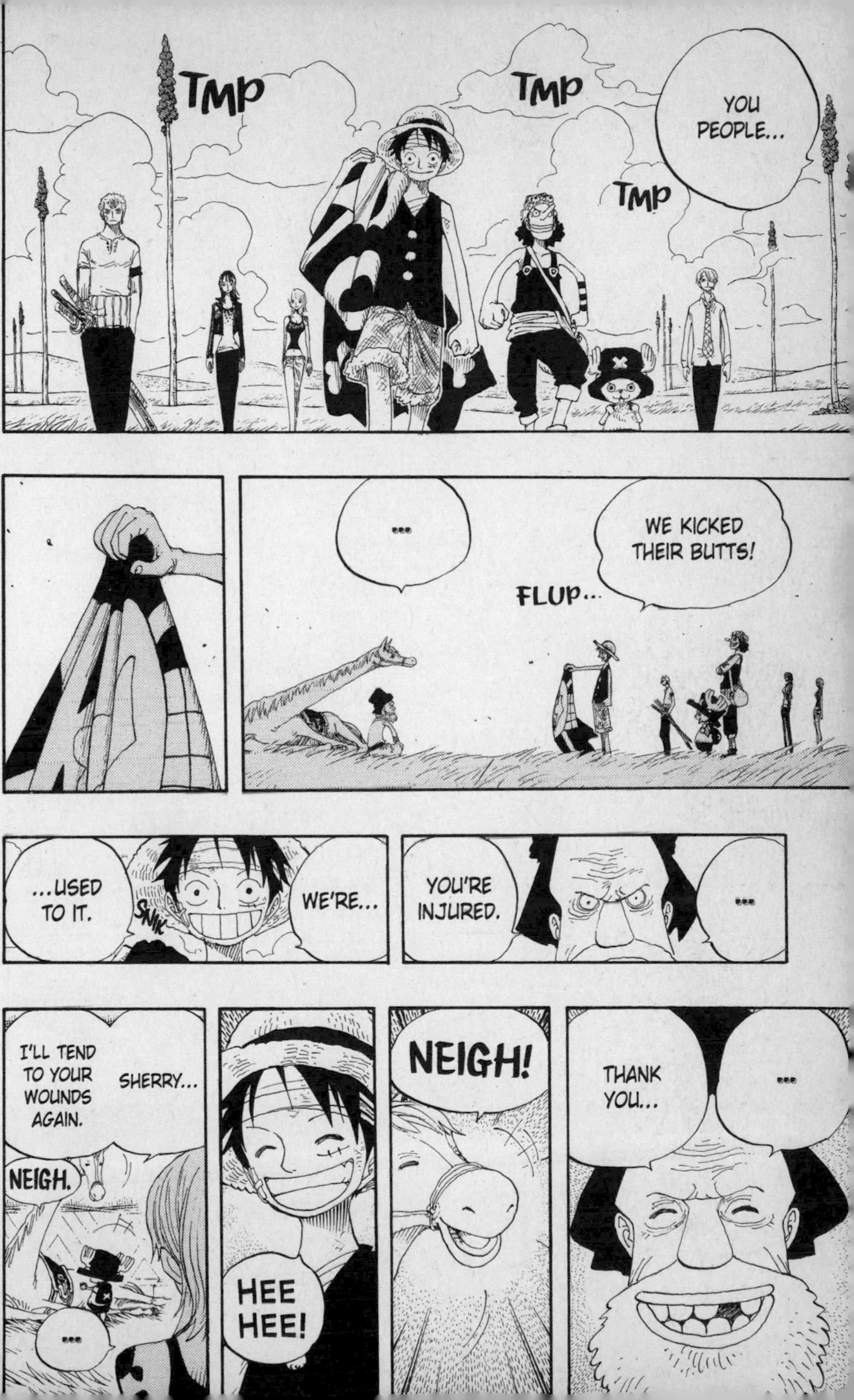
YOU PEOPLE...
TMP
TMP
TMP
WE KICKED THEIR BUTTS!
...
FLUP...
...
YOU'RE INJURED.
WE'RE...
SNIK
...USED TO IT.
...
THANK YOU...
NEIGH!
HEE HEE!
SHERRY...
I'LL TEND TO YOUR WOUNDS AGAIN.
NEIGH.
...

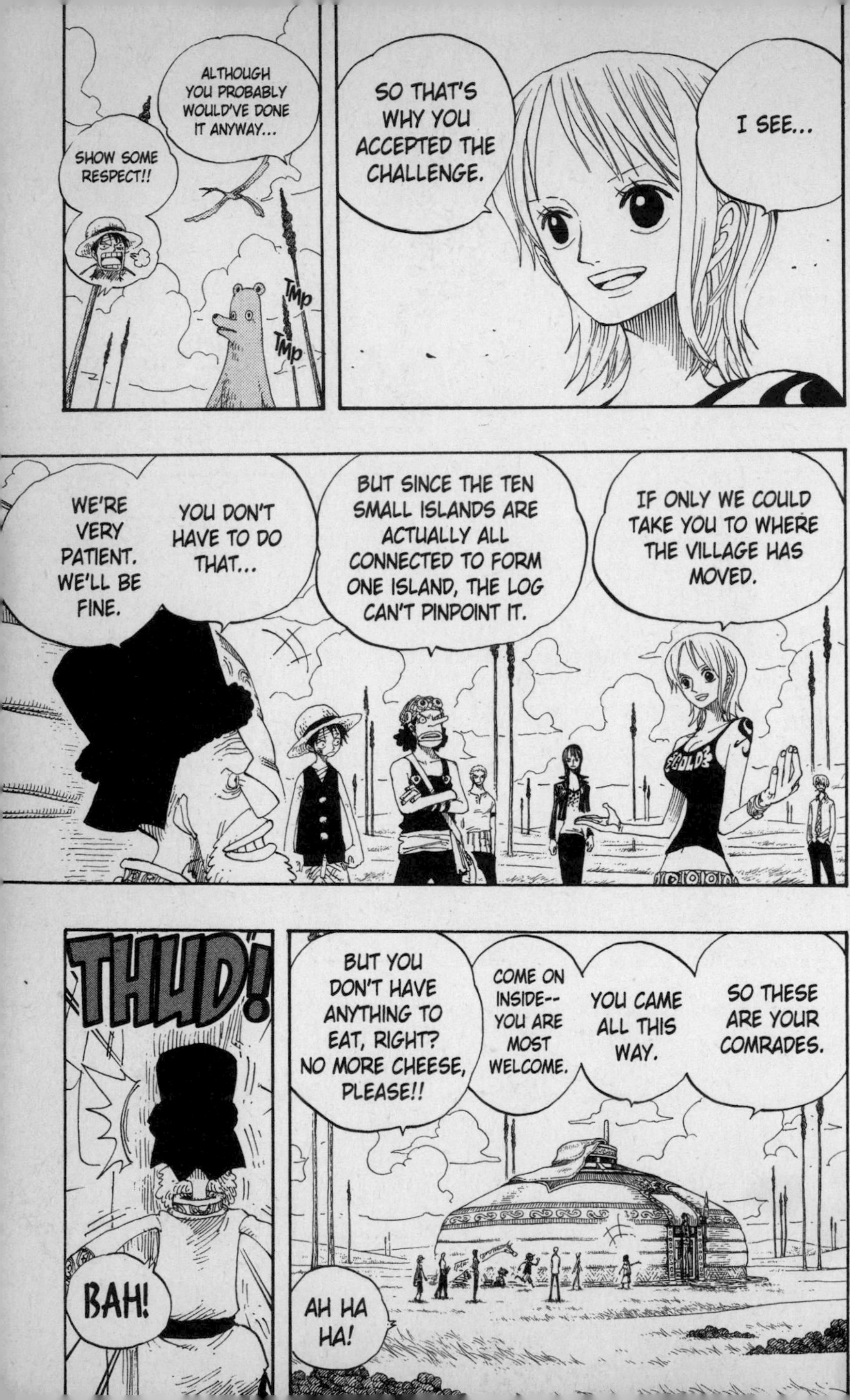
I SEE...
SO THAT'S WHY YOU ACCEPTED THE CHALLENGE.
ALTHOUGH YOU PROBABLY WOULD'VE DONE IT ANYWAY...
SHOW SOME RESPECT!!
TMp
TMp
IF ONLY WE COULD TAKE YOU TO WHERE THE VILLAGE HAS MOVED.
BUT SINCE THE TEN SMALL ISLANDS ARE ACTUALLY ALL CONNECTED TO FORM ONE ISLAND, THE LOG CAN'T PINPOINT IT.
YOU DON'T HAVE TO DO THAT...
WE'RE VERY PATIENT. WE'LL BE FINE.
SO THESE ARE YOUR COMRADES.
YOU CAME ALL THIS WAY.
COME ON INSIDE-- YOU ARE MOST WELCOME.
BUT YOU DON'T HAVE ANYTHING TO EAT, RIGHT? NO MORE CHEESE, PLEASE!!
AH HA HA!
THUD!
BAH!

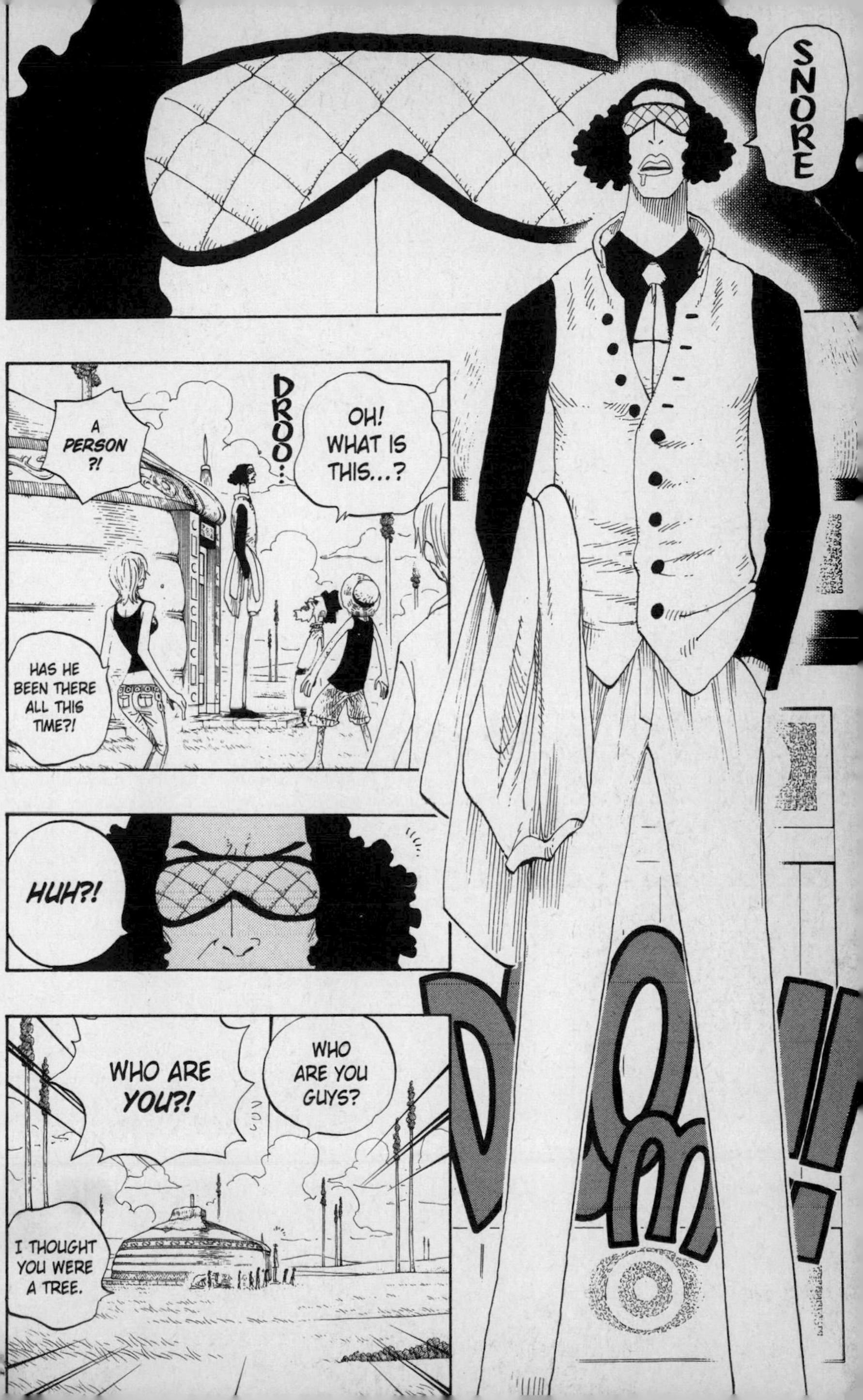
SNORE
DOOM!!
OH! WHAT IS THIS...?
DROO...
A PERSON ?!
HAS HE BEEN THERE ALL THIS TIME?!
HUH?!
WHO ARE YOU GUYS?
WHO ARE YOU?!
I THOUGHT YOU WERE A TREE.

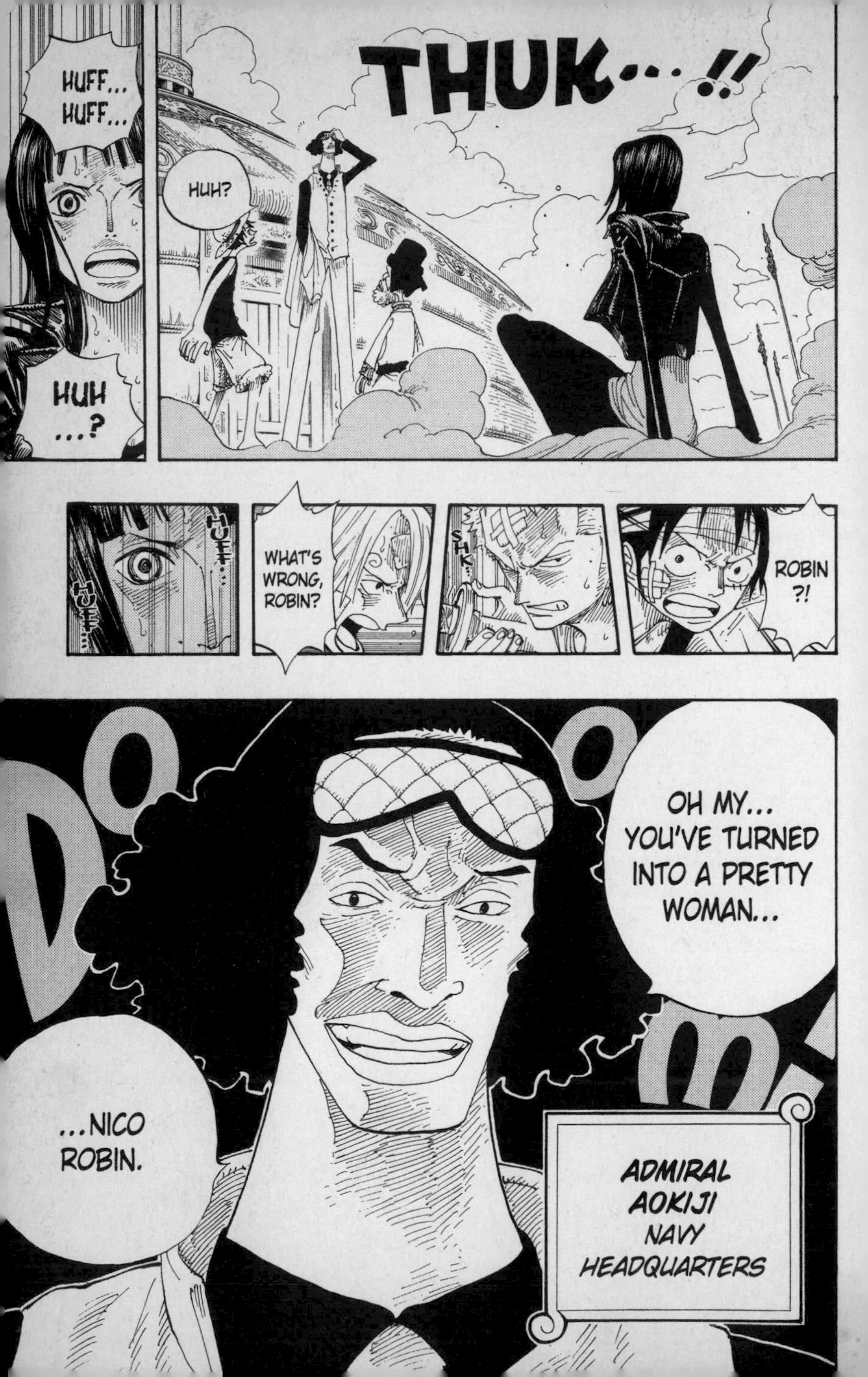
THUK...!!
HUH?
HUFF... HUFF...
HUH ...?
ROBIN ?!
SHK...
WHAT'S WRONG, ROBIN?
HUFF...
HUFF...
OH MY... YOU'VE TURNED INTO A PRETTY WOMAN...
...NICO ROBIN.
DOOM
ADMIRAL AOKIJI NAVY HEADQUARTERS

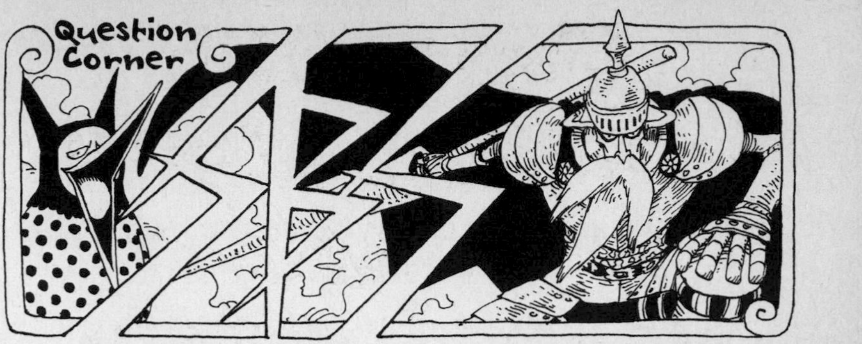
Question Corner

Q: Oda Sensei!! I have a question. What does "a believing heart" mean…?
--Someone Who Looks like Kimutaku

A: That's a good question. You must find the answer within yourself. It would be easy for me to answer (← doesn't know), but you yourself must encounter it in life and grasp at the answer (← doesn't know).

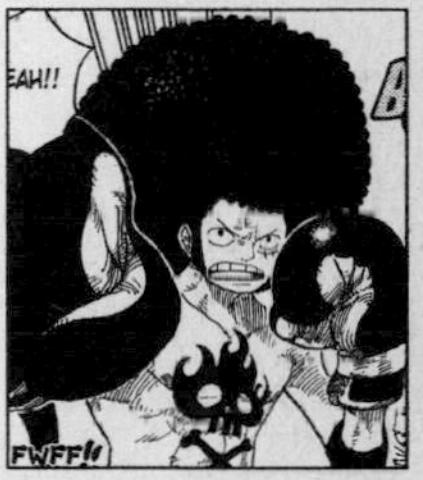
FWFF!!

Q: Hello. I always enjoy reading your manga. And here's my question. Once in a while, Sanji talks about how "Brother Soul" did this or that. What kind of soul does he mean? Is it yummy?
--Average Citizen

A: It tastes like pickled plum. As for what kind of soul... Here's an example: "Hey, yo! Aren't we awesome?!" "Yo, bro, you're lookin' good!" "What the heck does that mean, you jerk?! You're just as awesome!!" "Oh yeah, we're number one in this town!!" "Hahahaha."
It's that kind of soul.

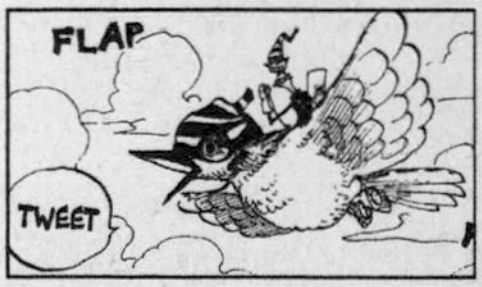
FLAP
TWEET

Q: Hello, Oda Sensei! I have a question. When that super-sparrow Chuchun eats, does he grow teeth like the super-duck Karoo? He's so cute I love him to bits. I want to know more about Chuchun. That's all!!
(P.S. I'm looking forward to the appearance of more super series species!)
--Super Silly

A: Yes, they have teeth. Their diet consists mainly of super-earthworms, super-sharks, super-football fish, etc.

Chapter 319:

ADMIRAL AOKIJI OF THE NAVY HEADQUARTERS

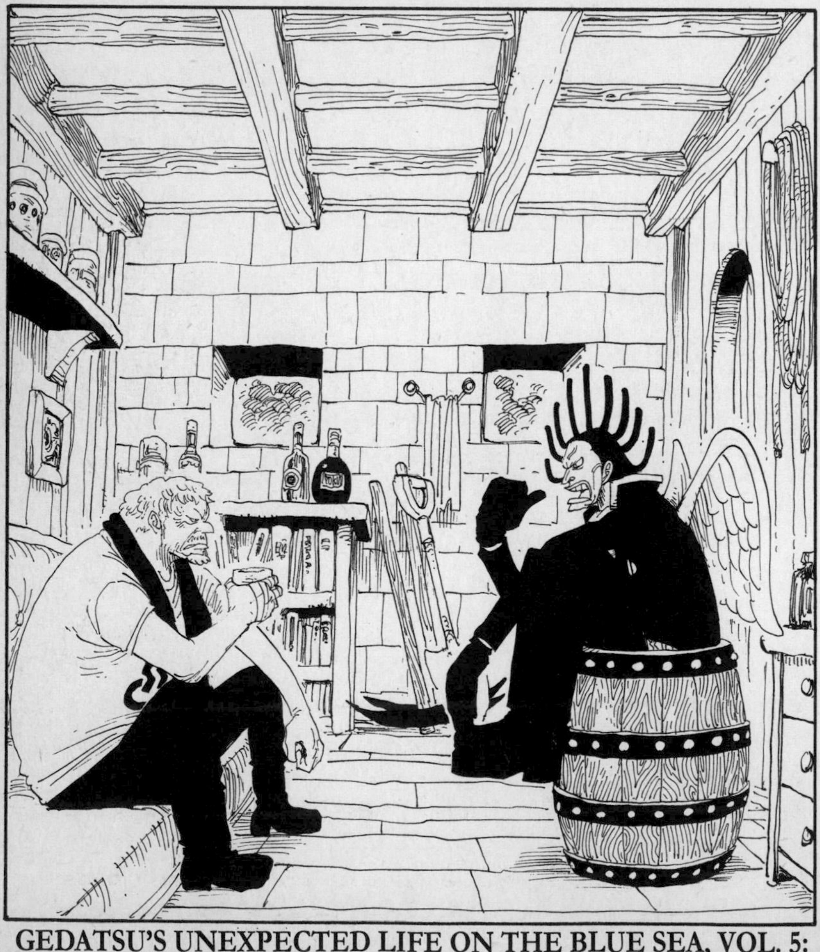

GEDATSU'S UNEXPECTED LIFE ON THE BLUE SEA, VOL. 5:
"I'VE DECIDED TO BECOME THE BOSS OF THE BLUE SEA"

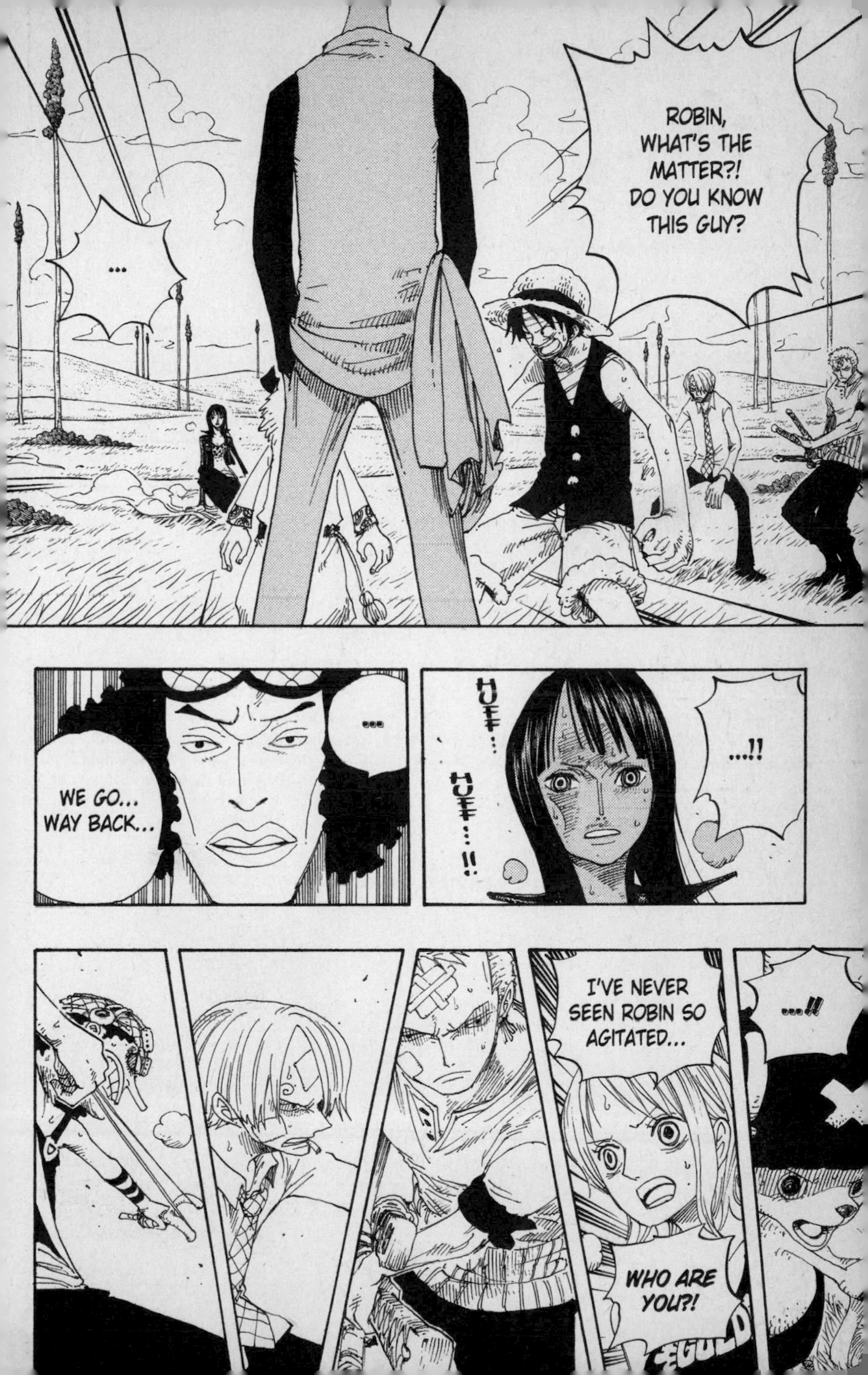
ROBIN, WHAT'S THE MATTER?! DO YOU KNOW THIS GUY?
...
...!!
HUFF...
HUFF...!!
...
WE GO... WAY BACK...
...!!
I'VE NEVER SEEN ROBIN SO AGITATED...
WHO ARE YOU?!

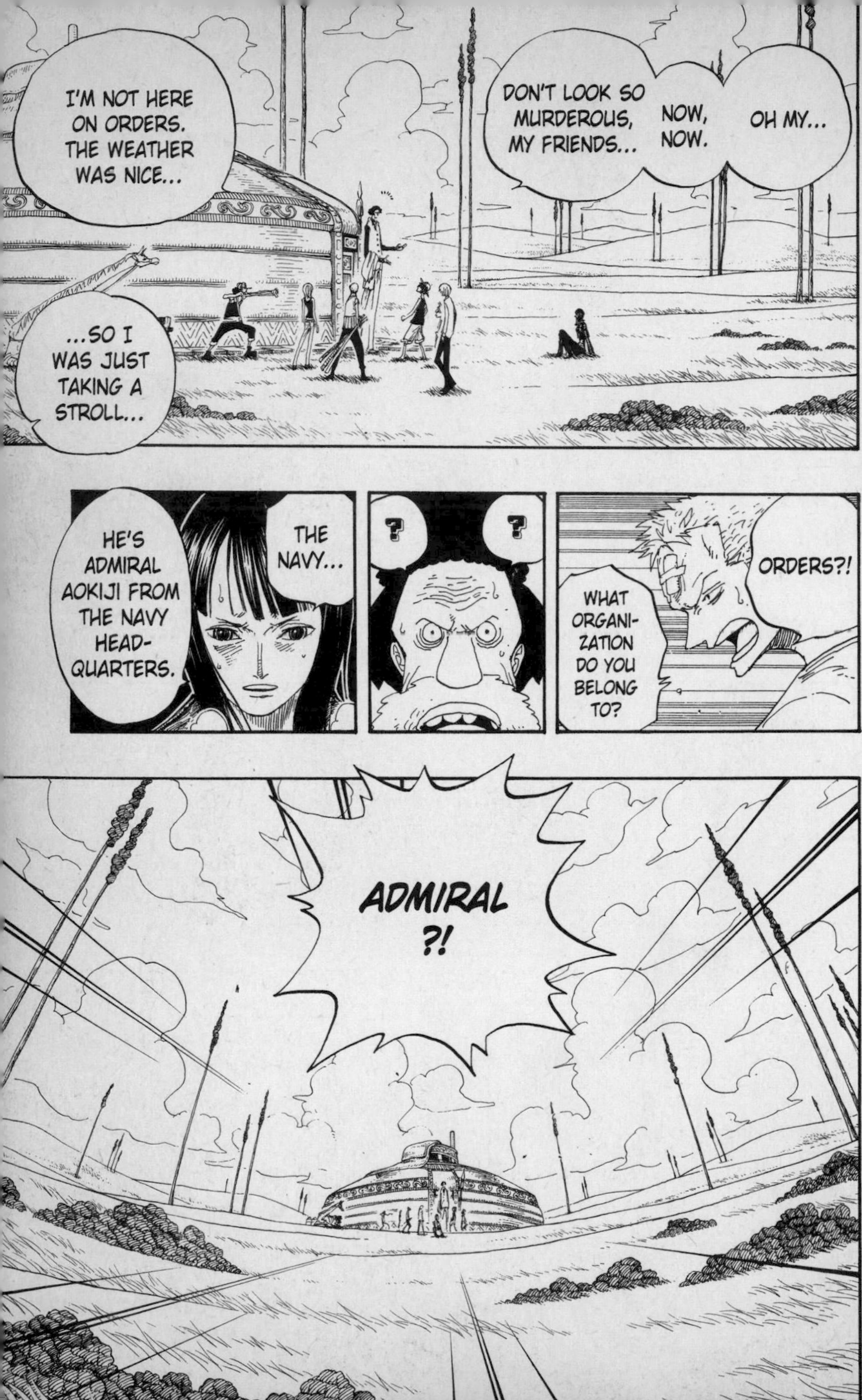
OH MY...
NOW, NOW.
DON'T LOOK SO MURDEROUS, MY FRIENDS...
I'M NOT HERE ON ORDERS. THE WEATHER WAS NICE...
...SO I WAS JUST TAKING A STROLL...
ORDERS?!
WHAT ORGANI-ZATION DO YOU BELONG TO?
?
?
THE NAVY...
HE'S ADMIRAL AOKIJI FROM THE NAVY HEAD-QUARTERS.
ADMIRAL ?!

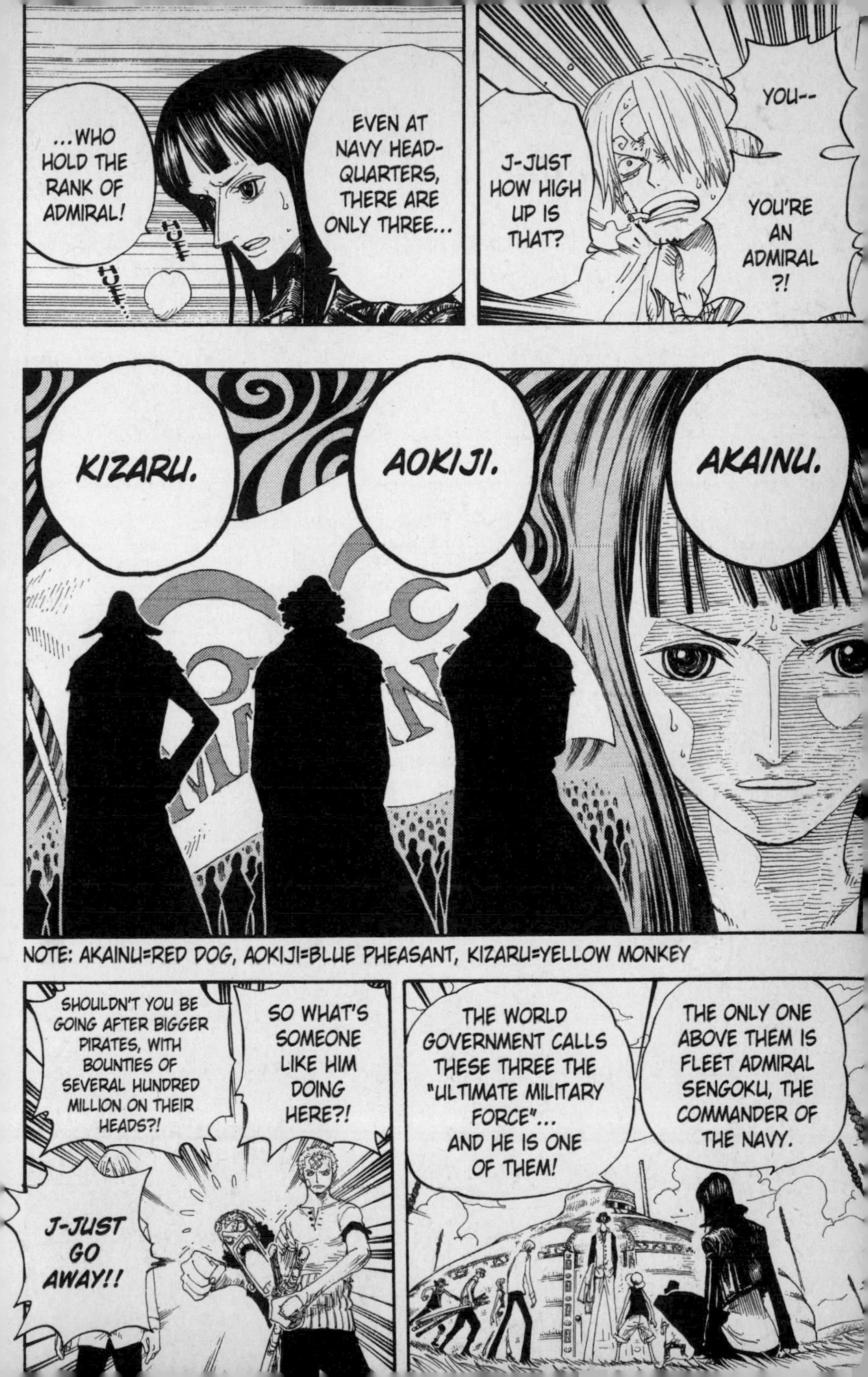
YOU--
YOU'RE AN ADMIRAL ?!
J-JUST HOW HIGH UP IS THAT?
EVEN AT NAVY HEAD-QUARTERS, THERE ARE ONLY THREE...
...WHO HOLD THE RANK OF ADMIRAL!
HUFF
HUFF...
AKAINU.
AOKIJI.
KIZARU.
NOTE: AKAINU=RED DOG, AOKIJI=BLUE PHEASANT, KIZARU=YELLOW MONKEY
THE ONLY ONE ABOVE THEM IS FLEET ADMIRAL SENGOKU, THE COMMANDER OF THE NAVY.
THE WORLD GOVERNMENT CALLS THESE THREE THE "ULTIMATE MILITARY FORCE"... AND HE IS ONE OF THEM!
SO WHAT'S SOMEONE LIKE HIM DOING HERE?!
SHOULDN'T YOU BE GOING AFTER BIGGER PIRATES, WITH BOUNTIES OF SEVERAL HUNDRED MILLION ON THEIR HEADS?!
J-JUST GO AWAY!!

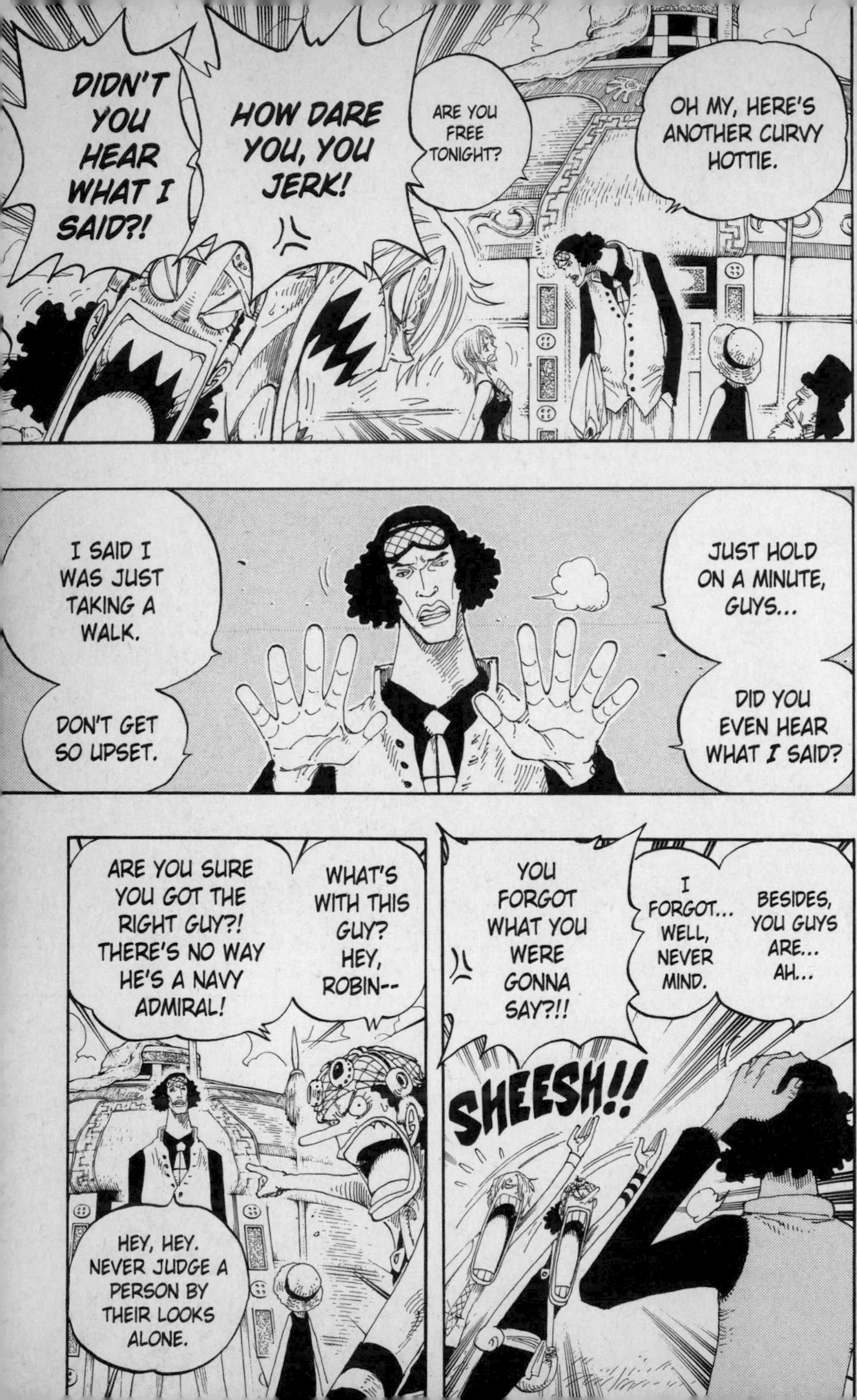
OH MY, HERE'S ANOTHER CURVY HOTTIE.
ARE YOU FREE TONIGHT?
HOW DARE YOU, YOU JERK!
DIDN'T YOU HEAR WHAT I SAID?!
JUST HOLD ON A MINUTE, GUYS...
DID YOU EVEN HEAR WHAT I SAID?
I SAID I WAS JUST TAKING A WALK.
DON'T GET SO UPSET.
BESIDES, YOU GUYS ARE... AH...
I FORGOT... WELL, NEVER MIND.
YOU FORGOT WHAT YOU WERE GONNA SAY?!!
SHEESH!!
WHAT'S WITH THIS GUY? HEY, ROBIN--
ARE YOU SURE YOU GOT THE RIGHT GUY?! THERE'S NO WAY HE'S A NAVY ADMIRAL!
HEY, HEY. NEVER JUDGE A PERSON BY THEIR LOOKS ALONE.

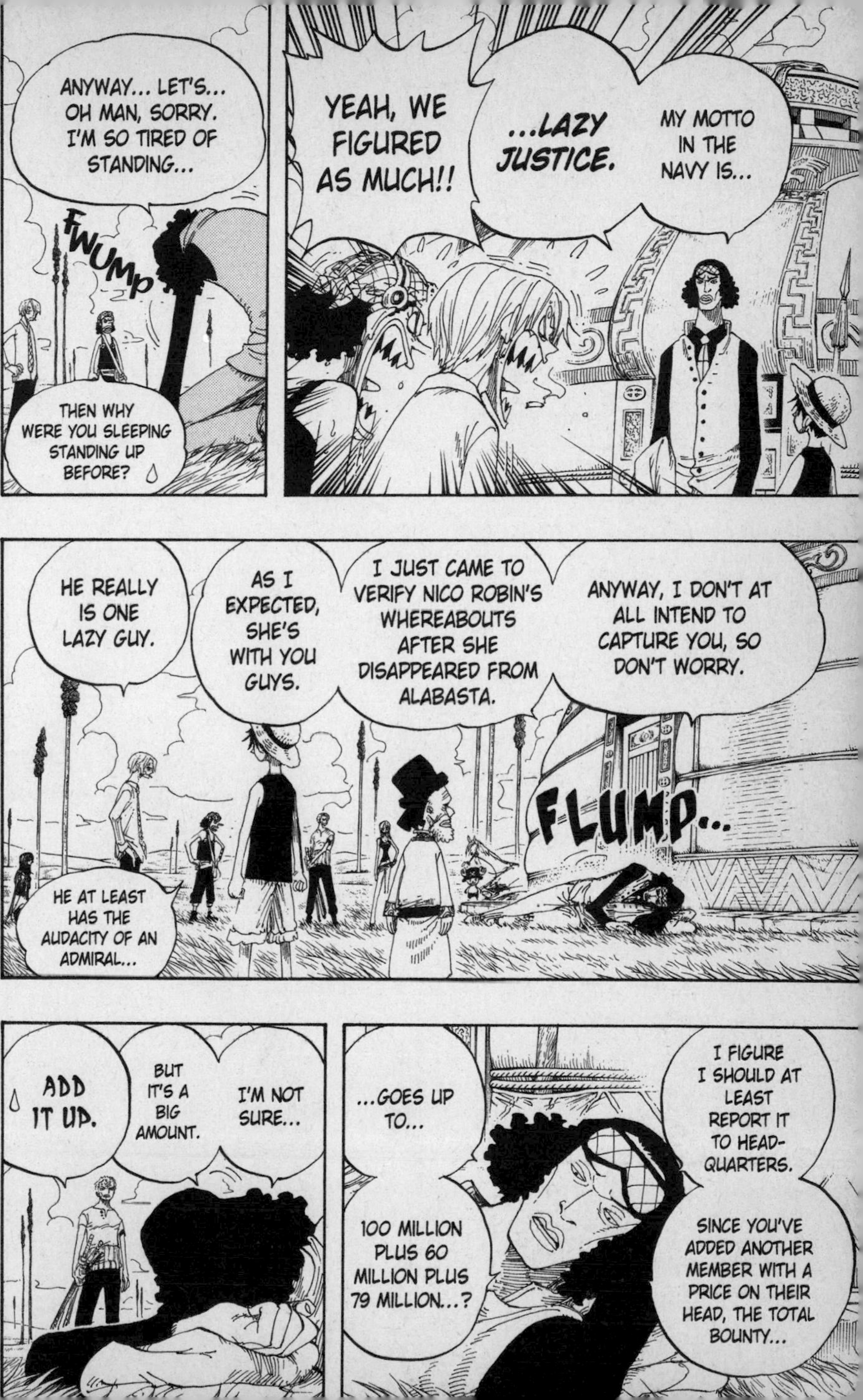
MY MOTTO IN THE NAVY IS...
...LAZY JUSTICE.
YEAH, WE FIGURED AS MUCH!!
ANYWAY... LET'S... OH MAN, SORRY. I'M SO TIRED OF STANDING...
FWUMP
THEN WHY WERE YOU SLEEPING STANDING UP BEFORE?
ANYWAY, I DON'T AT ALL INTEND TO CAPTURE YOU, SO DON'T WORRY.
I JUST CAME TO VERIFY NICO ROBIN'S WHEREABOUTS AFTER SHE DISAPPEARED FROM ALABASTA.
AS I EXPECTED, SHE'S WITH YOU GUYS.
FLUMP...
HE REALLY IS ONE LAZY GUY.
HE AT LEAST HAS THE AUDACITY OF AN ADMIRAL...
I FIGURE I SHOULD AT LEAST REPORT IT TO HEAD-QUARTERS.
SINCE YOU'VE ADDED ANOTHER MEMBER WITH A PRICE ON THEIR HEAD, THE TOTAL BOUNTY...
...GOES UP TO...
100 MILLION PLUS 60 MILLION PLUS 79 MILLION...?
I'M NOT SURE...
BUT IT'S A BIG AMOUNT.
ADD IT UP.

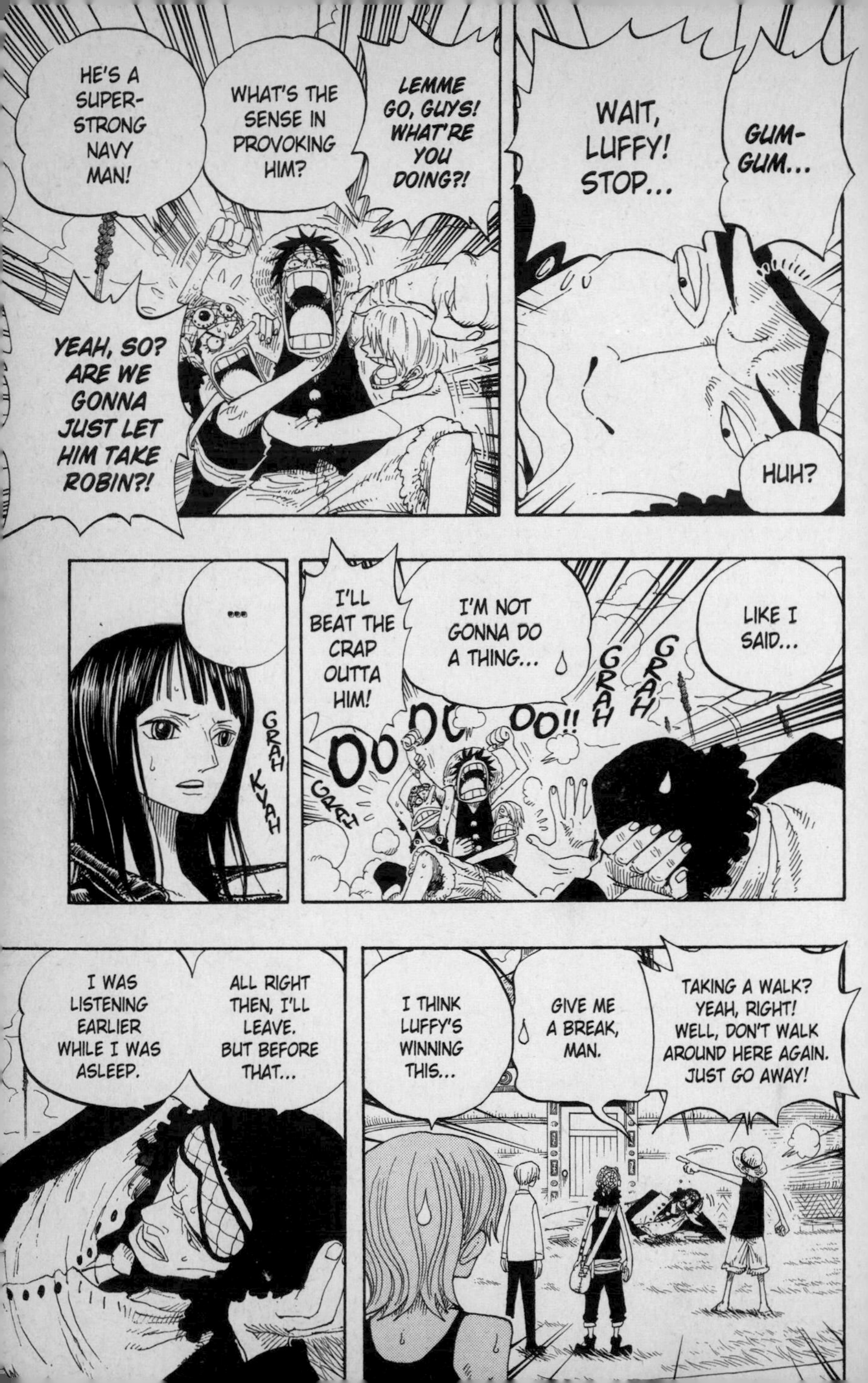
GUM-GUM...
WAIT, LUFFY! STOP...
HUH?
LEMME GO, GUYS! WHAT'RE YOU DOING?!
WHAT'S THE SENSE IN PROVOKING HIM?
HE'S A SUPER-STRONG NAVY MAN!
YEAH, SO? ARE WE GONNA JUST LET HIM TAKE ROBIN?!
LIKE I SAID...
GRAH
GRAH
I'M NOT GONNA DO A THING...
I'LL BEAT THE CRAP OUTTA HIM!
DOOOO!!
GRAH
...
GRAH
KYAH
TAKING A WALK? YEAH, RIGHT! WELL, DON'T WALK AROUND HERE AGAIN. JUST GO AWAY!
GIVE ME A BREAK, MAN.
I THINK LUFFY'S WINNING THIS...
ALL RIGHT THEN, I'LL LEAVE. BUT BEFORE THAT...
I WAS LISTENING EARLIER WHILE I WAS ASLEEP.

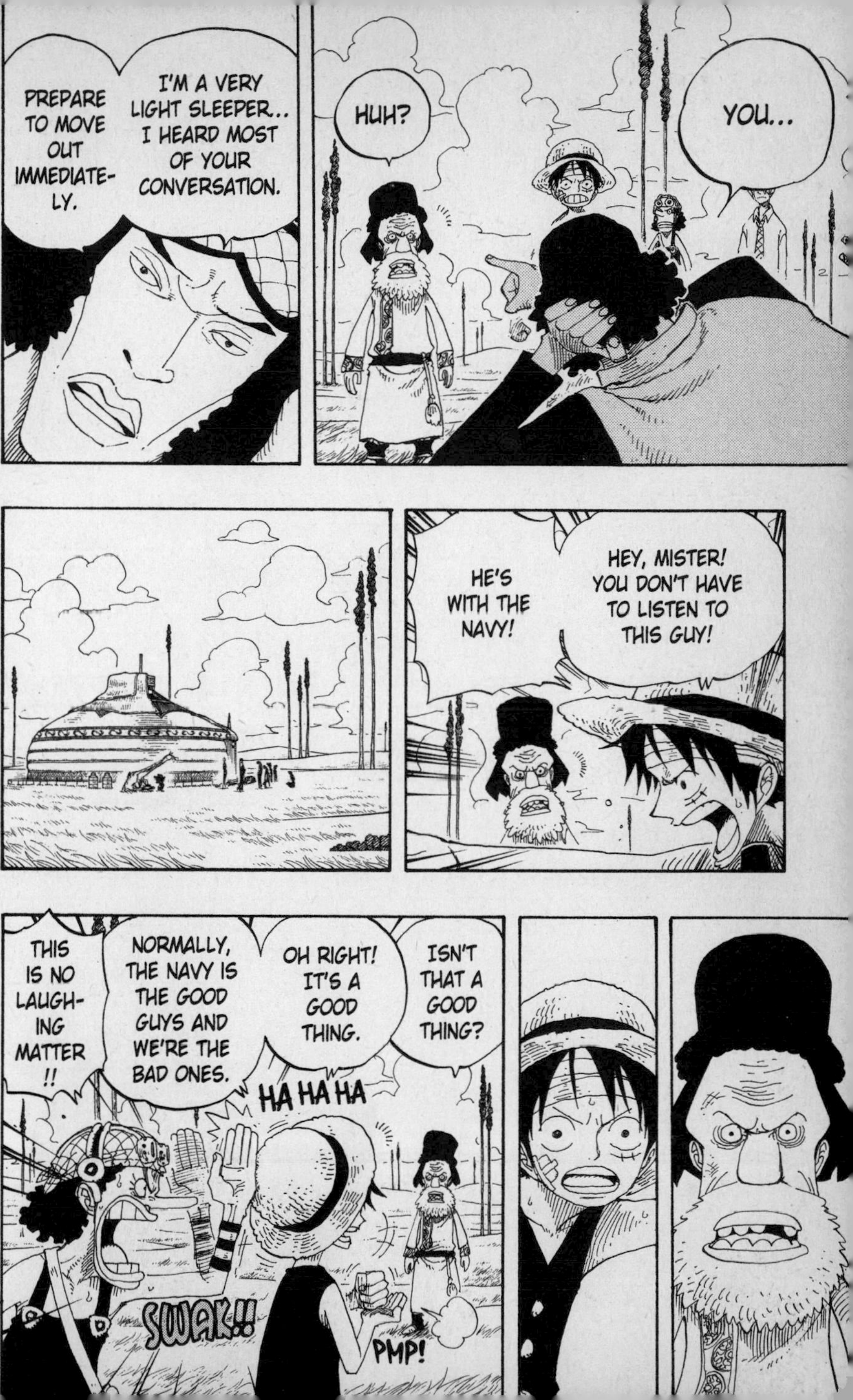
YOU...
HUH?
I'M A VERY LIGHT SLEEPER... I HEARD MOST OF YOUR CONVERSATION.
PREPARE TO MOVE OUT IMMEDIATE-LY.
HEY, MISTER! YOU DON'T HAVE TO LISTEN TO THIS GUY!
HE'S WITH THE NAVY!
ISN'T THAT A GOOD THING?
OH RIGHT! IT'S A GOOD THING.
HA HA HA
NORMALLY, THE NAVY IS THE GOOD GUYS AND WE'RE THE BAD ONES.
THIS IS NO LAUGH-ING MATTER !!
SWAK!!
PMP!

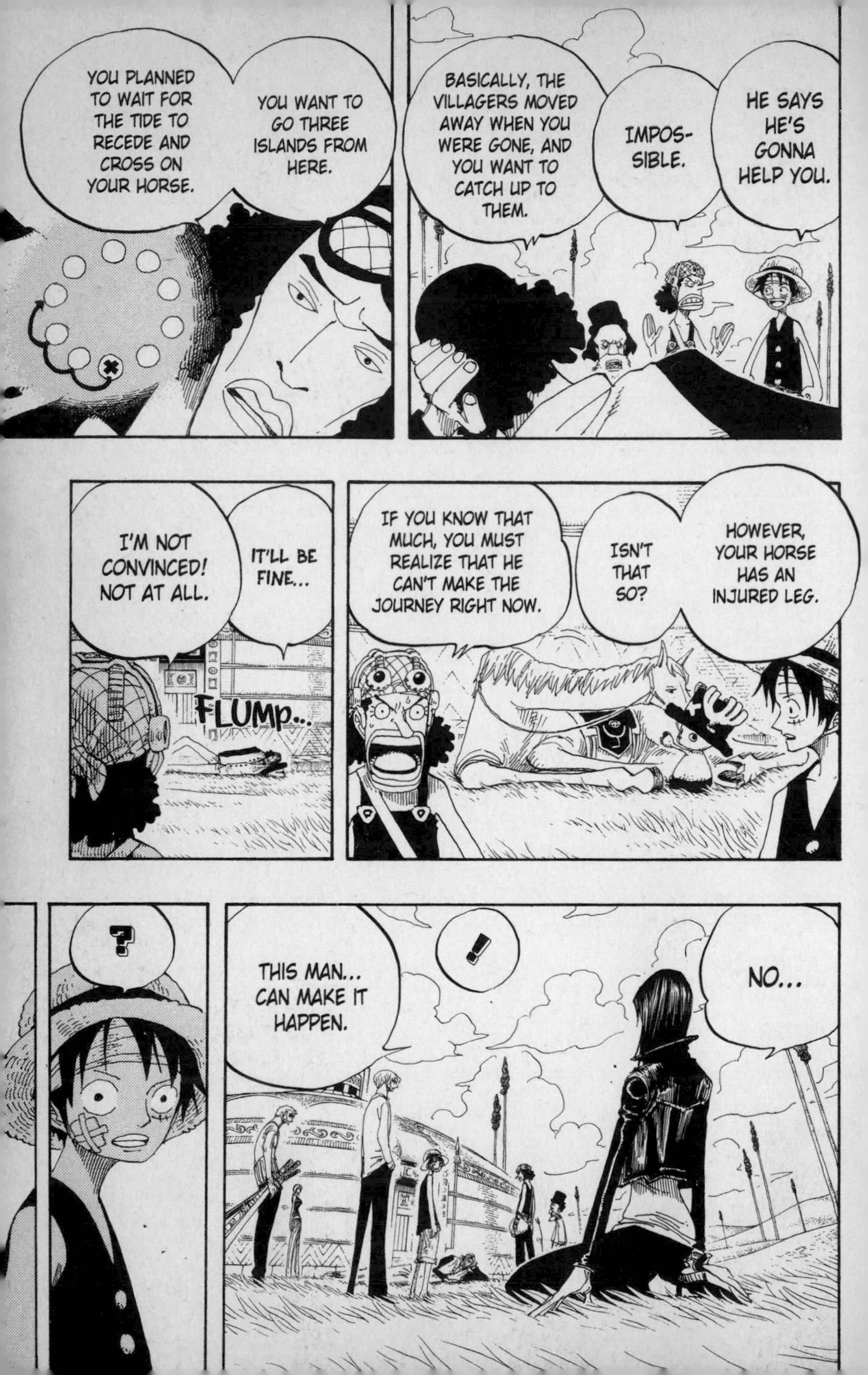
HE SAYS HE'S GONNA HELP YOU.
IMPOS- SIBLE.
BASICALLY, THE VILLAGERS MOVED AWAY WHEN YOU WERE GONE, AND YOU WANT TO CATCH UP TO THEM.
YOU WANT TO GO THREE ISLANDS FROM HERE.
YOU PLANNED TO WAIT FOR THE TIDE TO RECEDE AND CROSS ON YOUR HORSE.
HOWEVER, YOUR HORSE HAS AN INJURED LEG.
ISN'T THAT SO?
IF YOU KNOW THAT MUCH, YOU MUST REALIZE THAT HE CAN'T MAKE THE JOURNEY RIGHT NOW.
IT'LL BE FINE...
I'M NOT CONVINCED! NOT AT ALL.
FLUMP...
NO...
!
THIS MAN... CAN MAKE IT HAPPEN.
?

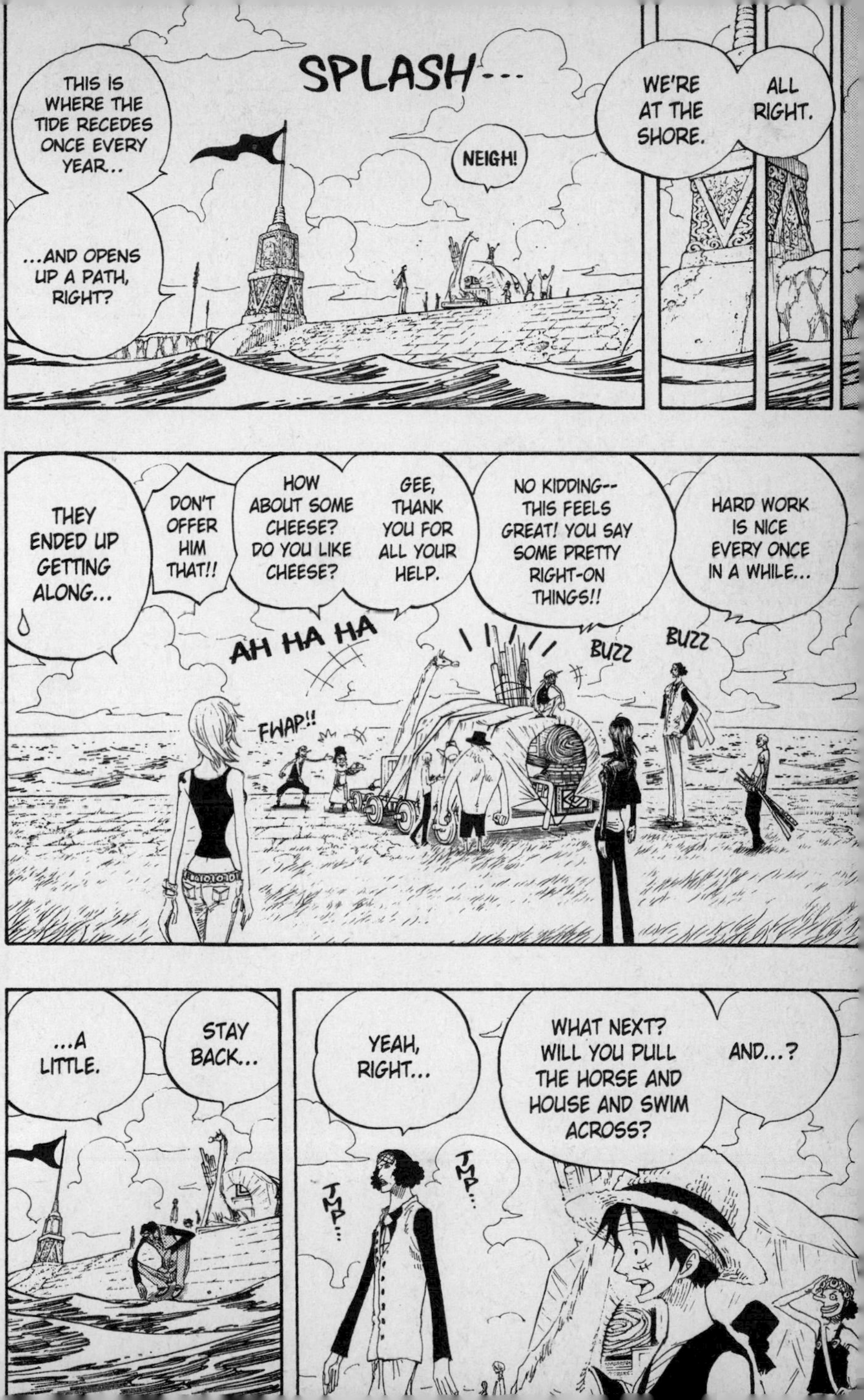
ALL RIGHT.
WE'RE AT THE SHORE.
SPLASH...
NEIGH!
THIS IS WHERE THE TIDE RECEDES ONCE EVERY YEAR...
...AND OPENS UP A PATH, RIGHT?
HARD WORK IS NICE EVERY ONCE IN A WHILE...
NO KIDDING-- THIS FEELS GREAT! YOU SAY SOME PRETTY RIGHT-ON THINGS!!
GEE, THANK YOU FOR ALL YOUR HELP.
HOW ABOUT SOME CHEESE? DO YOU LIKE CHEESE?
DON'T OFFER HIM THAT!!
THEY ENDED UP GETTING ALONG...
BUZZ
BUZZ
AH HA HA
FWAP!!
AND...?
WHAT NEXT? WILL YOU PULL THE HORSE AND HOUSE AND SWIM ACROSS?
YEAH, RIGHT...
TMP...
TMP...
STAY BACK...
...A LITTLE.

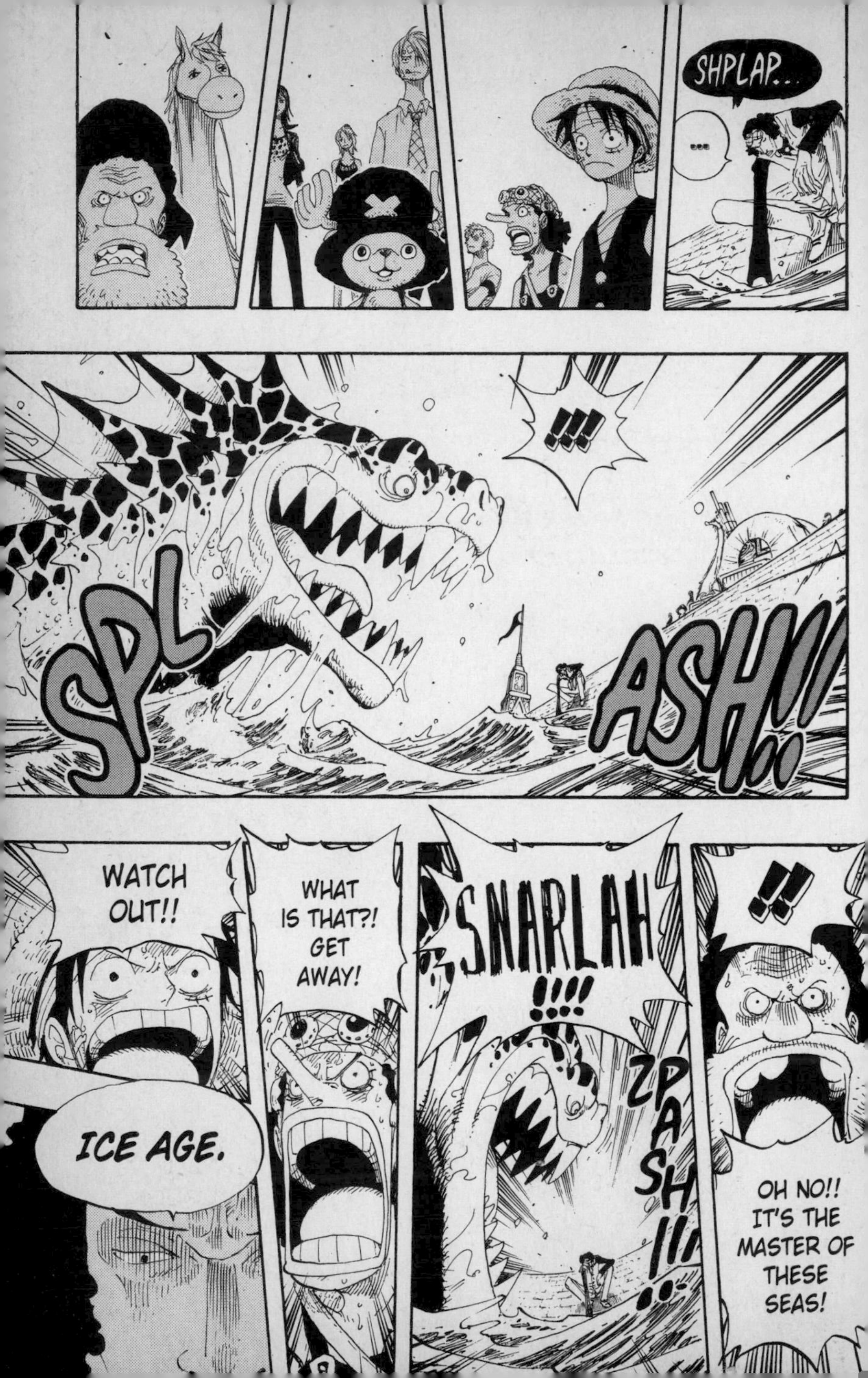
SHPLAP...
...
!!!
SPLASH!!
!!
OH NO!! IT'S THE MASTER OF THESE SEAS!
SNARLAH!!!!
ZPASH!!
WHAT IS THAT?! GET AWAY!
WATCH OUT!!
ICE AGE.

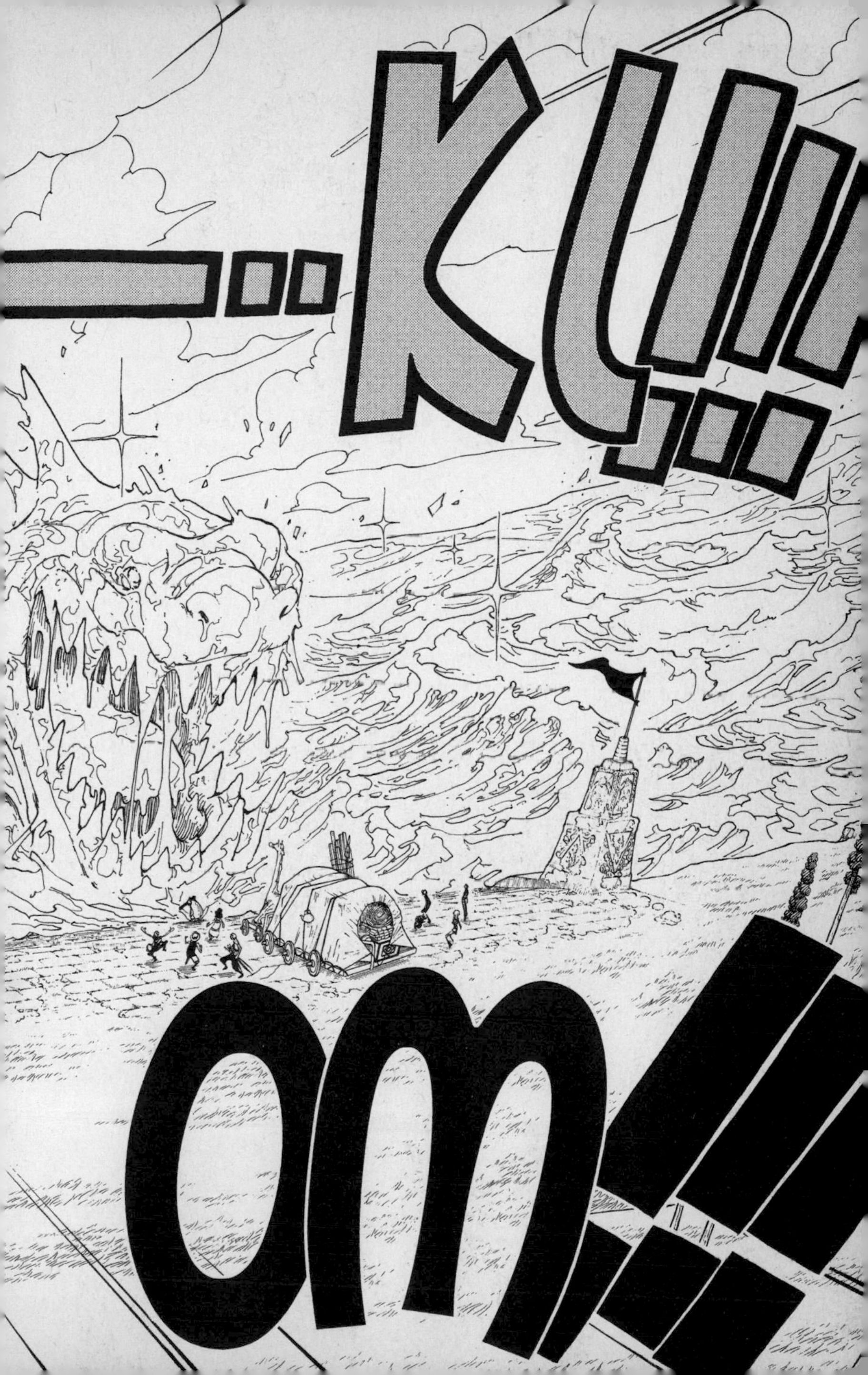
—..KU!!
OM!!

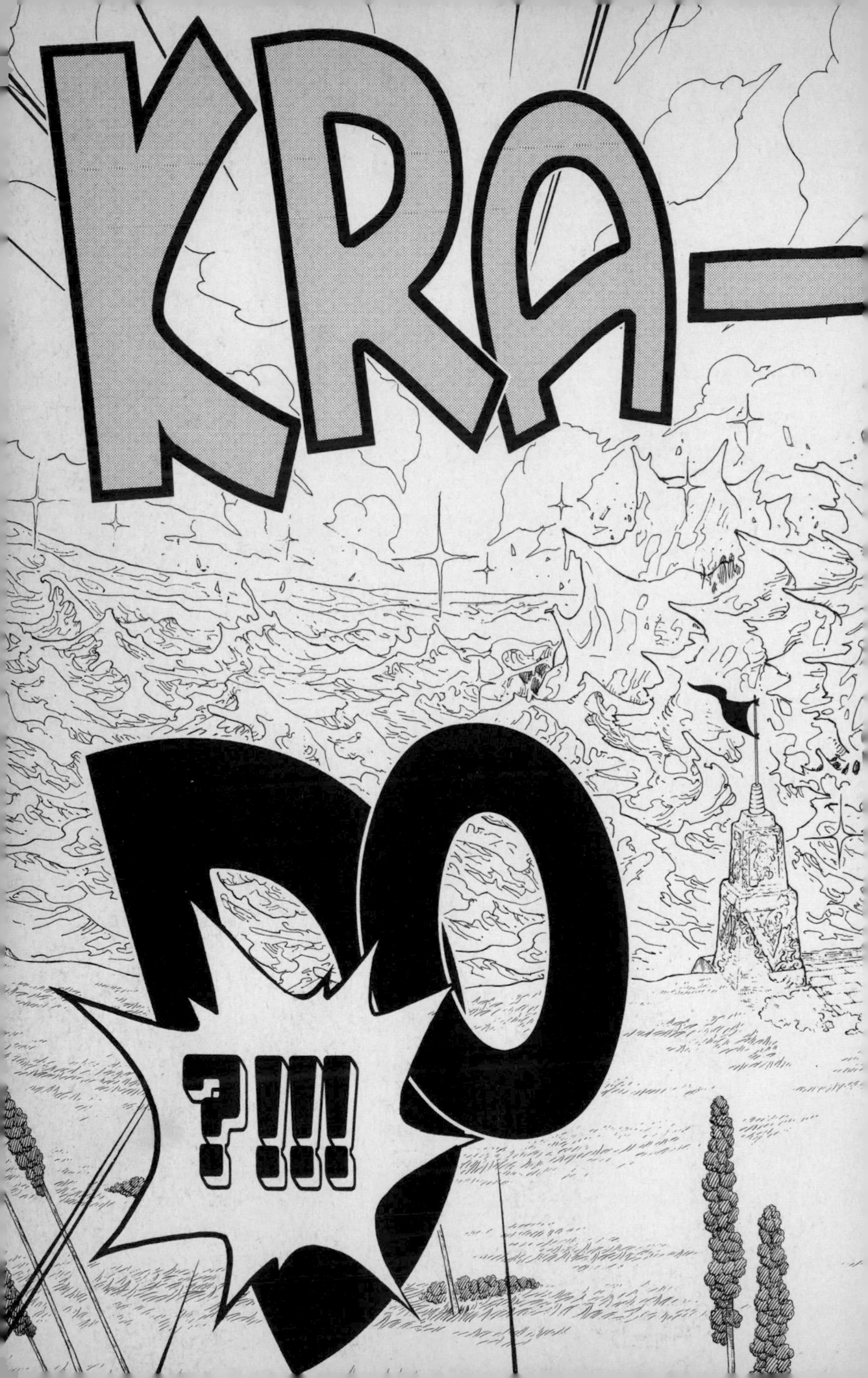
KRA-
KOOM
?!!!

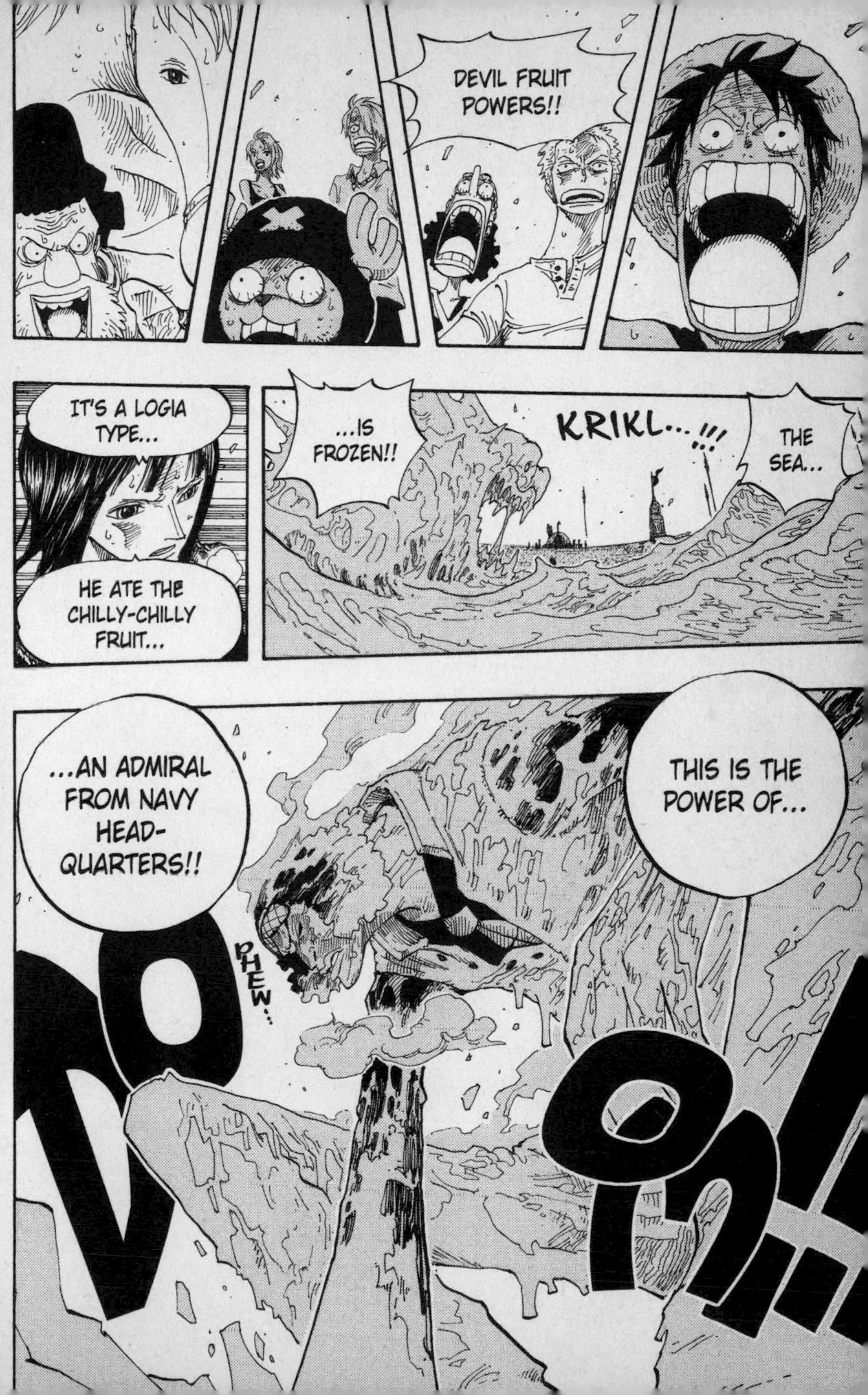
DEVIL FRUIT POWERS!!
THE SEA...
KRIKL...!!!
...IS FROZEN!!
IT'S A LOGIA TYPE...
HE ATE THE CHILLY-CHILLY FRUIT...
THIS IS THE POWER OF...
...AN ADMIRAL FROM NAVY HEAD-QUARTERS!!
PHEW...

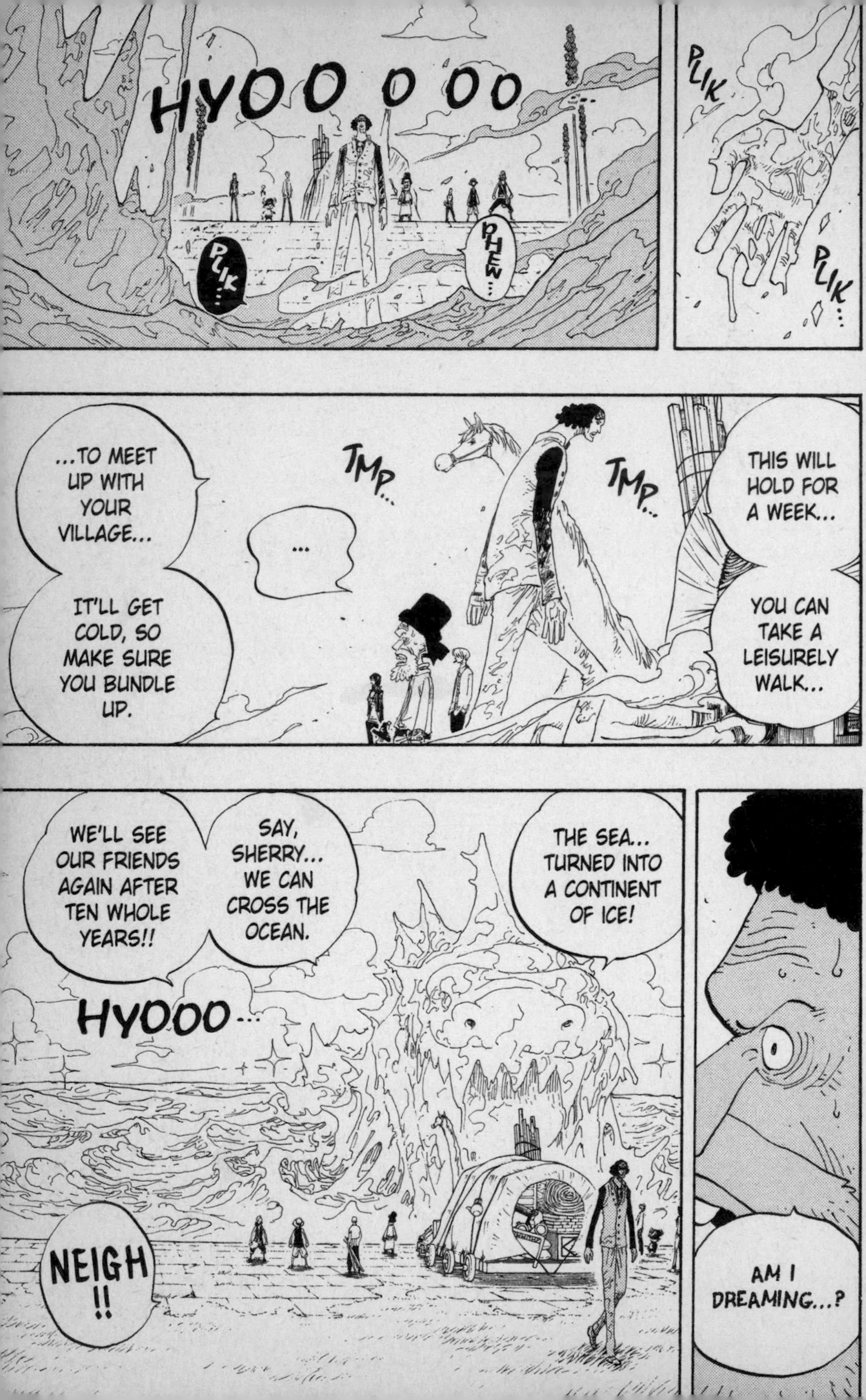
PLIK
PLIK...
HYOO O O OO
PHEW...
PLIK...
THIS WILL HOLD FOR A WEEK...
YOU CAN TAKE A LEISURELY WALK...
TMP...
TMP...
...
...TO MEET UP WITH YOUR VILLAGE...
IT'LL GET COLD, SO MAKE SURE YOU BUNDLE UP.
AM I DREAMING...?
THE SEA... TURNED INTO A CONTINENT OF ICE!
SAY, SHERRY... WE CAN CROSS THE OCEAN.
WE'LL SEE OUR FRIENDS AGAIN AFTER TEN WHOLE YEARS!!
HYOOO...
NEIGH!!

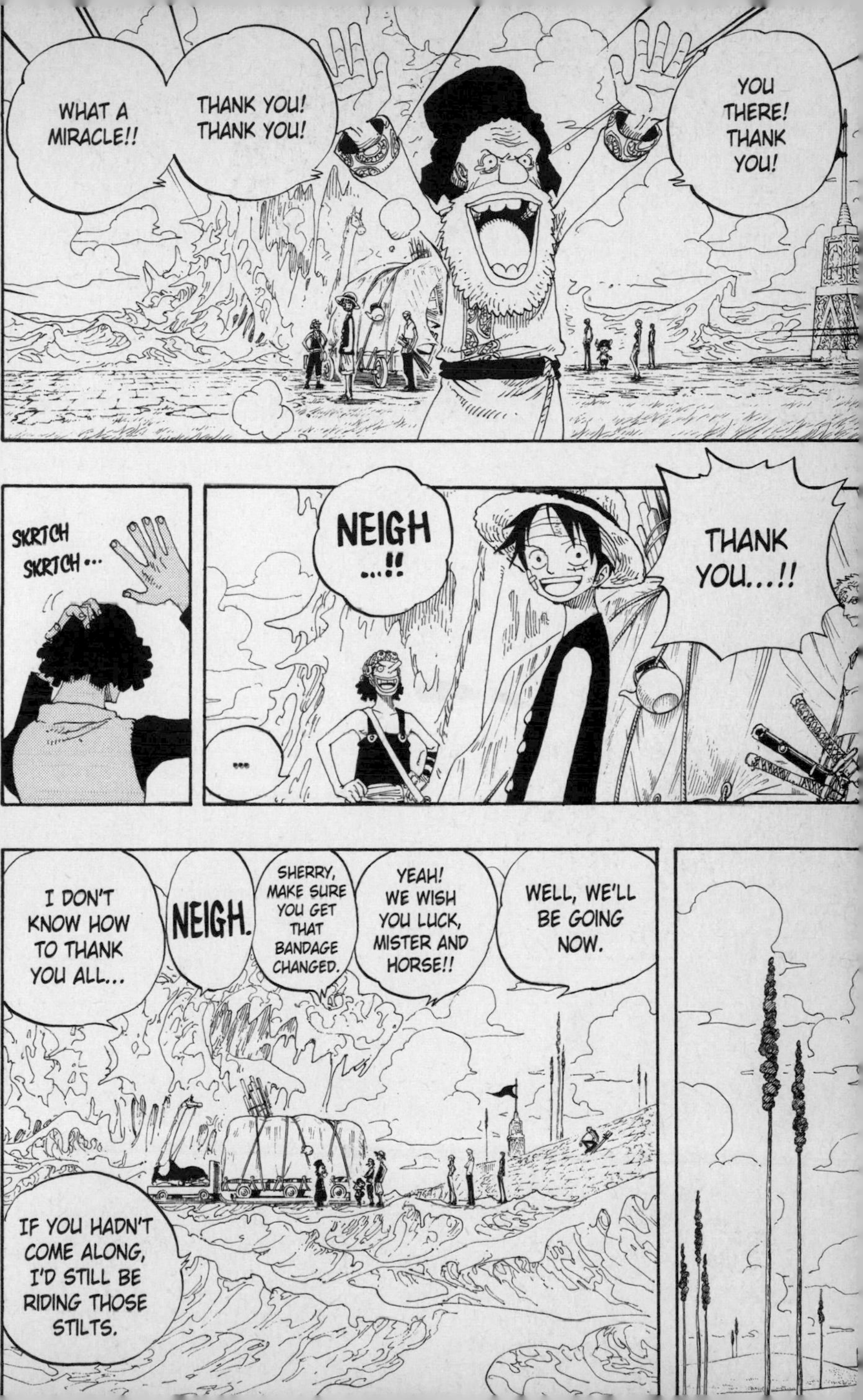
YOU THERE! THANK YOU!
THANK YOU! THANK YOU!
WHAT A MIRACLE!!
THANK YOU...!!
NEIGH ...!!
...
SKRTCH SKRTCH...
WELL, WE'LL BE GOING NOW.
YEAH! WE WISH YOU LUCK, MISTER AND HORSE!!
SHERRY, MAKE SURE YOU GET THAT BANDAGE CHANGED.
NEIGH.
I DON'T KNOW HOW TO THANK YOU ALL...
IF YOU HADN'T COME ALONG, I'D STILL BE RIDING THOSE STILTS.

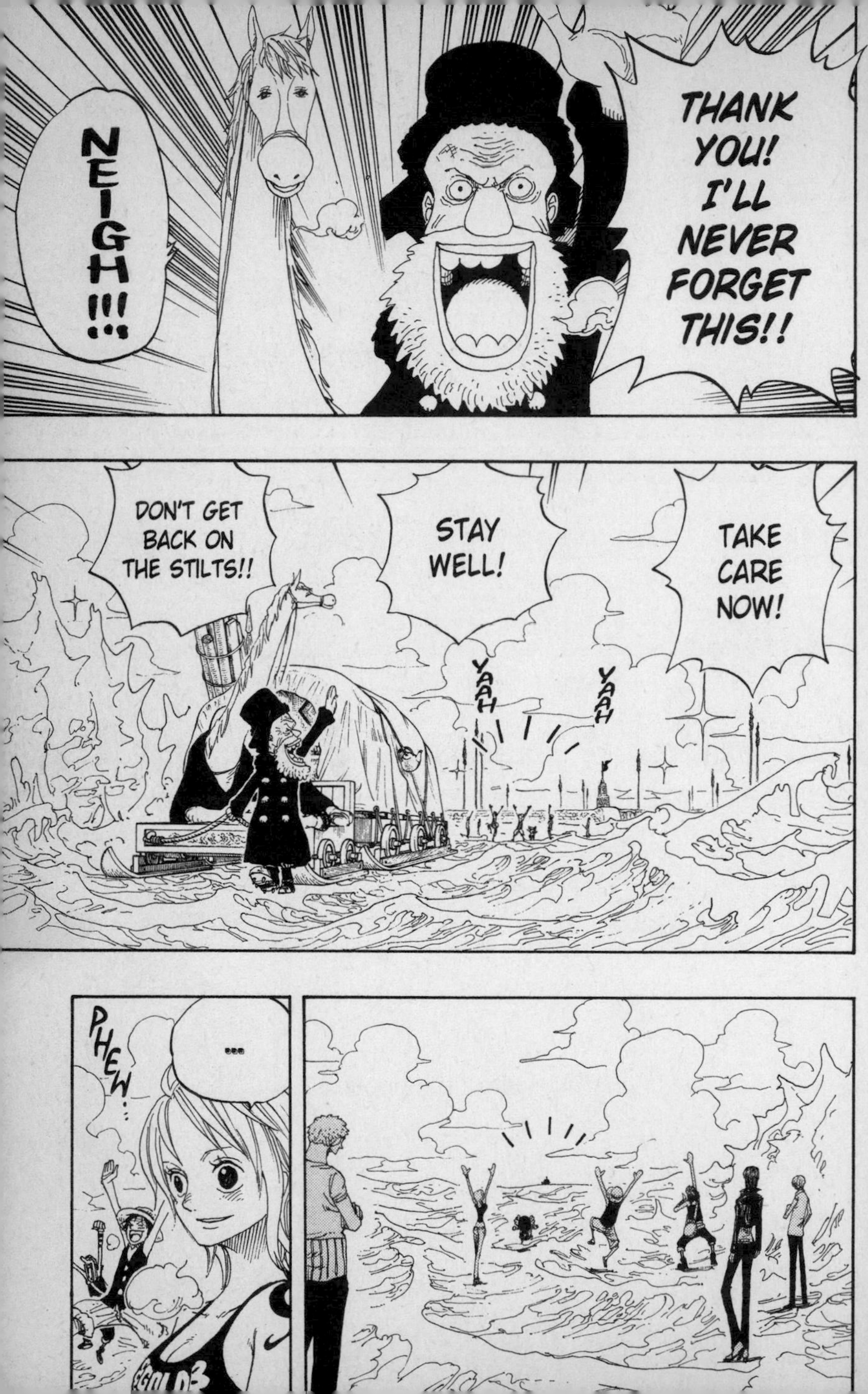
THANK YOU! I'LL NEVER FORGET THIS!!
NEIGH!!!
TAKE CARE NOW!
YAAAH
STAY WELL!
YAAH
DON'T GET BACK ON THE STILTS!!
...
PHEW...

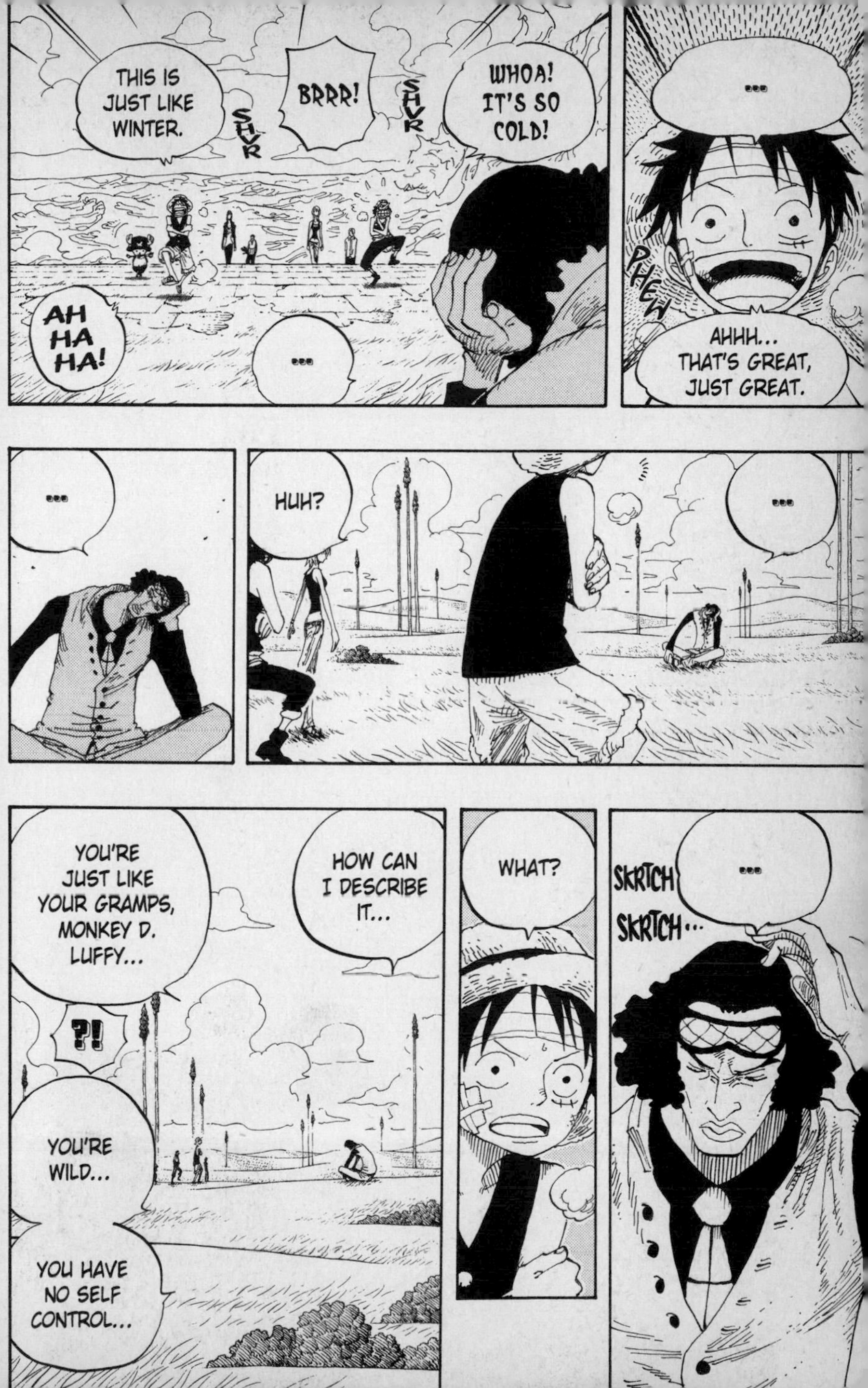
...
PHEW
AHHH... THAT'S GREAT, JUST GREAT.
WHOA! IT'S SO COLD!
SHVR
BRRR!
SHVR
THIS IS JUST LIKE WINTER.
...
AH HA HA!
...
HUH?
...
...
SKRTCH SKRTCH...
WHAT?
HOW CAN I DESCRIBE IT...
YOU'RE JUST LIKE YOUR GRAMPS, MONKEY D. LUFFY...
?!
YOU'RE WILD...
YOU HAVE NO SELF CONTROL...

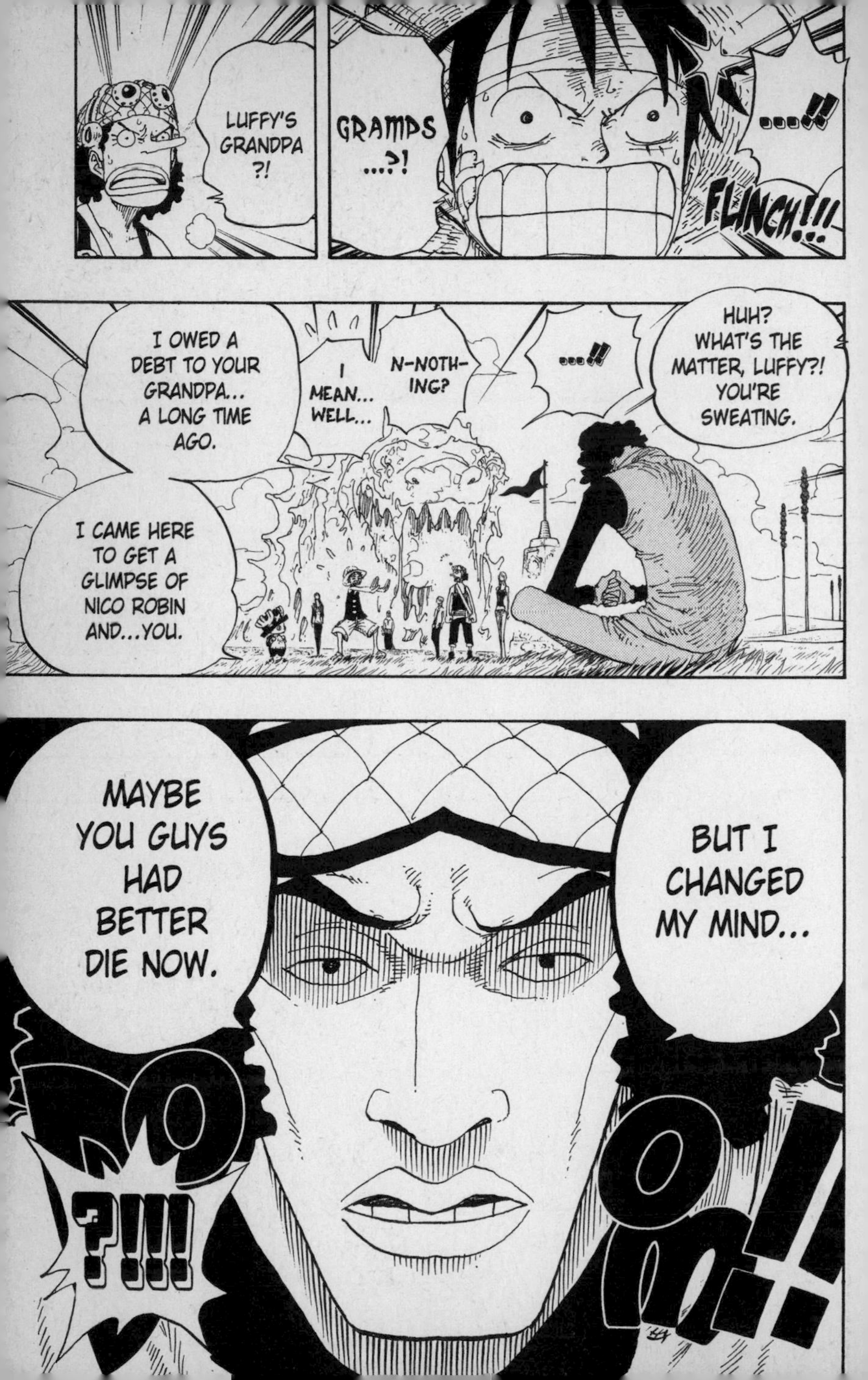
...!!
FLINCH!!!
GRAMPS ...?!
LUFFY'S GRANDPA ?!
HUH? WHAT'S THE MATTER, LUFFY?! YOU'RE SWEATING.
...!!
N-NOTHING?
I MEAN... WELL...
I OWED A DEBT TO YOUR GRANDPA... A LONG TIME AGO.
I CAME HERE TO GET A GLIMPSE OF NICO ROBIN AND...YOU.
BUT I CHANGED MY MIND...
MAYBE YOU GUYS HAD BETTER DIE NOW.
?!!!

Chapter 320:
ULTIMATE MILITARY FORCE

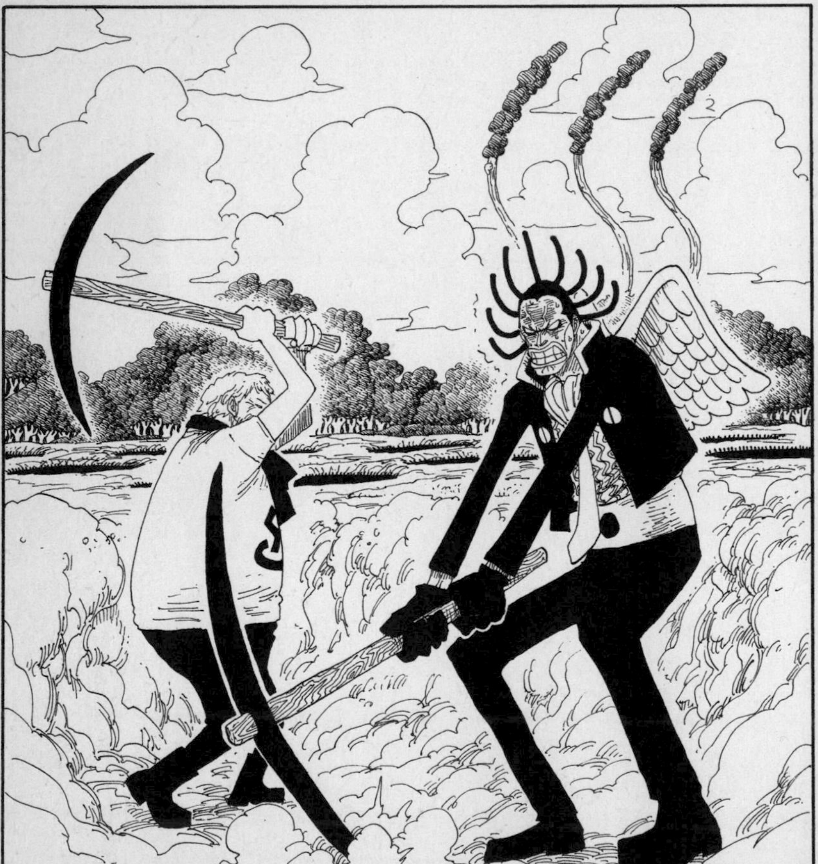

GEDATSU'S UNEXPECTED LIFE ON THE BLUE SEA, VOL. 6:
"DON'T FORGET TO BREATH WHEN YOU SPEND THE DAY DIGGING, MASTER GEDATSU"

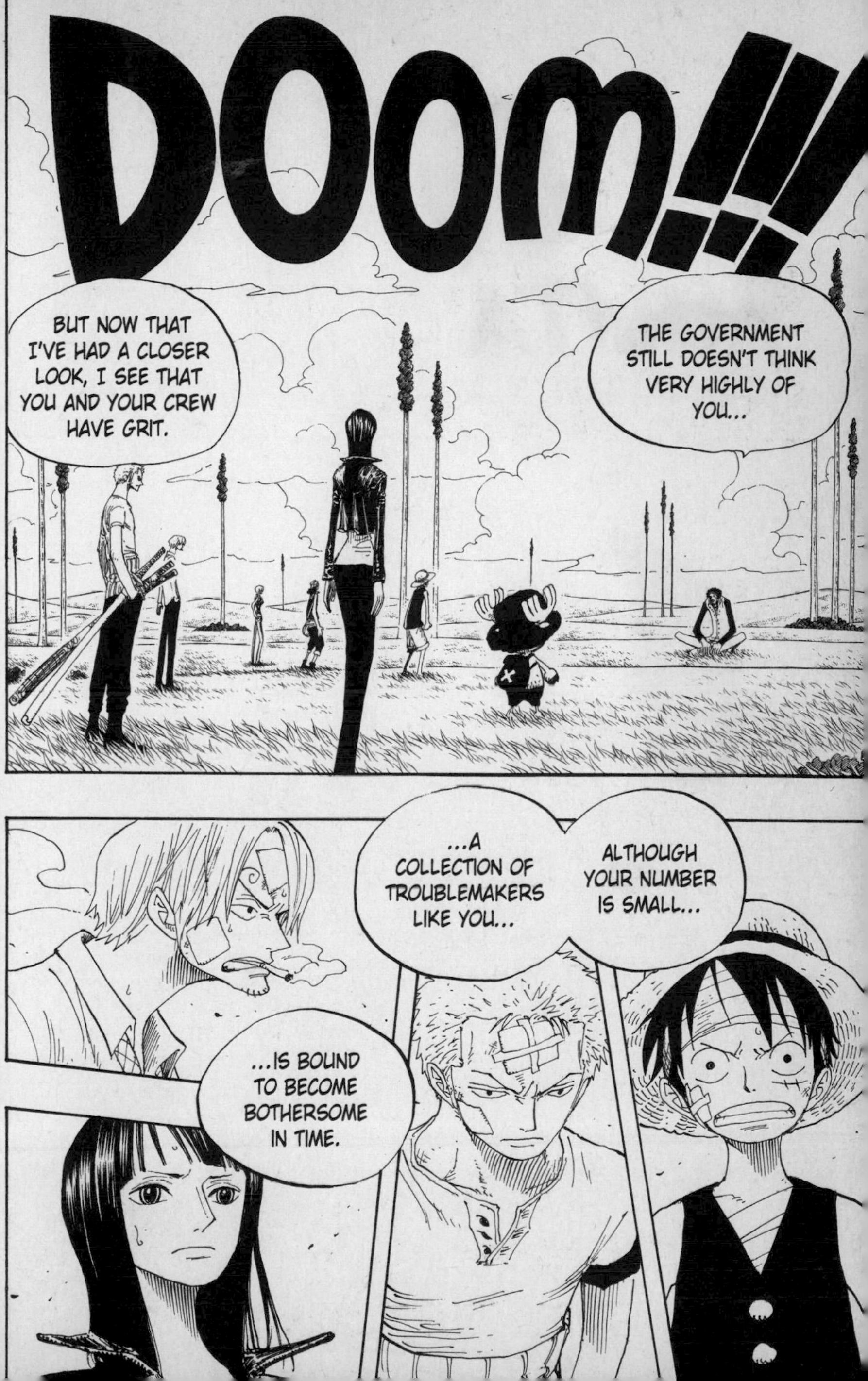
DOOM!!!
THE GOVERNMENT STILL DOESN'T THINK VERY HIGHLY OF YOU...
BUT NOW THAT I'VE HAD A CLOSER LOOK, I SEE THAT YOU AND YOUR CREW HAVE GRIT.
ALTHOUGH YOUR NUMBER IS SMALL...
...A COLLECTION OF TROUBLEMAKERS LIKE YOU...
...IS BOUND TO BECOME BOTHERSOME IN TIME.

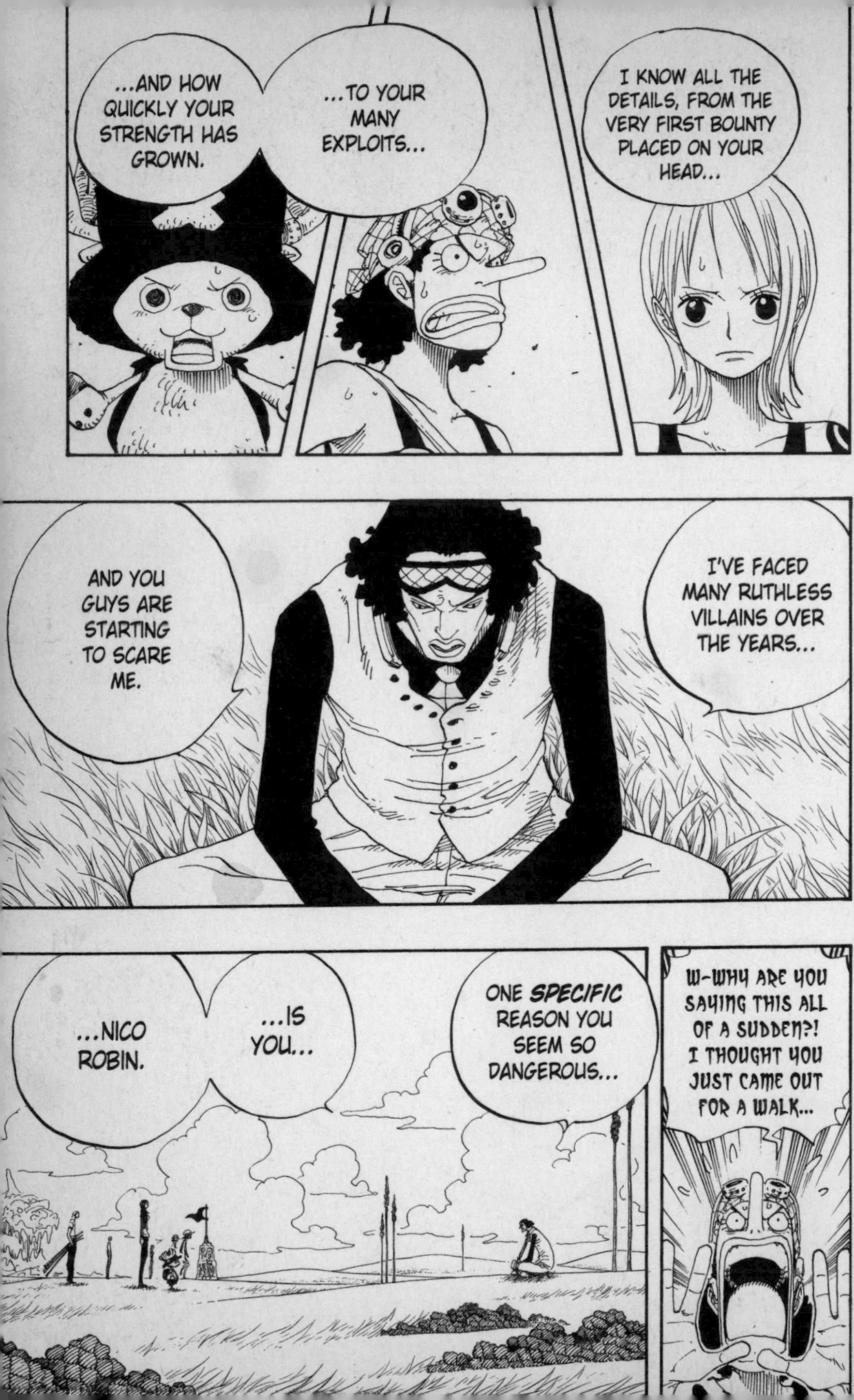
I KNOW ALL THE DETAILS, FROM THE VERY FIRST BOUNTY PLACED ON YOUR HEAD...
...TO YOUR MANY EXPLOITS...
...AND HOW QUICKLY YOUR STRENGTH HAS GROWN.
I'VE FACED MANY RUTHLESS VILLAINS OVER THE YEARS...
AND YOU GUYS ARE STARTING TO SCARE ME.
W-WHY ARE YOU SAYING THIS ALL OF A SUDDEN?! I THOUGHT YOU JUST CAME OUT FOR A WALK...
ONE *SPECIFIC* REASON YOU SEEM SO DANGEROUS...
...IS YOU...
...NICO ROBIN.

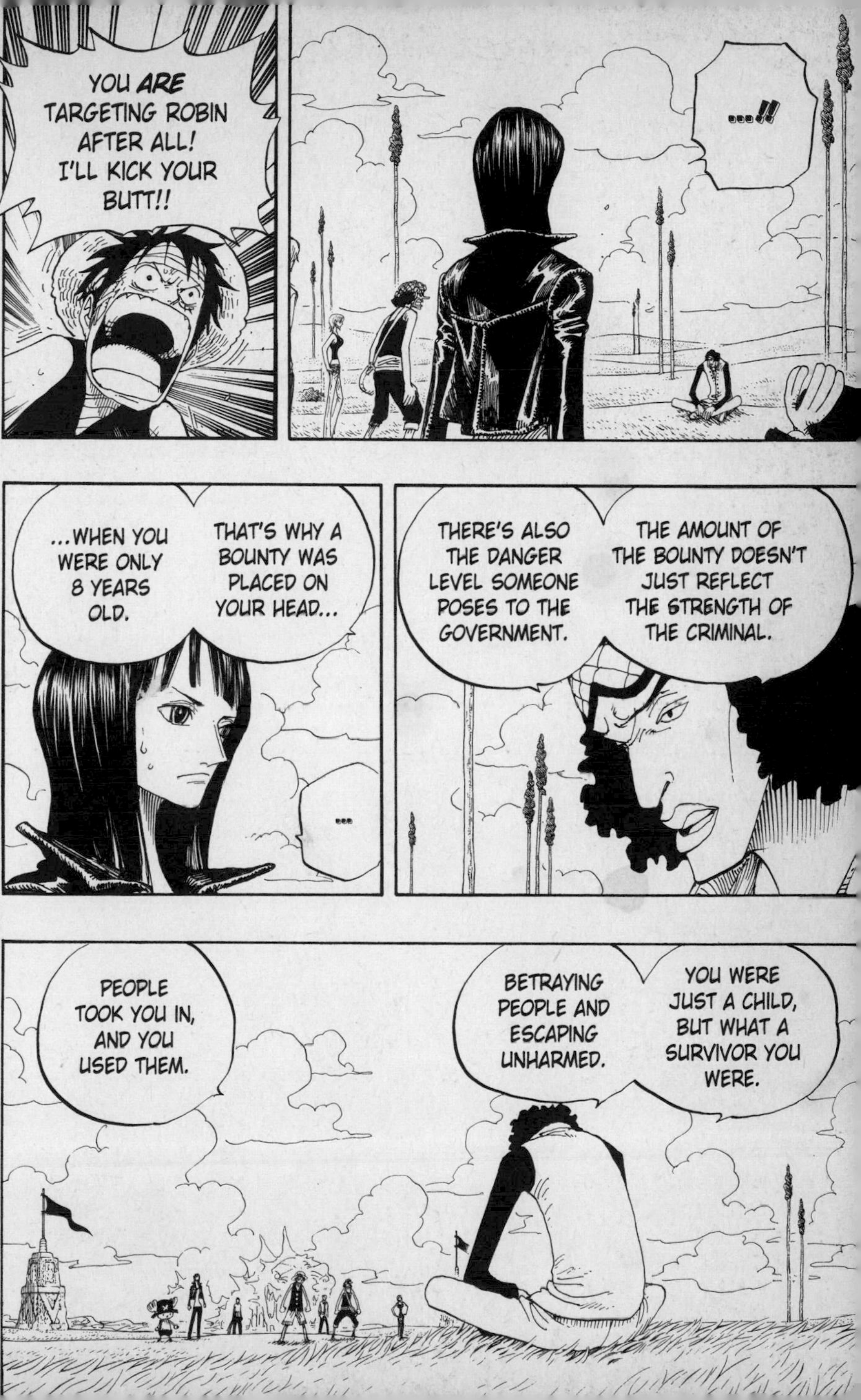
...!!
YOU ARE TARGETING ROBIN AFTER ALL! I'LL KICK YOUR BUTT!!
THE AMOUNT OF THE BOUNTY DOESN'T JUST REFLECT THE STRENGTH OF THE CRIMINAL.
THERE'S ALSO THE DANGER LEVEL SOMEONE POSES TO THE GOVERNMENT.
THAT'S WHY A BOUNTY WAS PLACED ON YOUR HEAD...
...WHEN YOU WERE ONLY 8 YEARS OLD.
...
YOU WERE JUST A CHILD, BUT WHAT A SURVIVOR YOU WERE.
BETRAYING PEOPLE AND ESCAPING UNHARMED.
PEOPLE TOOK YOU IN, AND YOU USED THEM.

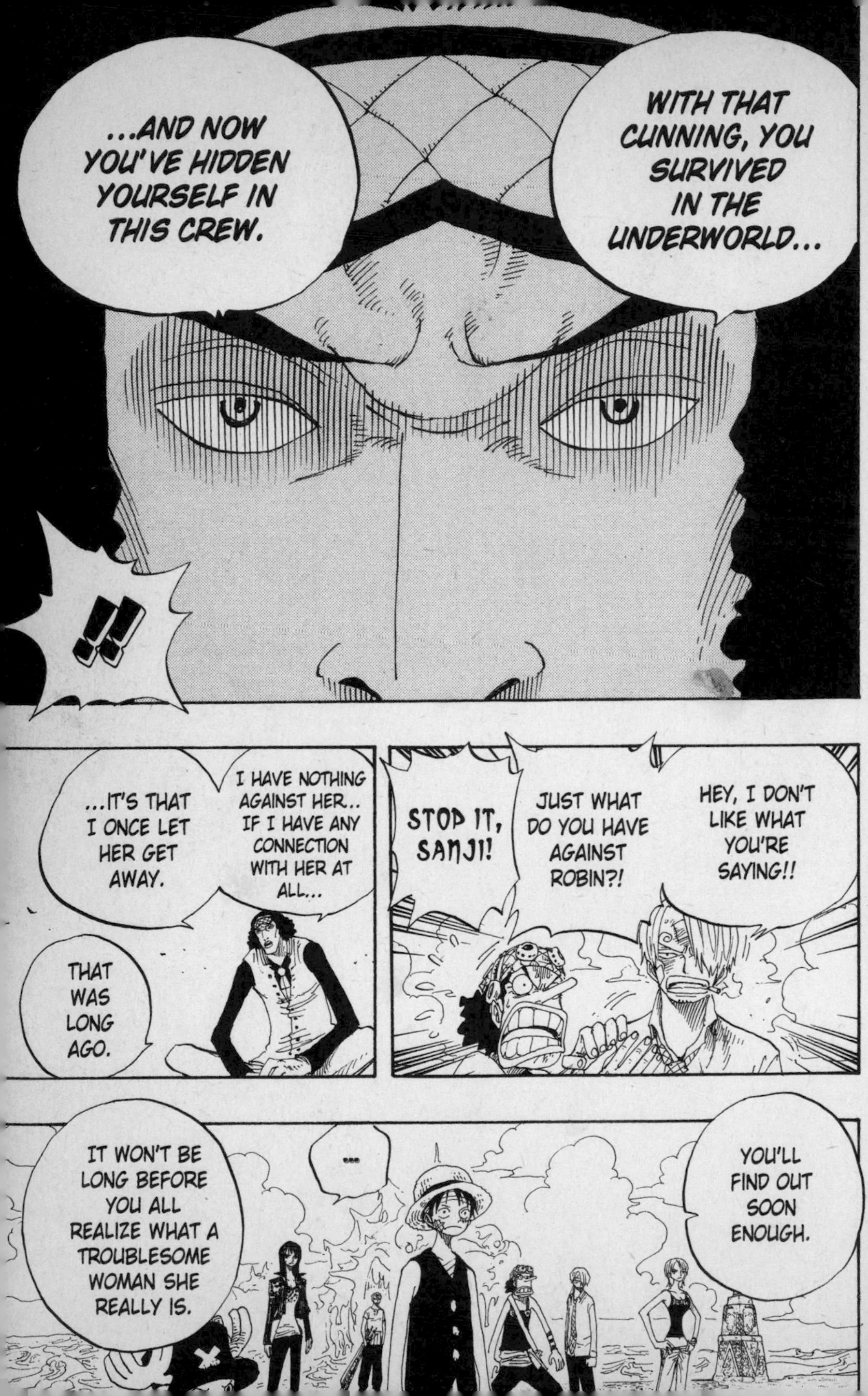
WITH THAT CUNNING, YOU SURVIVED IN THE UNDERWORLD...
...AND NOW YOU'VE HIDDEN YOURSELF IN THIS CREW.
!!
HEY, I DON'T LIKE WHAT YOU'RE SAYING!!
JUST WHAT DO YOU HAVE AGAINST ROBIN?!
STOP IT, SANJI!
I HAVE NOTHING AGAINST HER... IF I HAVE ANY CONNECTION WITH HER AT ALL...
...IT'S THAT I ONCE LET HER GET AWAY.
THAT WAS LONG AGO.
YOU'LL FIND OUT SOON ENOUGH.
...
IT WON'T BE LONG BEFORE YOU ALL REALIZE WHAT A TROUBLESOME WOMAN SHE REALLY IS.

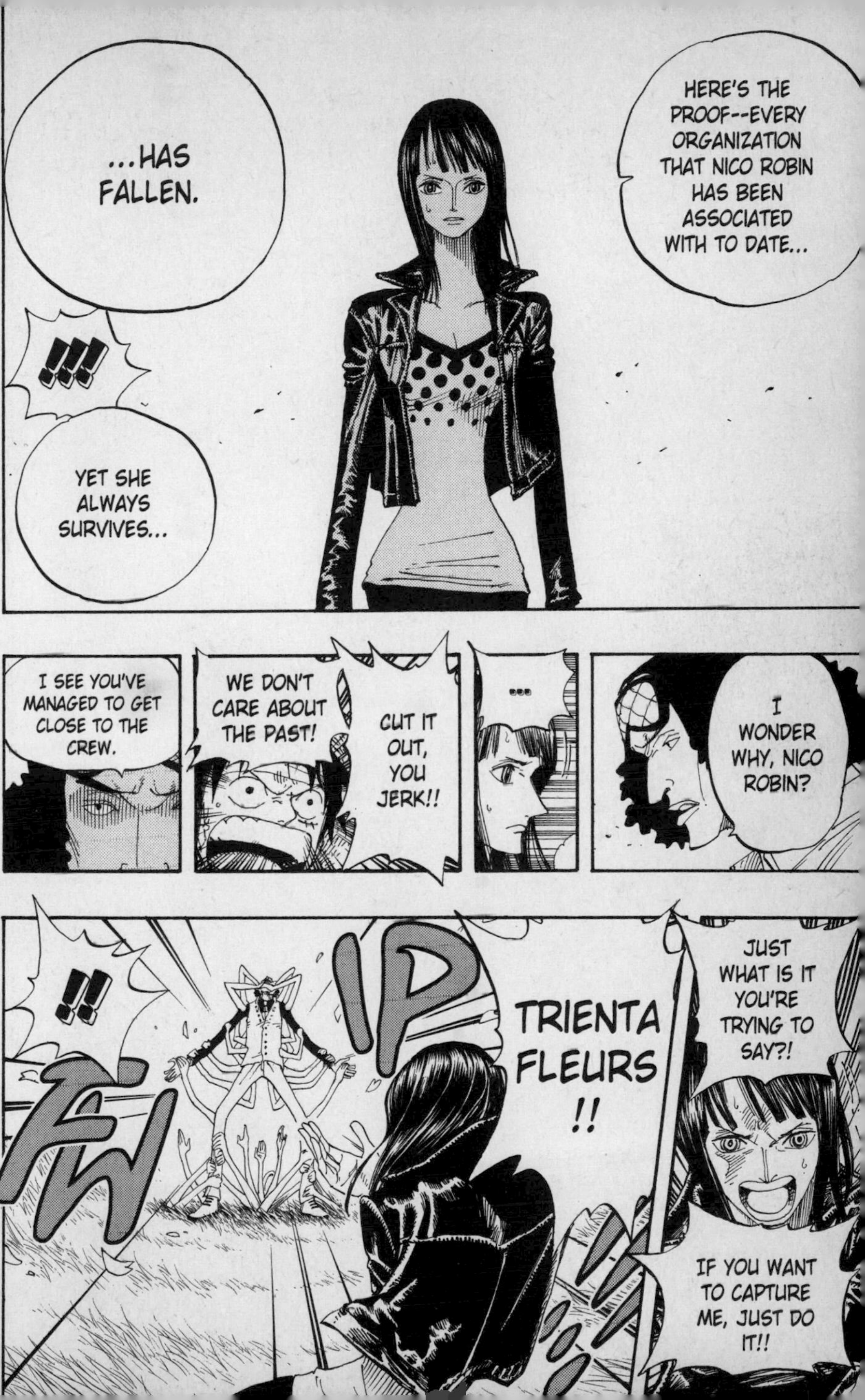
HERE'S THE PROOF--EVERY ORGANIZATION THAT NICO ROBIN HAS BEEN ASSOCIATED WITH TO DATE...
...HAS FALLEN.
!!!
YET SHE ALWAYS SURVIVES...
I WONDER WHY, NICO ROBIN?
...
CUT IT OUT, YOU JERK!!
WE DON'T CARE ABOUT THE PAST!
I SEE YOU'VE MANAGED TO GET CLOSE TO THE CREW.
JUST WHAT IS IT YOU'RE TRYING TO SAY?!
IF YOU WANT TO CAPTURE ME, JUST DO IT!!
TRIENTA FLEURS !!
!!

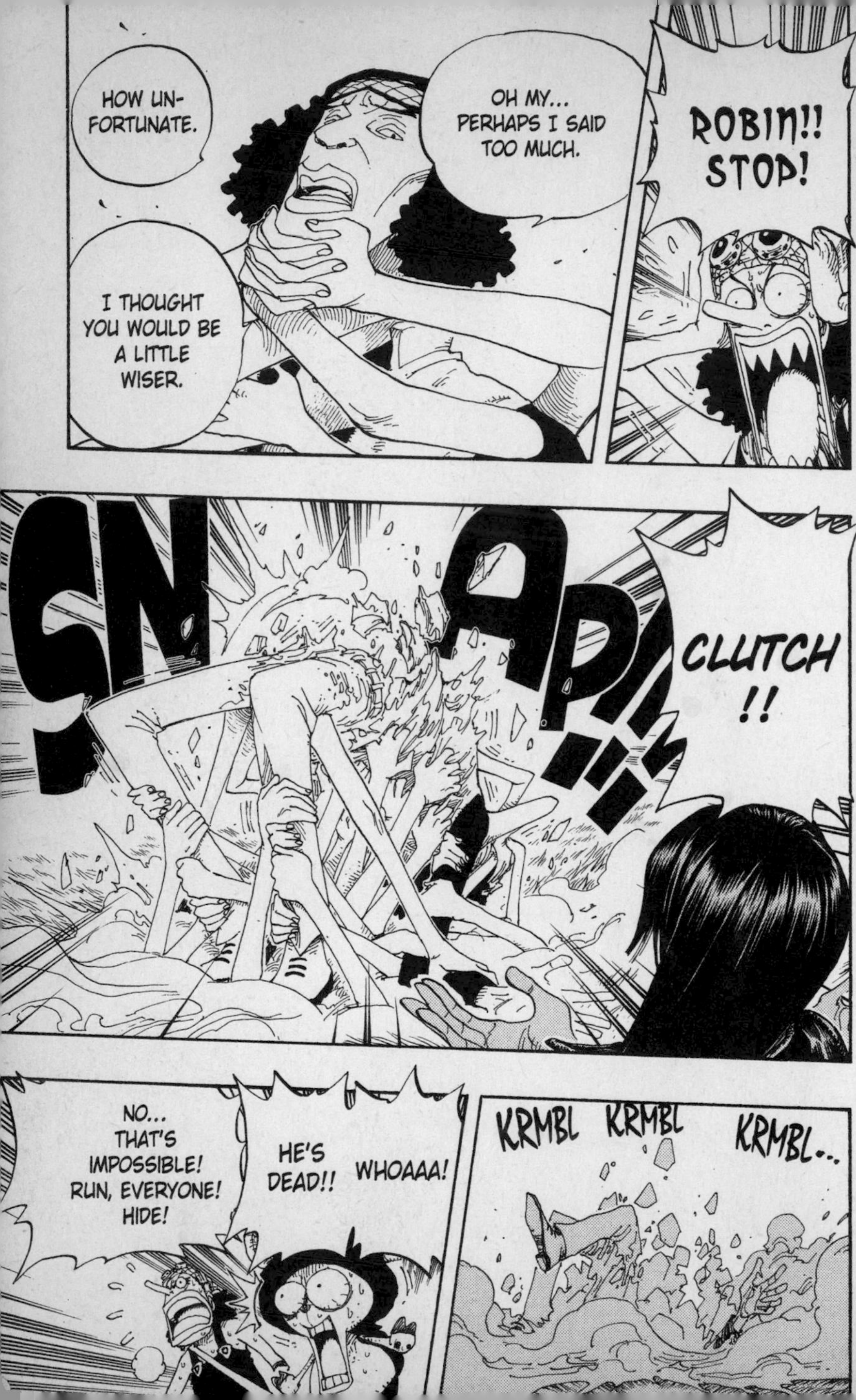
ROBIN!! STOP!
OH MY... PERHAPS I SAID TOO MUCH.
HOW UN-FORTUNATE.
I THOUGHT YOU WOULD BE A LITTLE WISER.
CLUTCH !!
SNAP!!
KRMBL KRMBL KRMBL...
WHOAAA!
HE'S DEAD!!
NO... THAT'S IMPOSSIBLE! RUN, EVERYONE! HIDE!

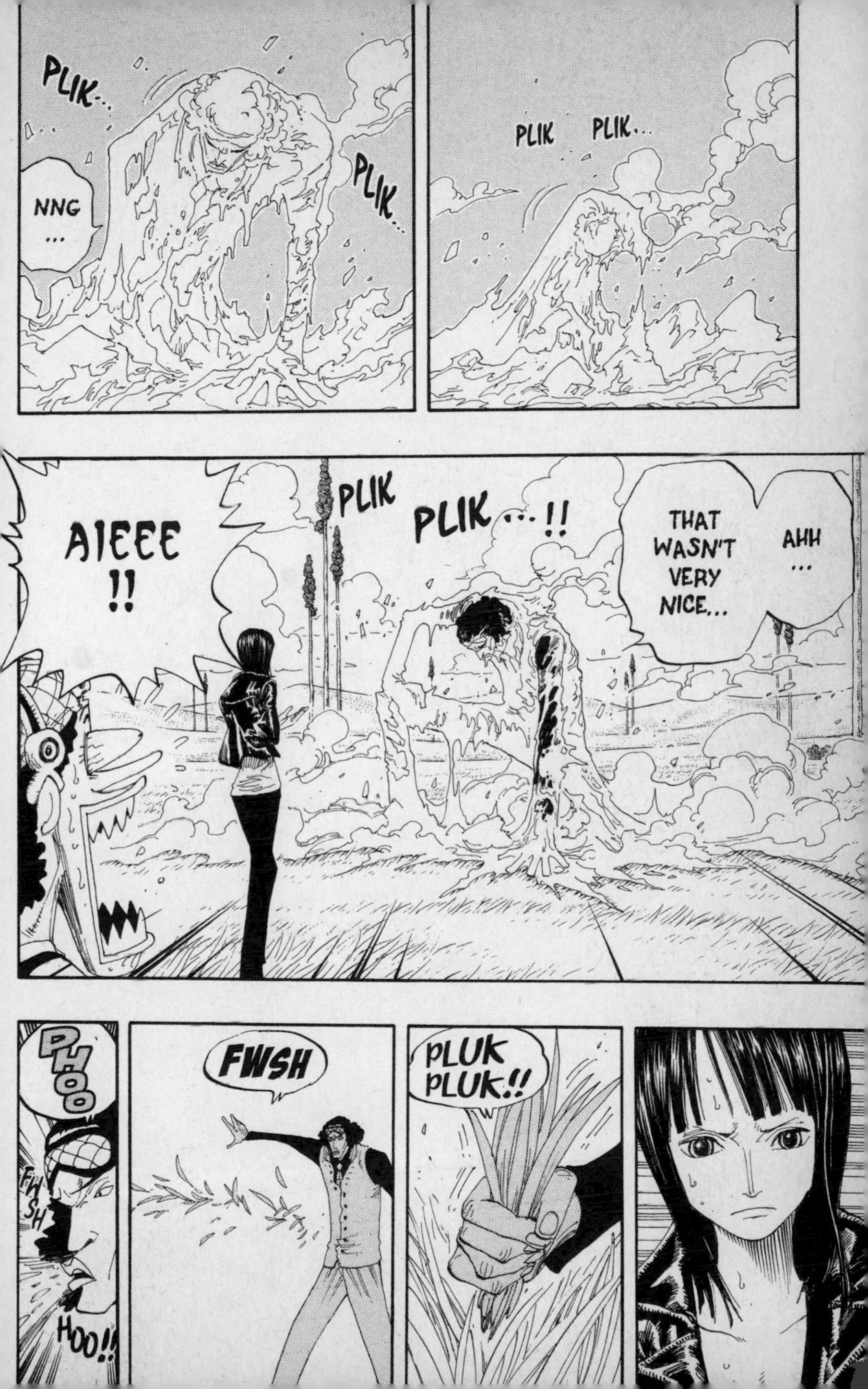
PLIK PLIK...
PLIK...
PLIK...
NNG ...
AHH ...
THAT WASN'T VERY NICE...
PLIK...!!
PLIK
AIEEE !!
PLUK PLUK!!
FWSH
PHOO
FWSH
HOO!!

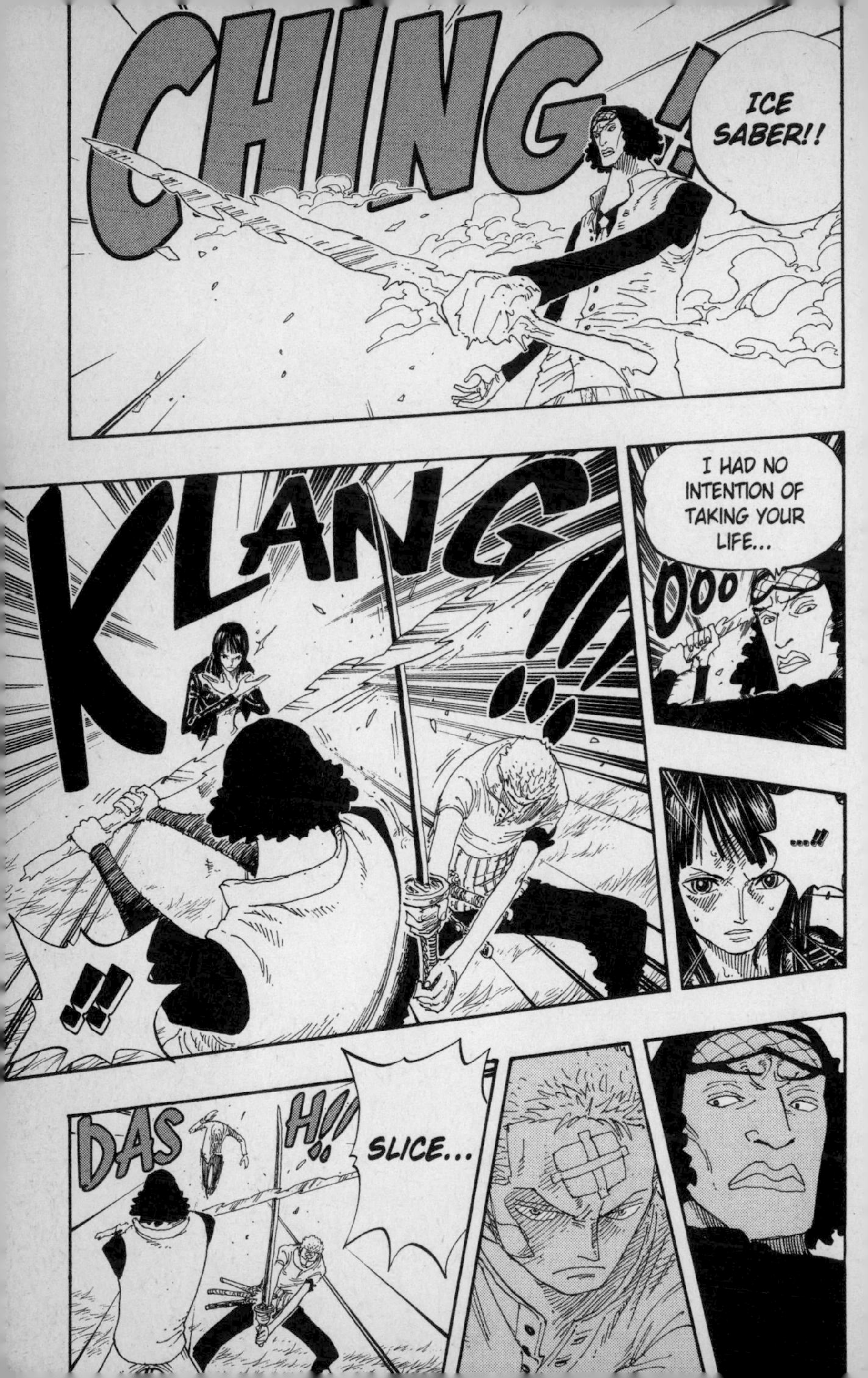
CHING!
ICE SABER!!
I HAD NO INTENTION OF TAKING YOUR LIFE...
...!!
KLANG!!
!!
DASH!!
SLICE...

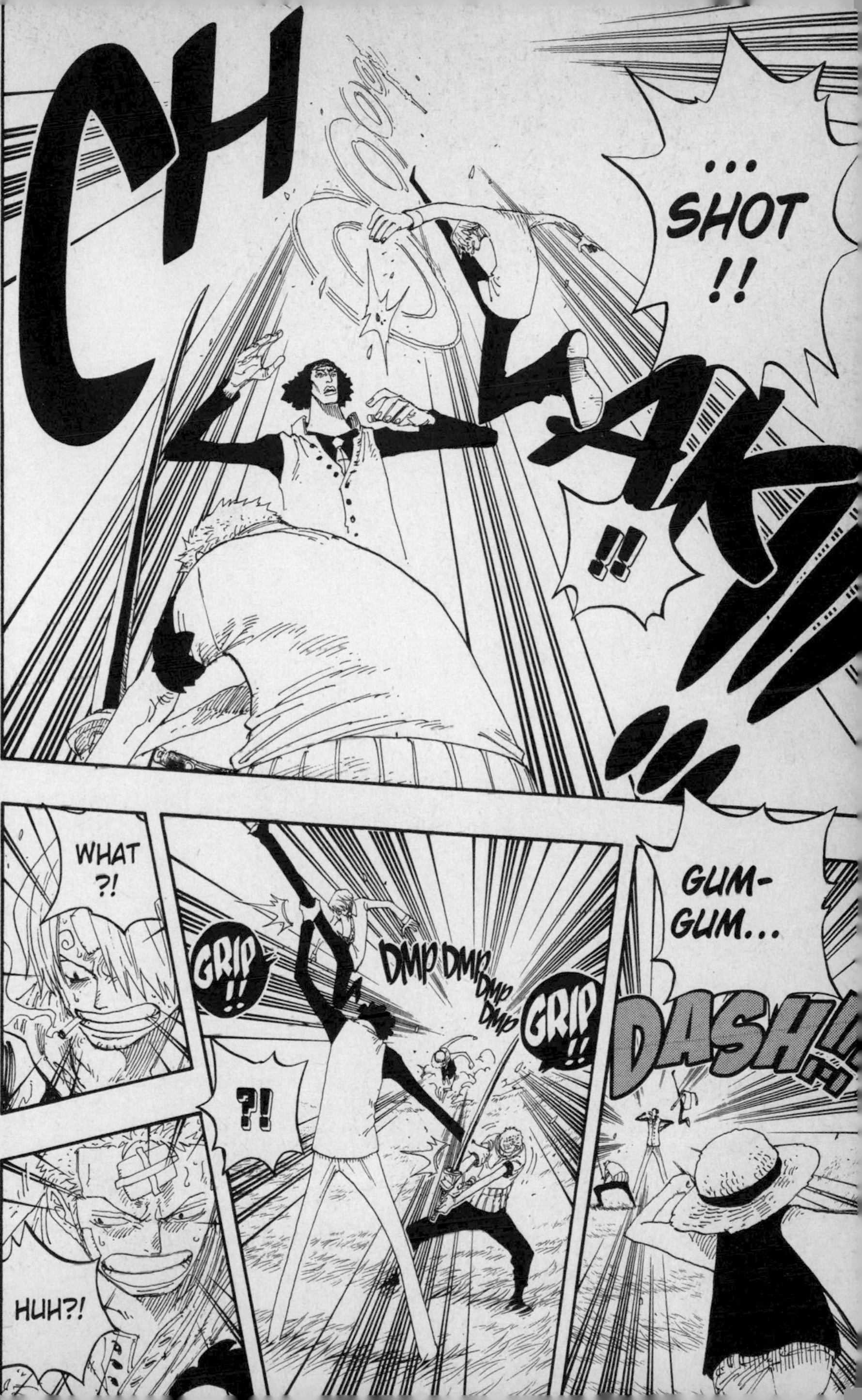
...SHOT!!
CH
AK!!
GUM-GUM...
DASH!!
GRIP!!
DMP DMP DMP DMP
GRIP!!
?!
WHAT?!
HUH?!

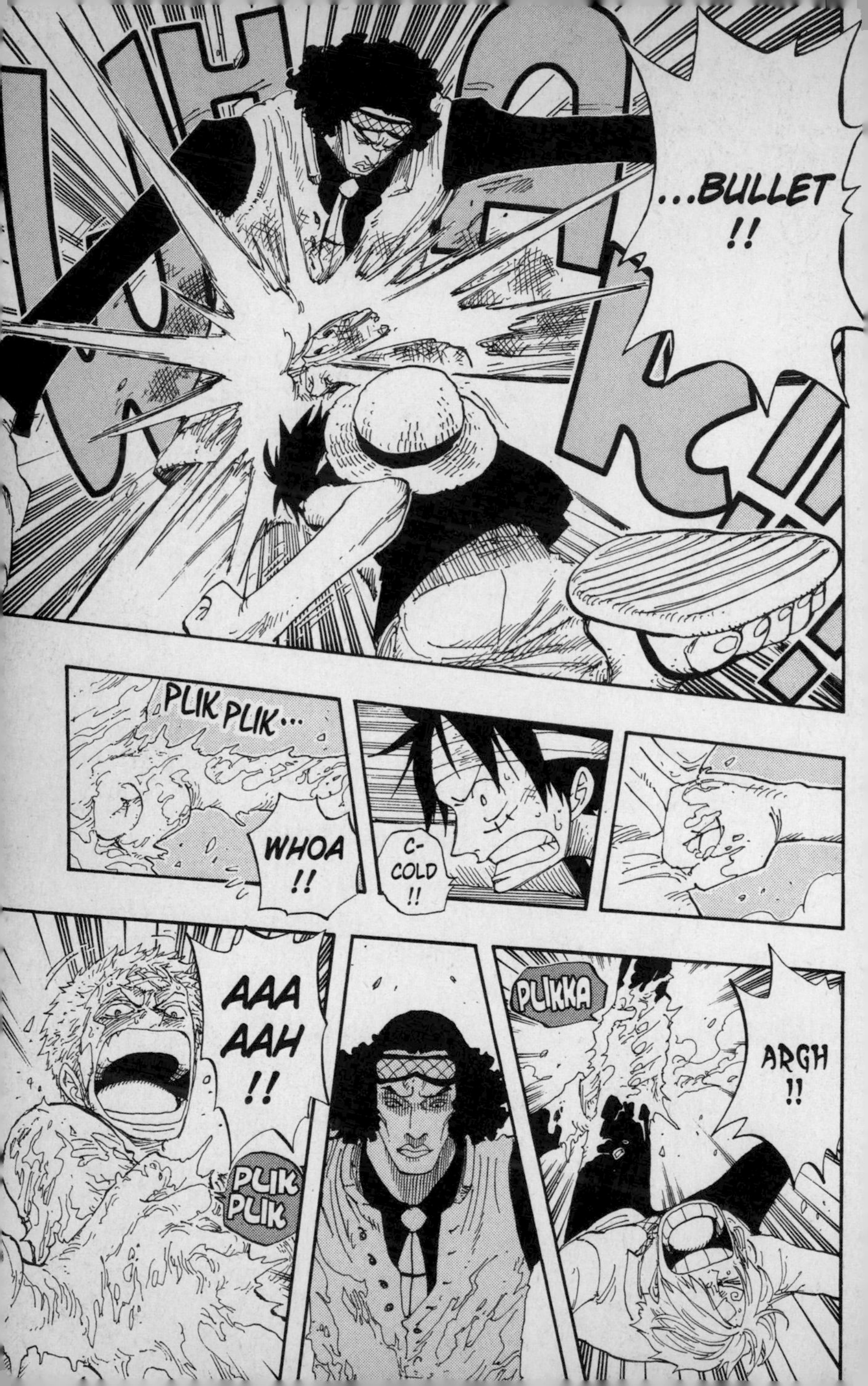
...BULLET !!
C- COLD !!
PLIK PLIK...
WHOA !!
PLIKKA
ARGH !!
AAA AAH !!
PLIK PLIK

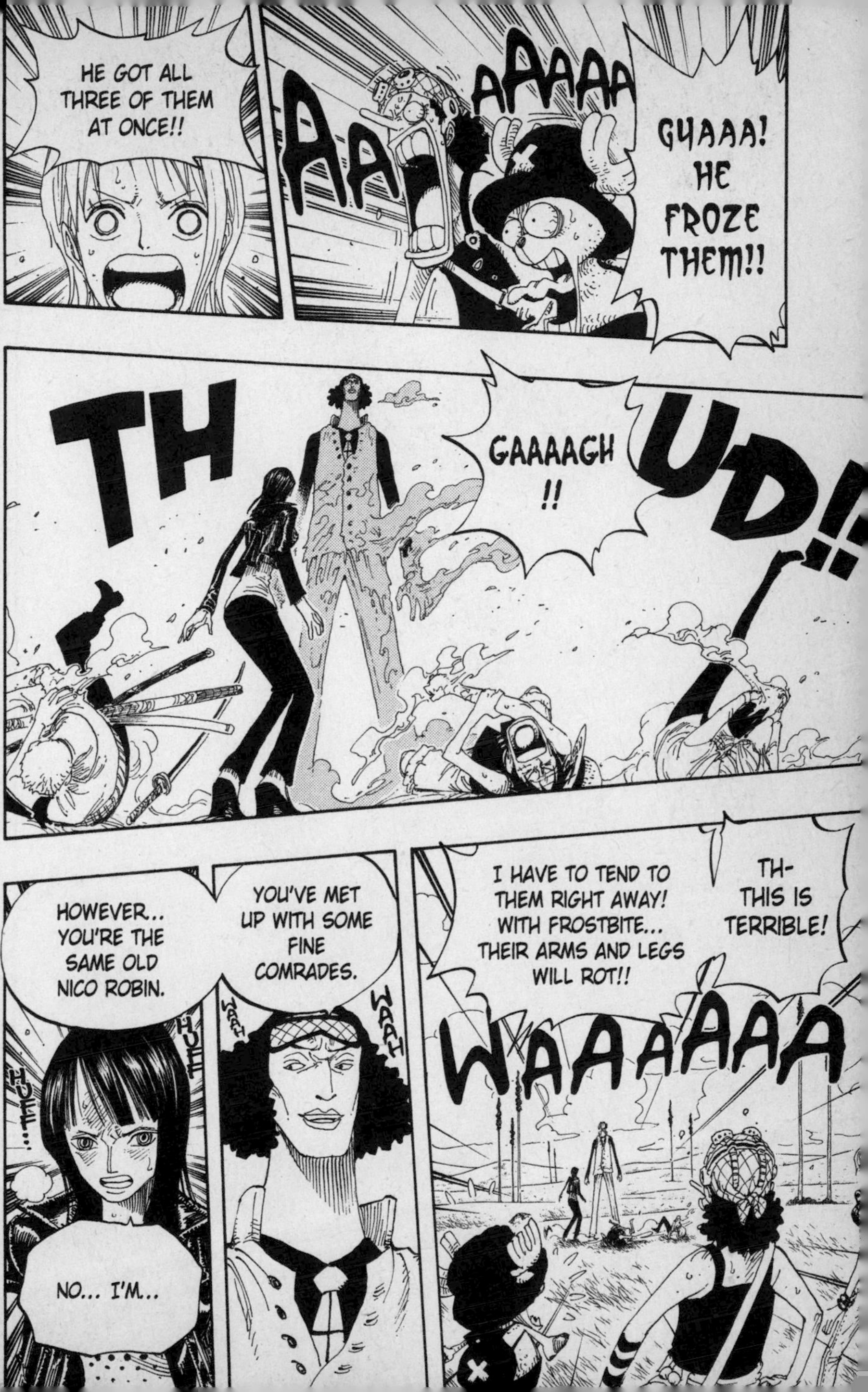
GYAAA! HE FROZE THEM!!
AA
AAAAA
HE GOT ALL THREE OF THEM AT ONCE!!
GAAAAGH !!
TH
UD!!
TH- THIS IS TERRIBLE!
I HAVE TO TEND TO THEM RIGHT AWAY! WITH FROSTBITE... THEIR ARMS AND LEGS WILL ROT!!
WAAAAAA
WAAH
WAAH
YOU'VE MET UP WITH SOME FINE COMRADES.
HOWEVER... YOU'RE THE SAME OLD NICO ROBIN.
HUFF
HUFF...
NO... I'M...

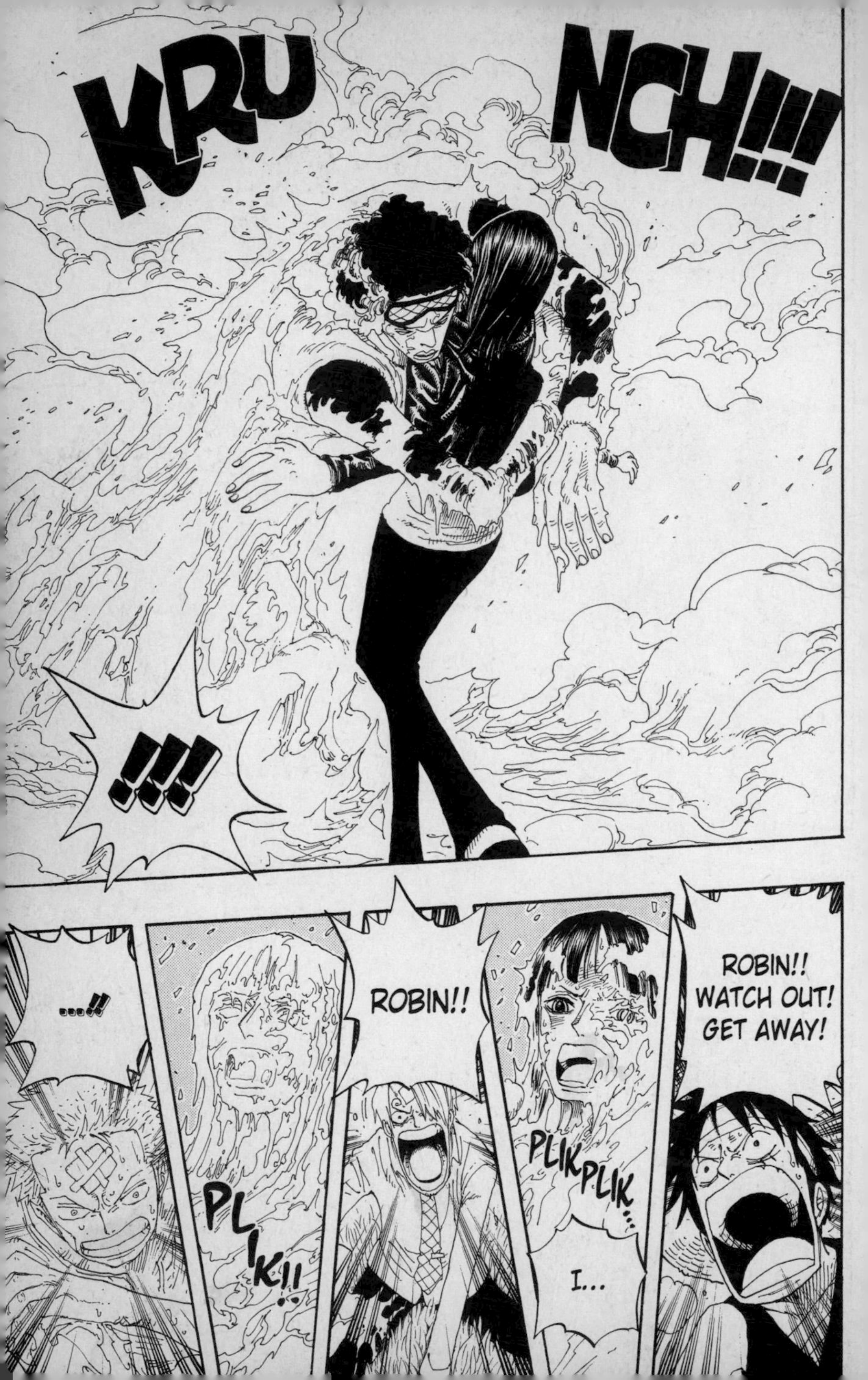
KRUNCH!!!
!!!
ROBIN!!
WATCH OUT!
GET AWAY!
PLIK PLIK...
I...
ROBIN!!
PLIK!!
...!!

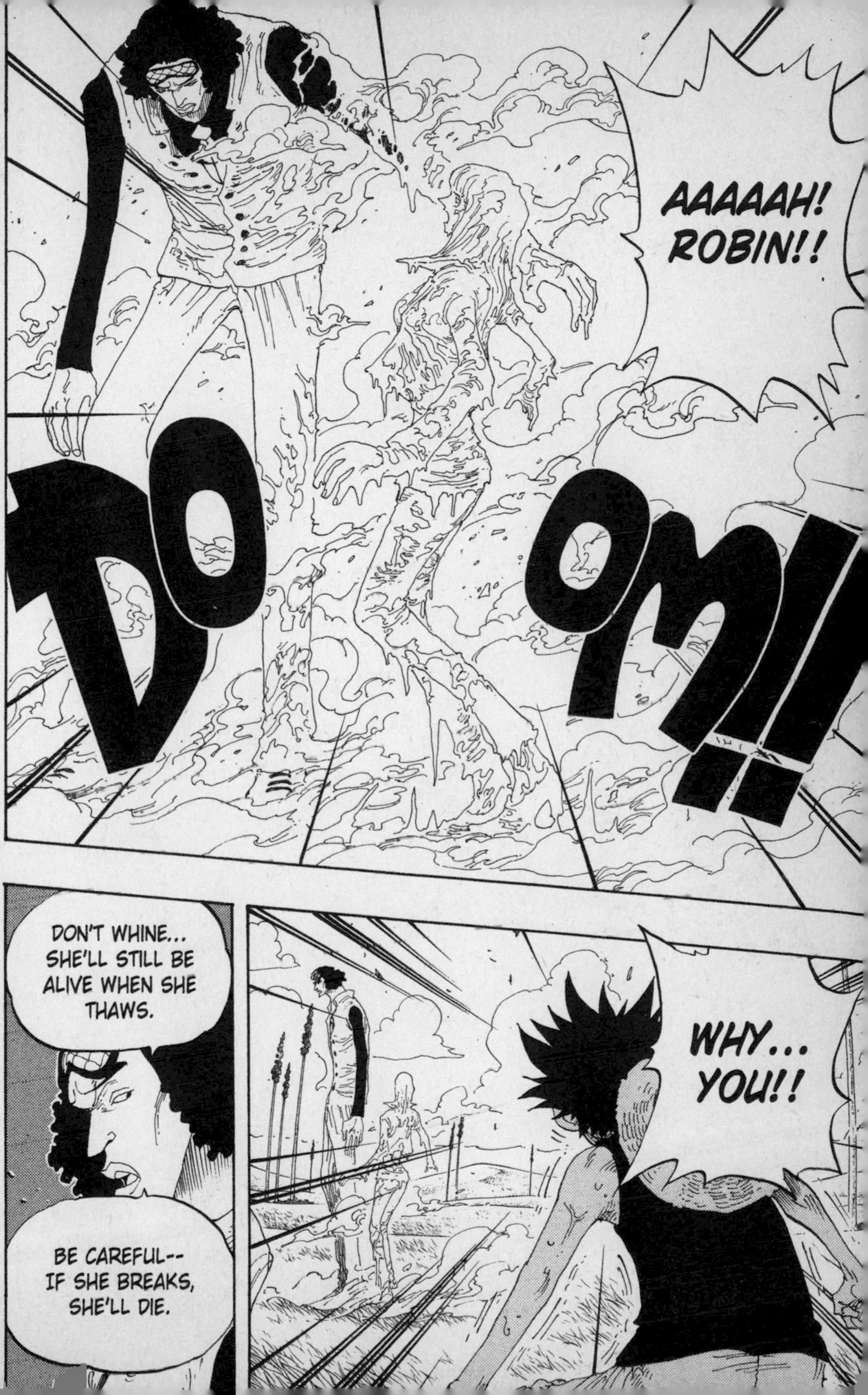
AAAAAH! ROBIN!!
DOOM!!
WHY... YOU!!
DON'T WHINE... SHE'LL STILL BE ALIVE WHEN SHE THAWS.
BE CAREFUL-- IF SHE BREAKS, SHE'LL DIE.

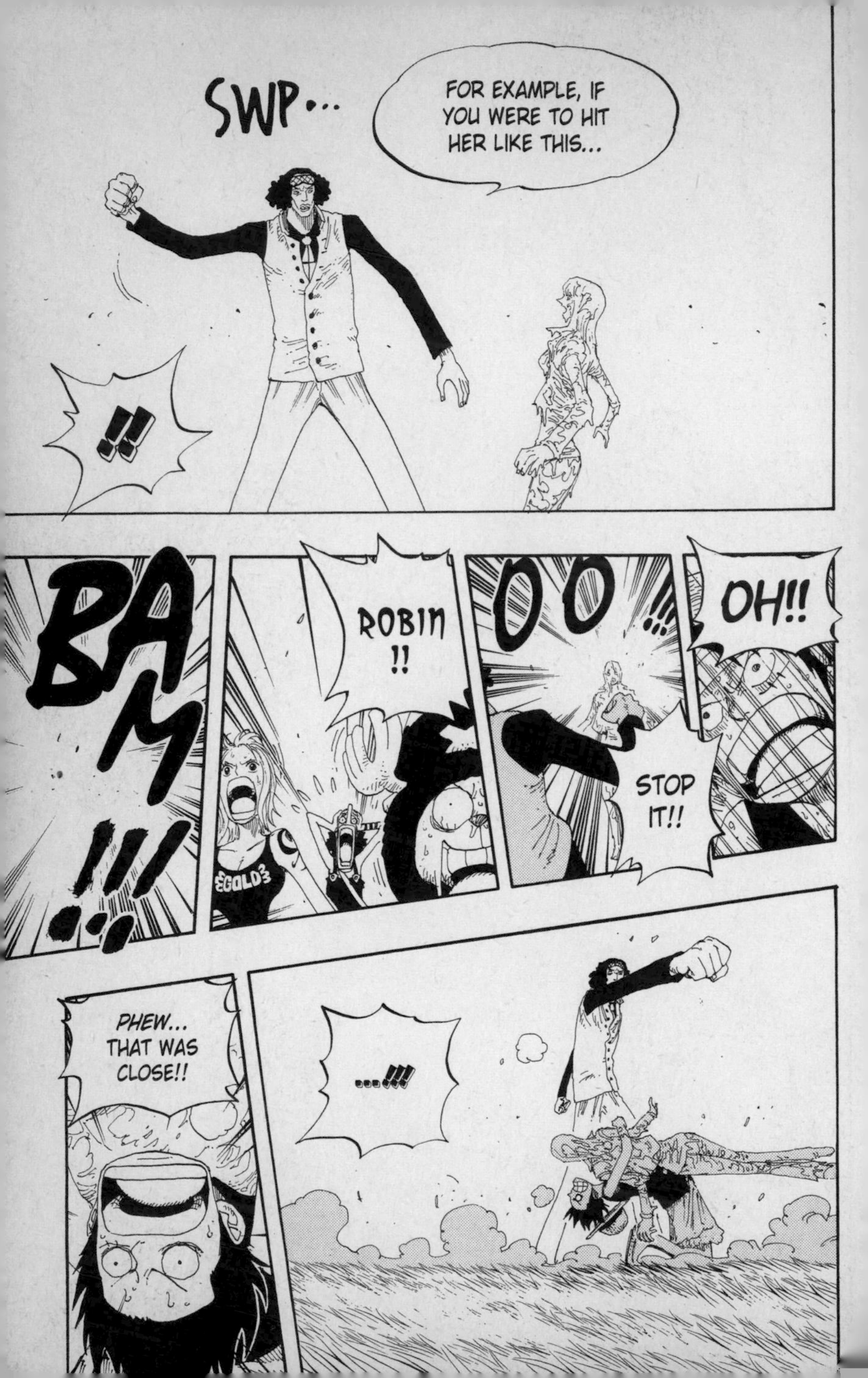

FOR EXAMPLE, IF YOU WERE TO HIT HER LIKE THIS...
SWP...
!!
OH!!
STOP IT!!
OO!!
ROBIN !!
BAM!!!
...!!!
PHEW... THAT WAS CLOSE!!

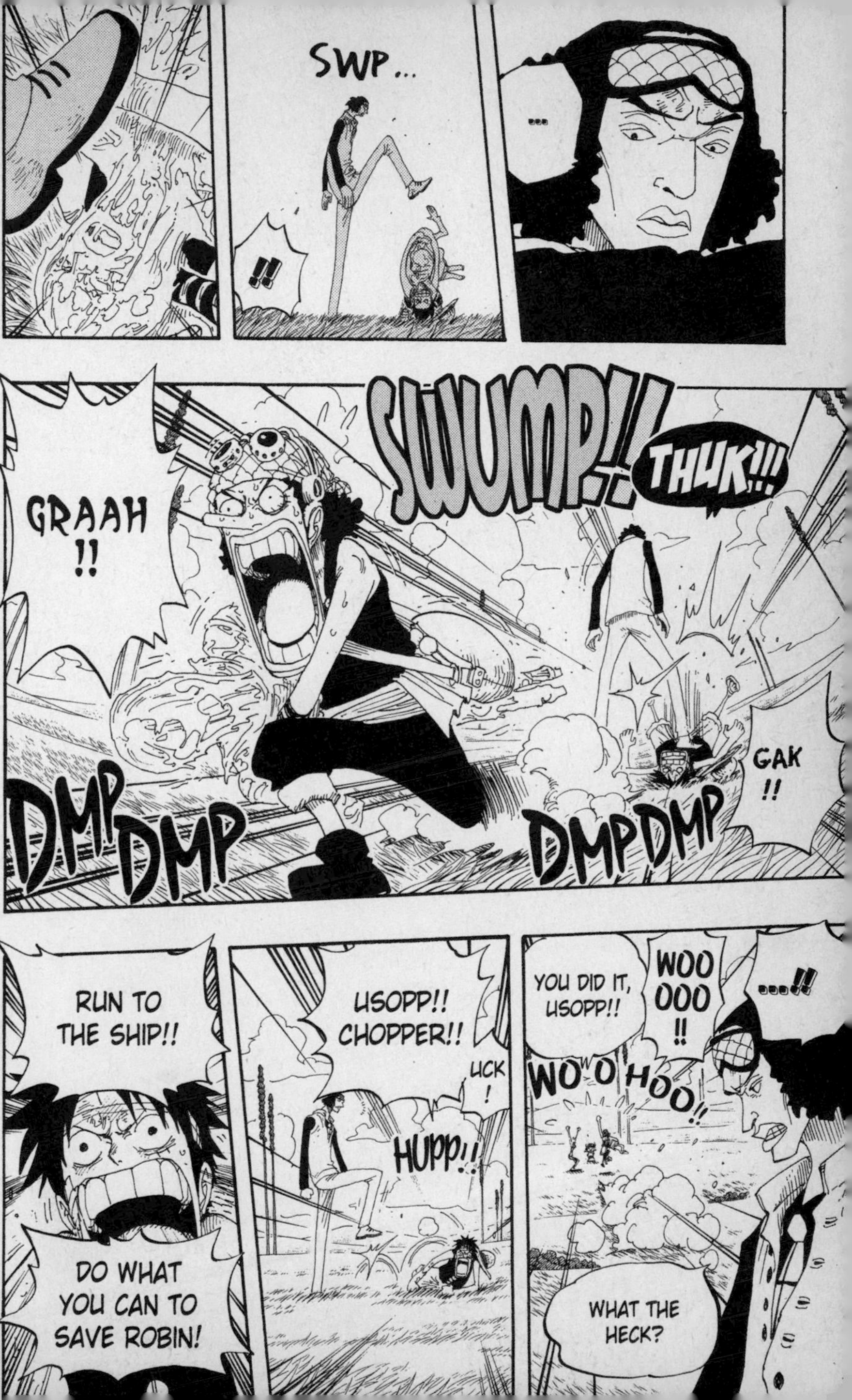
...
SWP...
!!
GAK !!
DMP DMP
THUK!!!
SWUMP!!
GRAAH !!
DMP DMP
...!!
WOO OOO !!
YOU DID IT, USOPP!!
WOO HOO!!
WHAT THE HECK?
USOPP!! CHOPPER!!
UCK !
HUPP!!
RUN TO THE SHIP!!
DO WHAT YOU CAN TO SAVE ROBIN!

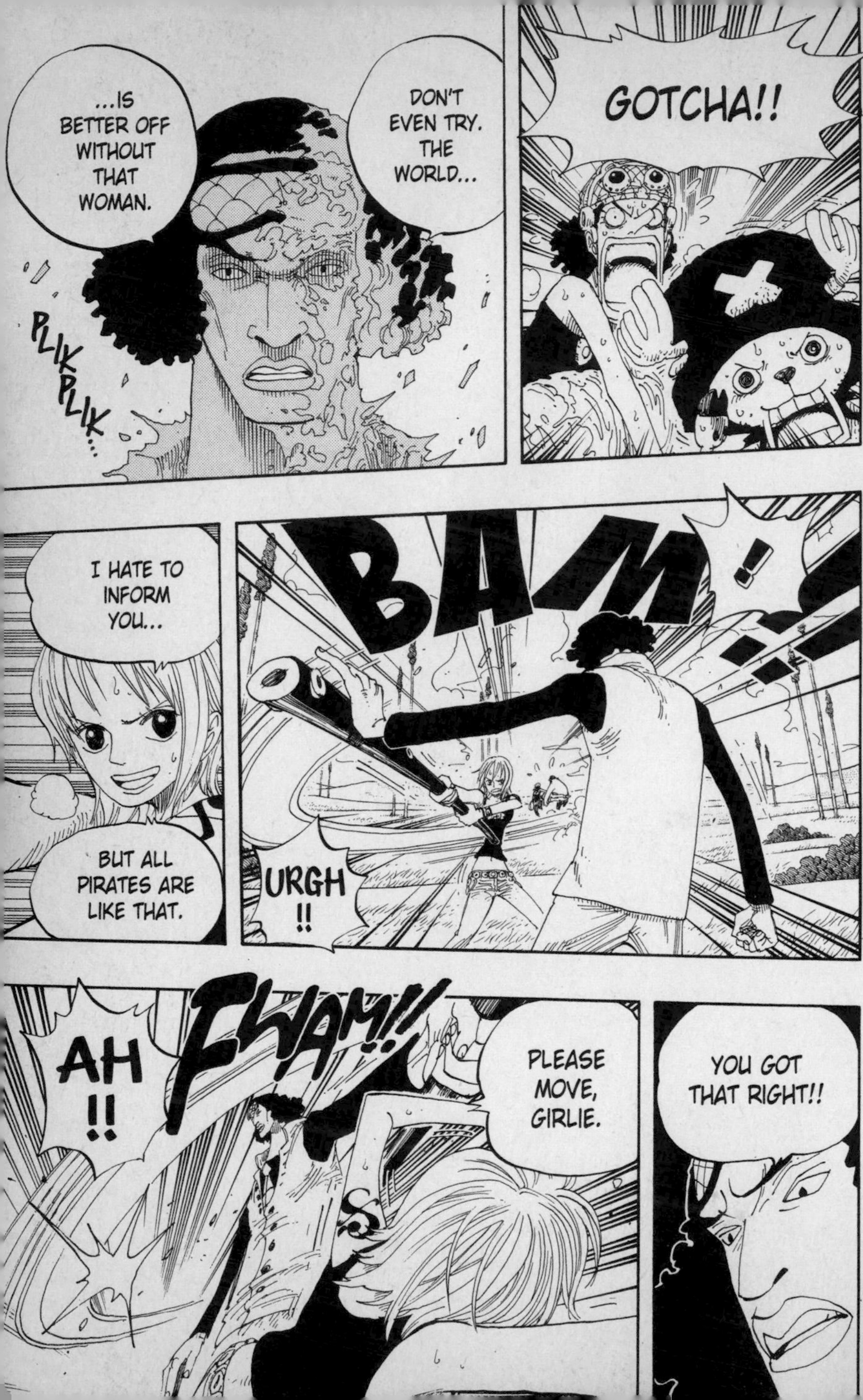
GOTCHA!!
DON'T EVEN TRY. THE WORLD...
...IS BETTER OFF WITHOUT THAT WOMAN.
PLIK PLIK...
BAM!!
URGH!!
I HATE TO INFORM YOU...
BUT ALL PIRATES ARE LIKE THAT.
YOU GOT THAT RIGHT!!
PLEASE MOVE, GIRLIE.
FWAM!!
AH!!

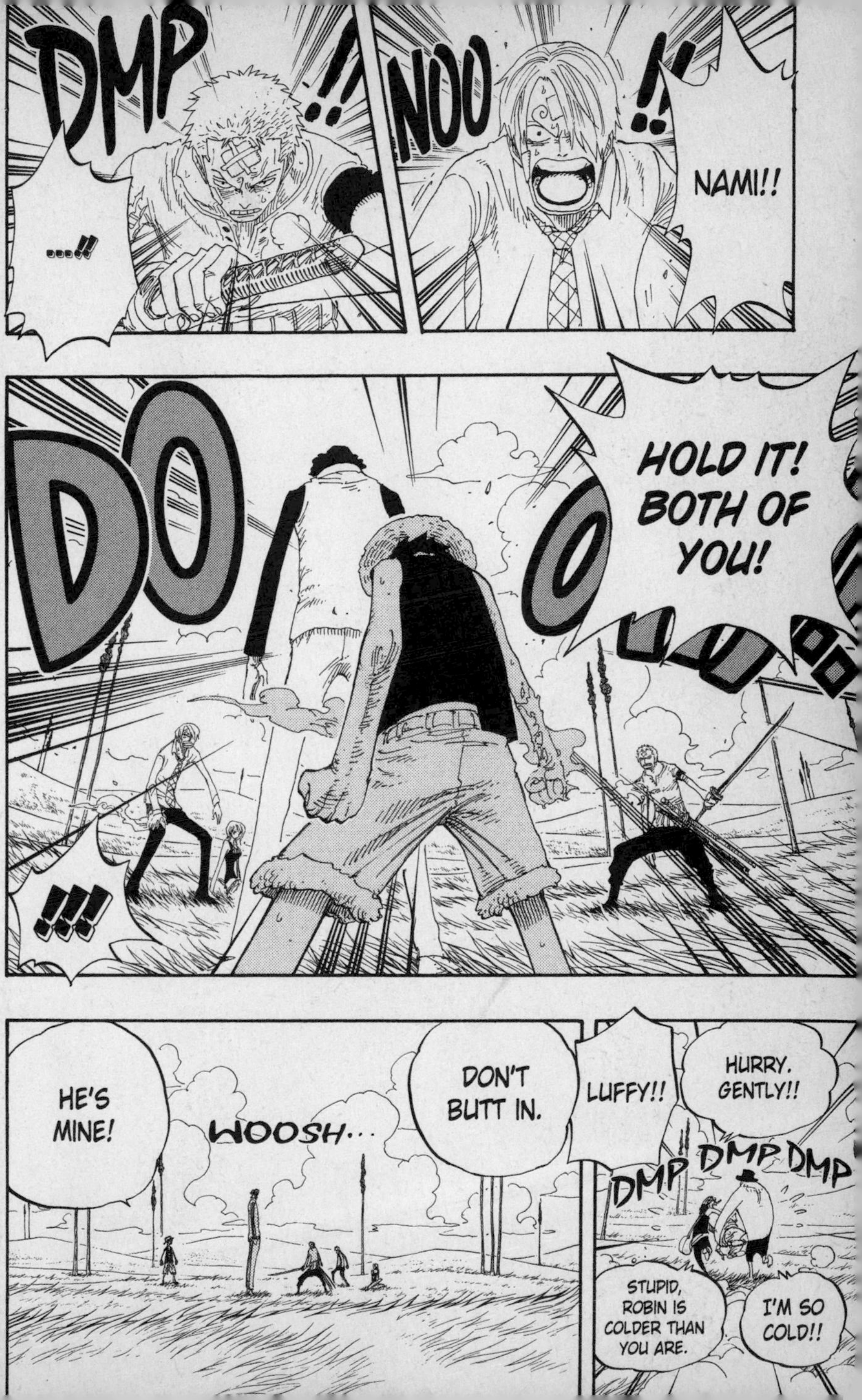
NOO !!
NAMI!!
DMP !!
...!!
HOLD IT! BOTH OF YOU!
DO
!!!
HURRY. GENTLY!!
LUFFY!!
DMP DMP DMP
I'M SO COLD!!
STUPID, ROBIN IS COLDER THAN YOU ARE.
DON'T BUTT IN.
WOOSH...
HE'S MINE!

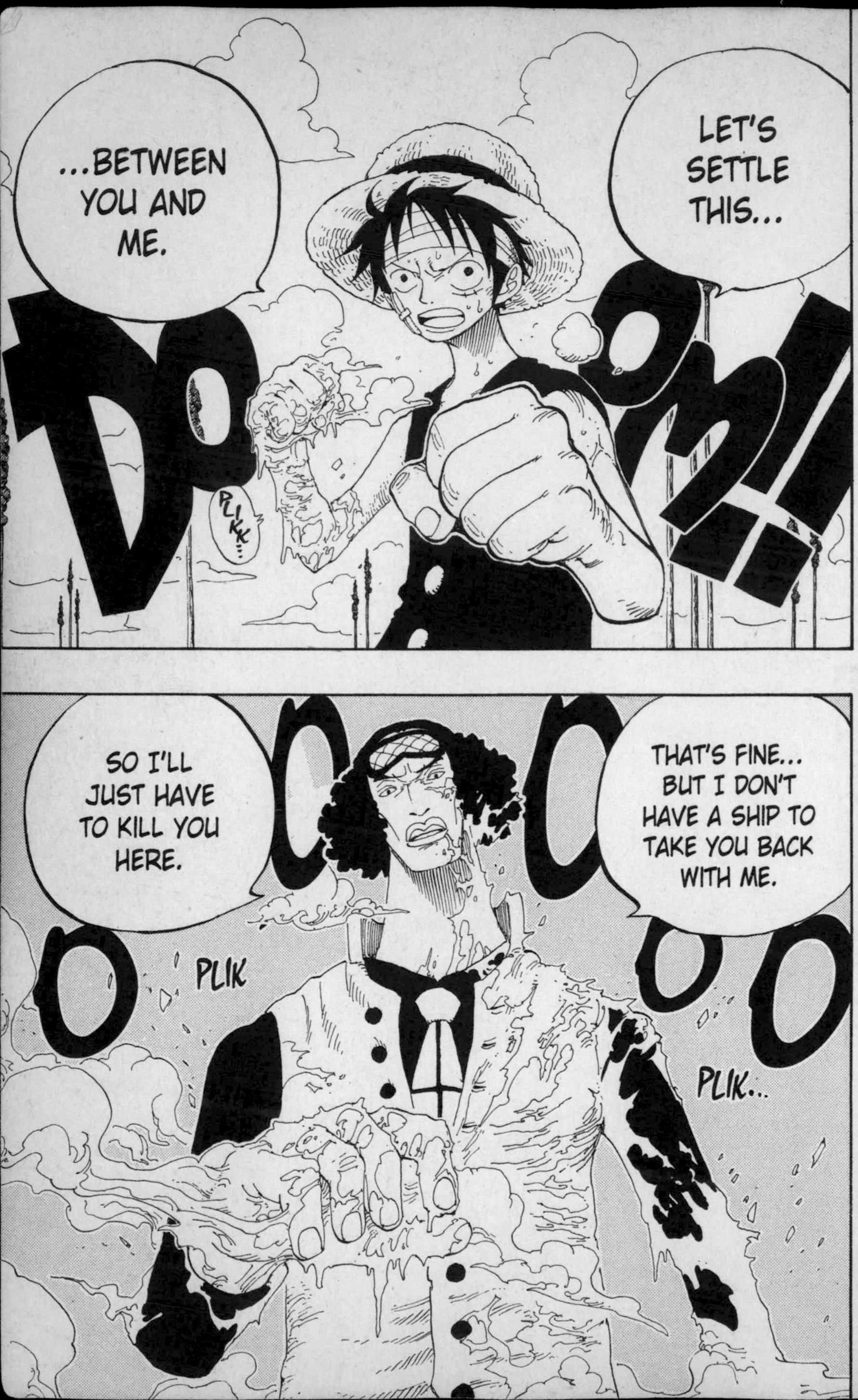
LET'S SETTLE THIS...
...BETWEEN YOU AND ME.
DOOM!!
PLIKK...
THAT'S FINE... BUT I DON'T HAVE A SHIP TO TAKE YOU BACK WITH ME.
SO I'LL JUST HAVE TO KILL YOU HERE.
PLIK...
PLIK

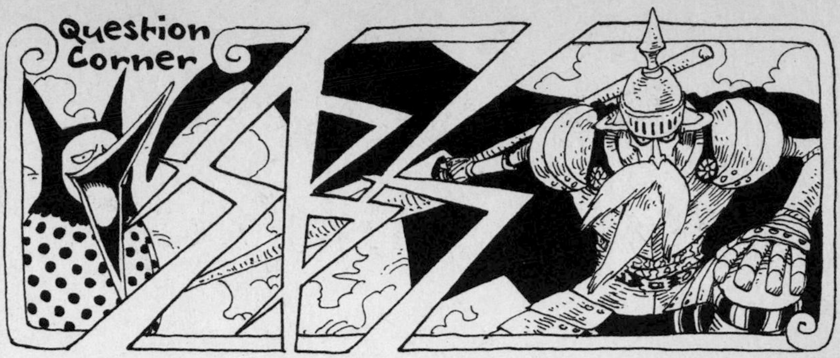
Question Corner

Q: On page 80 in vol. 9, is Navy Commodore Purinpurin--that man with the weird hairstyle--inspired by "The Purinpurin Story" show that aired in 1981?? I've been real curious about that.
Please let me know.
--Nana-chan

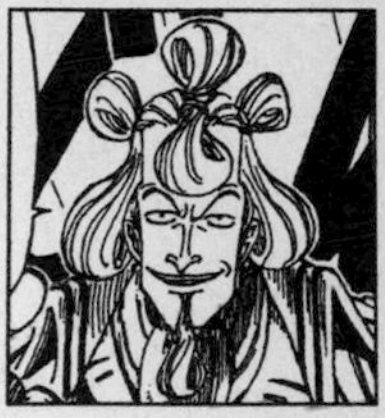

A: Oh, how nostalgic. I didn't get the idea from that--in fact, I barely remember it. And it wasn't like I liked it. It was a puppet program aimed at young girls, with a heroine named Purinpurin who was a princess. I guess she was named that because she was a princess.

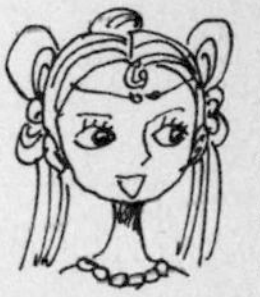
Geez, I don't remember her at all!

My older sister liked that show and watched it, so I remember seeing it and thinking what a funny name and funny hairstyle she had. You must have seen some reruns lately that made you think about this, eh, Nana-chan? Thank you.

Long ago, there were lots of puppet shows on television.

Chapter 321:

ONE-ON-ONE

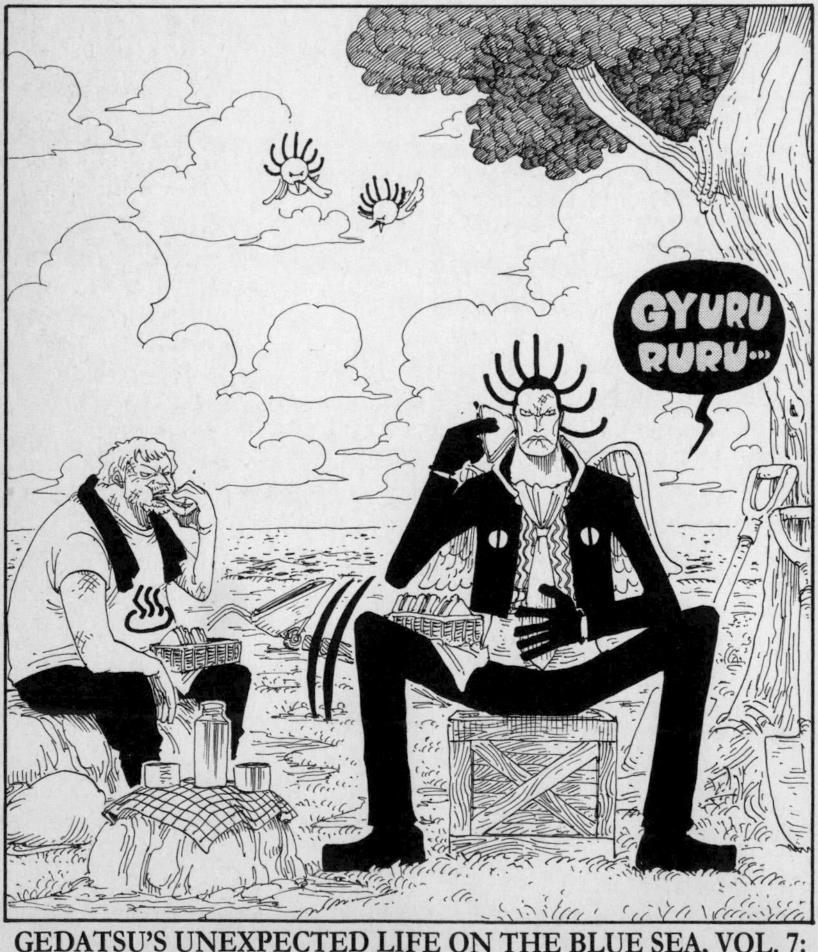
GYURU RURU...

GEDATSU'S UNEXPECTED LIFE ON THE BLUE SEA, VOL. 7:
"YOU HAVE TO EAT WITH YOUR MOUTH ON A DAY OF DIGGING, MASTER GEDATSU"

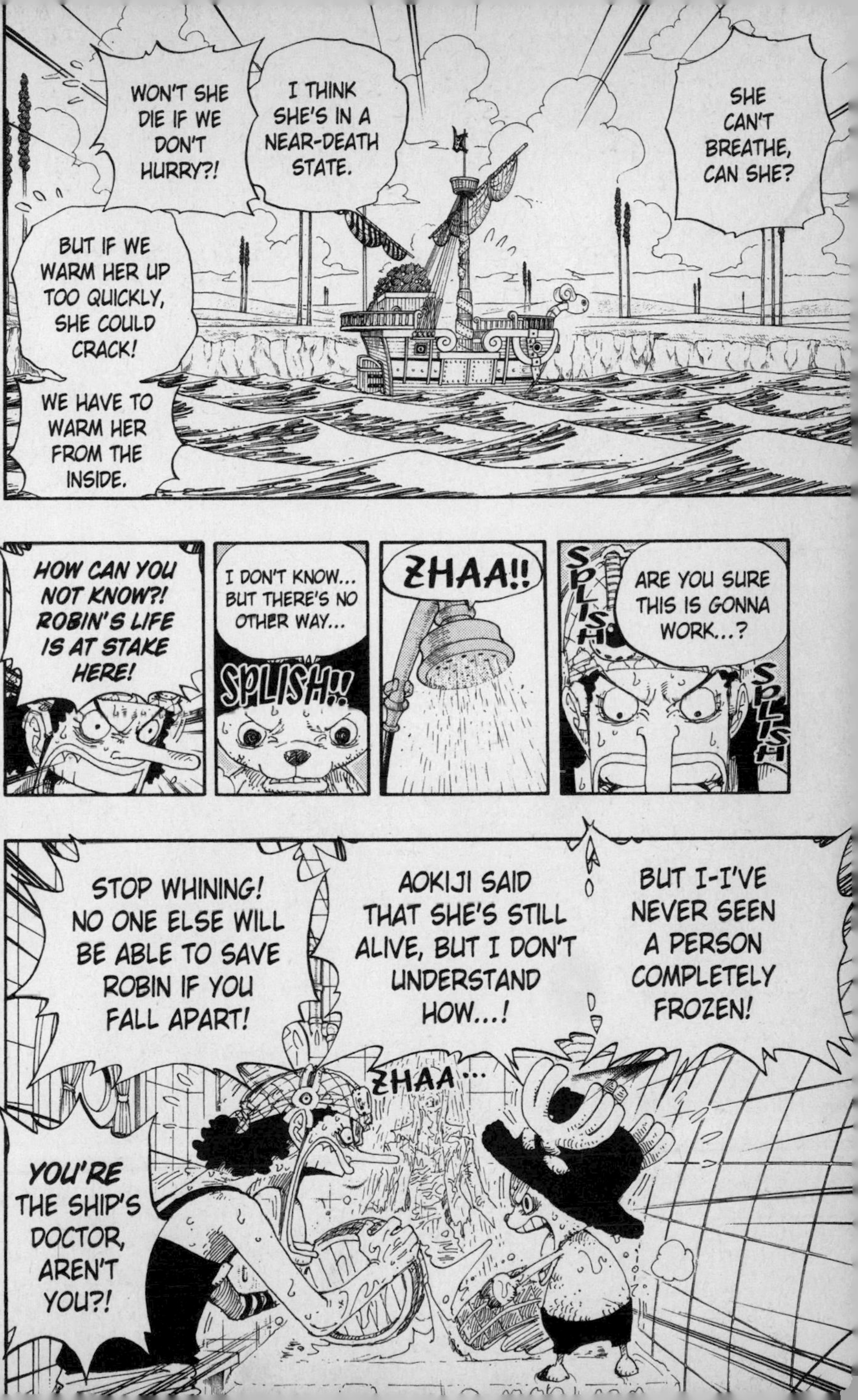
SHE CAN'T BREATHE, CAN SHE?
I THINK SHE'S IN A NEAR-DEATH STATE.
WON'T SHE DIE IF WE DON'T HURRY?!
BUT IF WE WARM HER UP TOO QUICKLY, SHE COULD CRACK!
WE HAVE TO WARM HER FROM THE INSIDE.
ARE YOU SURE THIS IS GONNA WORK...?
SPLISH
SPLISH
ZHAA!!
I DON'T KNOW... BUT THERE'S NO OTHER WAY...
SPLISH!!
HOW CAN YOU NOT KNOW?! ROBIN'S LIFE IS AT STAKE HERE!
BUT I-I'VE NEVER SEEN A PERSON COMPLETELY FROZEN!
AOKIJI SAID THAT SHE'S STILL ALIVE, BUT I DON'T UNDERSTAND HOW...!
STOP WHINING! NO ONE ELSE WILL BE ABLE TO SAVE ROBIN IF YOU FALL APART!
ZHAA...
YOU'RE THE SHIP'S DOCTOR, AREN'T YOU?!

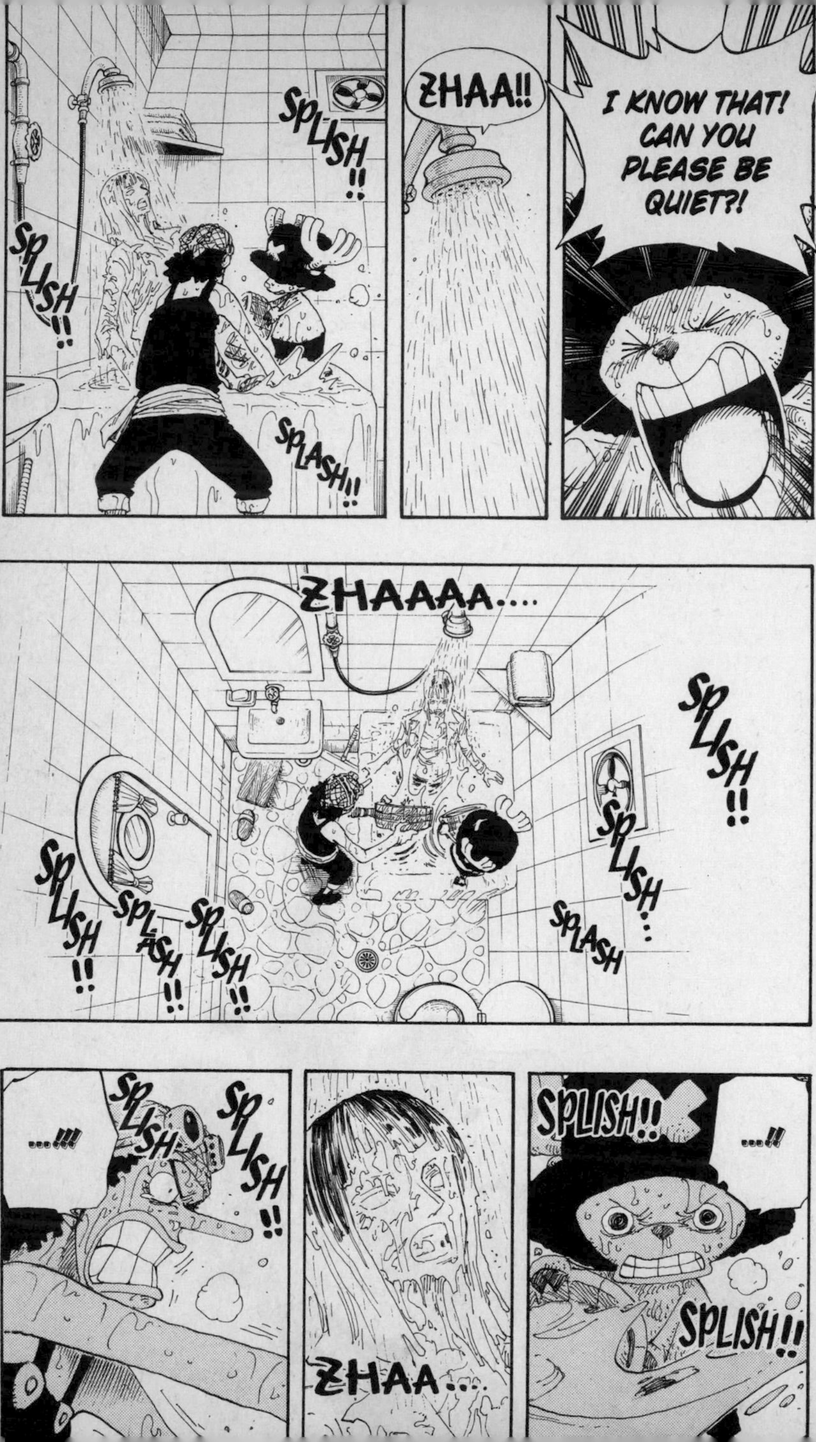
I KNOW THAT! CAN YOU PLEASE BE QUIET?!
ZHAA!!
SPLISH!!
SPLISH!!
SPLASH!!
ZHAAAA....
SPLISH!!
SPLISH..
SPLASH
SPLISH!!
SPLASH!!
SPLISH!!
SPLISH!!
...!!
SPLISH!!
ZHAA...
SPLISH
SPLISH!!
...!!!

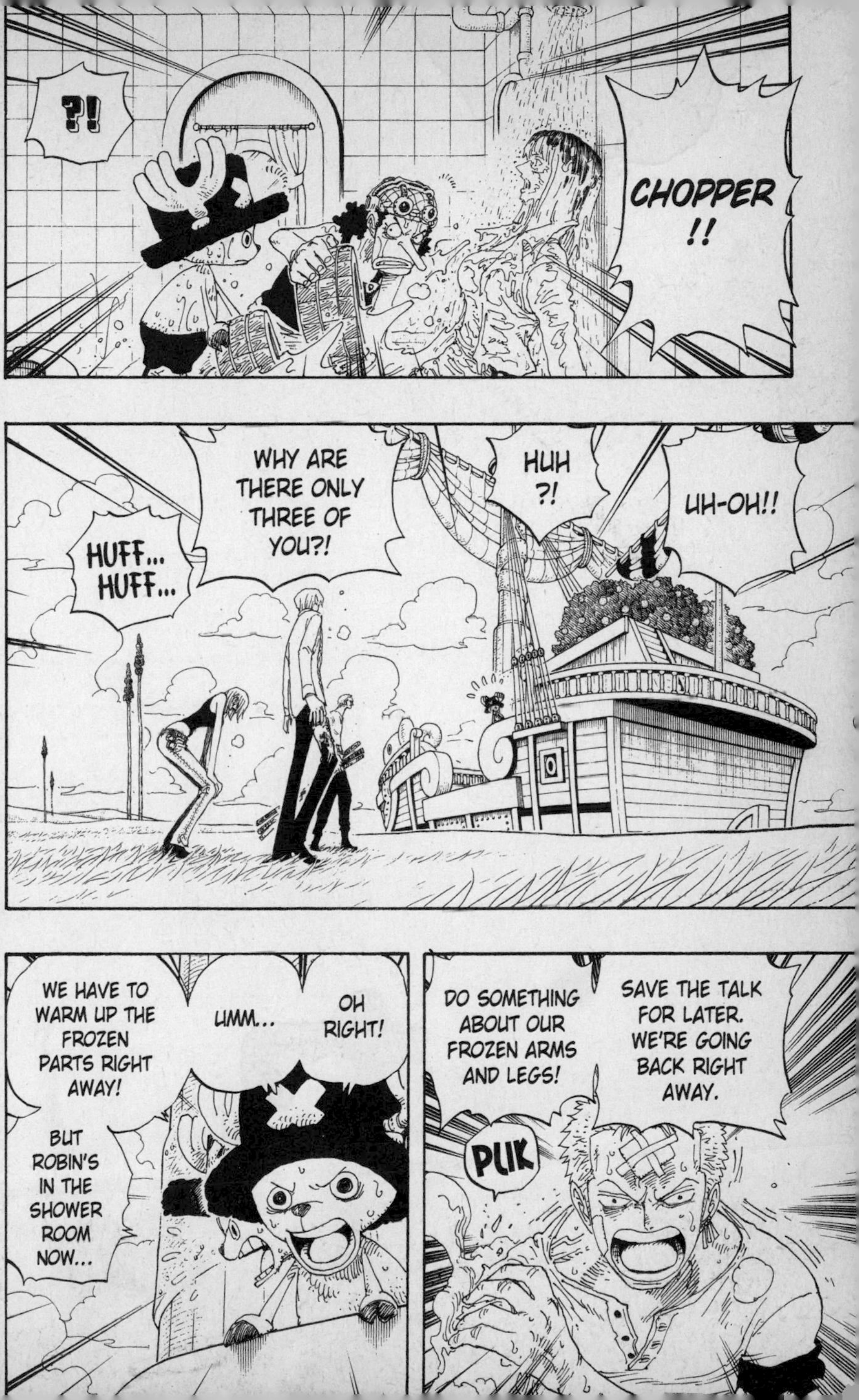
CHOPPER !!
?!
UH-OH!!
HUH ?!
WHY ARE THERE ONLY THREE OF YOU?!
HUFF... HUFF...
SAVE THE TALK FOR LATER. WE'RE GOING BACK RIGHT AWAY.
DO SOMETHING ABOUT OUR FROZEN ARMS AND LEGS!
PUK
OH RIGHT!
UMM...
WE HAVE TO WARM UP THE FROZEN PARTS RIGHT AWAY!
BUT ROBIN'S IN THE SHOWER ROOM NOW...

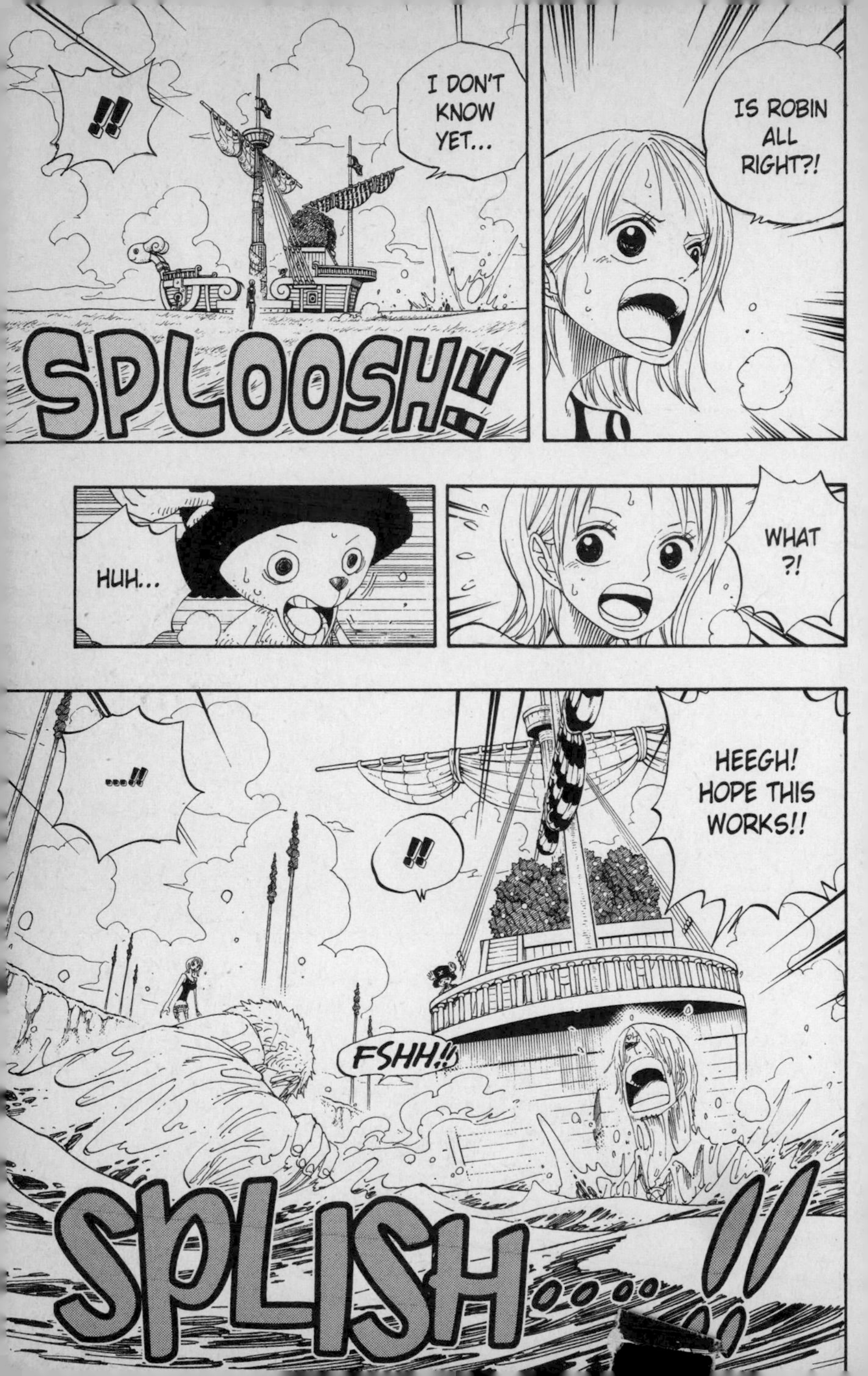
IS ROBIN ALL RIGHT?!
I DON'T KNOW YET...
!!
SPLOOSH!!
WHAT ?!
HUH...
HEEGH! HOPE THIS WORKS!!
!!
...!!
FSHH!!
SPLISH......!!

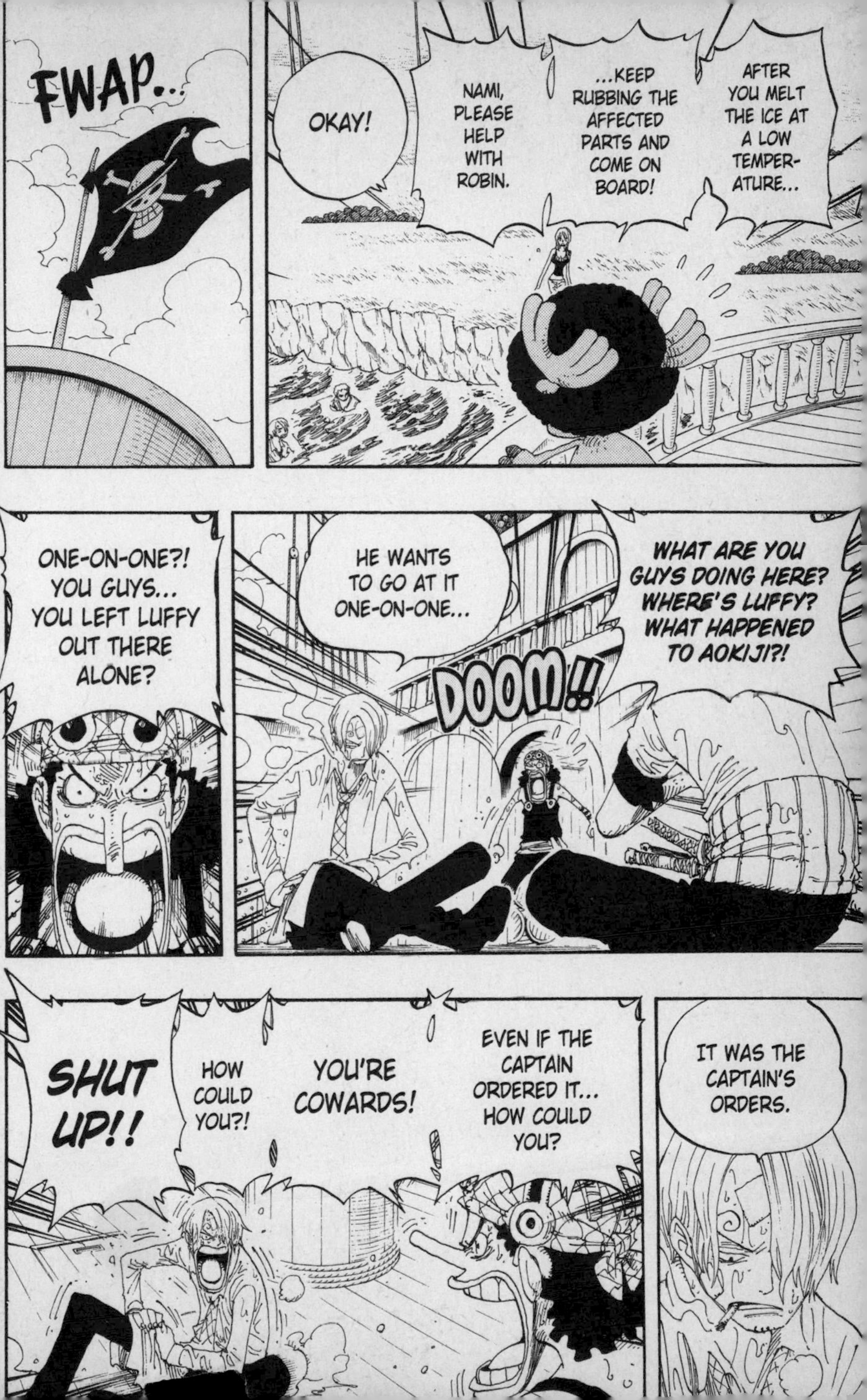
AFTER YOU MELT THE ICE AT A LOW TEMPERATURE...
...KEEP RUBBING THE AFFECTED PARTS AND COME ON BOARD!
NAMI, PLEASE HELP WITH ROBIN.
OKAY!
FWAP...
WHAT ARE YOU GUYS DOING HERE? WHERE'S LUFFY? WHAT HAPPENED TO AOKIJI?!
HE WANTS TO GO AT IT ONE-ON-ONE...
DOOM!!
ONE-ON-ONE?! YOU GUYS... YOU LEFT LUFFY OUT THERE ALONE?
IT WAS THE CAPTAIN'S ORDERS.
EVEN IF THE CAPTAIN ORDERED IT... HOW COULD YOU?
YOU'RE COWARDS!
HOW COULD YOU?!
SHUT UP!!

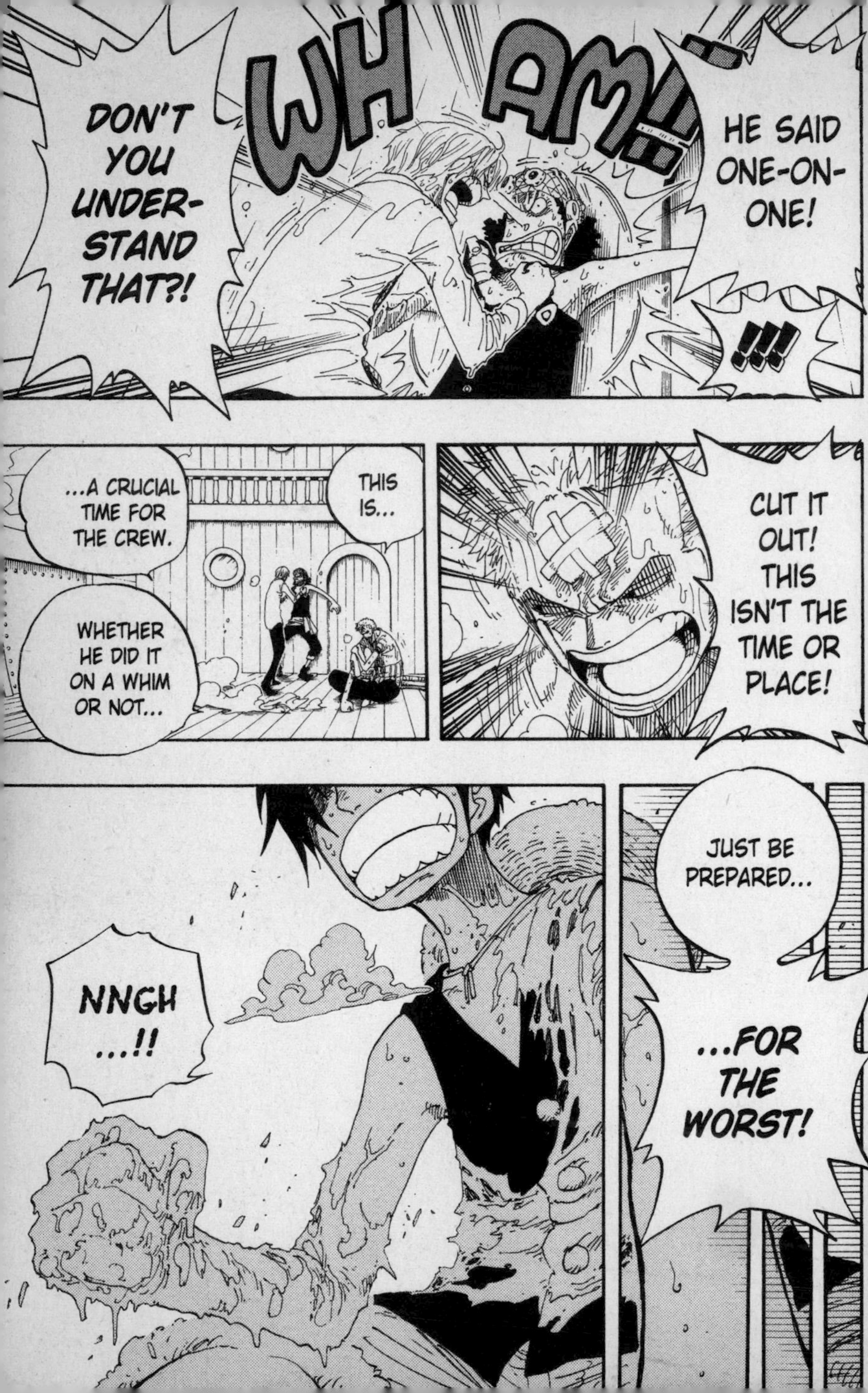
WHAM!!
HE SAID ONE-ON-ONE!
DON'T YOU UNDERSTAND THAT?!
!!!
CUT IT OUT! THIS ISN'T THE TIME OR PLACE!
THIS IS...
...A CRUCIAL TIME FOR THE CREW.
WHETHER HE DID IT ON A WHIM OR NOT...
JUST BE PREPARED...
...FOR THE WORST!
NNGH...!!

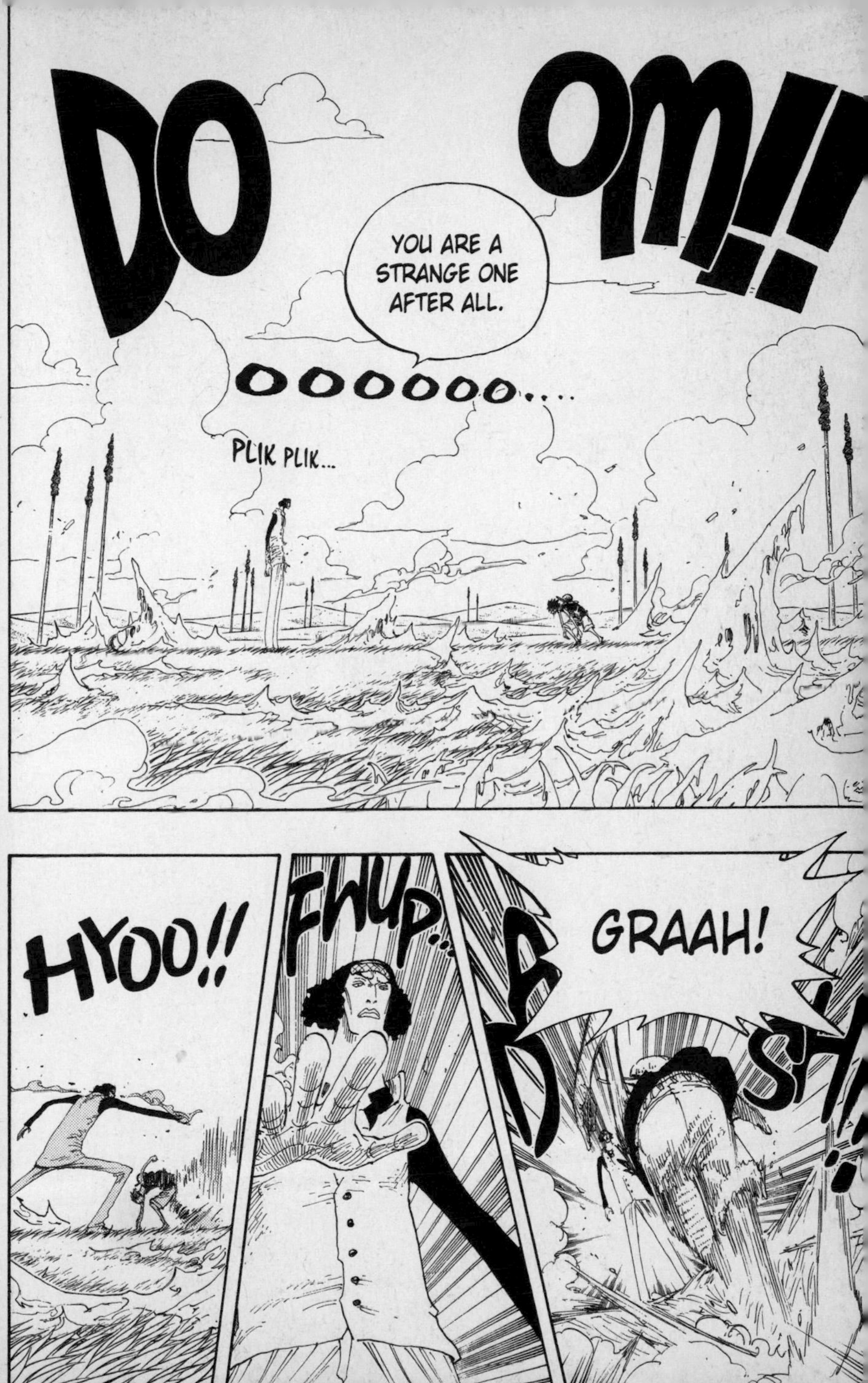
DO OM!!
YOU ARE A STRANGE ONE AFTER ALL.
OOOOOO....
PLIK PLIK...
GRAAH!
B
SH!!
FHUP...
HYOO!!

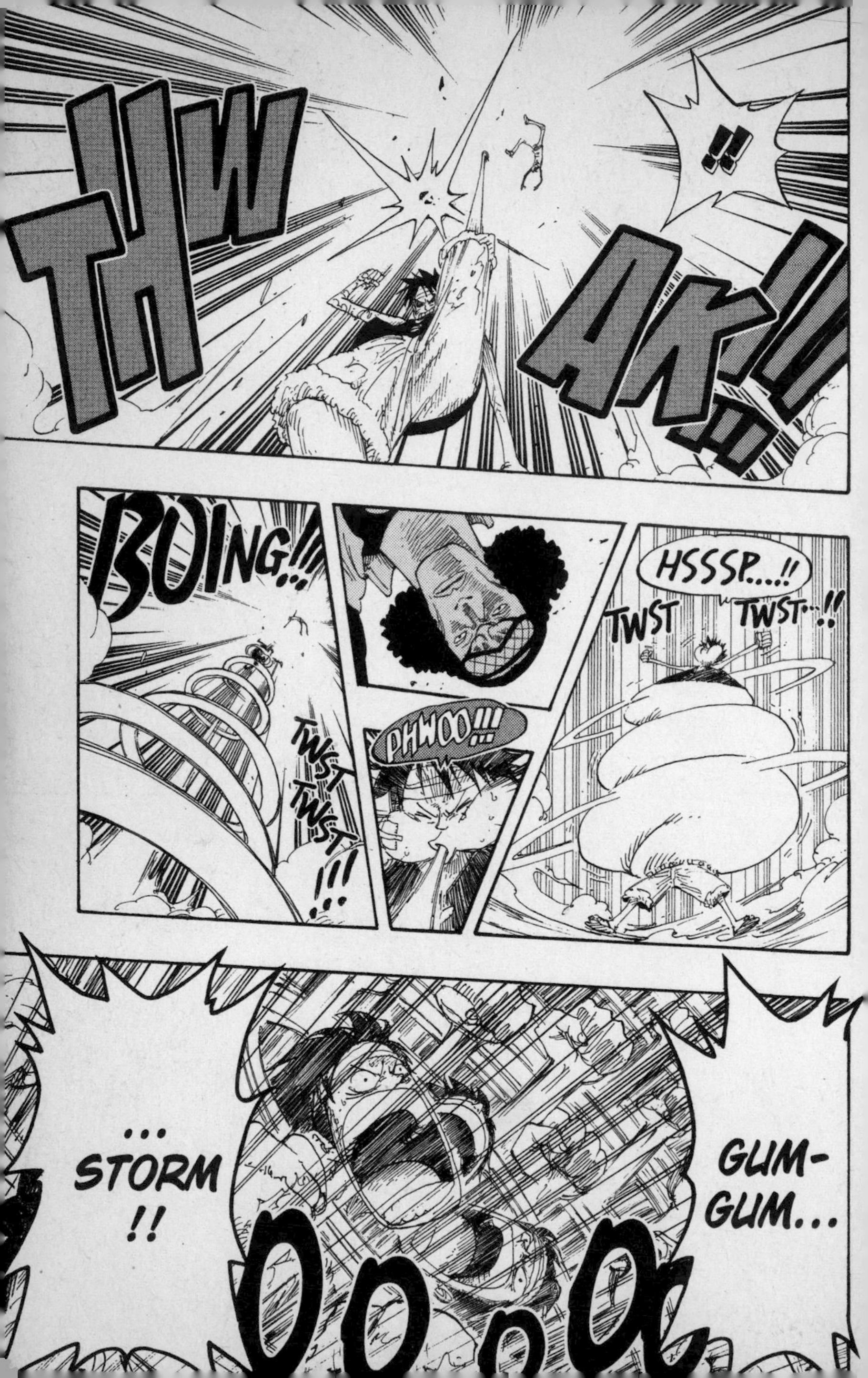
!!
THWAK!!
HSSSP...!!
TWST
TWST...!!
PHWOO!!!
BOING!!!
TWST TWST!!!
GUM-GUM...
...STORM!!

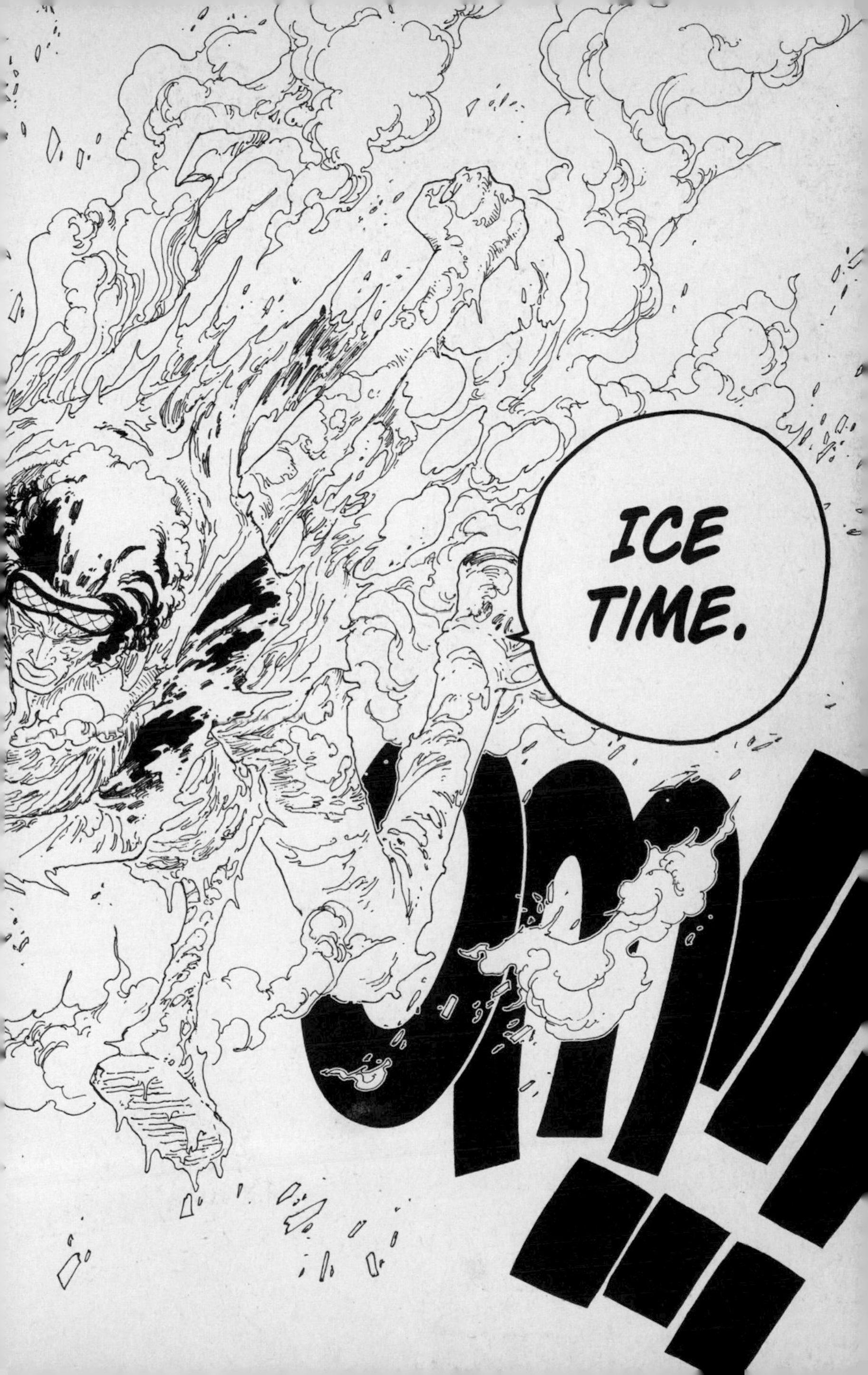
ICE TIME.

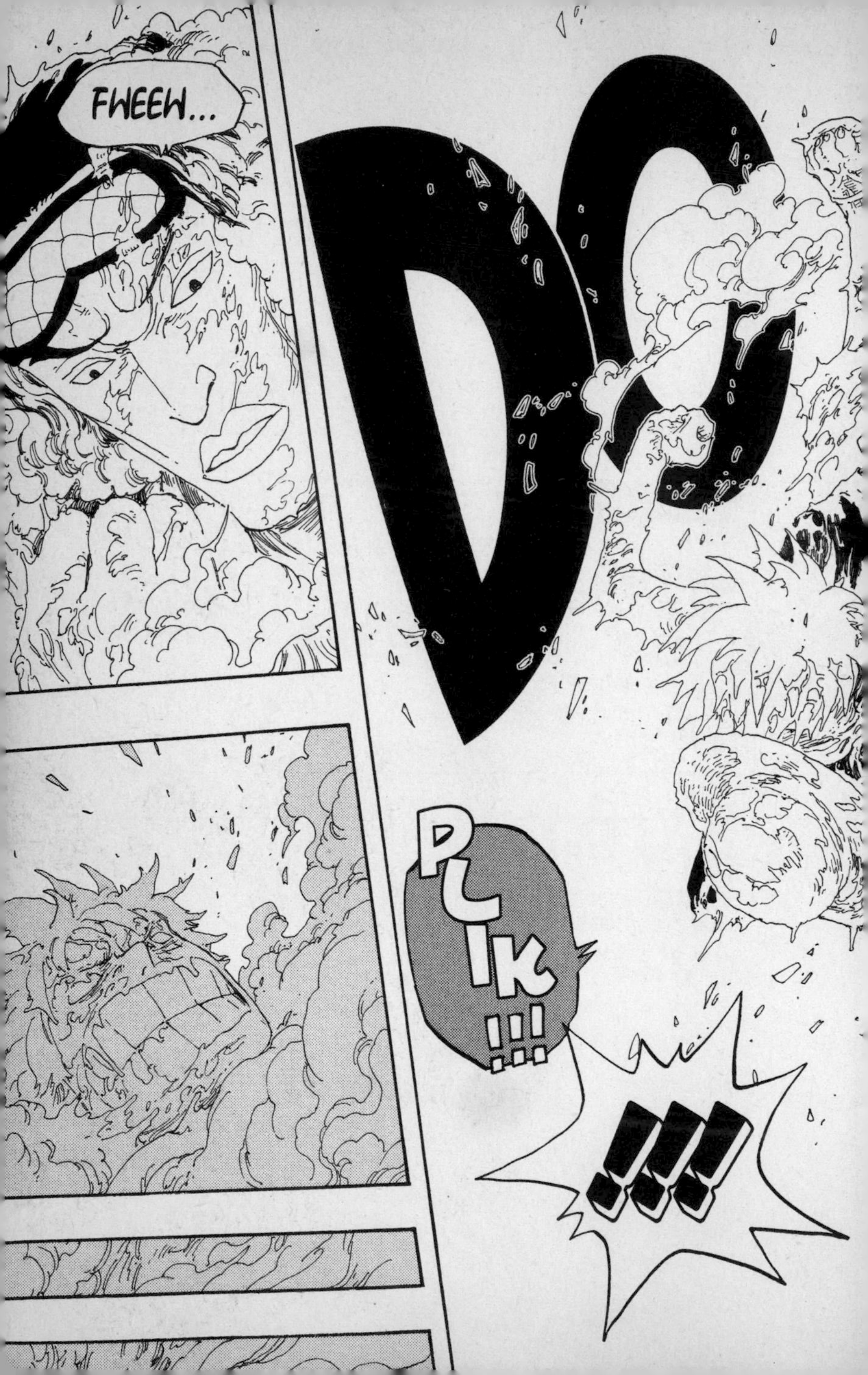
DO
PLIK!!!
!!!
FWEEW...

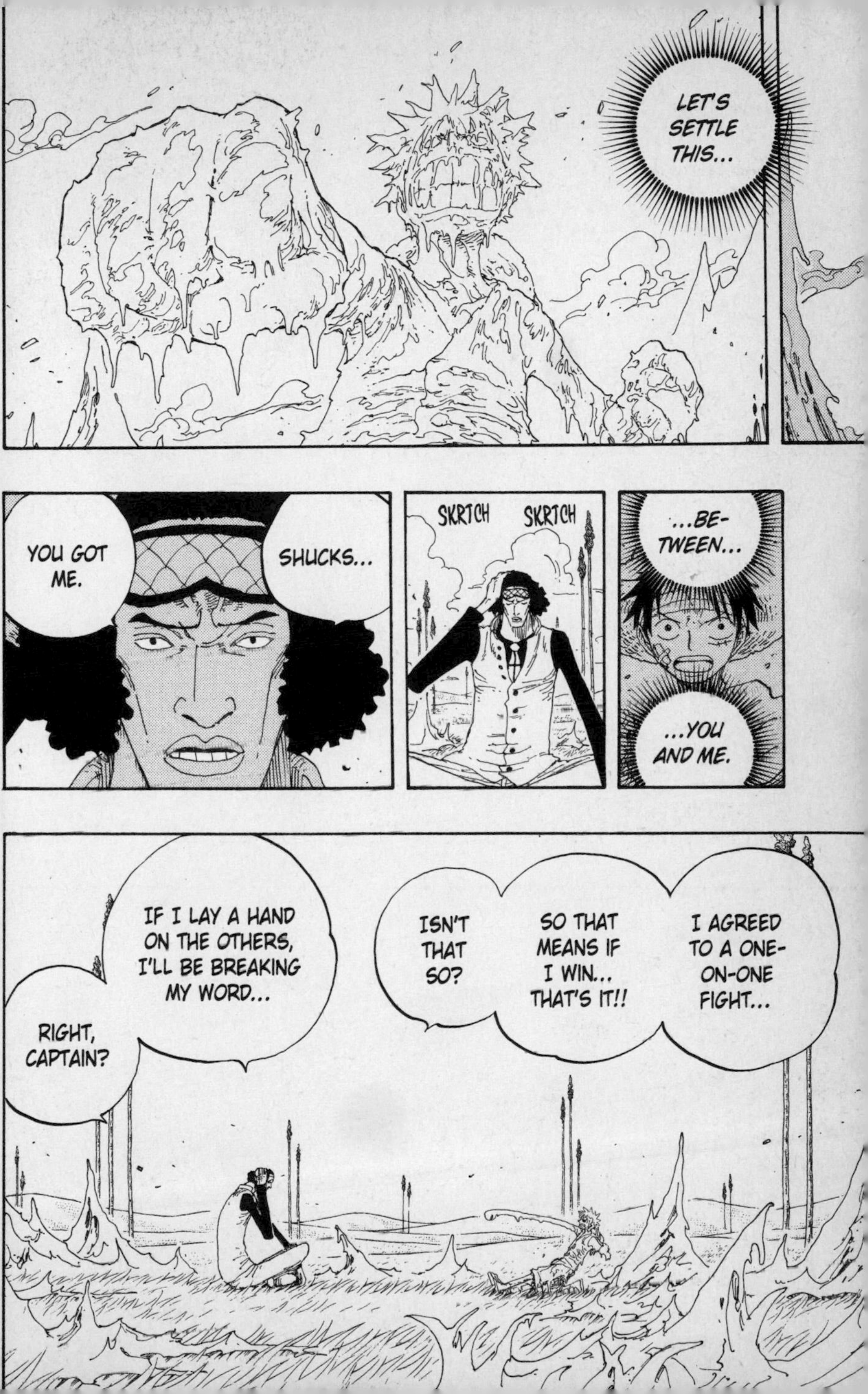
LET'S SETTLE THIS...
...BE-TWEEN...
...YOU AND ME.
SKRTCH SKRTCH
SHUCKS...
YOU GOT ME.
I AGREED TO A ONE-ON-ONE FIGHT...
SO THAT MEANS IF I WIN... THAT'S IT!!
ISN'T THAT SO?
IF I LAY A HAND ON THE OTHERS, I'LL BE BREAKING MY WORD...
RIGHT, CAPTAIN?

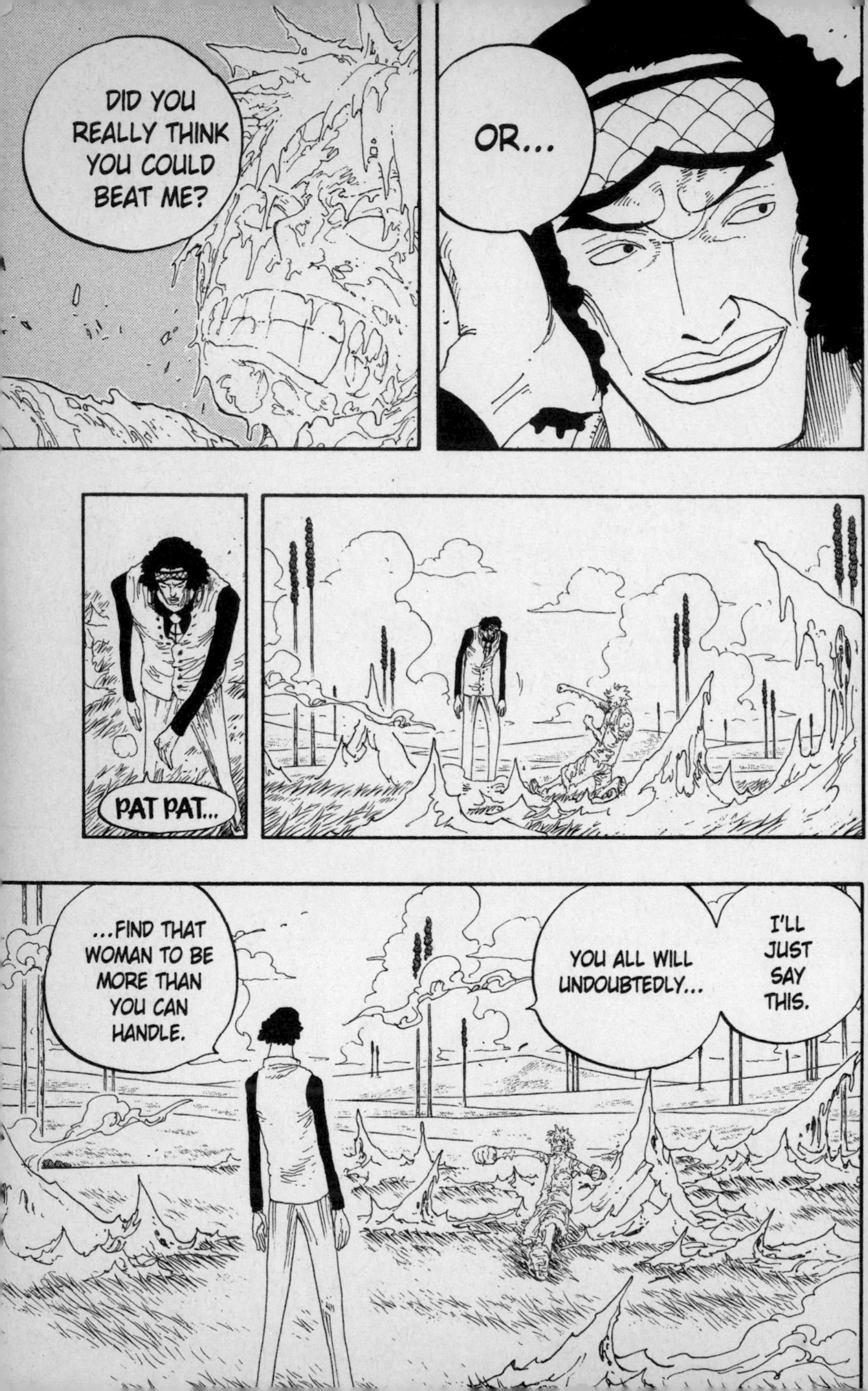
OR...
DID YOU REALLY THINK YOU COULD BEAT ME?
PAT PAT...
I'LL JUST SAY THIS.
YOU ALL WILL UNDOUBTEDLY...
...FIND THAT WOMAN TO BE MORE THAN YOU CAN HANDLE.

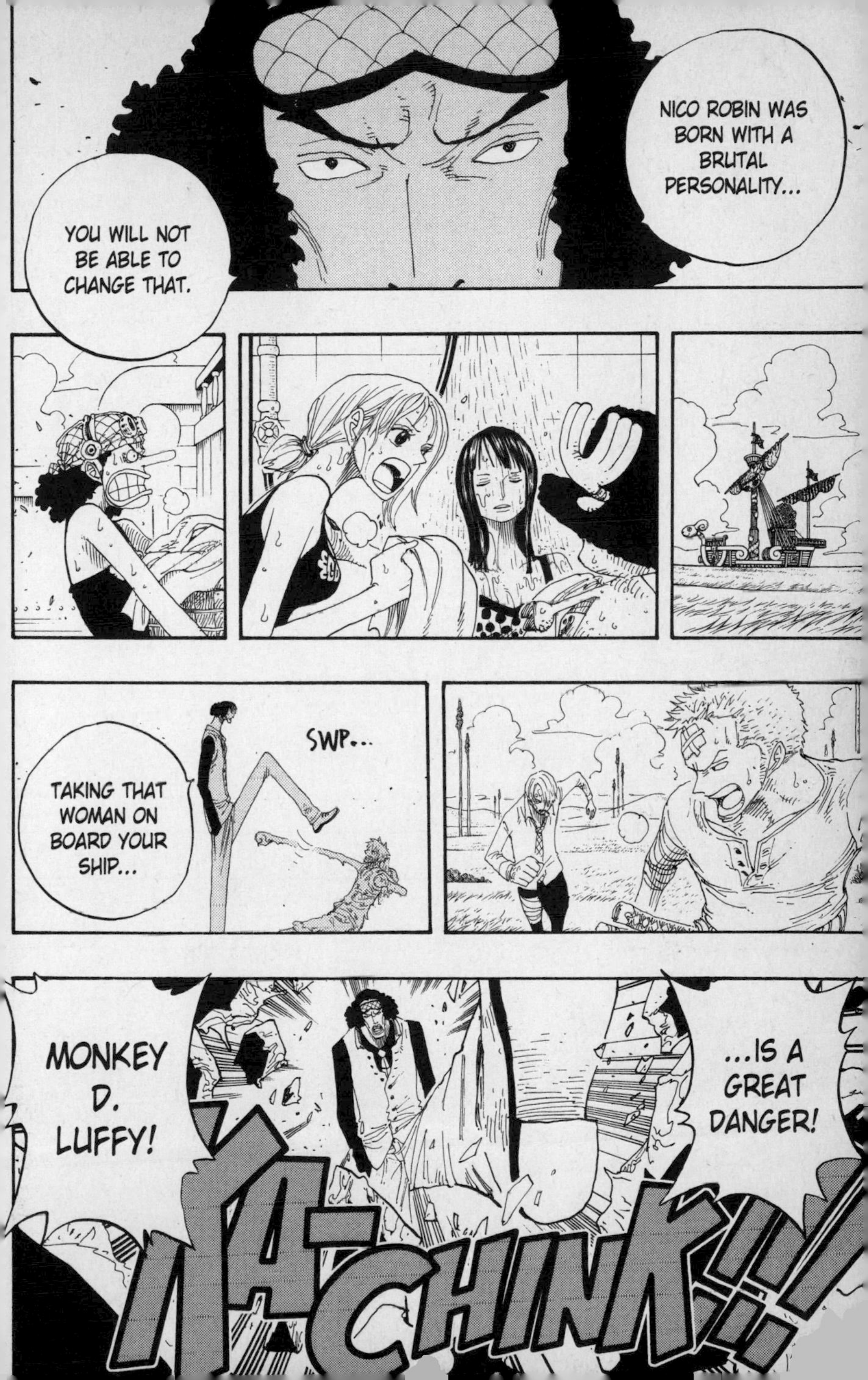
NICO ROBIN WAS BORN WITH A BRUTAL PERSONALITY...
YOU WILL NOT BE ABLE TO CHANGE THAT.
SWP...
TAKING THAT WOMAN ON BOARD YOUR SHIP...
...IS A GREAT DANGER!
MONKEY D. LUFFY!
YA-CHINK!!!

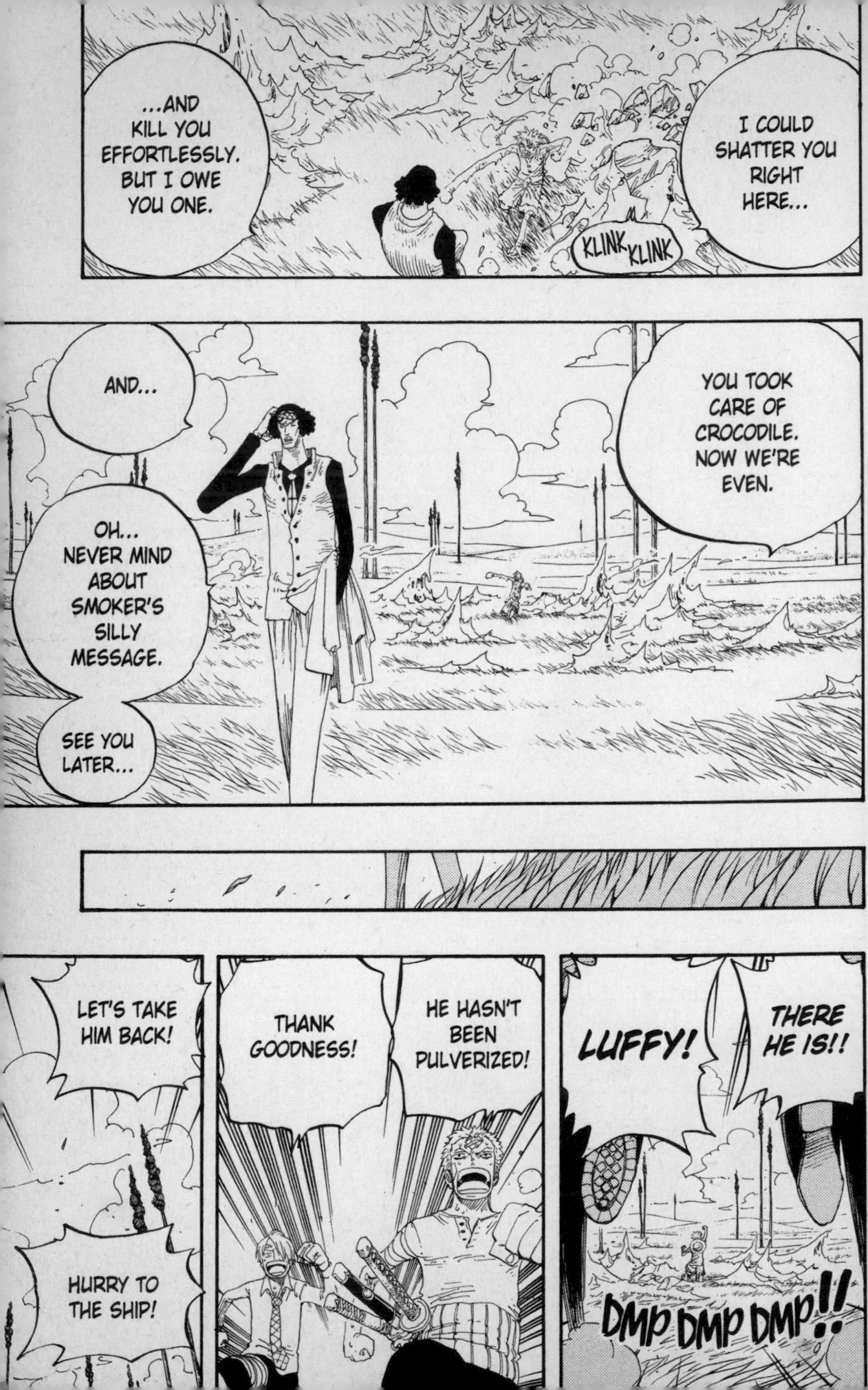
I COULD SHATTER YOU RIGHT HERE...
KLINK KLINK
...AND KILL YOU EFFORTLESSLY. BUT I OWE YOU ONE.
YOU TOOK CARE OF CROCODILE. NOW WE'RE EVEN.
AND...
OH... NEVER MIND ABOUT SMOKER'S SILLY MESSAGE.
SEE YOU LATER...
THERE HE IS!!
LUFFY!
DMP DMP DMP!!
HE HASN'T BEEN PULVERIZED!
THANK GOODNESS!
LET'S TAKE HIM BACK!
HURRY TO THE SHIP!

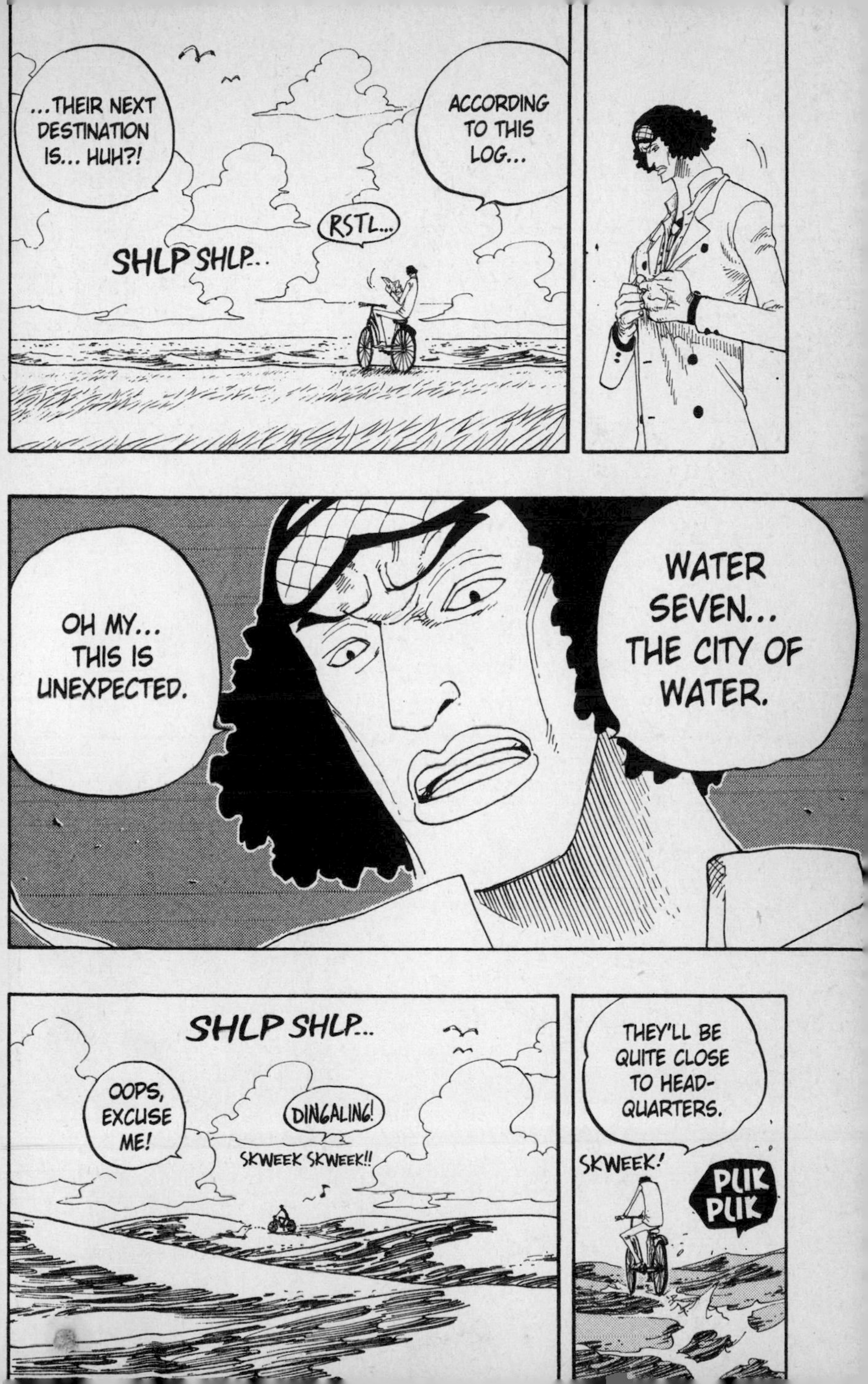
ACCORDING TO THIS LOG...
...THEIR NEXT DESTINATION IS... HUH?!
RSTL...
SHLP SHLP...
WATER SEVEN... THE CITY OF WATER.
OH MY... THIS IS UNEXPECTED.
THEY'LL BE QUITE CLOSE TO HEAD-QUARTERS.
PUK PUK
SKWEEK!
SHLP SHLP...
DINGALING!
OOPS, EXCUSE ME!
SKWEEK SKWEEK!!

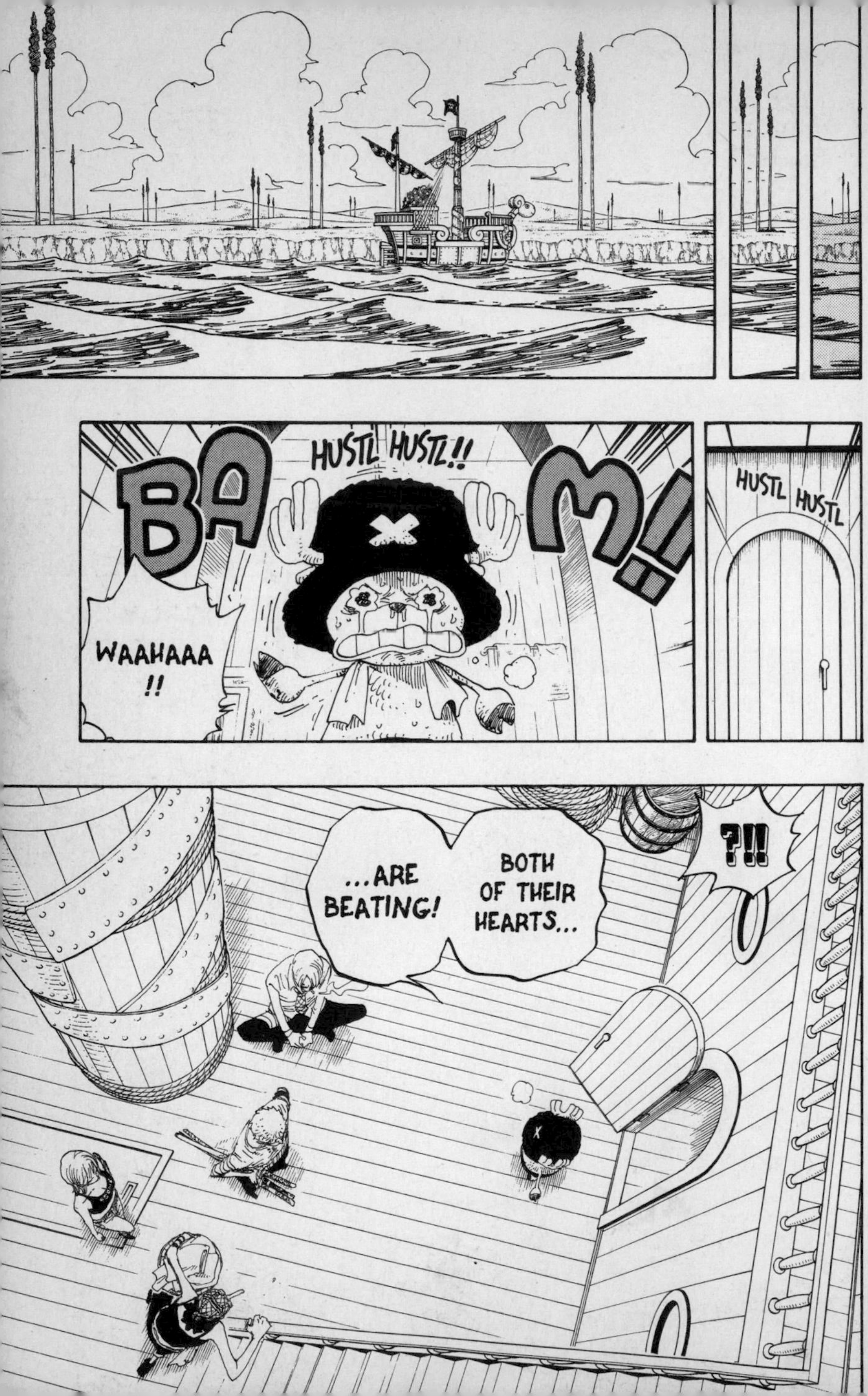
HUSTL HUSTL
HUSTL HUSTL!!
BAM!!
WAAHAAA!!
?!!
BOTH OF THEIR HEARTS...
...ARE BEATING!

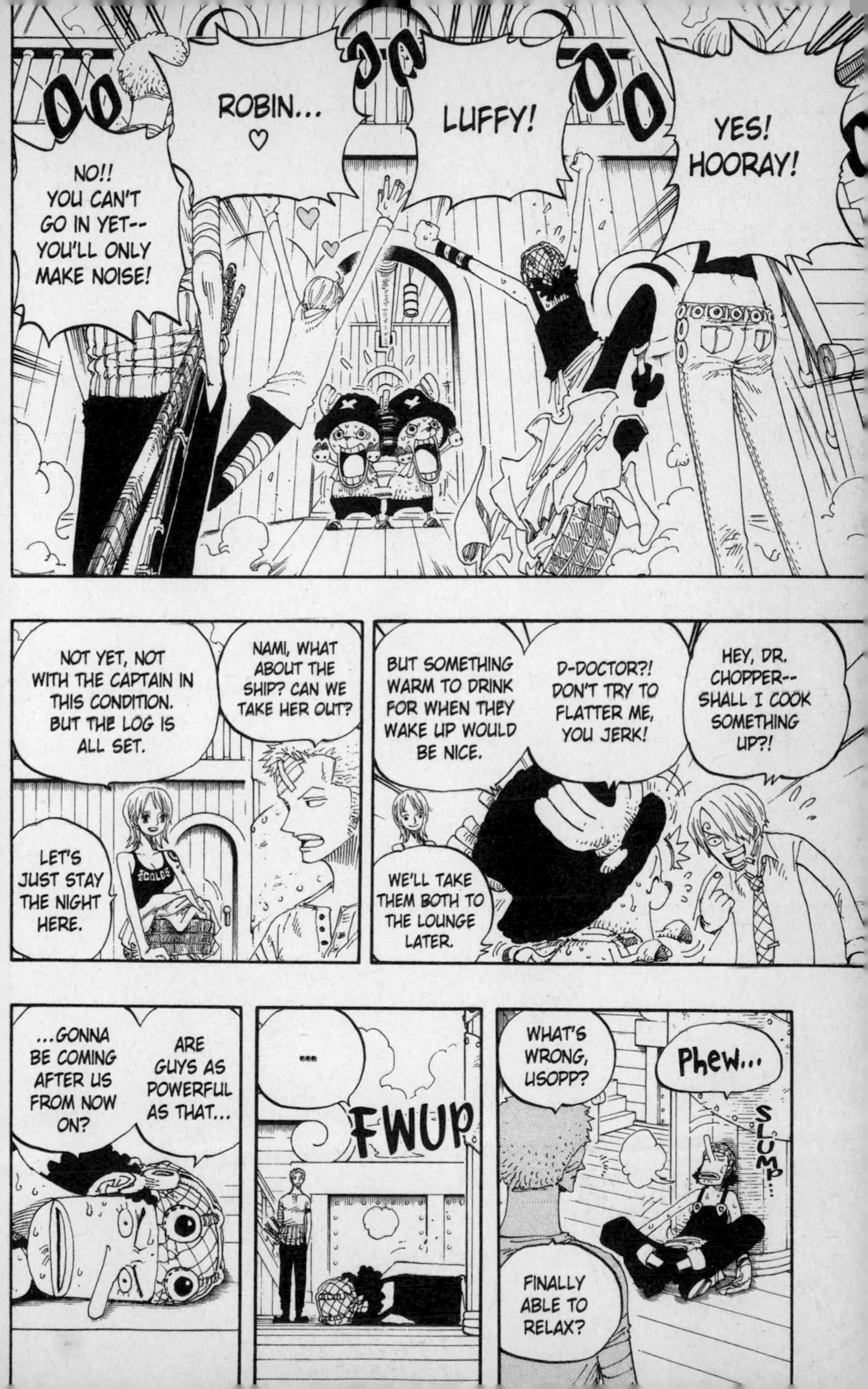
YES! HOORAY!
LUFFY!
ROBIN... ♡
NO!! YOU CAN'T GO IN YET-- YOU'LL ONLY MAKE NOISE!
HEY, DR. CHOPPER-- SHALL I COOK SOMETHING UP?!
D-DOCTOR?! DON'T TRY TO FLATTER ME, YOU JERK!
BUT SOMETHING WARM TO DRINK FOR WHEN THEY WAKE UP WOULD BE NICE.
WE'LL TAKE THEM BOTH TO THE LOUNGE LATER.
NAMI, WHAT ABOUT THE SHIP? CAN WE TAKE HER OUT?
NOT YET, NOT WITH THE CAPTAIN IN THIS CONDITION. BUT THE LOG IS ALL SET.
LET'S JUST STAY THE NIGHT HERE.
Phew...
SLUMP...
WHAT'S WRONG, USOPP?
FINALLY ABLE TO RELAX?
...
FWUP
ARE GUYS AS POWERFUL AS THAT...
...GONNA BE COMING AFTER US FROM NOW ON?

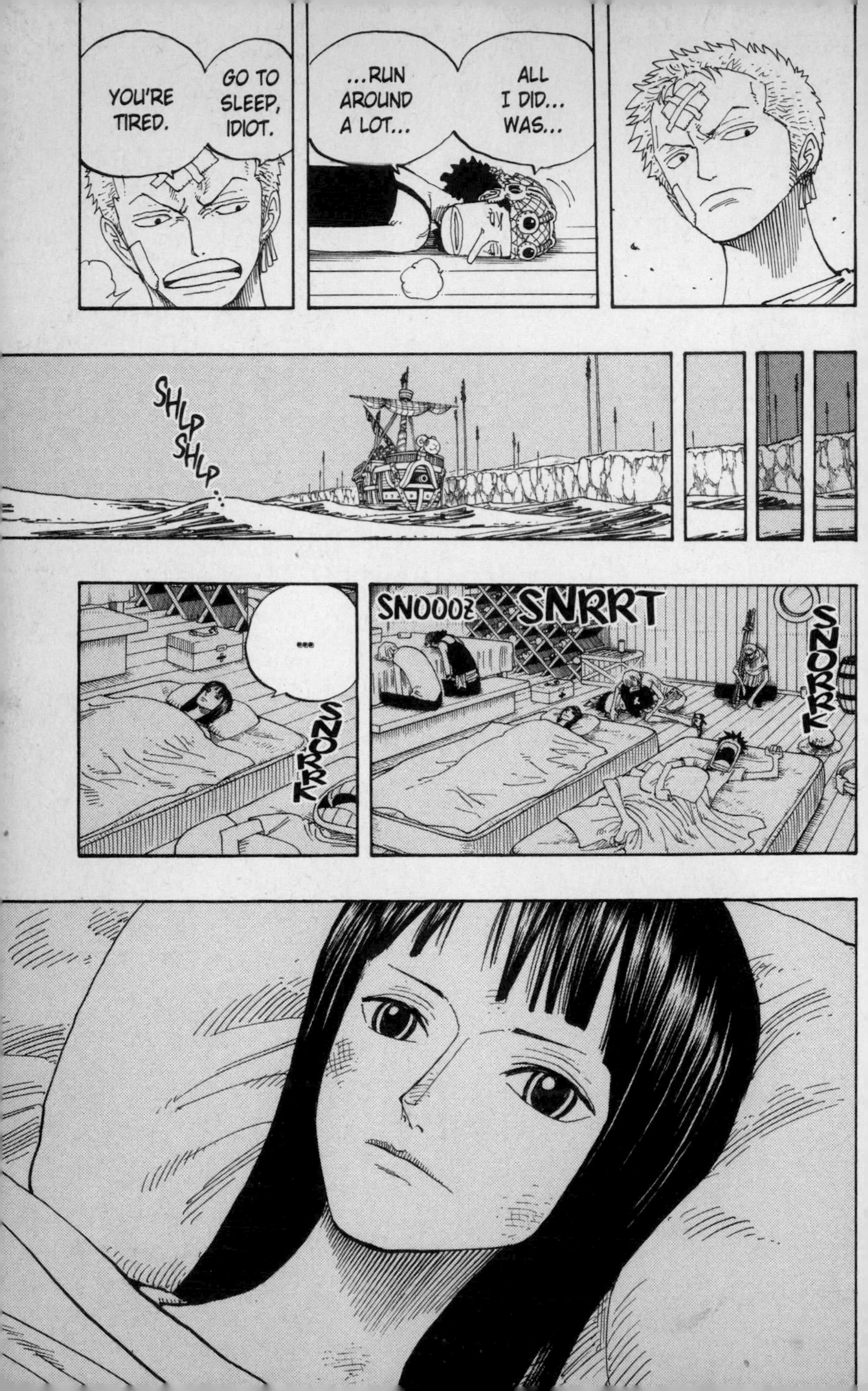
ALL I DID... WAS...
...RUN AROUND A LOT...
GO TO SLEEP, IDIOT.
YOU'RE TIRED.
SHLP SHLP...
SNORRK
SNRRT
SNOOOZ
...
SNORRK

Chapter 322:
PUFFING TOM

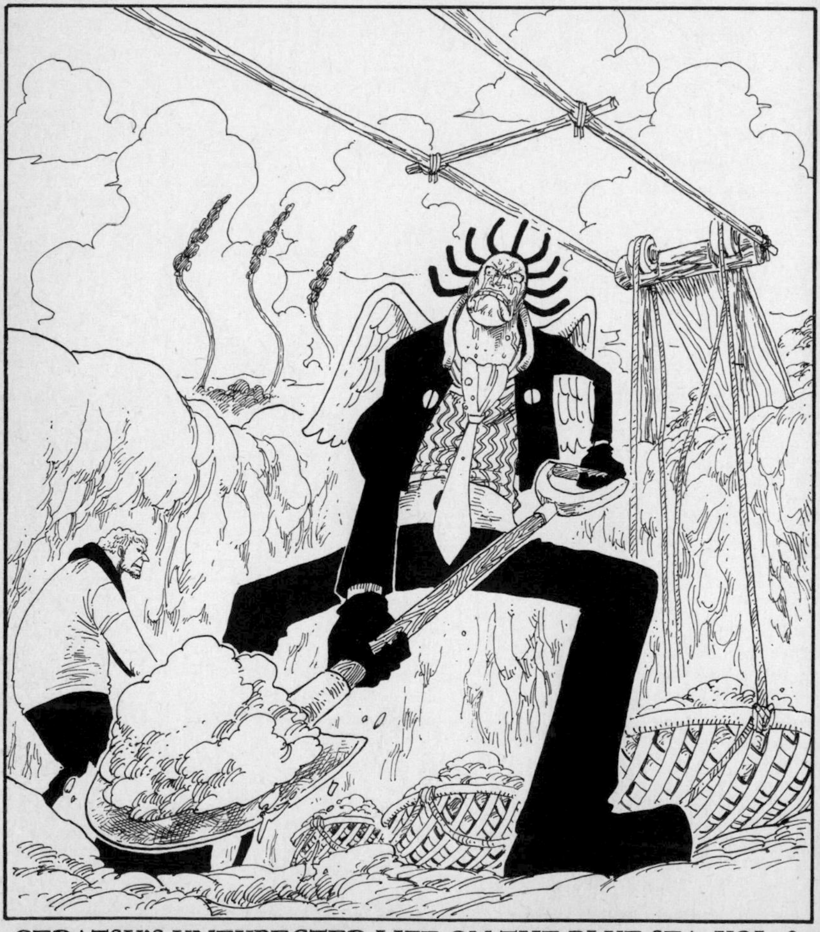

GEDATSU'S UNEXPECTED LIFE ON THE BLUE SEA, VOL. 8: "DON'T FORGET TO BLINK WHILE YOU DIG, MASTER GEDATSU"

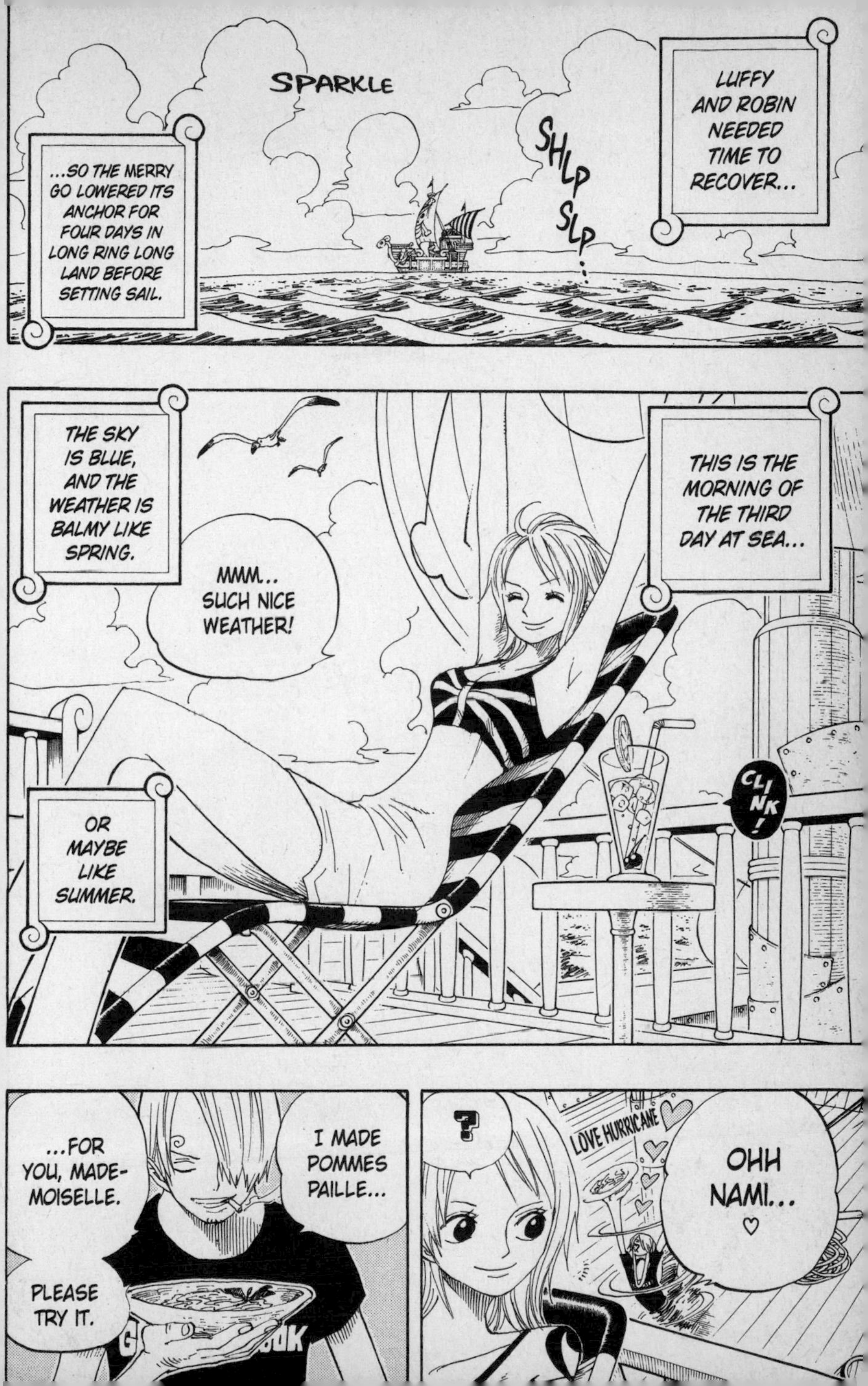
LUFFY AND ROBIN NEEDED TIME TO RECOVER...
SHLP SLP...
SPARKLE
...SO THE MERRY GO LOWERED ITS ANCHOR FOR FOUR DAYS IN LONG RING LONG LAND BEFORE SETTING SAIL.
THIS IS THE MORNING OF THE THIRD DAY AT SEA...
THE SKY IS BLUE, AND THE WEATHER IS BALMY LIKE SPRING.
MMM... SUCH NICE WEATHER!
CLINK!
OR MAYBE LIKE SUMMER.
OHH NAMI... ♡
LOVE HURRICANE
?
I MADE POMMES PAILLE...
...FOR YOU, MADEMOISELLE.
PLEASE TRY IT.

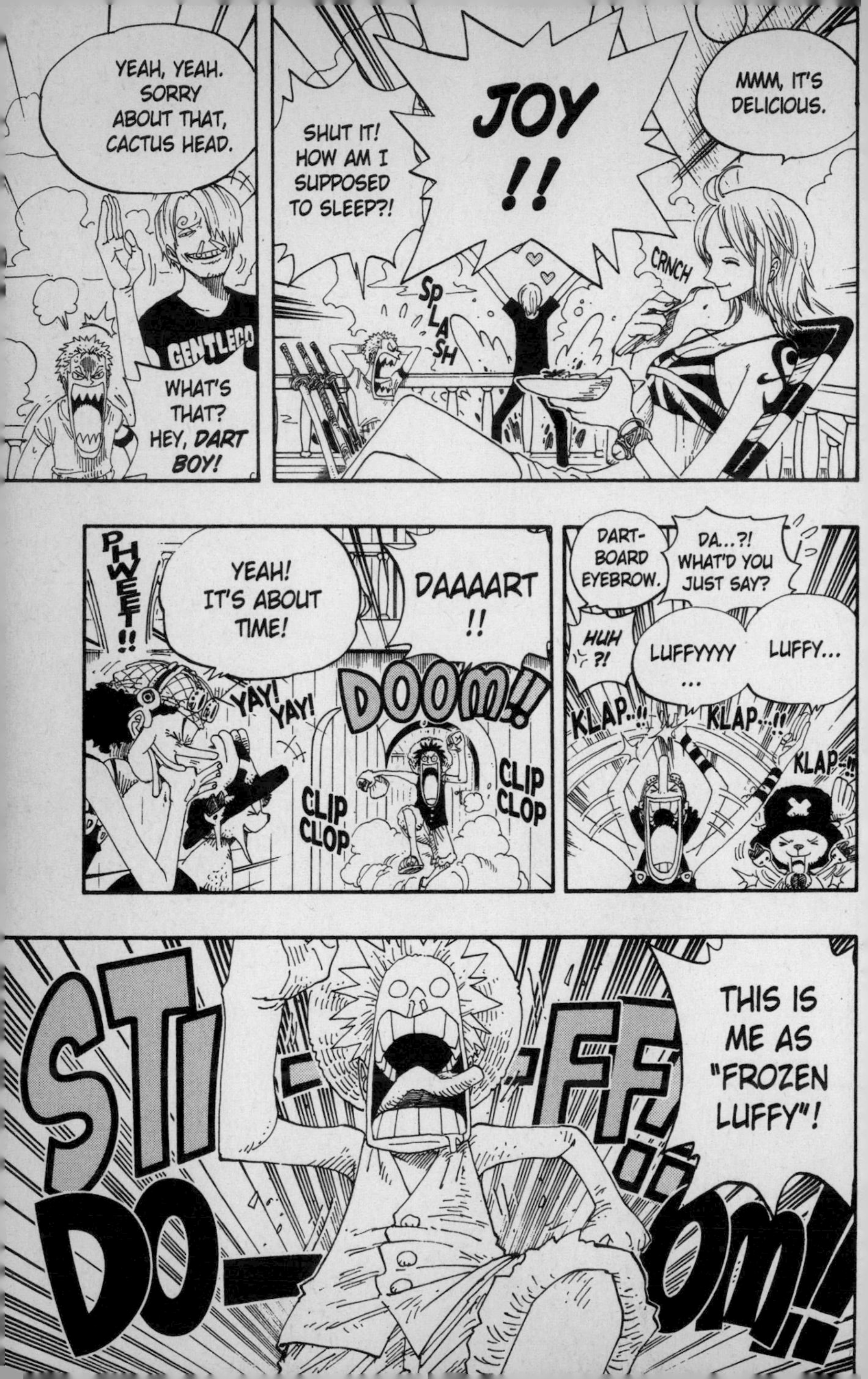
MMM, IT'S DELICIOUS.
CRNCH
JOY!!
SHUT IT! HOW AM I SUPPOSED TO SLEEP?!
SPLASH
YEAH, YEAH. SORRY ABOUT THAT, CACTUS HEAD.
GENTLECO
WHAT'S THAT? HEY, DART BOY!
DA...?! WHAT'D YOU JUST SAY?
DART-BOARD EYEBROW.
LUFFY...
LUFFYYYY...
HUH?!
KLAP..!!
KLAP..!!
KLAP..!!
DAAAART!!
YEAH! IT'S ABOUT TIME!
PHWEET!!
YAY! YAY!
DOOM!!
CLIP CLOP
CLIP CLOP
THIS IS ME AS "FROZEN LUFFY"!
STI-FF!!
DO-OM!!

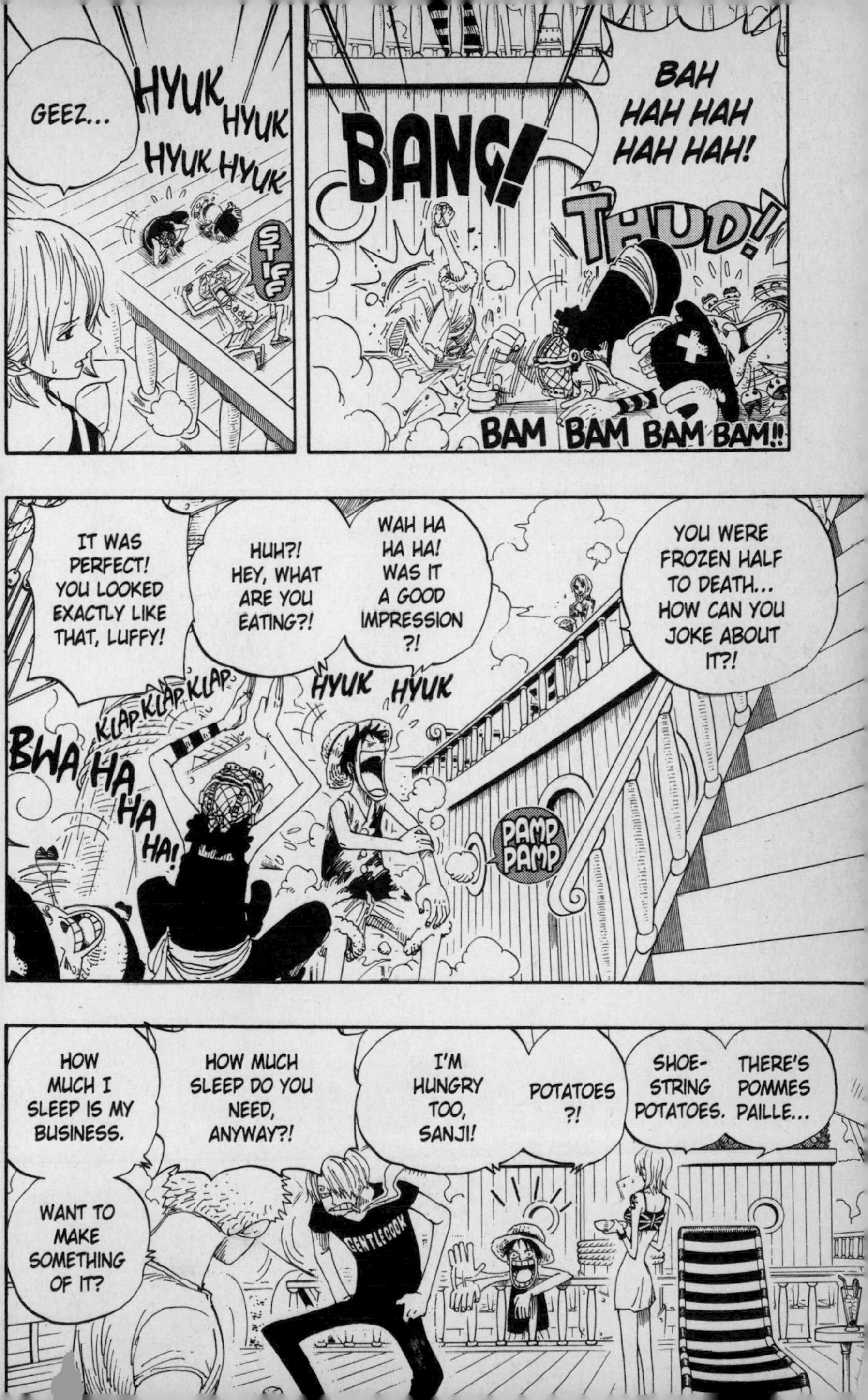
BAH HAH HAH HAH HAH!
BANG!
THUD!
BAM BAM BAM BAM!!
GEEZ...
HYUK HYUK HYUK HYUK
STIFF
YOU WERE FROZEN HALF TO DEATH... HOW CAN YOU JOKE ABOUT IT?!
PAMP PAMP
WAH HA HA HA! WAS IT A GOOD IMPRESSION?!
HUH?! HEY, WHAT ARE YOU EATING?!
HYUK HYUK
IT WAS PERFECT! YOU LOOKED EXACTLY LIKE THAT, LUFFY!
KLAP KLAP KLAP
BWA HA HA HA HA!
THERE'S POMMES PAILLE...
SHOE-STRING POTATOES.
POTATOES?!
I'M HUNGRY TOO, SANJI!
HOW MUCH SLEEP DO YOU NEED, ANYWAY?!
HOW MUCH I SLEEP IS MY BUSINESS.
WANT TO MAKE SOMETHING OF IT?

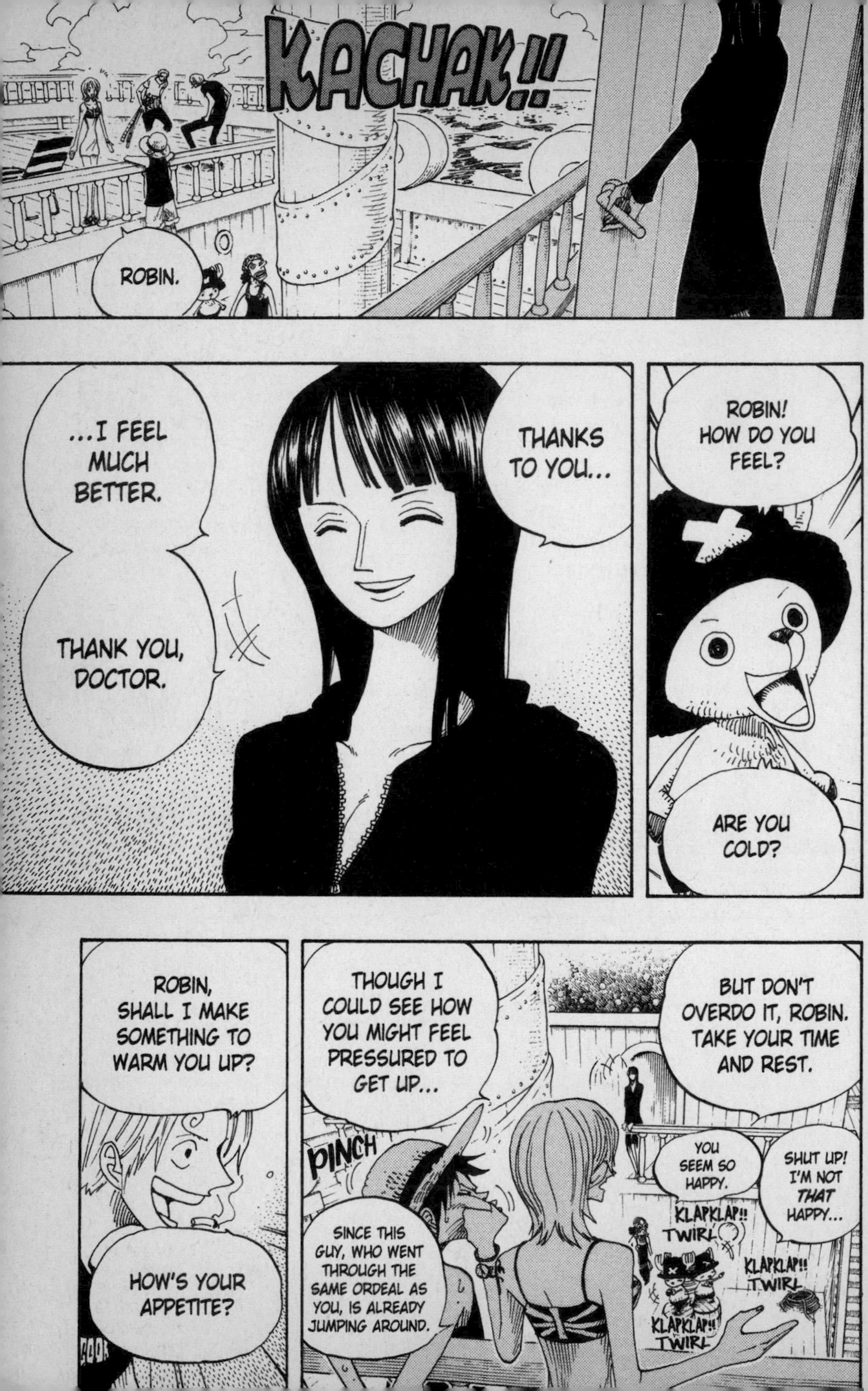
KACHAK!!
ROBIN.
ROBIN! HOW DO YOU FEEL?
ARE YOU COLD?
THANKS TO YOU...
...I FEEL MUCH BETTER.
THANK YOU, DOCTOR.
BUT DON'T OVERDO IT, ROBIN. TAKE YOUR TIME AND REST.
THOUGH I COULD SEE HOW YOU MIGHT FEEL PRESSURED TO GET UP...
PINCH
SINCE THIS GUY, WHO WENT THROUGH THE SAME ORDEAL AS YOU, IS ALREADY JUMPING AROUND.
YOU SEEM SO HAPPY.
SHUT UP! I'M NOT *THAT* HAPPY...
KLAPKLAP!! TWIRL
KLAPKLAP!! TWIRL
KLAPKLAP!! TWIRL
ROBIN, SHALL I MAKE SOMETHING TO WARM YOU UP?
HOW'S YOUR APPETITE?

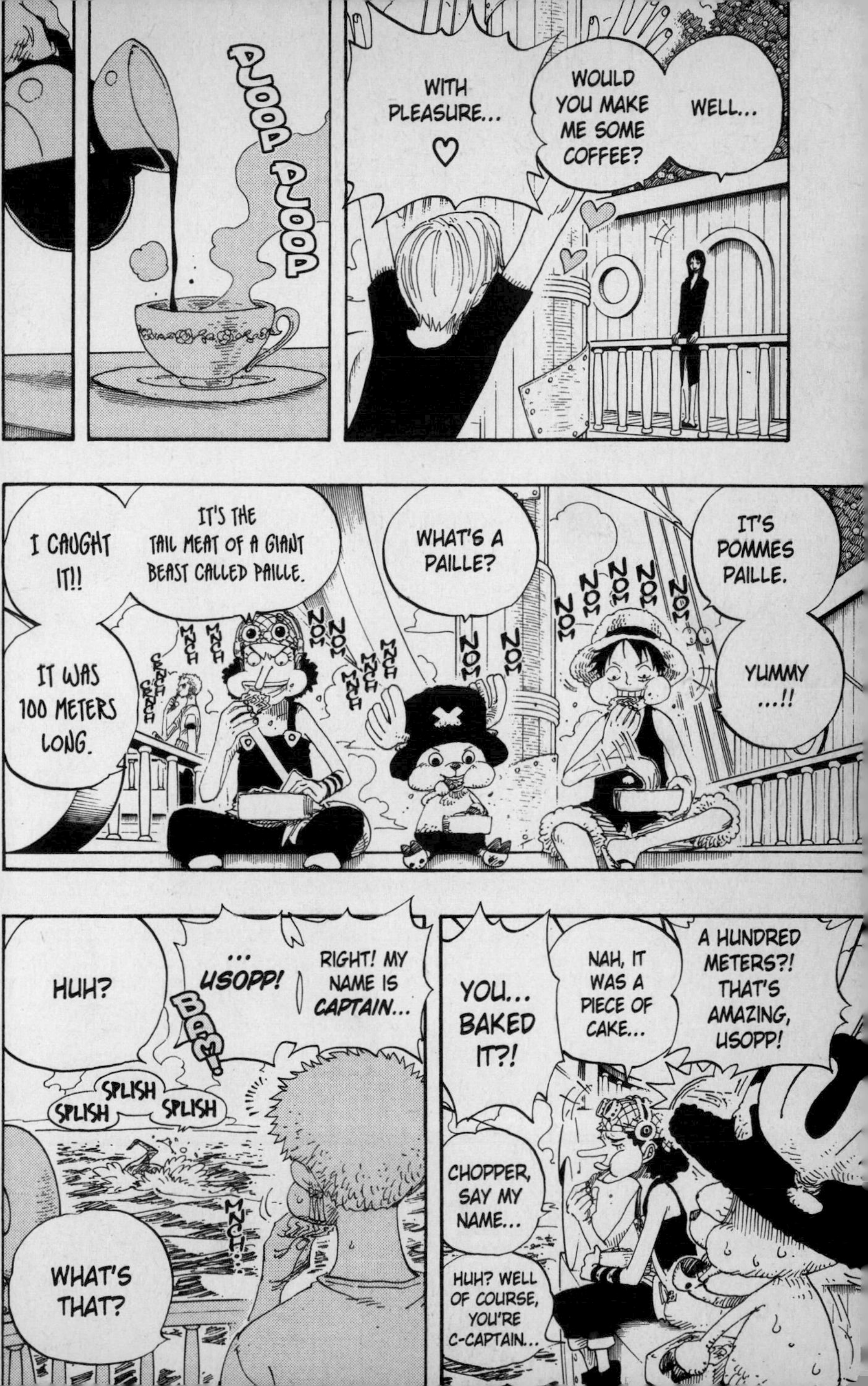
WELL...
WOULD YOU MAKE ME SOME COFFEE?
WITH PLEASURE... ♥
PLOOP PLOOP
IT'S POMMES PAILLE.
YUMMY ...!!
NOM NOM NOM NOM NOM NOM
WHAT'S A PAILLE?
NOM NOM
MNCH MNCH
NOM NOM
IT'S THE TAIL MEAT OF A GIANT BEAST CALLED PAILLE.
I CAUGHT IT!!
IT WAS 100 METERS LONG.
MNCH MNCH
CRNCH CRNCH
A HUNDRED METERS?! THAT'S AMAZING, USOPP!
NAH, IT WAS A PIECE OF CAKE...
YOU... BAKED IT?!
CHOPPER, SAY MY NAME...
HUH? WELL OF COURSE, YOU'RE C-CAPTAIN...
RIGHT! MY NAME IS CAPTAIN...
... USOPP!
BAM!
HUH?
SPLISH SPLISH SPLISH
MNCH...
WHAT'S THAT?

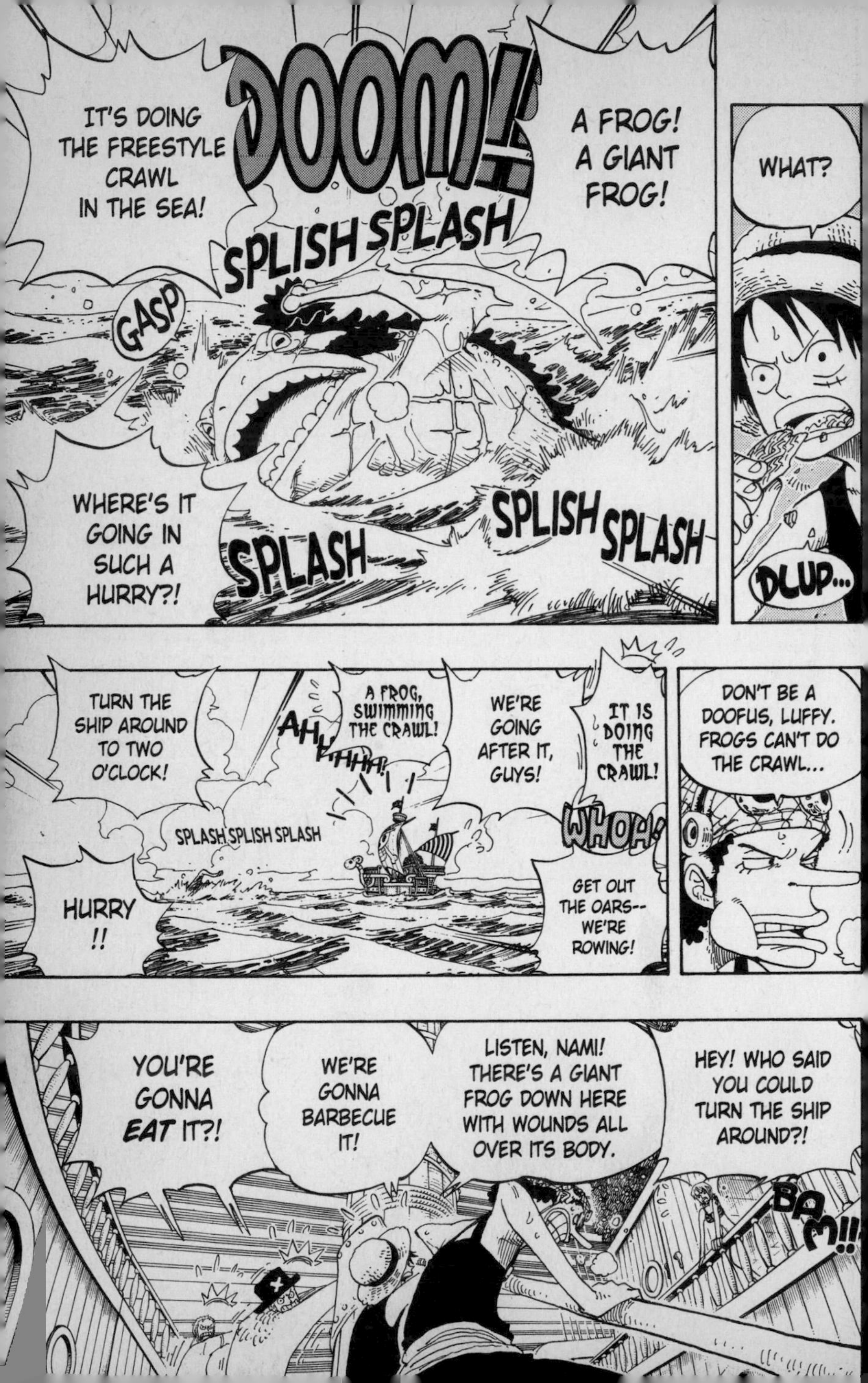
WHAT?
DLUP...
A FROG! A GIANT FROG!
DOOM!!
IT'S DOING THE FREESTYLE CRAWL IN THE SEA!
SPLISH SPLASH
GASP
SPLISH SPLASH
SPLASH
WHERE'S IT GOING IN SUCH A HURRY?!
DON'T BE A DOOFUS, LUFFY. FROGS CAN'T DO THE CRAWL...
IT IS DOING THE CRAWL!
WE'RE GOING AFTER IT, GUYS!
A FROG, SWIMMING THE CRAWL!
AHHHHH!
TURN THE SHIP AROUND TO TWO O'CLOCK!
WHOA!
GET OUT THE OARS-- WE'RE ROWING!
SPLASH SPLISH SPLASH
HURRY !!
HEY! WHO SAID YOU COULD TURN THE SHIP AROUND?!
BAM!!
LISTEN, NAMI! THERE'S A GIANT FROG DOWN HERE WITH WOUNDS ALL OVER ITS BODY.
WE'RE GONNA BARBECUE IT!
YOU'RE GONNA EAT IT?!

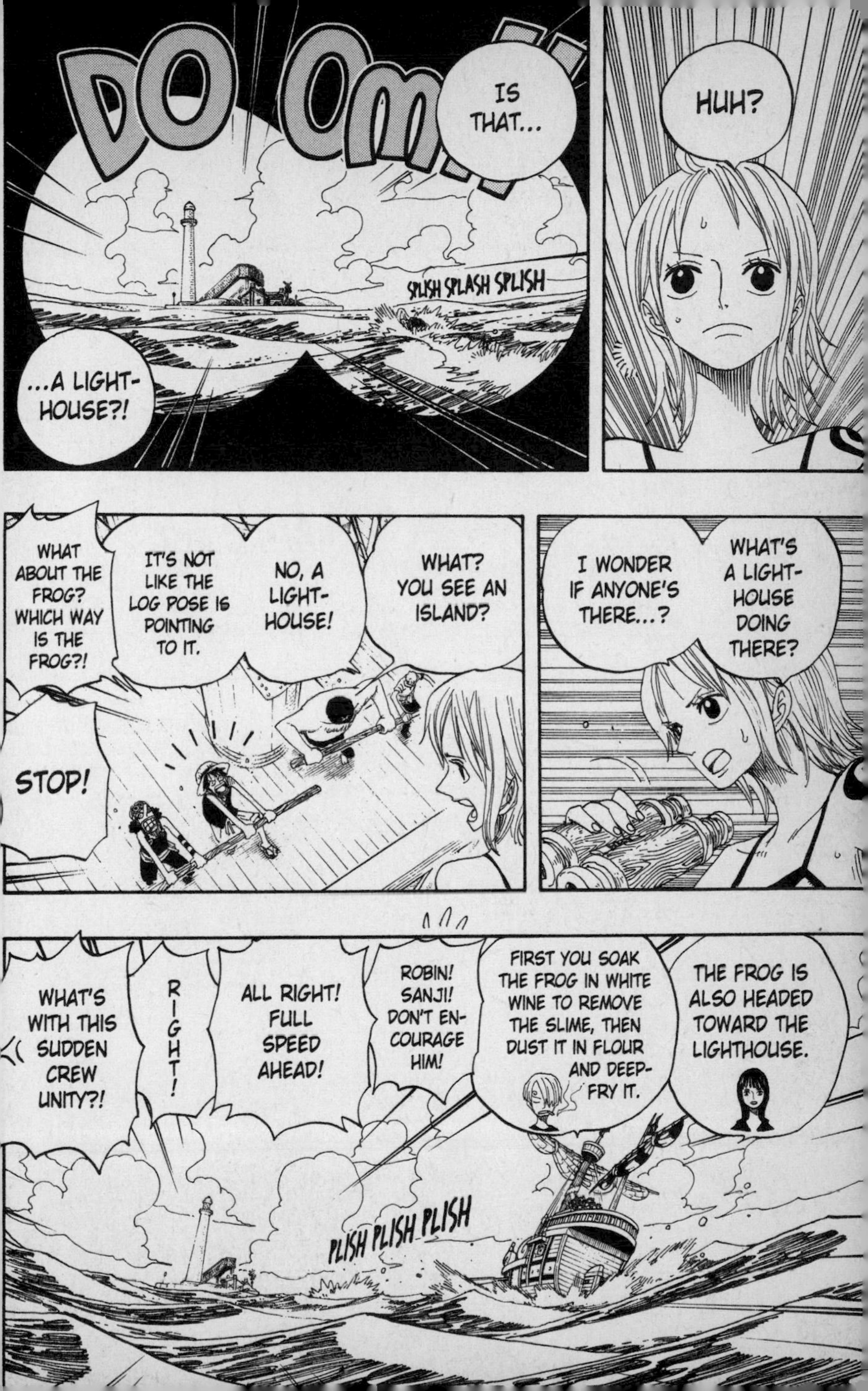
HUH?
DOOM!!
IS THAT...
SPLISH SPLASH SPLISH
...A LIGHTHOUSE?!
WHAT'S A LIGHTHOUSE DOING THERE?
I WONDER IF ANYONE'S THERE...?
WHAT? YOU SEE AN ISLAND?
NO, A LIGHTHOUSE!
IT'S NOT LIKE THE LOG POSE IS POINTING TO IT.
WHAT ABOUT THE FROG? WHICH WAY IS THE FROG?!
STOP!
THE FROG IS ALSO HEADED TOWARD THE LIGHTHOUSE.
FIRST YOU SOAK THE FROG IN WHITE WINE TO REMOVE THE SLIME, THEN DUST IT IN FLOUR AND DEEP-FRY IT.
ROBIN! SANJI! DON'T ENCOURAGE HIM!
ALL RIGHT! FULL SPEED AHEAD!
RIGHT!
WHAT'S WITH THIS SUDDEN CREW UNITY?!
PLISH PLISH PLISH

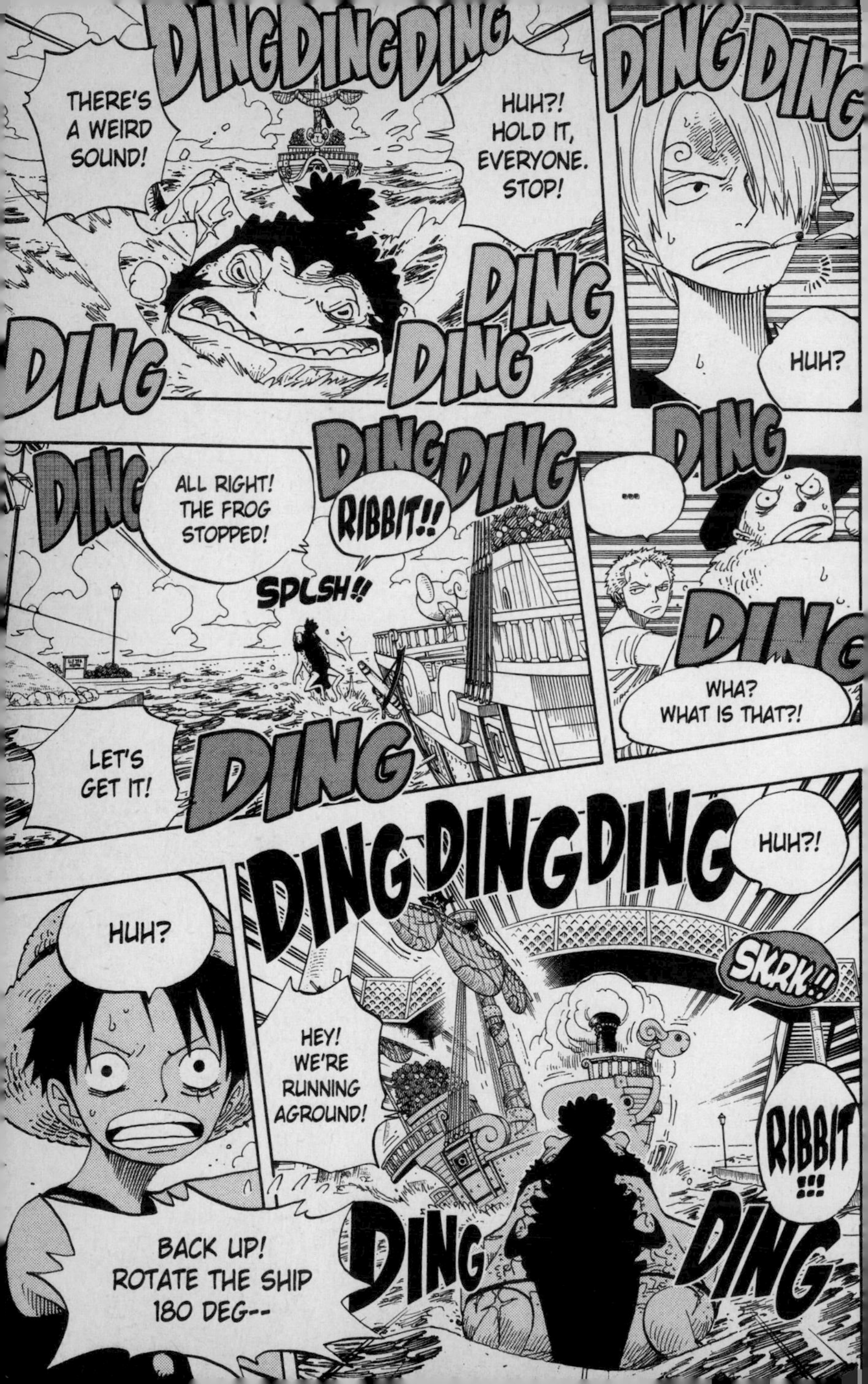
DING DING
DING
HUH?
DING DING DING
HUH?! HOLD IT, EVERYONE. STOP!
THERE'S A WEIRD SOUND!
DING DING
DING
DING
...
DING
WHA? WHAT IS THAT?!
DING DING
RIBBIT!!
ALL RIGHT! THE FROG STOPPED!
DING
SPLSH!!
DING
LET'S GET IT!
DING DING DING
HUH?!
SKRK!!
RIBBIT!!!
HEY! WE'RE RUNNING AGROUND!
DING
DING
HUH?
BACK UP! ROTATE THE SHIP 180 DEG--

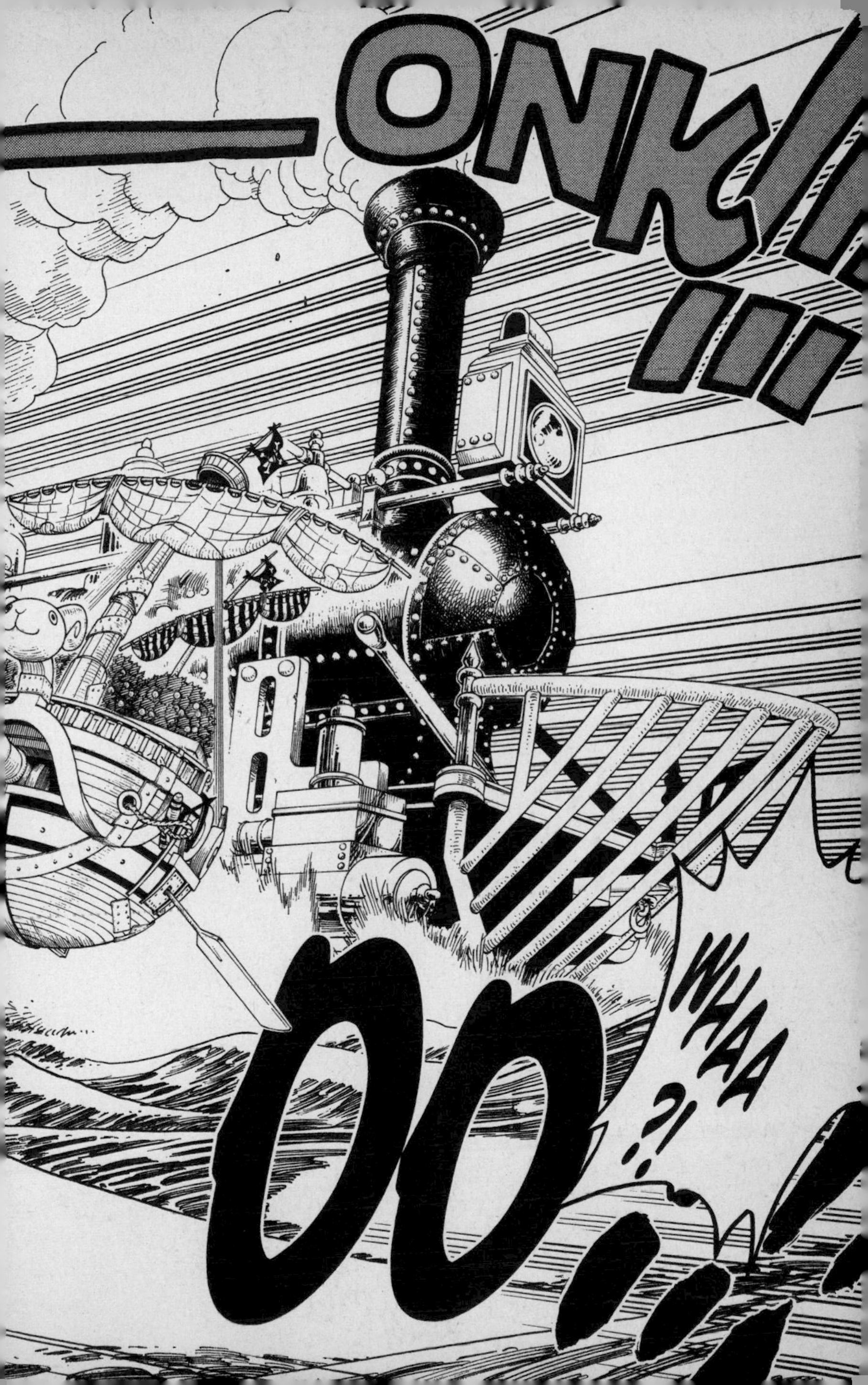
—ONK!!!!
WHAA ?!
OO...!!

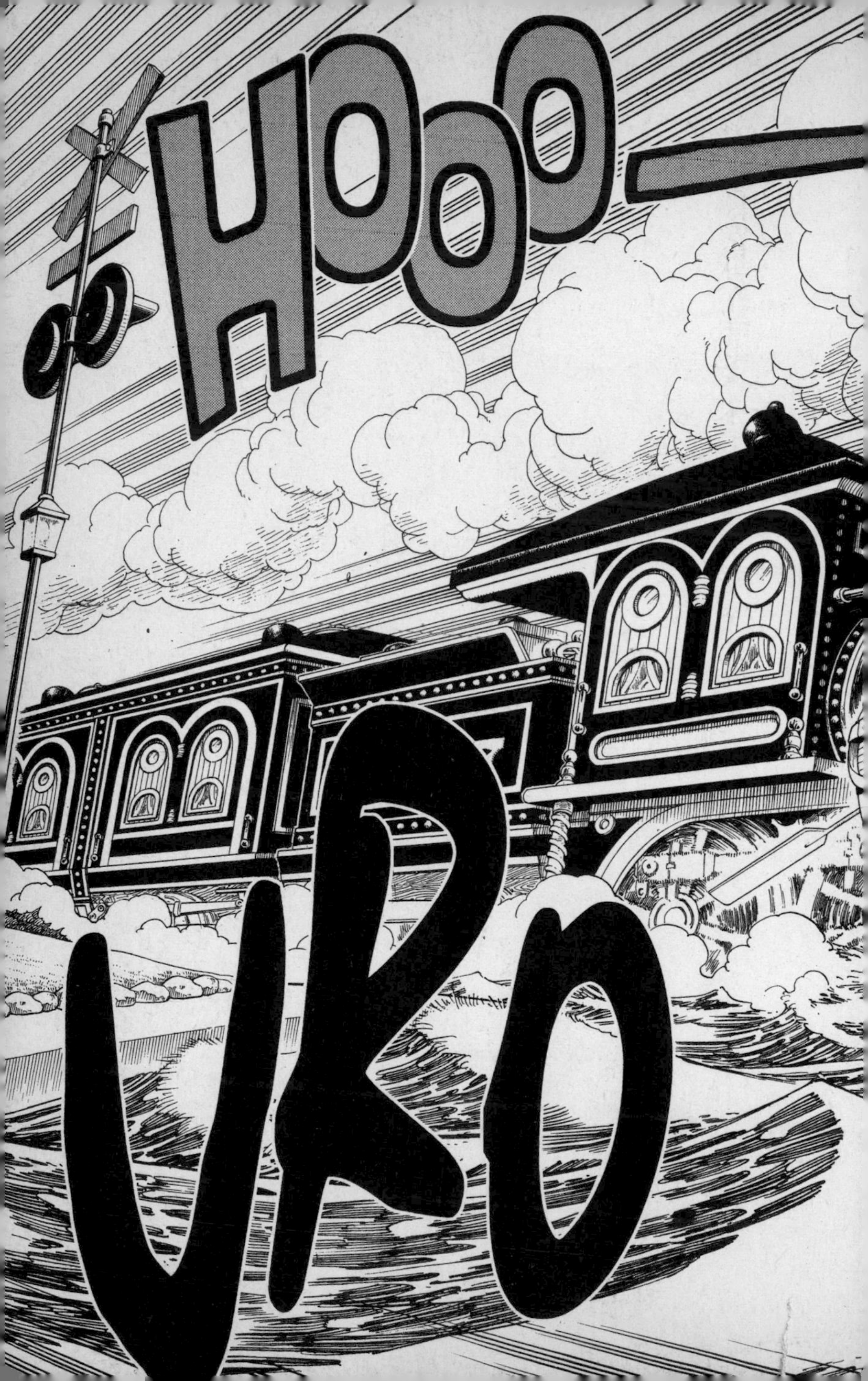
HOOO—
VRO

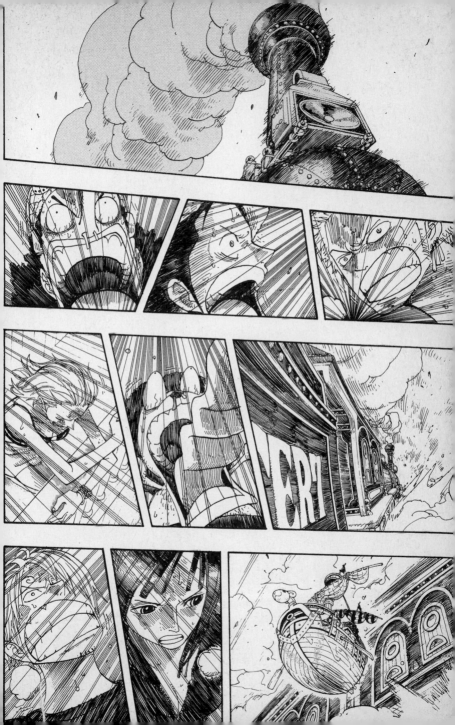

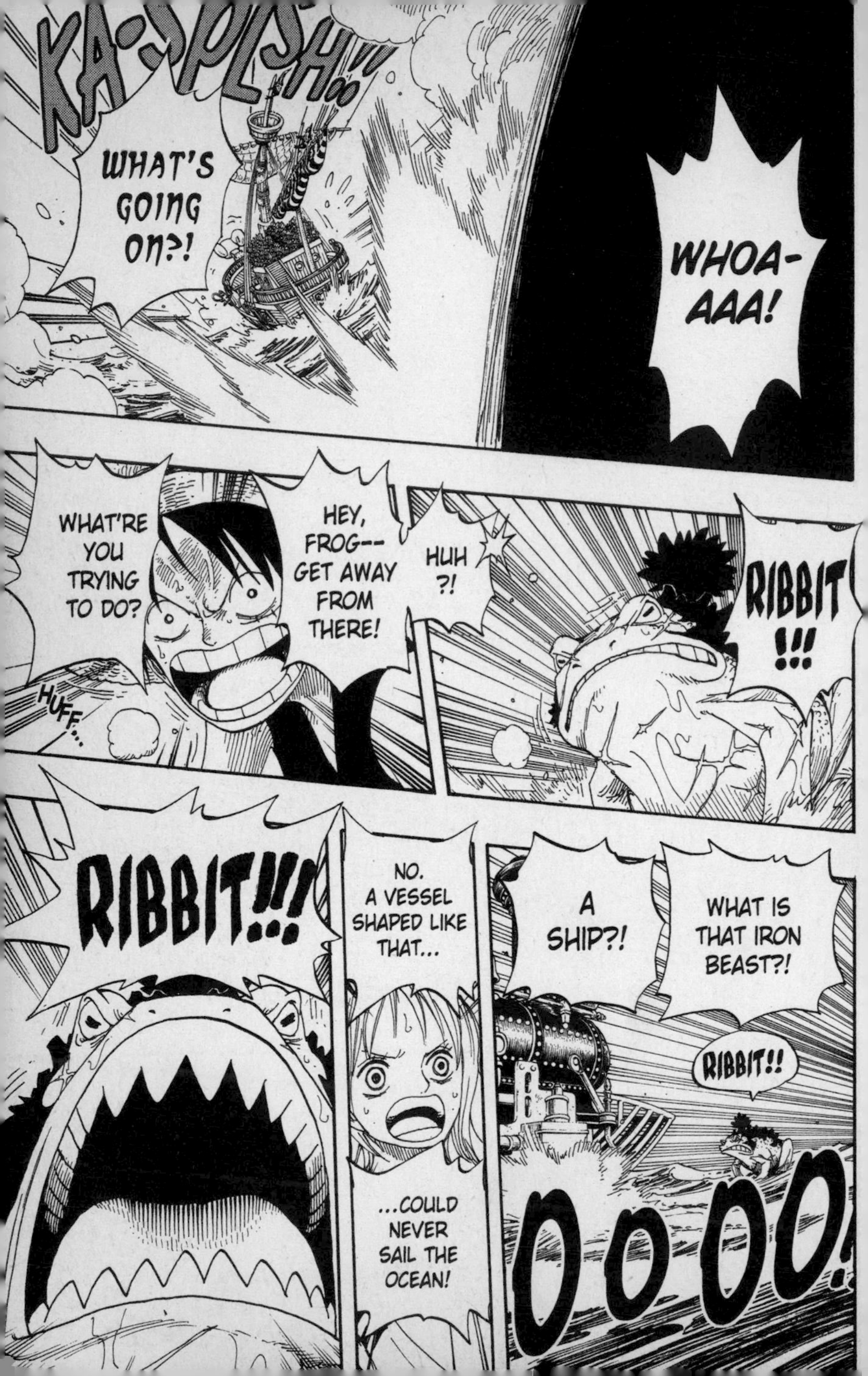
WHOA-AAA!
KA-SPLSH!!
WHAT'S GOING ON?!
RIBBIT!!!
HUH?!
HEY, FROG-- GET AWAY FROM THERE!
WHAT'RE YOU TRYING TO DO?
HUFF...
WHAT IS THAT IRON BEAST?!
A SHIP?!
RIBBIT!!
OOOOO!
NO. A VESSEL SHAPED LIKE THAT...
...COULD NEVER SAIL THE OCEAN!
RIBBIT!!!

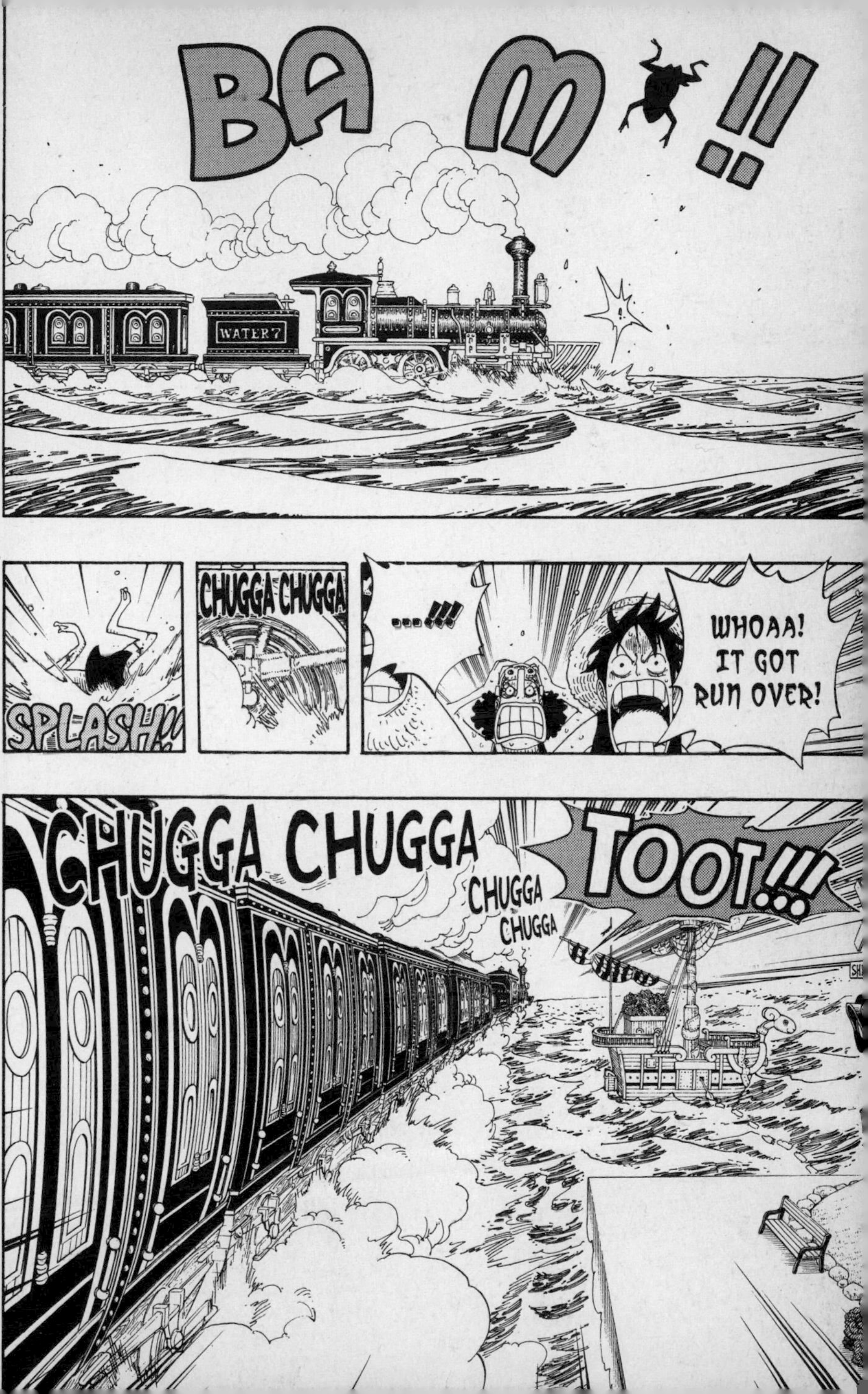
BAM!!
WHOAA! IT GOT RUN OVER!
...!!!
CHUGGA CHUGGA
SPLASH!!
TOOT!!!
CHUGGA CHUGGA
CHUGGA CHUGGA
WATER 7

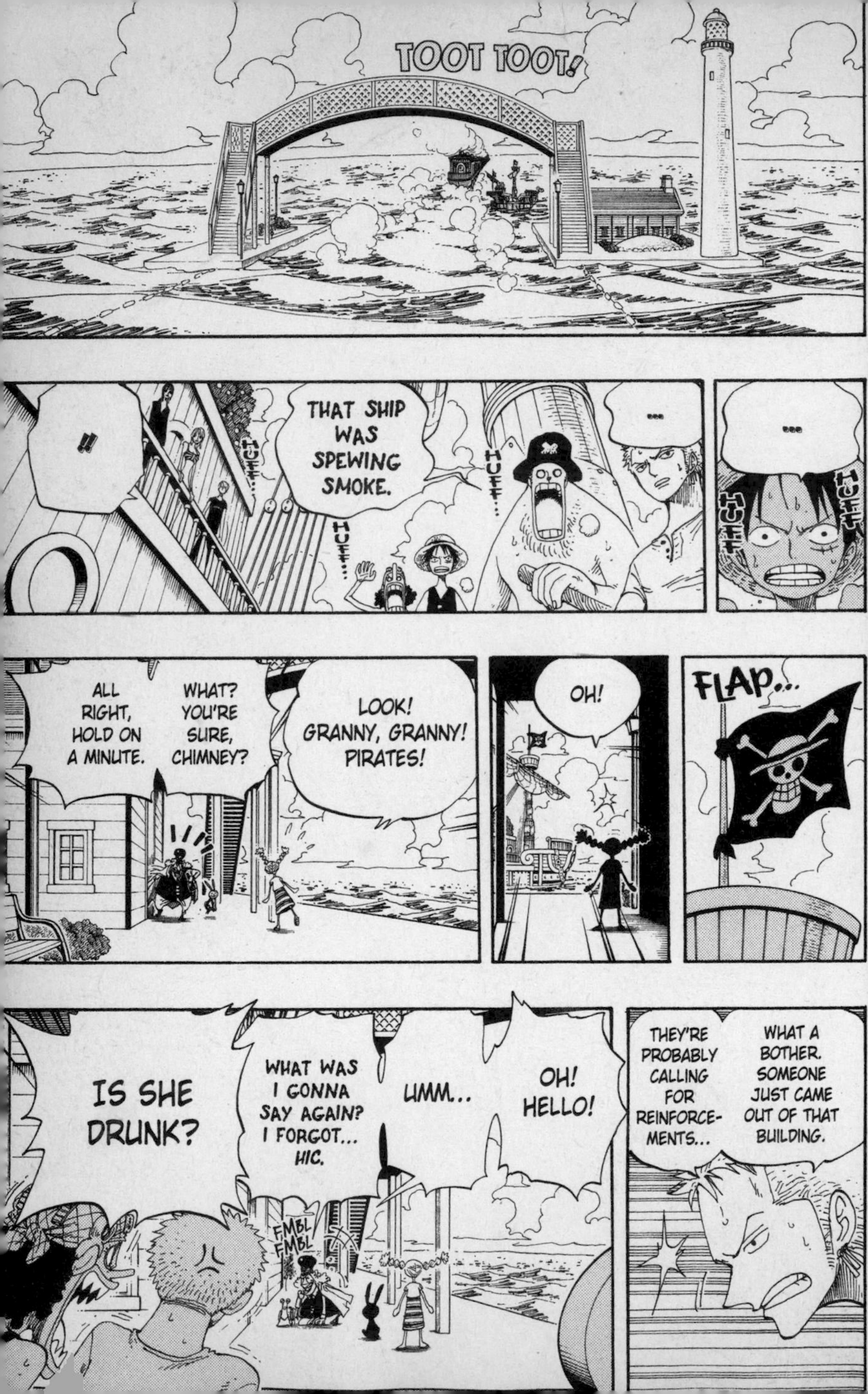
TOOT TOOT!
...
HUFF HUFF
...
HUFF...
THAT SHIP WAS SPEWING SMOKE.
HUFF...
HUFF...
!!
FLAP...
OH!
LOOK! GRANNY, GRANNY! PIRATES!
WHAT? YOU'RE SURE, CHIMNEY?
ALL RIGHT, HOLD ON A MINUTE.
WHAT A BOTHER. SOMEONE JUST CAME OUT OF THAT BUILDING.
THEY'RE PROBABLY CALLING FOR REINFORCEMENTS...
OH! HELLO!
UMM...
WHAT WAS I GONNA SAY AGAIN? I FORGOT... HIC.
FMBL FMBL
IS SHE DRUNK?

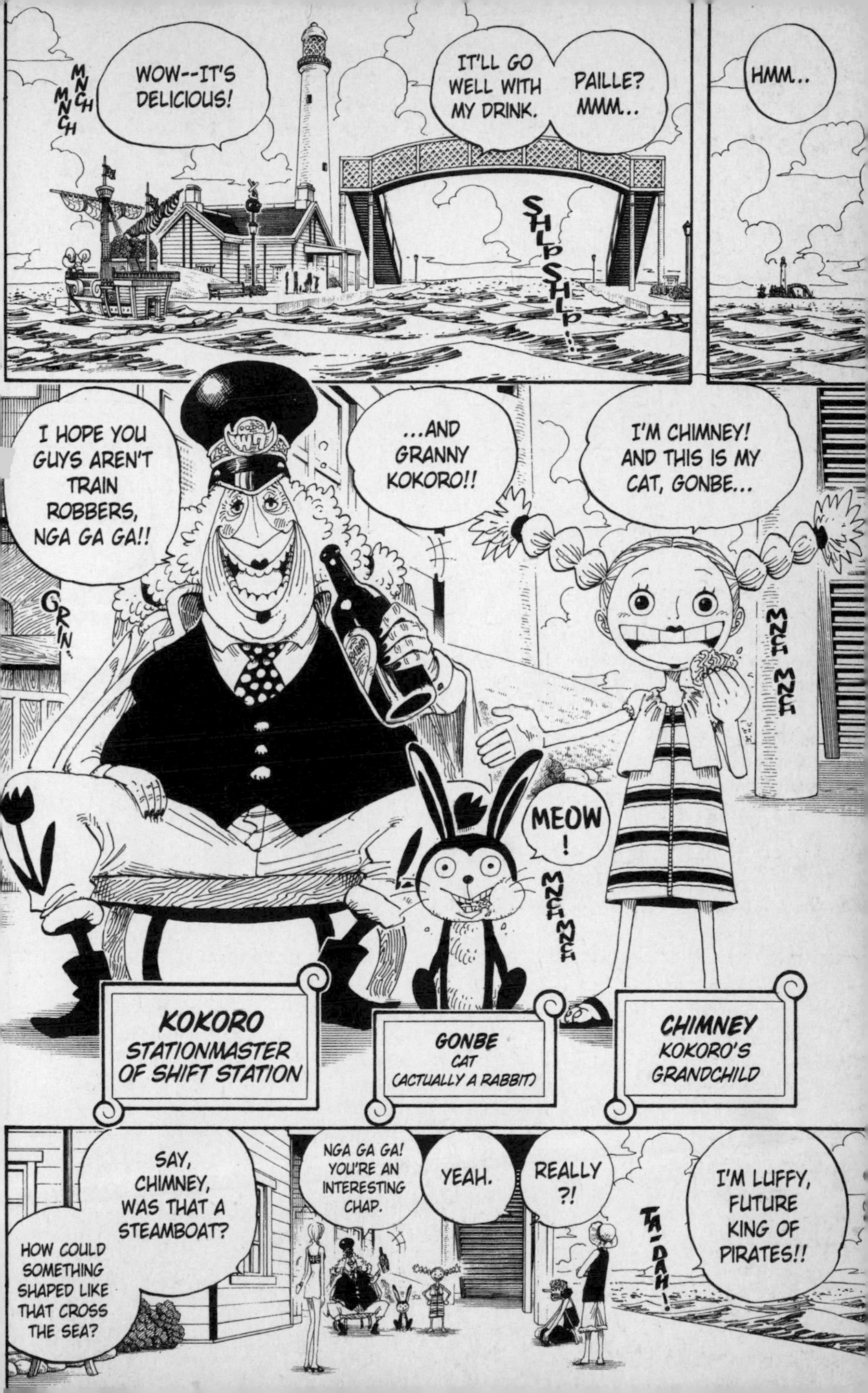
HMM...
PAILLE? MMM...
IT'LL GO WELL WITH MY DRINK.
SHLP SHLP...
WOW--IT'S DELICIOUS!
MNCH MNCH
I'M CHIMNEY! AND THIS IS MY CAT, GONBE...
MNCH MNCH
...AND GRANNY KOKORO!!
I HOPE YOU GUYS AREN'T TRAIN ROBBERS, NGA GA GA!!
GRIN...
MEOW!
MNCH MNCH
CHIMNEY
KOKORO'S GRANDCHILD
GONBE
CAT (ACTUALLY A RABBIT)
KOKORO
STATIONMASTER OF SHIFT STATION
I'M LUFFY, FUTURE KING OF PIRATES!!
TA-DAH!
REALLY?!
YEAH.
NGA GA GA! YOU'RE AN INTERESTING CHAP.
SAY, CHIMNEY, WAS THAT A STEAMBOAT?
HOW COULD SOMETHING SHAPED LIKE THAT CROSS THE SEA?

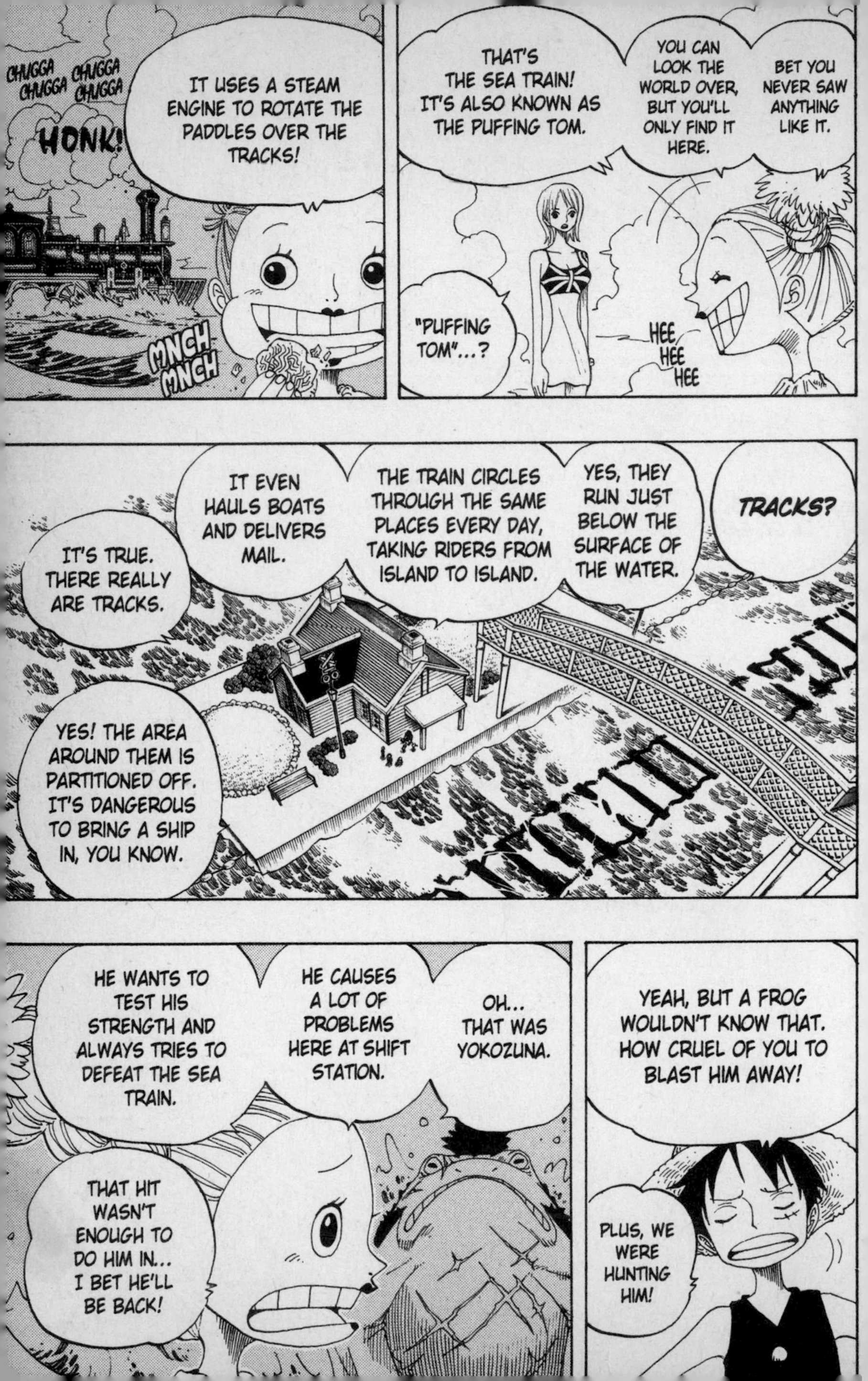
BET YOU NEVER SAW ANYTHING LIKE IT.
YOU CAN LOOK THE WORLD OVER, BUT YOU'LL ONLY FIND IT HERE.
THAT'S THE SEA TRAIN! IT'S ALSO KNOWN AS THE PUFFING TOM.
HEE HEE HEE
"PUFFING TOM"...?
IT USES A STEAM ENGINE TO ROTATE THE PADDLES OVER THE TRACKS!
CHUGGA CHUGGA CHUGGA CHUGGA
HONK!
MNCH MNCH
TRACKS?
YES, THEY RUN JUST BELOW THE SURFACE OF THE WATER.
THE TRAIN CIRCLES THROUGH THE SAME PLACES EVERY DAY, TAKING RIDERS FROM ISLAND TO ISLAND.
IT EVEN HAULS BOATS AND DELIVERS MAIL.
IT'S TRUE. THERE REALLY ARE TRACKS.
YES! THE AREA AROUND THEM IS PARTITIONED OFF. IT'S DANGEROUS TO BRING A SHIP IN, YOU KNOW.
YEAH, BUT A FROG WOULDN'T KNOW THAT. HOW CRUEL OF YOU TO BLAST HIM AWAY!
PLUS, WE WERE HUNTING HIM!
OH... THAT WAS YOKOZUNA.
HE CAUSES A LOT OF PROBLEMS HERE AT SHIFT STATION.
HE WANTS TO TEST HIS STRENGTH AND ALWAYS TRIES TO DEFEAT THE SEA TRAIN.
THAT HIT WASN'T ENOUGH TO DO HIM IN... I BET HE'LL BE BACK!

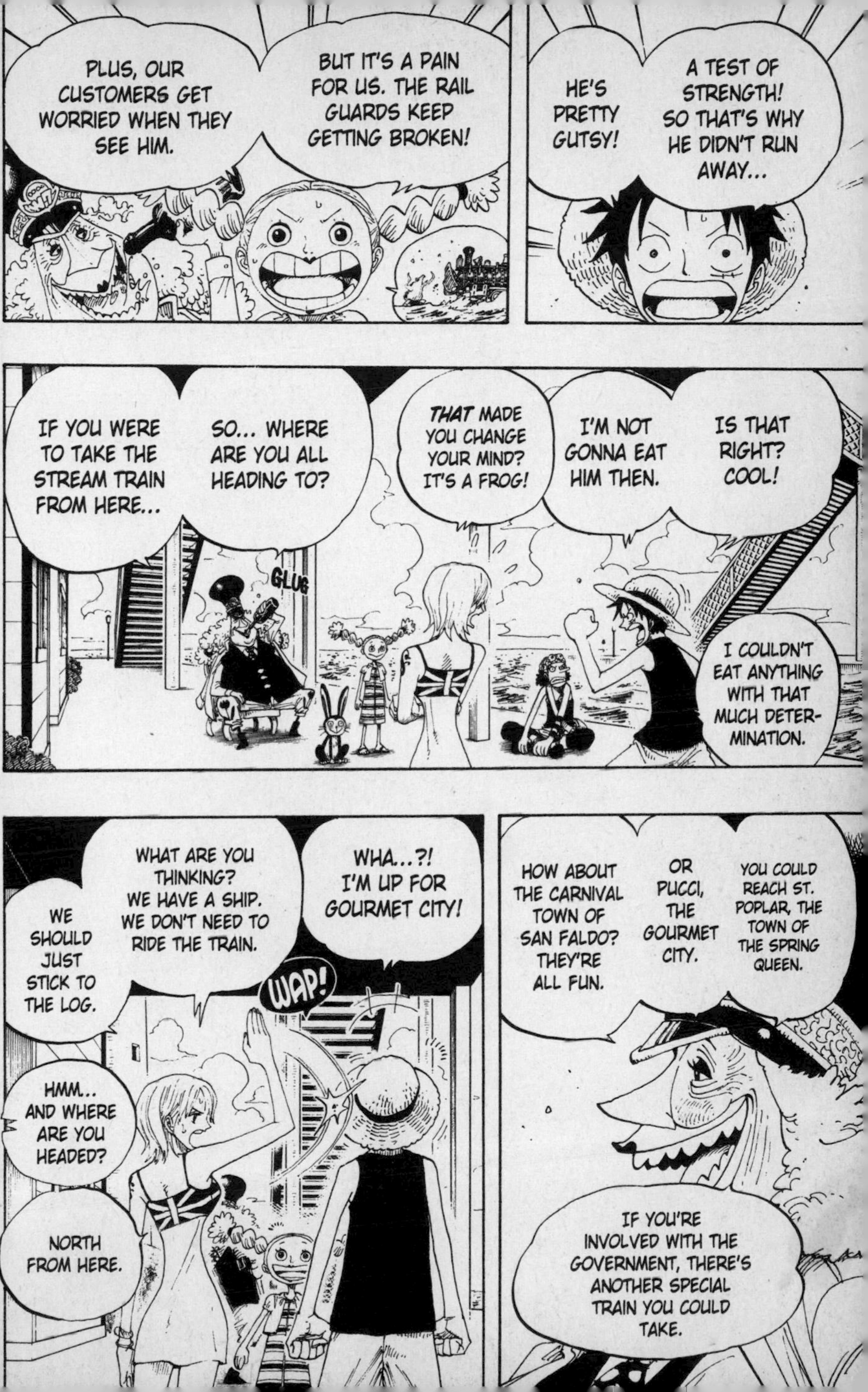
A TEST OF STRENGTH! SO THAT'S WHY HE DIDN'T RUN AWAY...
HE'S PRETTY GUTSY!
BUT IT'S A PAIN FOR US. THE RAIL GUARDS KEEP GETTING BROKEN!
PLUS, OUR CUSTOMERS GET WORRIED WHEN THEY SEE HIM.
IS THAT RIGHT? COOL!
I'M NOT GONNA EAT HIM THEN.
I COULDN'T EAT ANYTHING WITH THAT MUCH DETERMINATION.
THAT MADE YOU CHANGE YOUR MIND? IT'S A FROG!
GLUG
SO... WHERE ARE YOU ALL HEADING TO?
IF YOU WERE TO TAKE THE STREAM TRAIN FROM HERE...
YOU COULD REACH ST. POPLAR, THE TOWN OF THE SPRING QUEEN.
OR PUCCI, THE GOURMET CITY.
HOW ABOUT THE CARNIVAL TOWN OF SAN FALDO? THEY'RE ALL FUN.
IF YOU'RE INVOLVED WITH THE GOVERNMENT, THERE'S ANOTHER SPECIAL TRAIN YOU COULD TAKE.
WHA...?! I'M UP FOR GOURMET CITY!
WAP!
WHAT ARE YOU THINKING? WE HAVE A SHIP. WE DON'T NEED TO RIDE THE TRAIN.
WE SHOULD JUST STICK TO THE LOG.
HMM... AND WHERE ARE YOU HEADED?
NORTH FROM HERE.

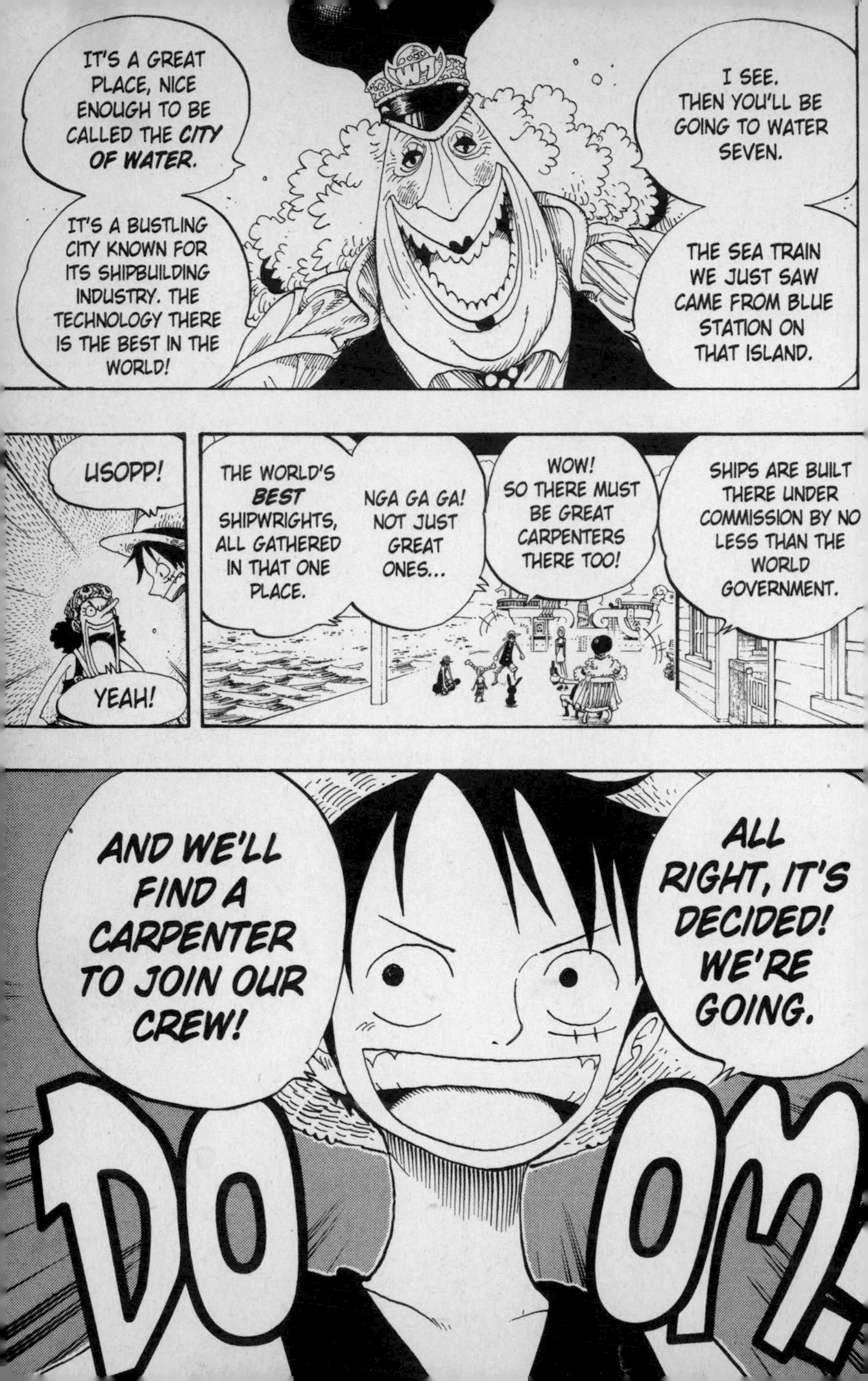
I SEE. THEN YOU'LL BE GOING TO WATER SEVEN.
THE SEA TRAIN WE JUST SAW CAME FROM BLUE STATION ON THAT ISLAND.
IT'S A GREAT PLACE, NICE ENOUGH TO BE CALLED THE *CITY OF WATER*.
IT'S A BUSTLING CITY KNOWN FOR ITS SHIPBUILDING INDUSTRY. THE TECHNOLOGY THERE IS THE BEST IN THE WORLD!
SHIPS ARE BUILT THERE UNDER COMMISSION BY NO LESS THAN THE WORLD GOVERNMENT.
WOW! SO THERE MUST BE GREAT CARPENTERS THERE TOO!
NGA GA GA! NOT JUST GREAT ONES...
THE WORLD'S *BEST* SHIPWRIGHTS, ALL GATHERED IN THAT ONE PLACE.
USOPP!
YEAH!
ALL RIGHT, IT'S DECIDED! WE'RE GOING.
AND WE'LL FIND A CARPENTER TO JOIN OUR CREW!
DOOM.

Chapter 323: THE CITY OF WATER, WATER SEVEN

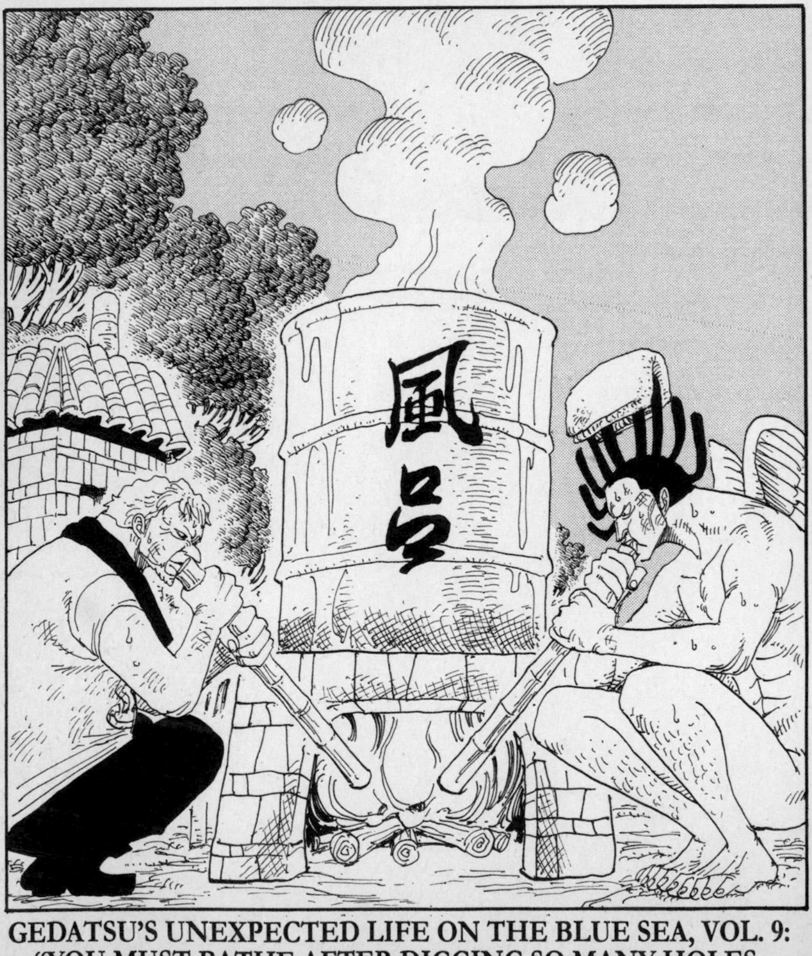
KANJI SAYS "BATH"--ED.
風呂

GEDATSU'S UNEXPECTED LIFE ON THE BLUE SEA, VOL. 9: "YOU MUST BATHE AFTER DIGGING SO MANY HOLES, MASTER GEDATSU"

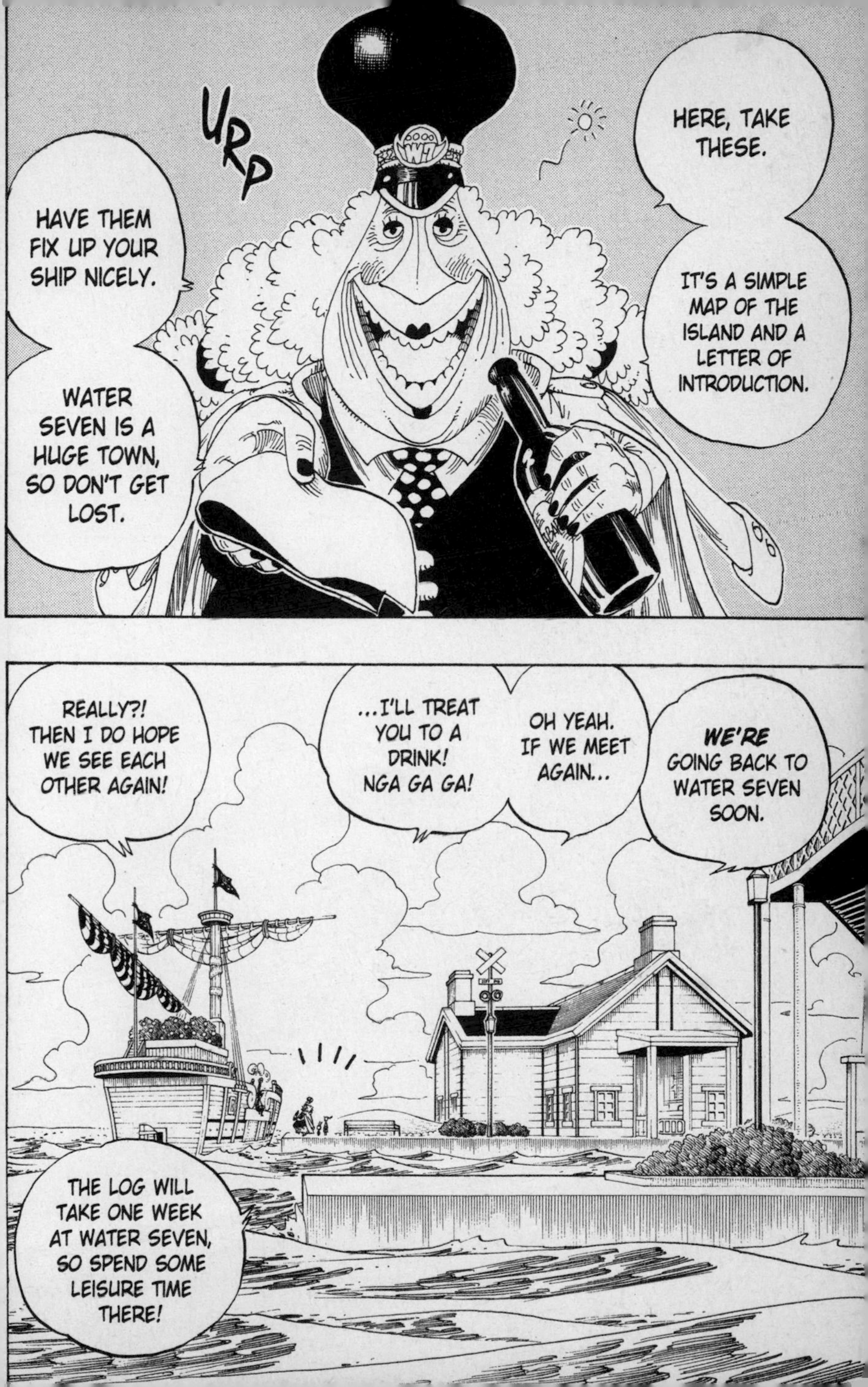
HERE, TAKE THESE.
IT'S A SIMPLE MAP OF THE ISLAND AND A LETTER OF INTRODUCTION.
URP
HAVE THEM FIX UP YOUR SHIP NICELY.
WATER SEVEN IS A HUGE TOWN, SO DON'T GET LOST.
WE'RE GOING BACK TO WATER SEVEN SOON.
OH YEAH. IF WE MEET AGAIN...
...I'LL TREAT YOU TO A DRINK! NGA GA GA!
REALLY?! THEN I DO HOPE WE SEE EACH OTHER AGAIN!
THE LOG WILL TAKE ONE WEEK AT WATER SEVEN, SO SPEND SOME LEISURE TIME THERE!

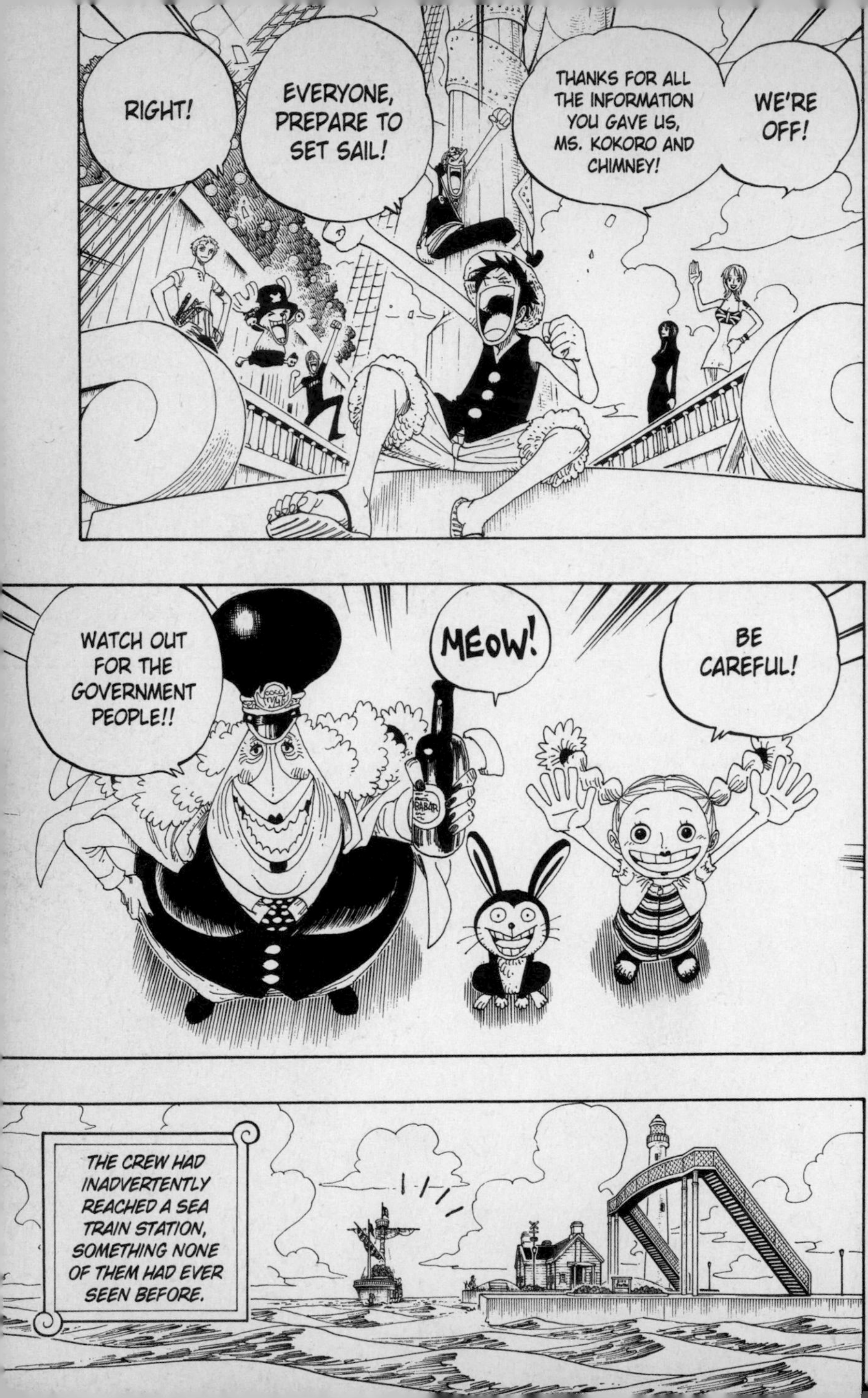
WE'RE OFF!
THANKS FOR ALL THE INFORMATION YOU GAVE US, MS. KOKORO AND CHIMNEY!
EVERYONE, PREPARE TO SET SAIL!
RIGHT!
BE CAREFUL!
MEOW!
WATCH OUT FOR THE GOVERNMENT PEOPLE!!
THE CREW HAD INADVERTENTLY REACHED A SEA TRAIN STATION, SOMETHING NONE OF THEM HAD EVER SEEN BEFORE.

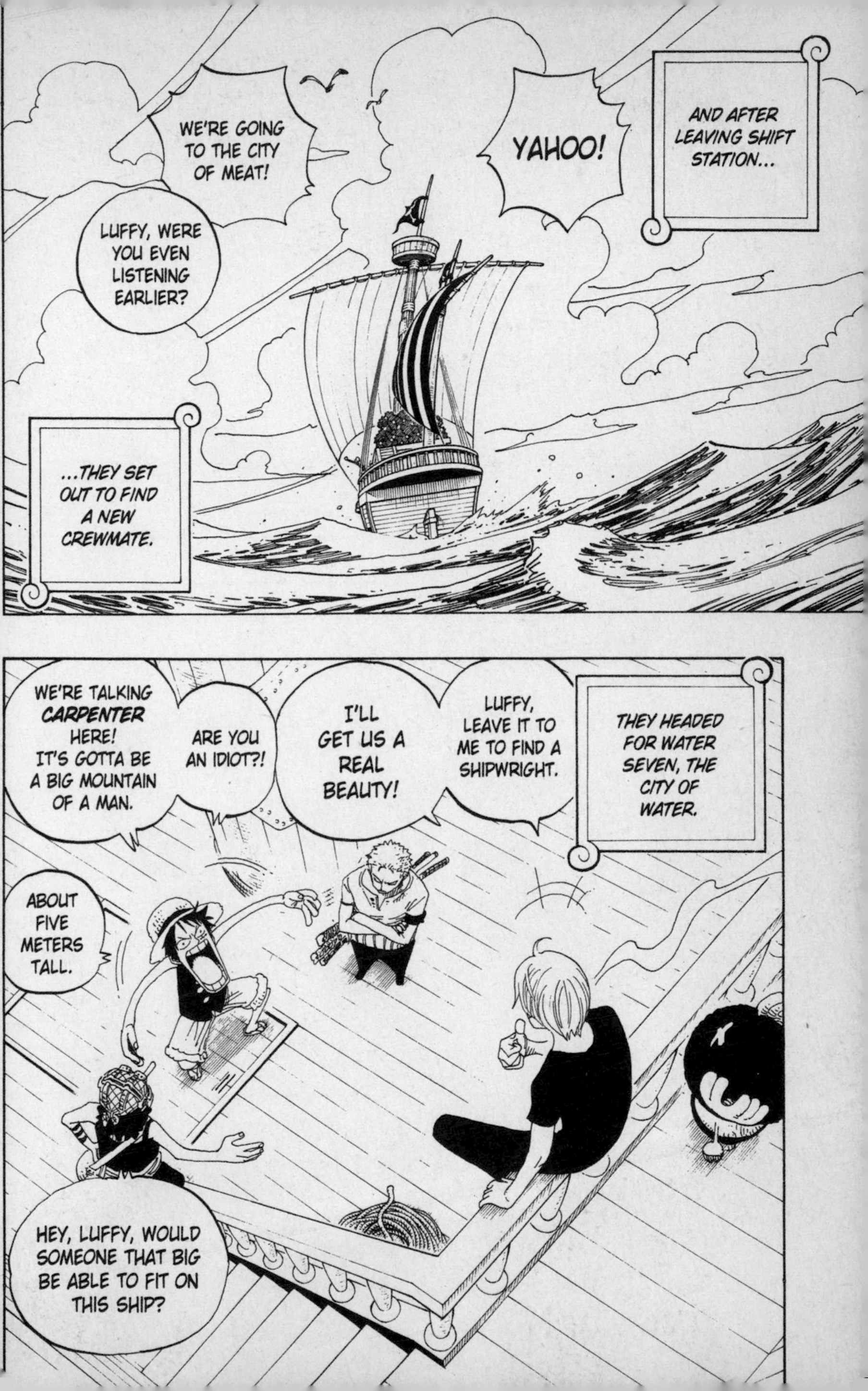
AND AFTER LEAVING SHIFT STATION...
YAHOO!
WE'RE GOING TO THE CITY OF MEAT!
LUFFY, WERE YOU EVEN LISTENING EARLIER?
...THEY SET OUT TO FIND A NEW CREWMATE.
THEY HEADED FOR WATER SEVEN, THE CITY OF WATER.
LUFFY, LEAVE IT TO ME TO FIND A SHIPWRIGHT.
I'LL GET US A REAL BEAUTY!
ARE YOU AN IDIOT?!
WE'RE TALKING **CARPENTER** HERE! IT'S GOTTA BE A BIG MOUNTAIN OF A MAN.
ABOUT FIVE METERS TALL.
HEY, LUFFY, WOULD SOMEONE THAT BIG BE ABLE TO FIT ON THIS SHIP?

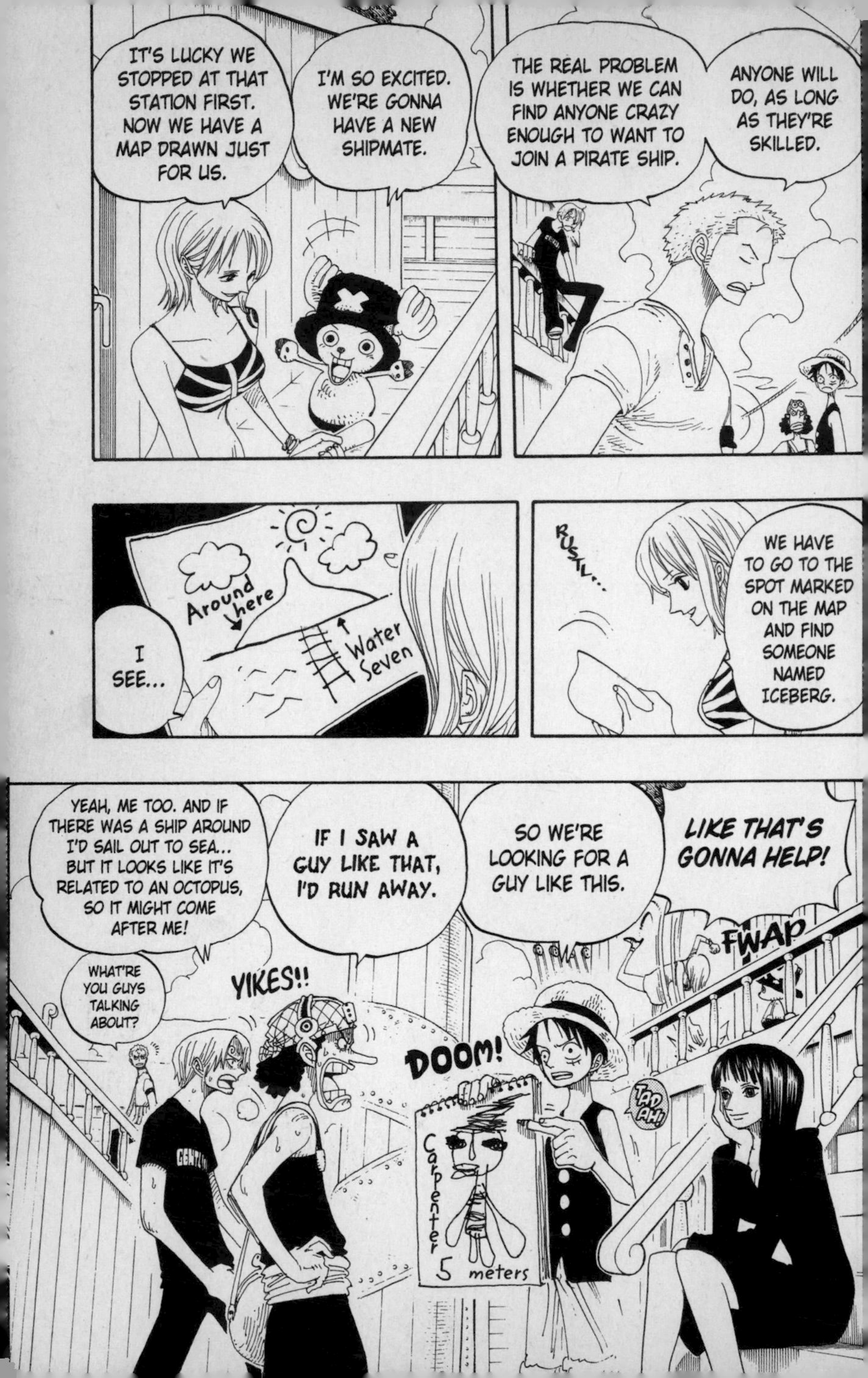
ANYONE WILL DO, AS LONG AS THEY'RE SKILLED.
THE REAL PROBLEM IS WHETHER WE CAN FIND ANYONE CRAZY ENOUGH TO WANT TO JOIN A PIRATE SHIP.
I'M SO EXCITED. WE'RE GONNA HAVE A NEW SHIPMATE.
IT'S LUCKY WE STOPPED AT THAT STATION FIRST. NOW WE HAVE A MAP DRAWN JUST FOR US.
WE HAVE TO GO TO THE SPOT MARKED ON THE MAP AND FIND SOMEONE NAMED ICEBERG.
RUSTL...
Around here
Water Seven
I SEE...
LIKE THAT'S GONNA HELP!
FWAP
SO WE'RE LOOKING FOR A GUY LIKE THIS.
TADAH!
DOOM!
Carpenter
5 meters
IF I SAW A GUY LIKE THAT, I'D RUN AWAY.
YIKES!!
YEAH, ME TOO. AND IF THERE WAS A SHIP AROUND I'D SAIL OUT TO SEA... BUT IT LOOKS LIKE IT'S RELATED TO AN OCTOPUS, SO IT MIGHT COME AFTER ME!
WHAT'RE YOU GUYS TALKING ABOUT?

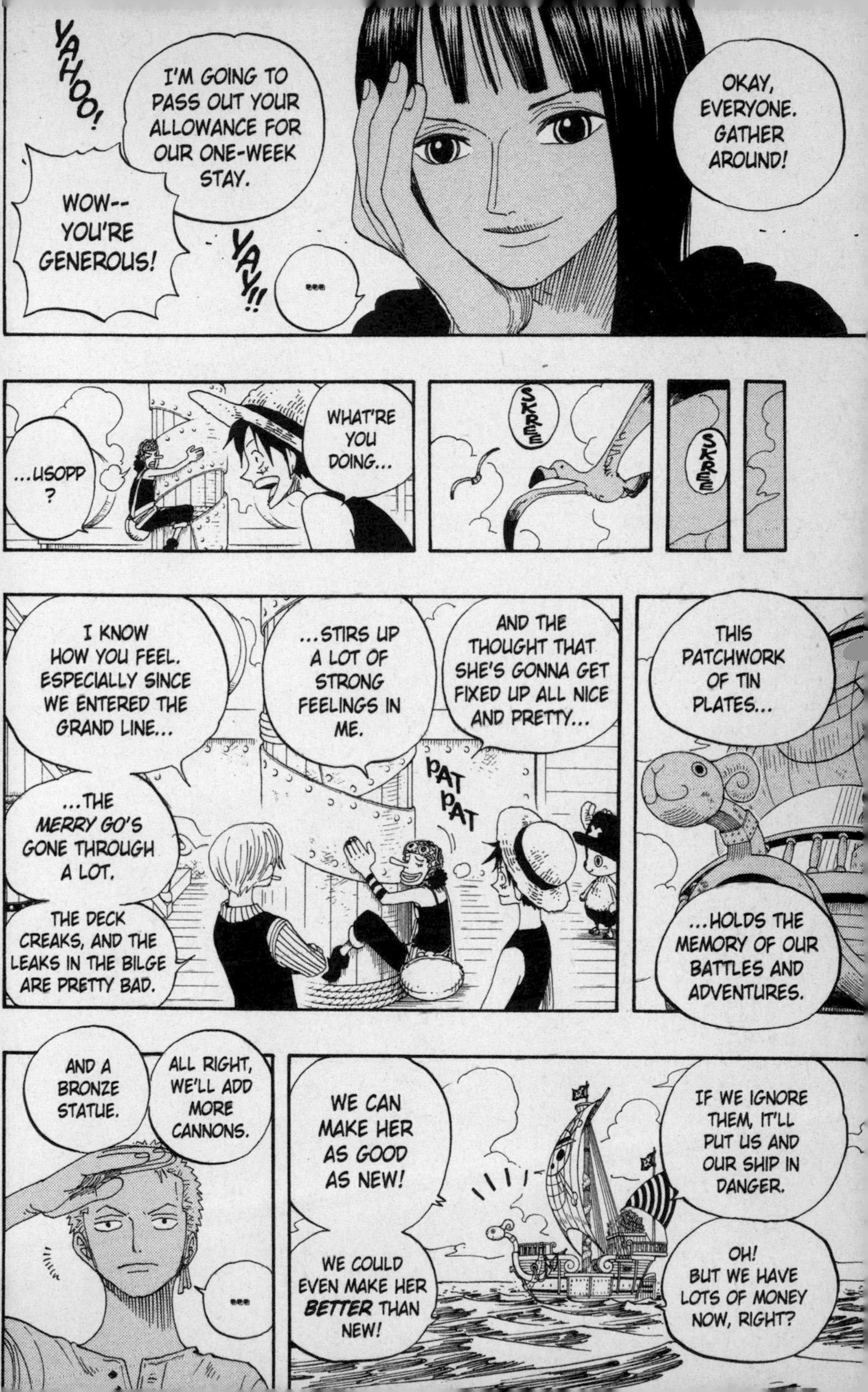
OKAY, EVERYONE. GATHER AROUND!
I'M GOING TO PASS OUT YOUR ALLOWANCE FOR OUR ONE-WEEK STAY.
YAHOO!
YAY!!
...
WOW-- YOU'RE GENEROUS!
SKREE
SKREE
WHAT'RE YOU DOING...
...USOPP ?
THIS PATCHWORK OF TIN PLATES...
...HOLDS THE MEMORY OF OUR BATTLES AND ADVENTURES.
AND THE THOUGHT THAT SHE'S GONNA GET FIXED UP ALL NICE AND PRETTY...
...STIRS UP A LOT OF STRONG FEELINGS IN ME.
I KNOW HOW YOU FEEL. ESPECIALLY SINCE WE ENTERED THE GRAND LINE...
PAT PAT
...THE *MERRY GO'S* GONE THROUGH A LOT.
THE DECK CREAKS, AND THE LEAKS IN THE BILGE ARE PRETTY BAD.
IF WE IGNORE THEM, IT'LL PUT US AND OUR SHIP IN DANGER.
WE CAN MAKE HER AS GOOD AS NEW!
OH! BUT WE HAVE LOTS OF MONEY NOW, RIGHT?
WE COULD EVEN MAKE HER ***BETTER*** THAN NEW!
ALL RIGHT, WE'LL ADD MORE CANNONS.
AND A BRONZE STATUE.
...

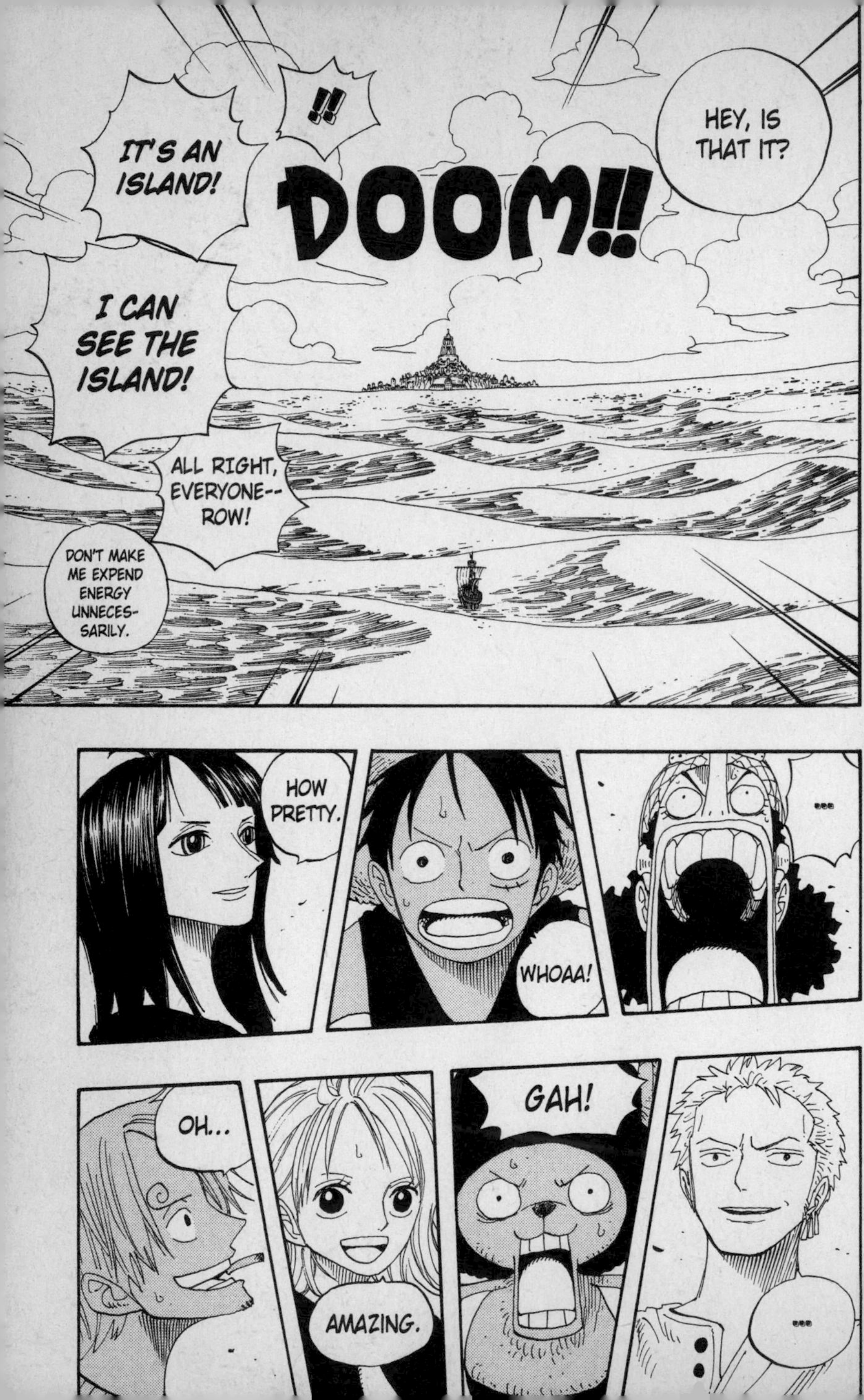
HEY, IS THAT IT?
!!
DOOM!!
IT'S AN ISLAND!
I CAN SEE THE ISLAND!
ALL RIGHT, EVERYONE-- ROW!
DON'T MAKE ME EXPEND ENERGY UNNECES-SARILY.
...
WHOAA!
HOW PRETTY.
...
GAH!
AMAZING.
OH...

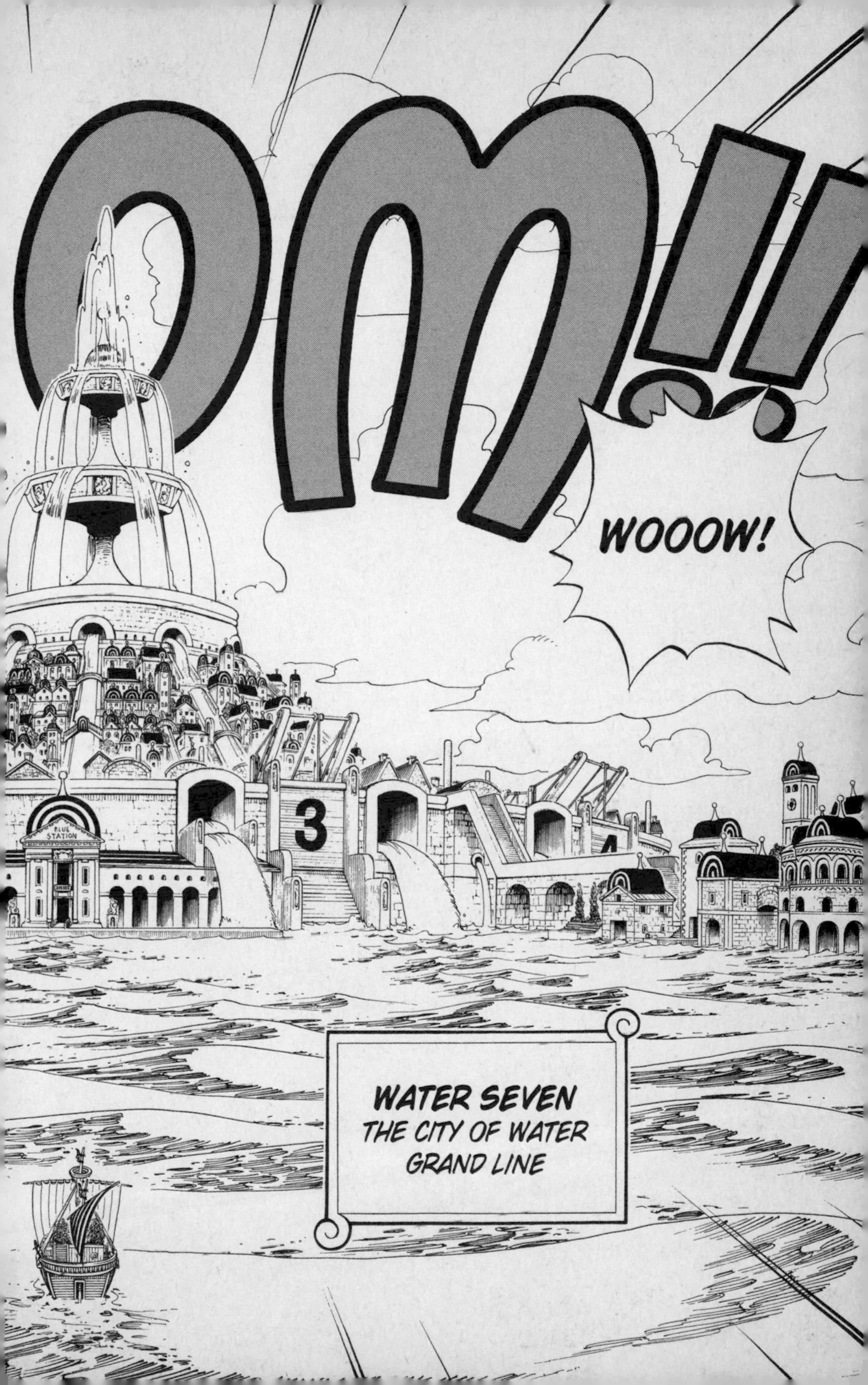
WOW!!
WOOOW!
BLUE STATION
3
WATER SEVEN
THE CITY OF WATER
GRAND LINE

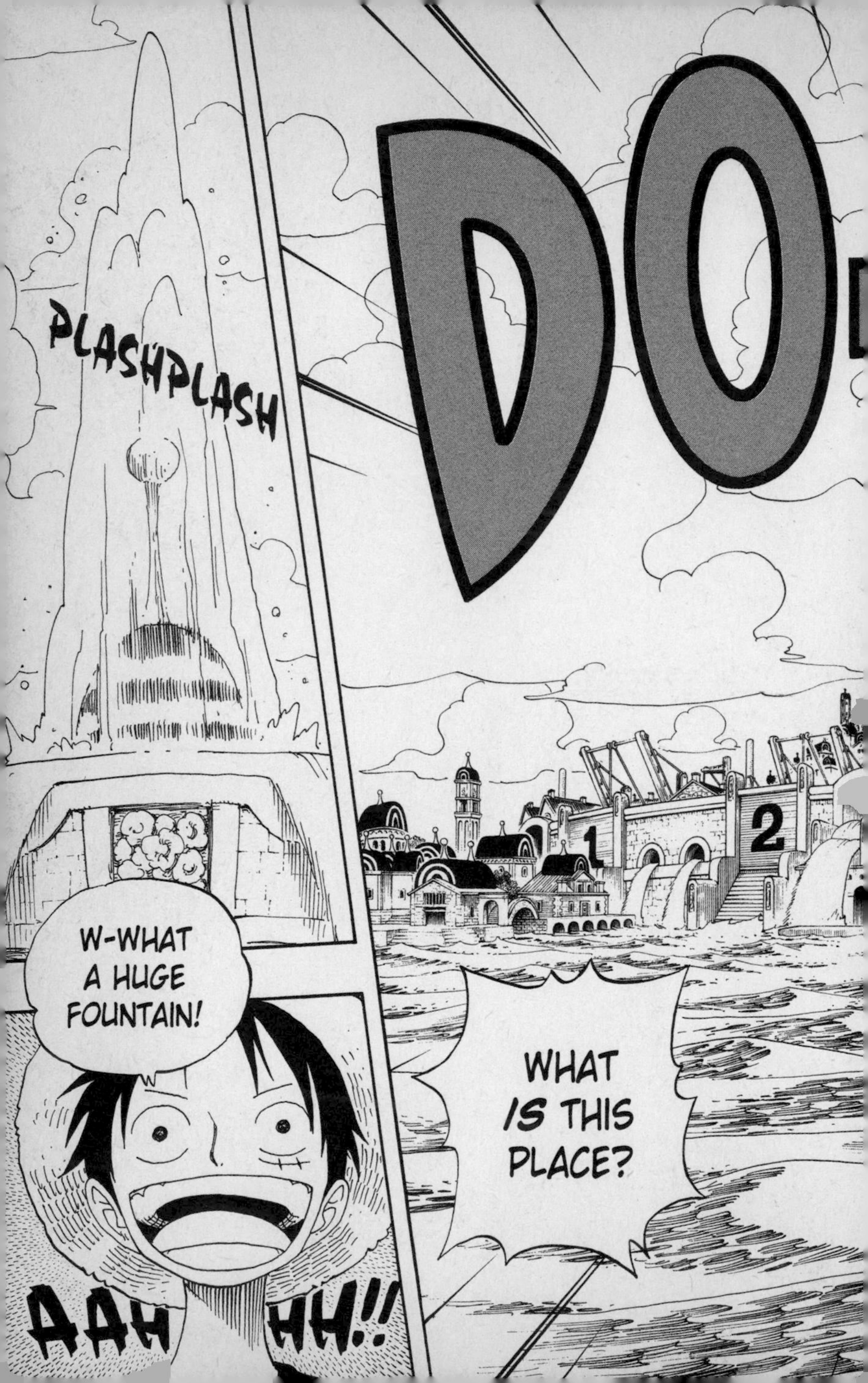
DO
1
2
WHAT IS THIS PLACE?
PLASHPLASH
W-WHAT A HUGE FOUNTAIN!
AAH HH!!

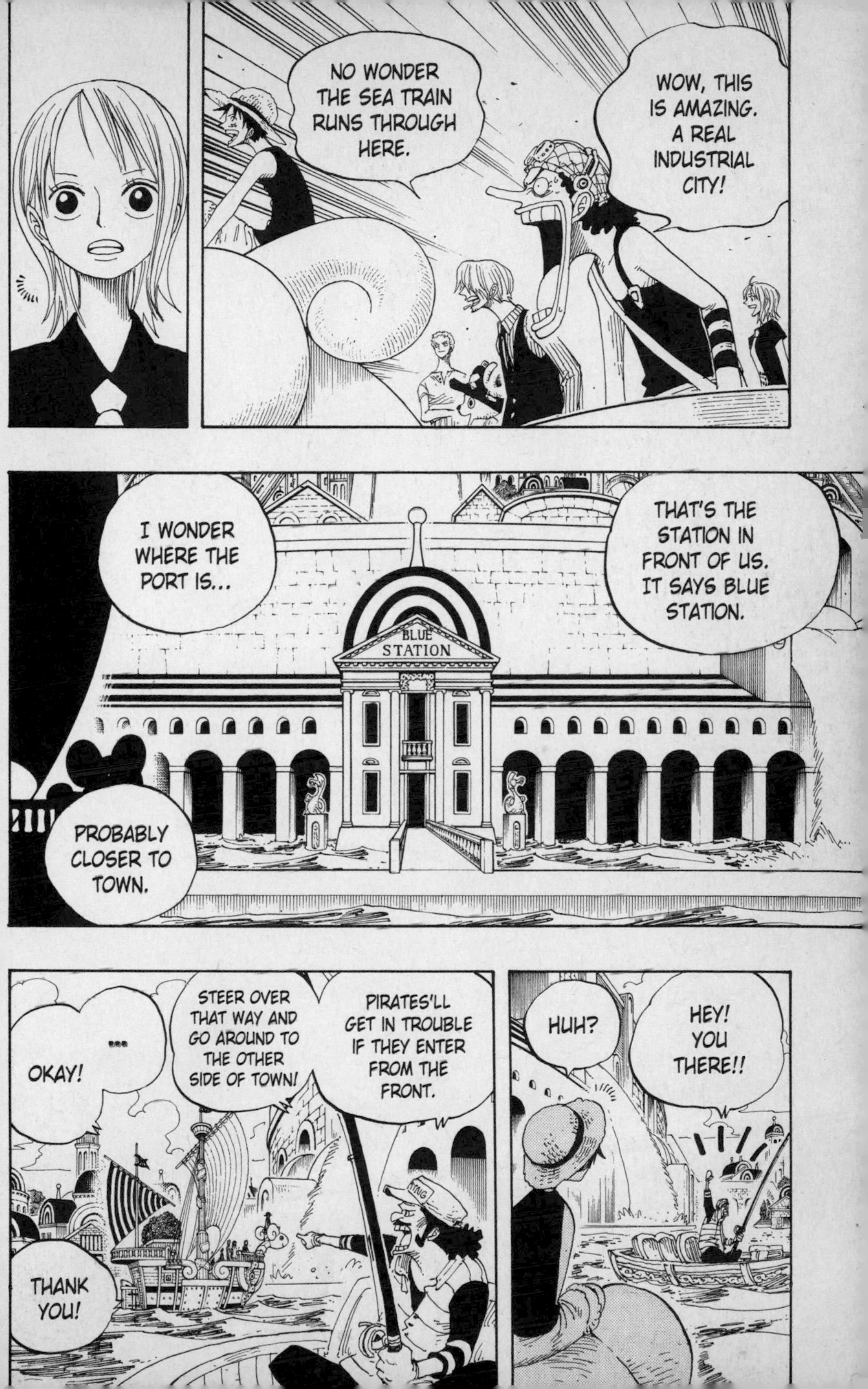
WOW, THIS IS AMAZING. A REAL INDUSTRIAL CITY!
NO WONDER THE SEA TRAIN RUNS THROUGH HERE.
THAT'S THE STATION IN FRONT OF US. IT SAYS BLUE STATION.
BLUE STATION
I WONDER WHERE THE PORT IS...
PROBABLY CLOSER TO TOWN.
HEY! YOU THERE!!
HUH?
PIRATES'LL GET IN TROUBLE IF THEY ENTER FROM THE FRONT.
STEER OVER THAT WAY AND GO AROUND TO THE OTHER SIDE OF TOWN!
...
OKAY!
THANK YOU!

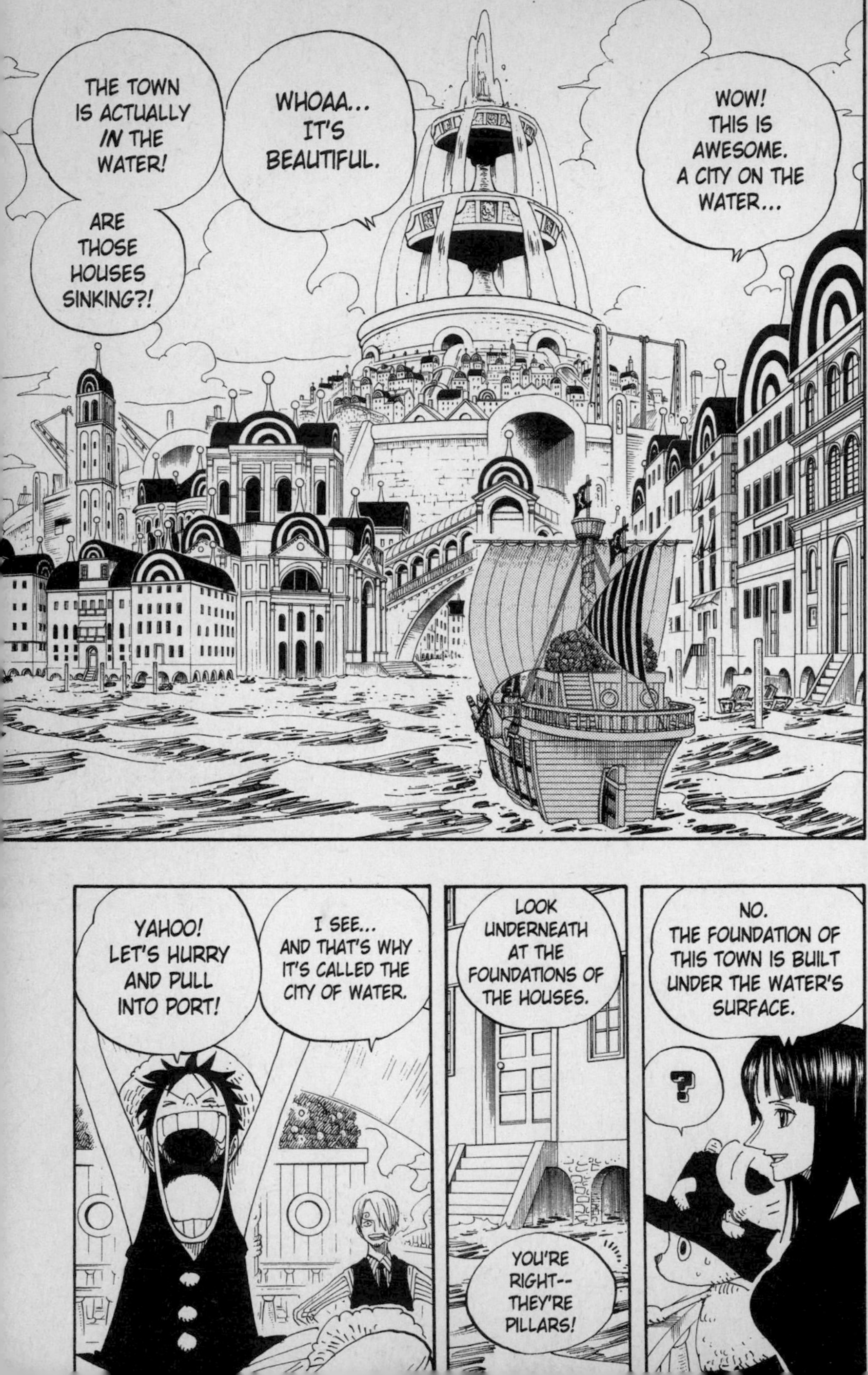
WOW! THIS IS AWESOME. A CITY ON THE WATER...
WHOAA... IT'S BEAUTIFUL.
THE TOWN IS ACTUALLY *IN* THE WATER!
ARE THOSE HOUSES SINKING?!
NO. THE FOUNDATION OF THIS TOWN IS BUILT UNDER THE WATER'S SURFACE.
?
LOOK UNDERNEATH AT THE FOUNDATIONS OF THE HOUSES.
YOU'RE RIGHT-- THEY'RE PILLARS!
I SEE... AND THAT'S WHY IT'S CALLED THE CITY OF WATER.
YAHOO! LET'S HURRY AND PULL INTO PORT!

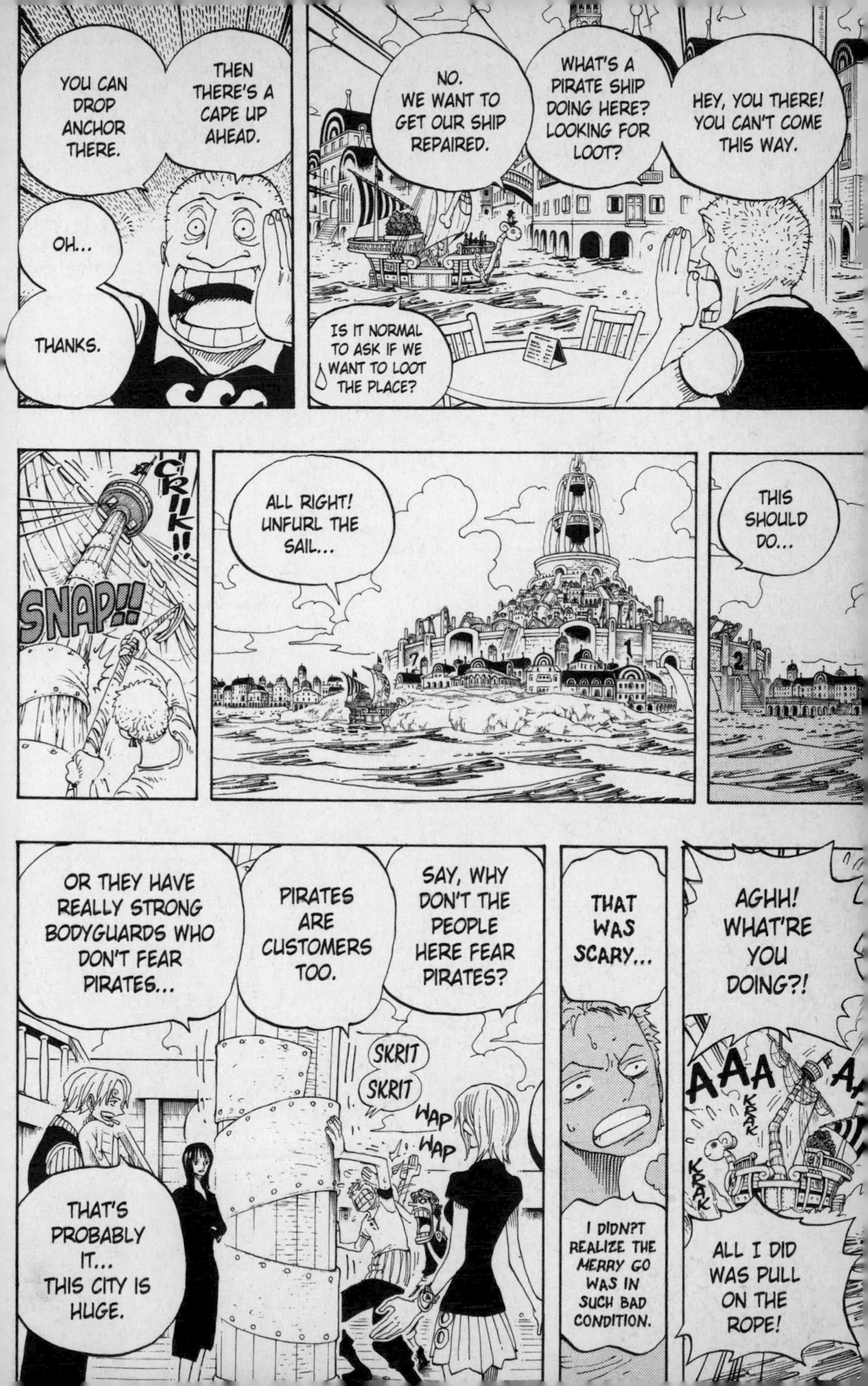
HEY, YOU THERE! YOU CAN'T COME THIS WAY.
WHAT'S A PIRATE SHIP DOING HERE? LOOKING FOR LOOT?
NO. WE WANT TO GET OUR SHIP REPAIRED.
IS IT NORMAL TO ASK IF WE WANT TO LOOT THE PLACE?
THEN THERE'S A CAPE UP AHEAD.
YOU CAN DROP ANCHOR THERE.
OH...
THANKS.
THIS SHOULD DO...
ALL RIGHT! UNFURL THE SAIL...
CRIIK!!
SNAP!!
AGHH! WHAT'RE YOU DOING?!
AAA
KRAK
KRAK
ALL I DID WAS PULL ON THE ROPE!
THAT WAS SCARY...
I DIDN?T REALIZE THE MERRY GO WAS IN SUCH BAD CONDITION.
SAY, WHY DON'T THE PEOPLE HERE FEAR PIRATES?
PIRATES ARE CUSTOMERS TOO.
OR THEY HAVE REALLY STRONG BODYGUARDS WHO DON'T FEAR PIRATES...
SKRIT
SKRIT
WAP
WAP
THAT'S PROBABLY IT... THIS CITY IS HUGE.

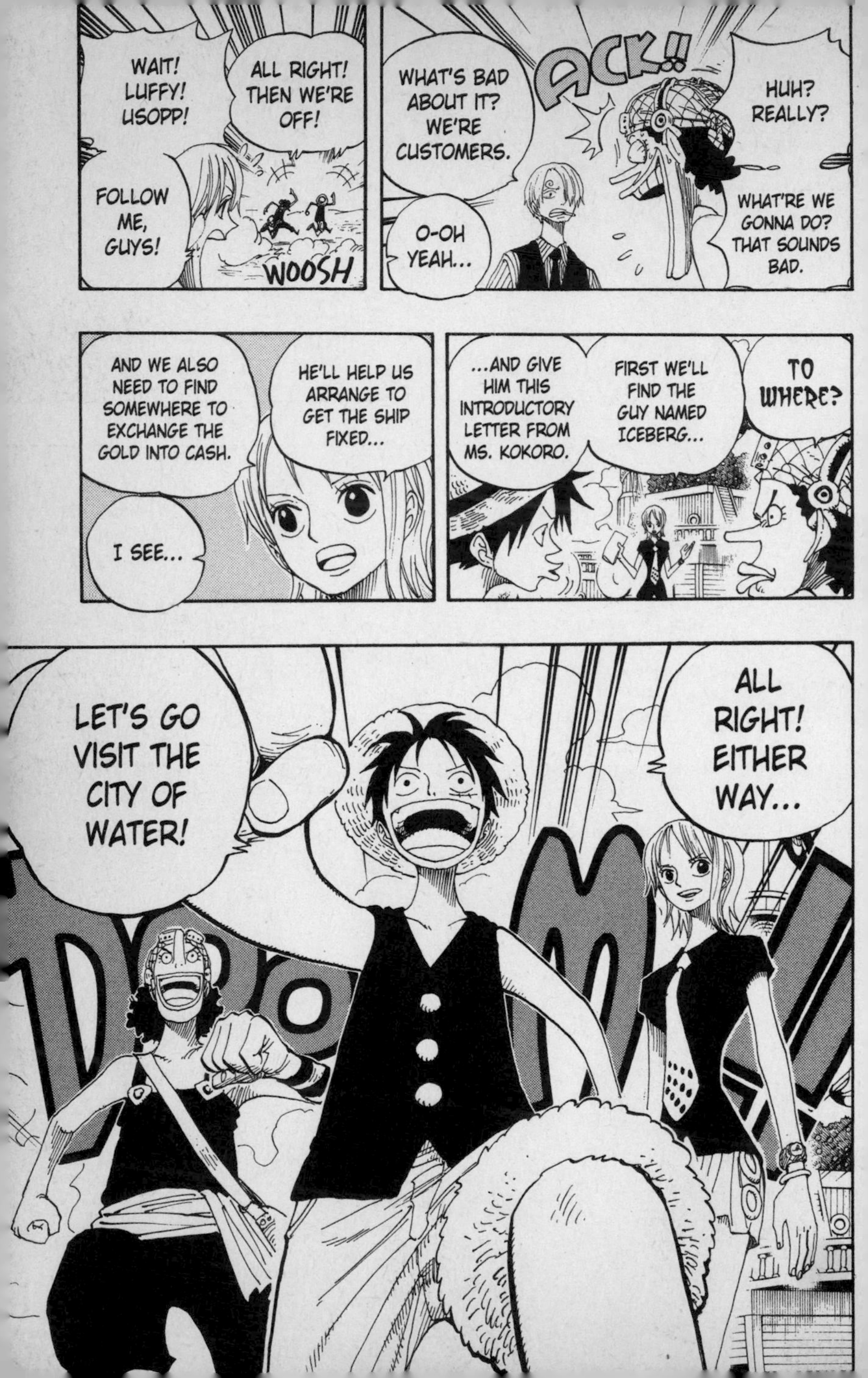
HUH? REALLY?
WHAT'RE WE GONNA DO? THAT SOUNDS BAD.
ACK!!
WHAT'S BAD ABOUT IT? WE'RE CUSTOMERS.
O-OH YEAH...
ALL RIGHT! THEN WE'RE OFF!
WAIT! LUFFY! USOPP!
FOLLOW ME, GUYS!
WOOSH
TO WHERE?
FIRST WE'LL FIND THE GUY NAMED ICEBERG...
...AND GIVE HIM THIS INTRODUCTORY LETTER FROM MS. KOKORO.
HE'LL HELP US ARRANGE TO GET THE SHIP FIXED...
AND WE ALSO NEED TO FIND SOMEWHERE TO EXCHANGE THE GOLD INTO CASH.
I SEE...
ALL RIGHT! EITHER WAY...
LET'S GO VISIT THE CITY OF WATER!

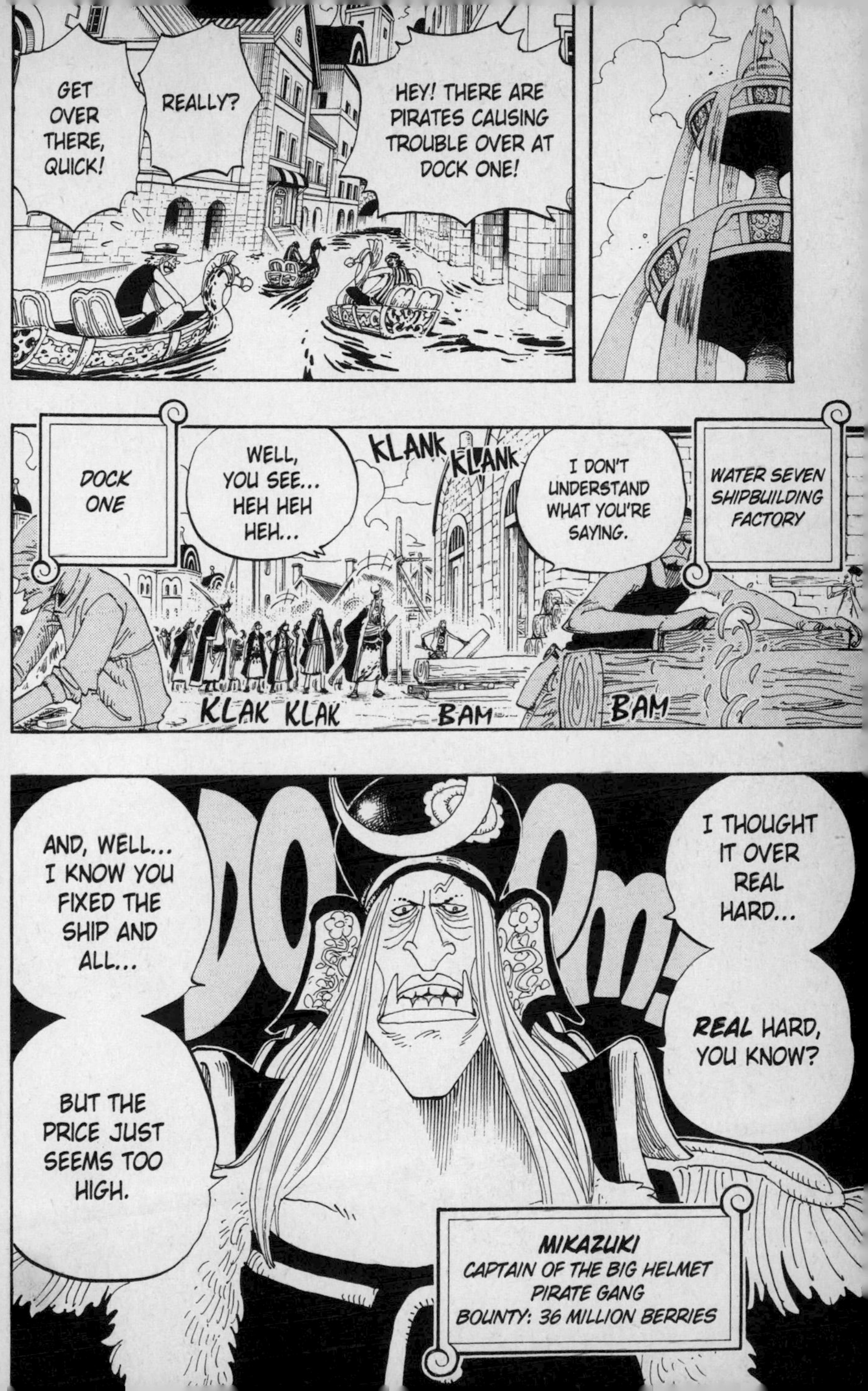
HEY! THERE ARE PIRATES CAUSING TROUBLE OVER AT DOCK ONE!
REALLY?
GET OVER THERE, QUICK!
WATER SEVEN SHIPBUILDING FACTORY
I DON'T UNDERSTAND WHAT YOU'RE SAYING.
KLANK KLANK
WELL, YOU SEE... HEH HEH HEH...
DOCK ONE
BAM
BAM
KLAK KLAK
I THOUGHT IT OVER REAL HARD...
REAL HARD, YOU KNOW?
DOOM
AND, WELL... I KNOW YOU FIXED THE SHIP AND ALL...
BUT THE PRICE JUST SEEMS TOO HIGH.
MIKAZUKI
CAPTAIN OF THE BIG HELMET PIRATE GANG
BOUNTY: 36 MILLION BERRIES

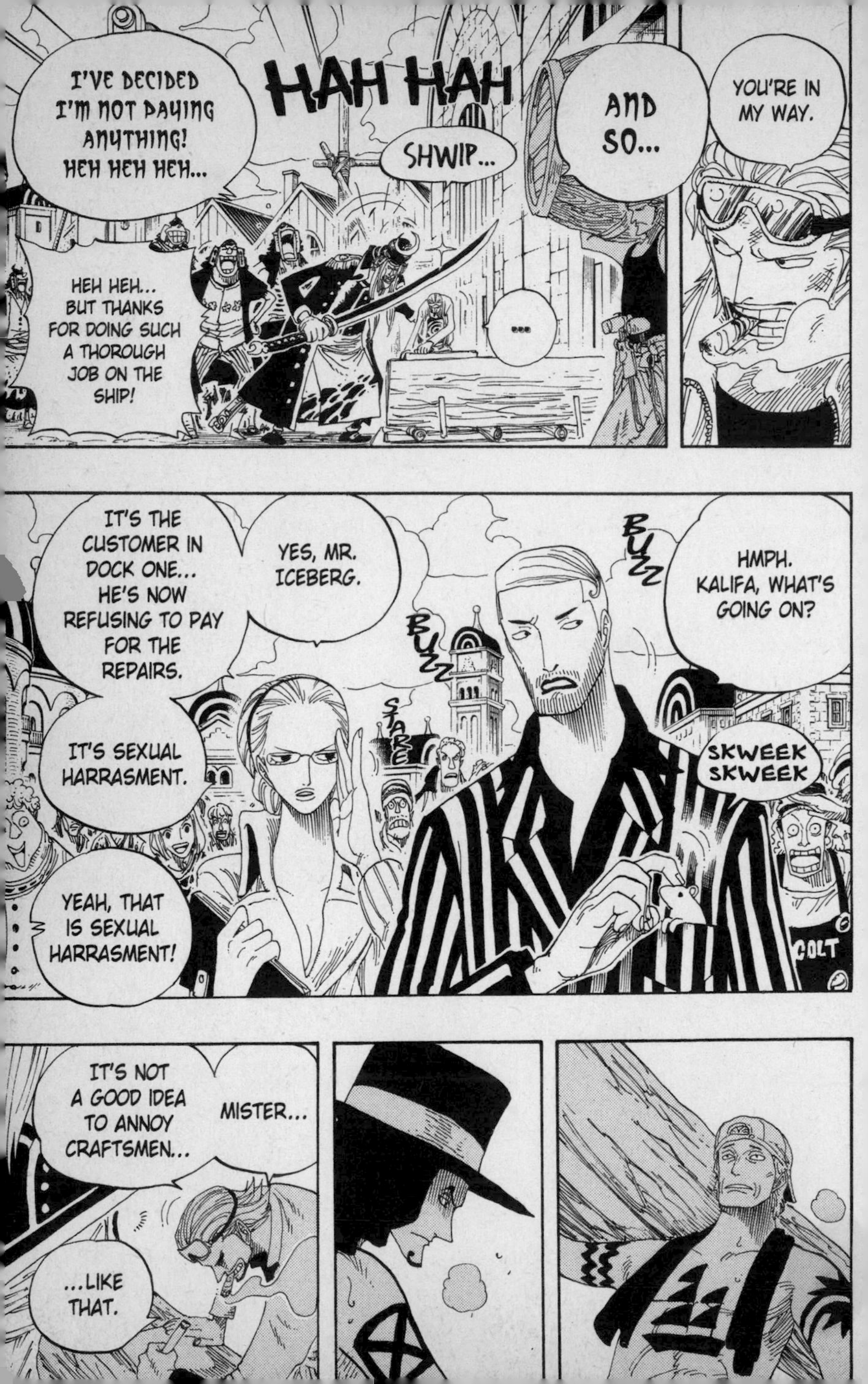
YOU'RE IN MY WAY.
AND SO...
SHWIP...
HAH HAH
I'VE DECIDED I'M NOT PAYING ANYTHING! HEH HEH HEH...
...
HEH HEH... BUT THANKS FOR DOING SUCH A THOROUGH JOB ON THE SHIP!
HMPH. KALIFA, WHAT'S GOING ON?
BUZZ
BUZZ
YES, MR. ICEBERG.
IT'S THE CUSTOMER IN DOCK ONE... HE'S NOW REFUSING TO PAY FOR THE REPAIRS.
STARE
SKWEEK SKWEEK
COLT
IT'S SEXUAL HARRASMENT.
YEAH, THAT IS SEXUAL HARRASMENT!
MISTER...
IT'S NOT A GOOD IDEA TO ANNOY CRAFTSMEN...
...LIKE THAT.

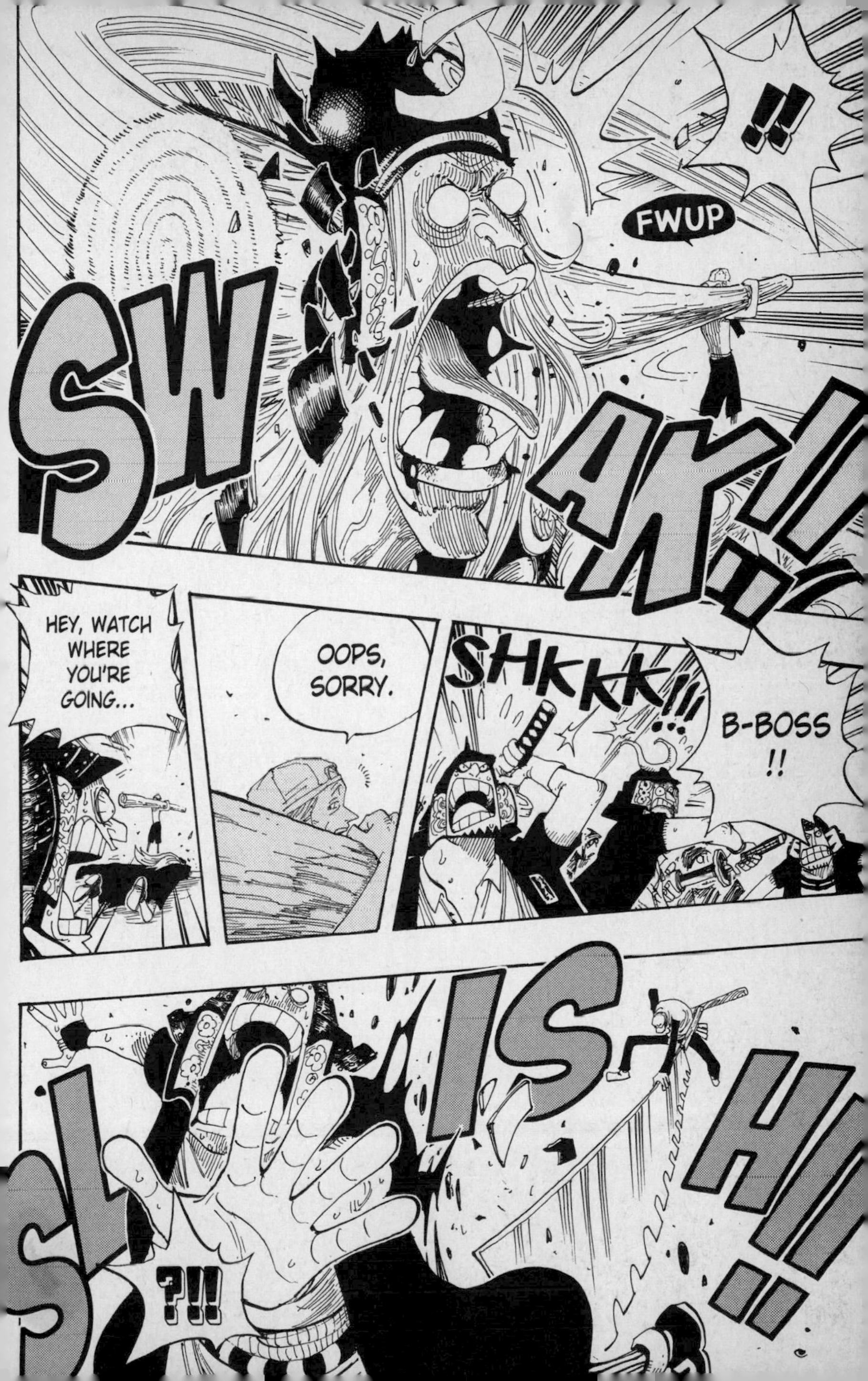
!!
FWUP
SWAK!!
HEY, WATCH WHERE YOU'RE GOING...
OOPS, SORRY.
SHKKK!!!
B-BOSS !!
SLISH!!
?!!

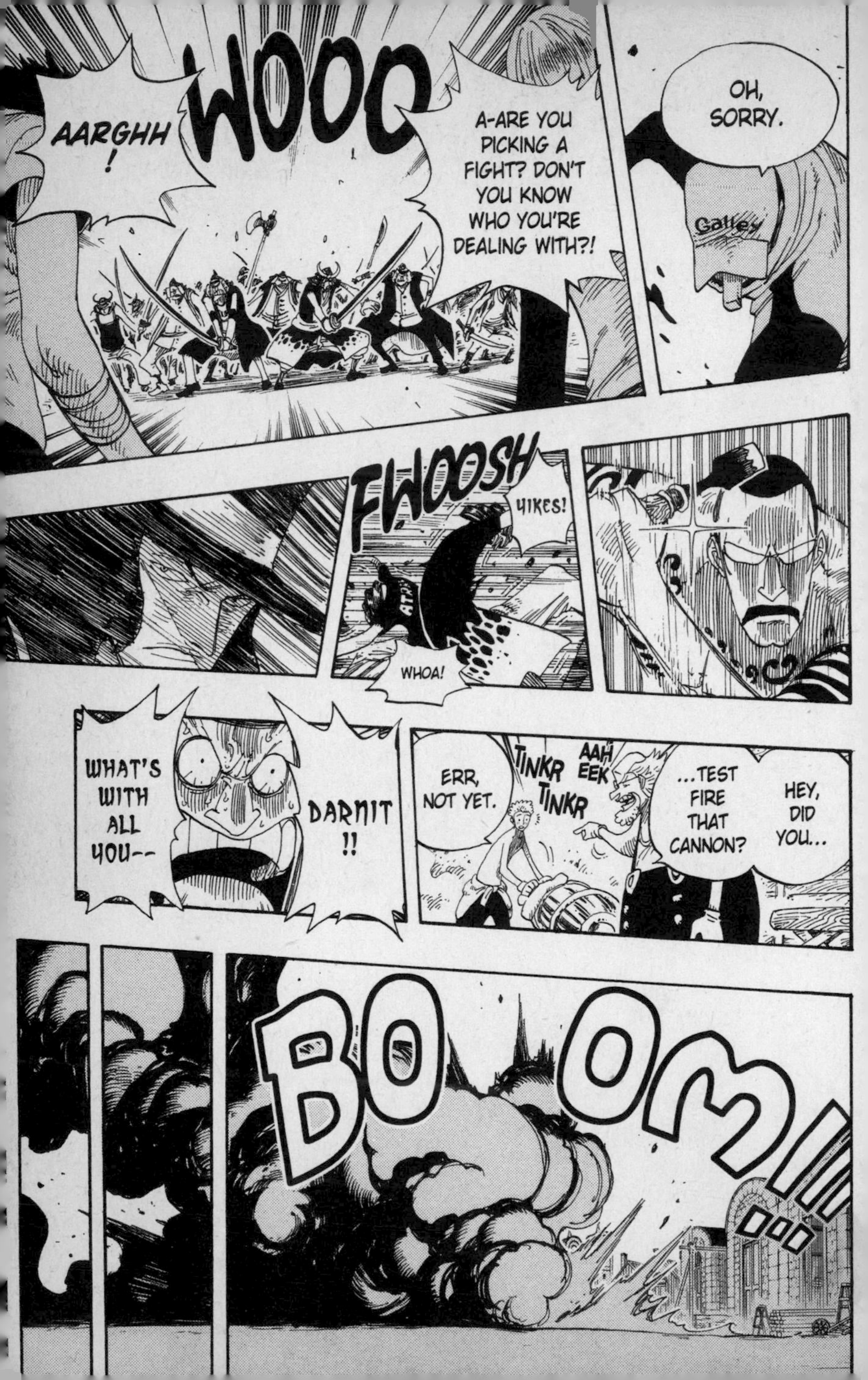
OH, SORRY.
Galley
A-ARE YOU PICKING A FIGHT? DON'T YOU KNOW WHO YOU'RE DEALING WITH?!
WOOO
AARGHH!
FWOOSH
YIKES!
WHOA!
HEY, DID YOU...
...TEST FIRE THAT CANNON?
AAH EEK
TINKR TINKR
ERR, NOT YET.
DARNIT!!
WHAT'S WITH ALL YOU--
BOOM!!!

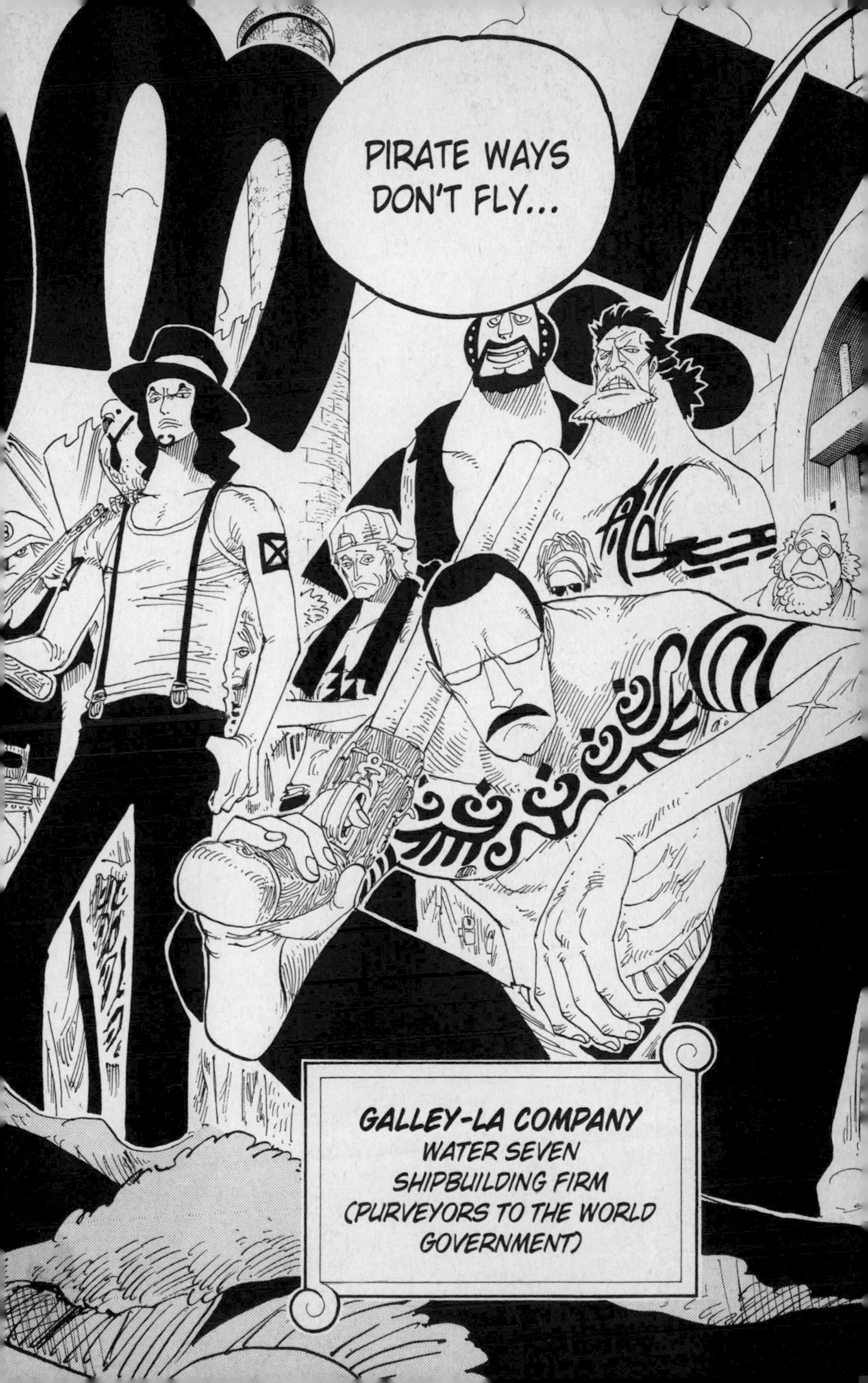
PIRATE WAYS DON'T FLY...
GALLEY-LA COMPANY
WATER SEVEN
SHIPBUILDING FIRM
(PURVEYORS TO THE WORLD
GOVERNMENT)

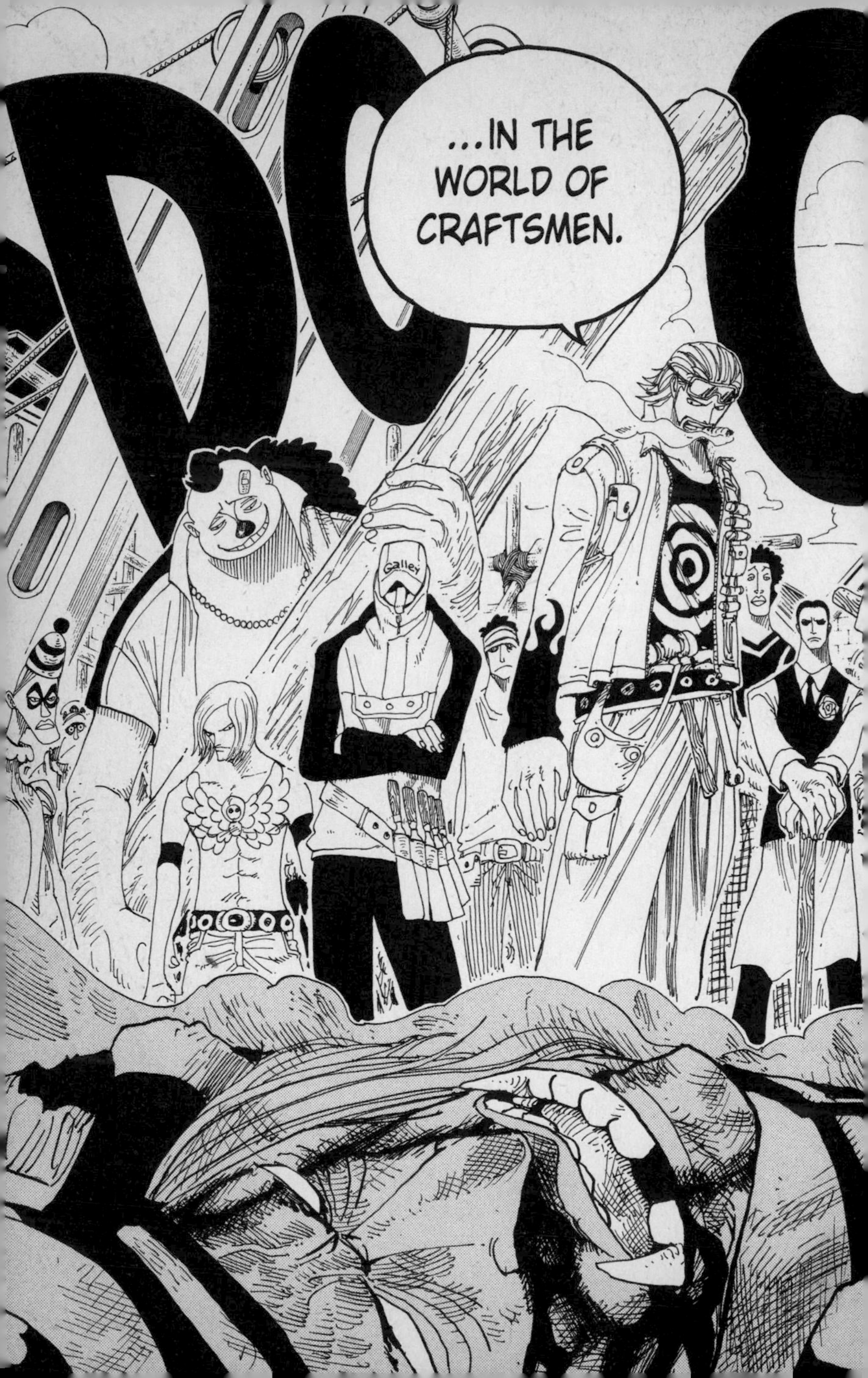
...IN THE WORLD OF CRAFTSMEN.
Galley

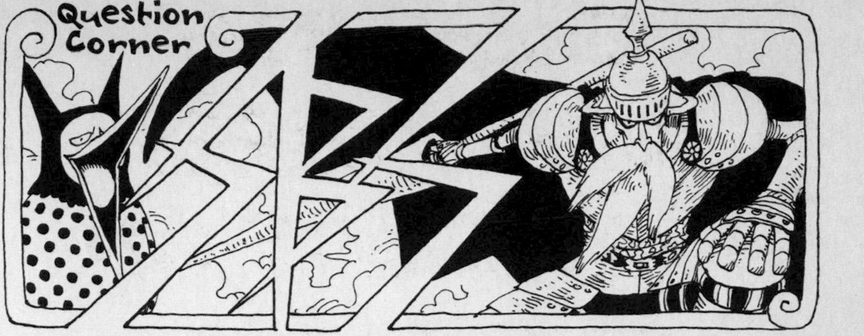
Question Corner

Q: Hello, Oda Sensei. I enjoy reading *One Piece*. Anyway, here's the thing. In vol. 33, page 168, in the second panel, there are all sorts of wigs in the closet, and I'm just itching to see Luffy try them all on!
Please, Oda Sensei!! Please!!
--Naopee

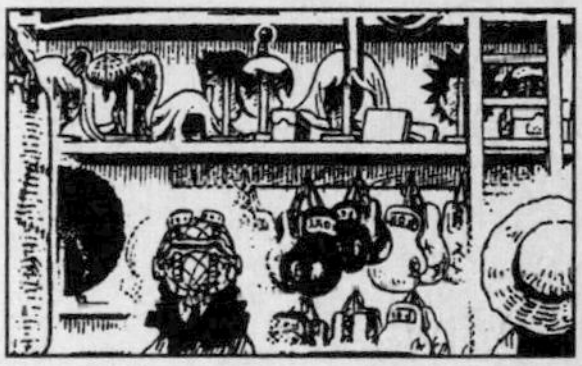

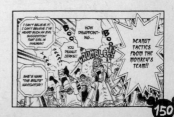

A: You're right, there were many strange costumes there. I left that room to Y-san, one of my staffers. He's a father of one and loves Sailor MXXn. Actually, my office is full of weirdos.
Luffy looks strong no matter which wig he wears.

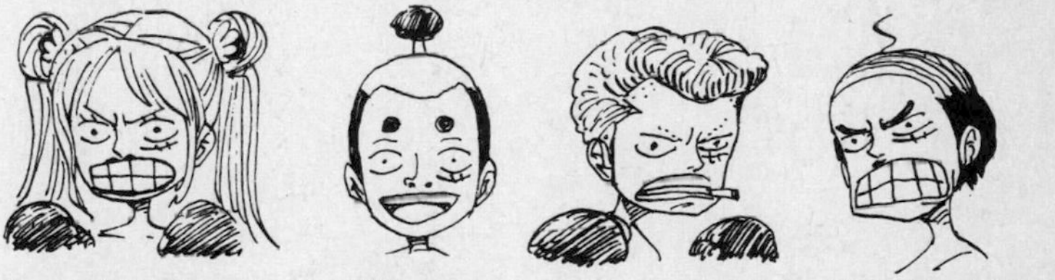

Beautiful Female Warrior Luffy Moon

Moronic Feudal Lord Luffy

Greaser Luffy

Old Man Luffy

Q: In the Davy Back Fight in volume 33, page 152, there's mention of a "Peanut strategy." How come it's called "peanut"?
--Kissa

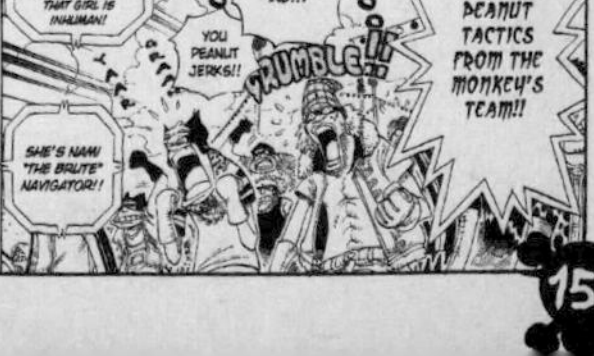
PEANUT TACTICS FROM THE MONKEY'S TEAM!!
BOOO!!
HOW DISAPPOINTING...
RUMBLE!!
YOU PEANUT JERKS!!
BOOO
I CAN'T BELIEVE IT! I CAN'T BELIEVE I'VE HEARD SUCH AN EVIL SUGGESTION! THAT GIRL IS INHUMAN!
SHE'S NAMI "THE BRUTE" NAVIGATOR!!

A: Well... I used it to sound sort of like "cowardly." Just to fit the mood. I mean, I have nothing against peanuts. Peanuts from Chiba are yummy.

Chapter 324: ADVENTURES IN THE CITY ON THE WATER

GAKIN !!!

GEDATSU'S UNEXPECTED LIFE ON THE BLUE SEA, VOL. 10: "STAND ON THE GROUND WHILE YOU DIG, MASTER GEDATSU"

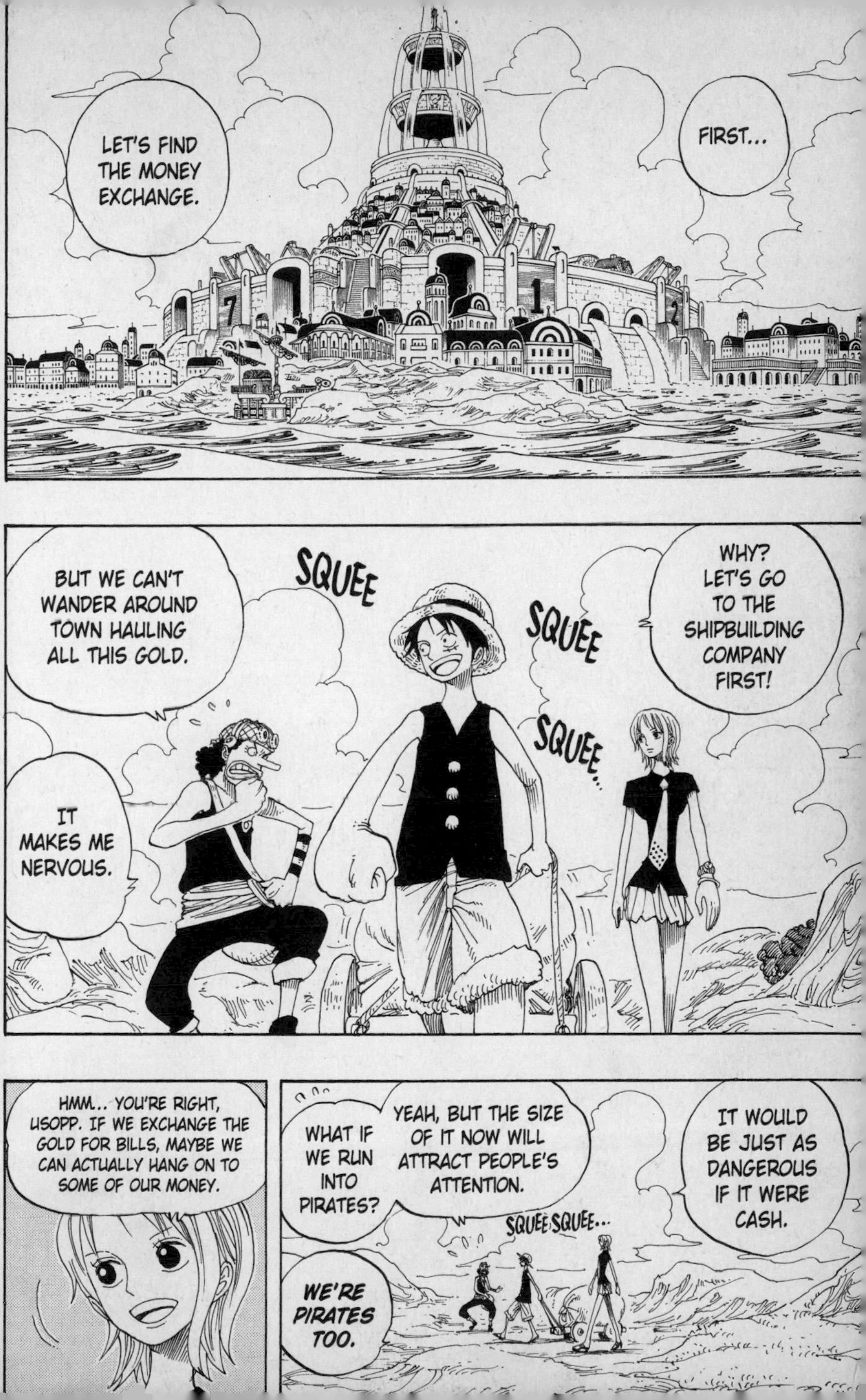
FIRST...
LET'S FIND THE MONEY EXCHANGE.
WHY? LET'S GO TO THE SHIPBUILDING COMPANY FIRST!
SQUEE
SQUEE
SQUEE...
BUT WE CAN'T WANDER AROUND TOWN HAULING ALL THIS GOLD.
IT MAKES ME NERVOUS.
IT WOULD BE JUST AS DANGEROUS IF IT WERE CASH.
YEAH, BUT THE SIZE OF IT NOW WILL ATTRACT PEOPLE'S ATTENTION.
WHAT IF WE RUN INTO PIRATES?
SQUEE SQUEE...
WE'RE PIRATES TOO.
HMM.. YOU'RE RIGHT, USOPP. IF WE EXCHANGE THE GOLD FOR BILLS, MAYBE WE CAN ACTUALLY HANG ON TO SOME OF OUR MONEY.

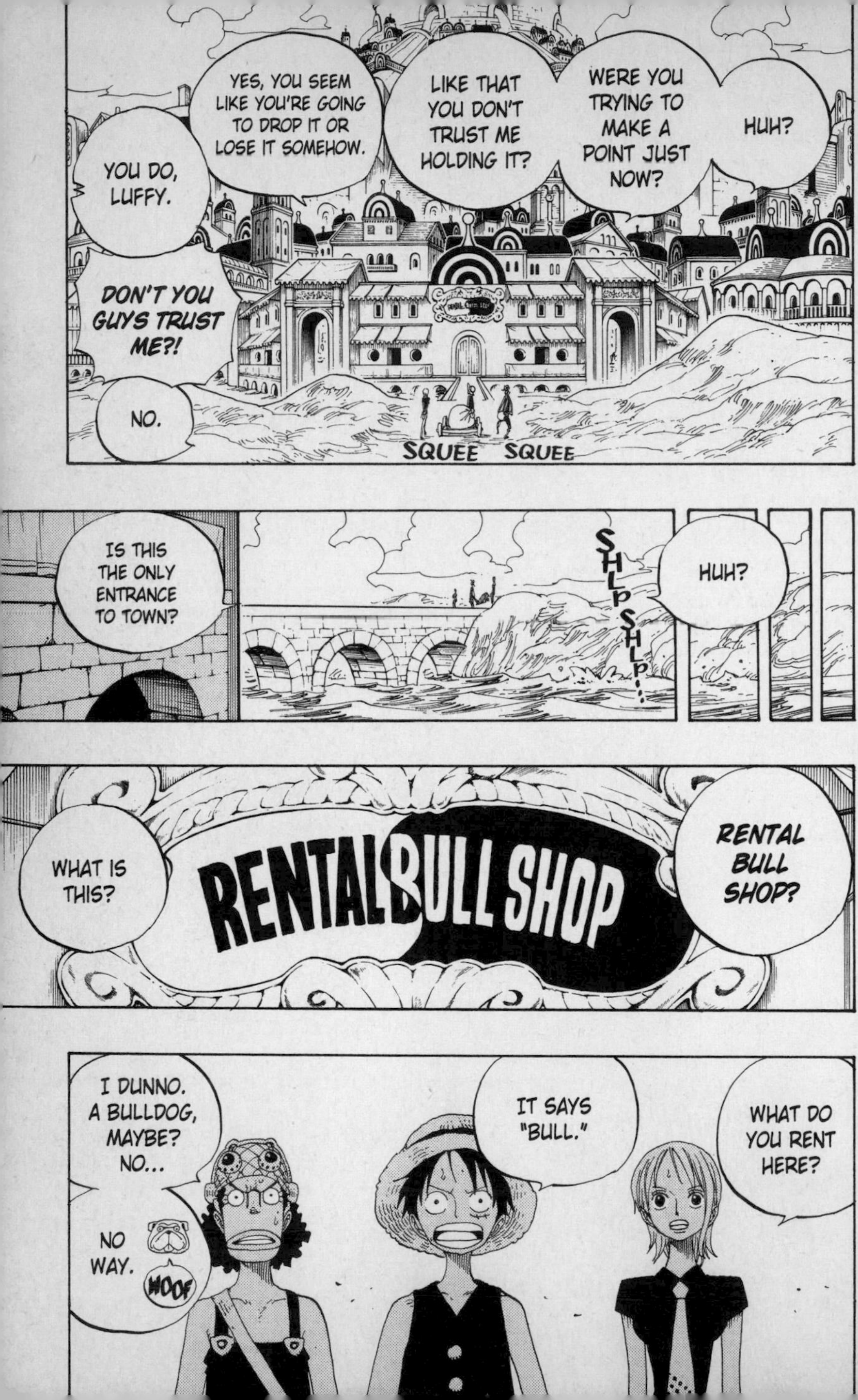
HUH?
WERE YOU TRYING TO MAKE A POINT JUST NOW?
LIKE THAT YOU DON'T TRUST ME HOLDING IT?
YES, YOU SEEM LIKE YOU'RE GOING TO DROP IT OR LOSE IT SOMEHOW.
YOU DO, LUFFY.
DON'T YOU GUYS TRUST ME?!
NO.
SQUEE SQUEE
HUH?
SHLP SHLP...
IS THIS THE ONLY ENTRANCE TO TOWN?
RENTAL BULL SHOP?
RENTAL BULL SHOP
WHAT IS THIS?
WHAT DO YOU RENT HERE?
IT SAYS "BULL."
I DUNNO. A BULLDOG, MAYBE? NO...
NO WAY.
WOOF

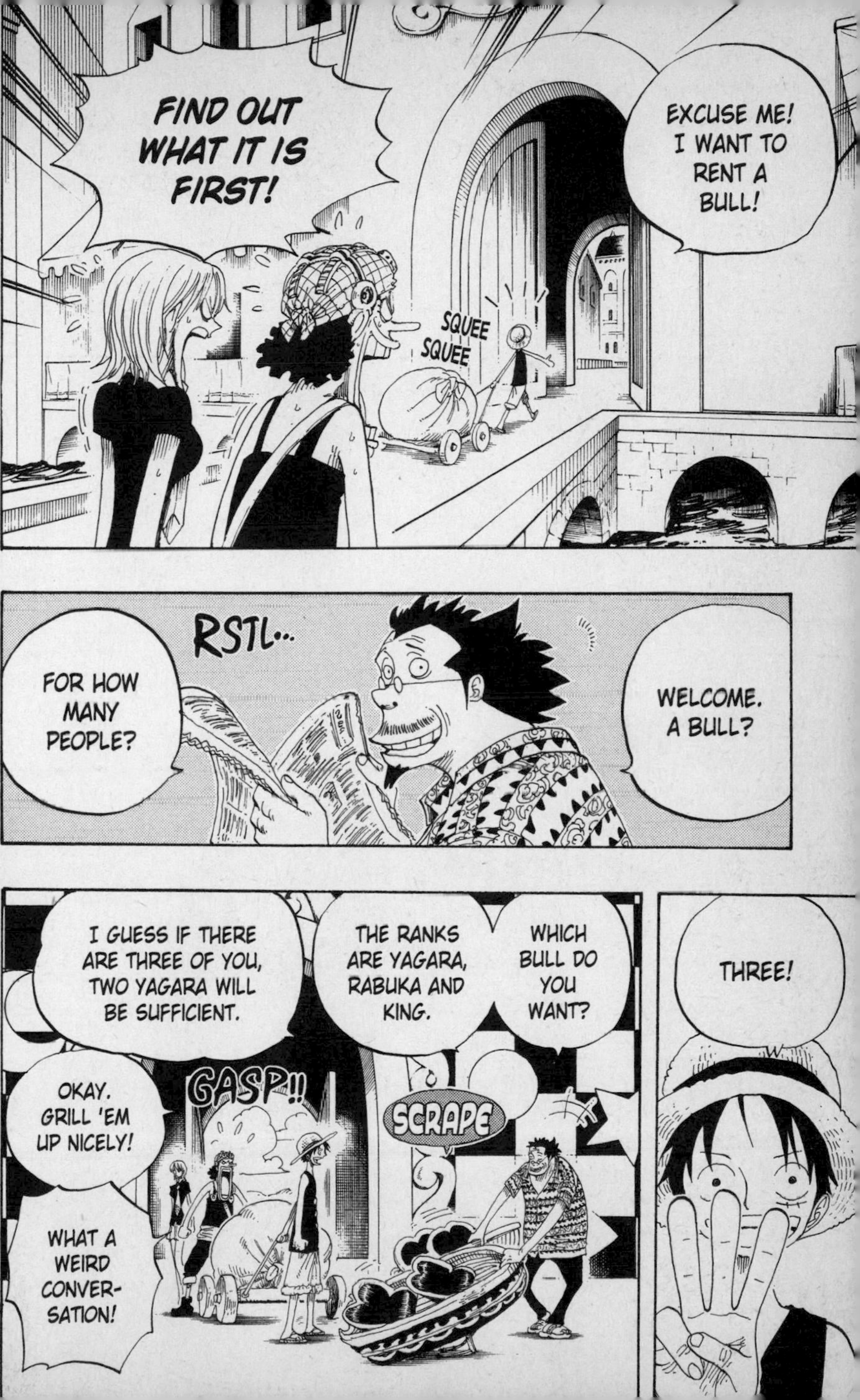
EXCUSE ME! I WANT TO RENT A BULL!
FIND OUT WHAT IT IS FIRST!
SQUEE SQUEE
WELCOME. A BULL?
RSTL...
FOR HOW MANY PEOPLE?
THREE!
WHICH BULL DO YOU WANT?
THE RANKS ARE YAGARA, RABUKA AND KING.
I GUESS IF THERE ARE THREE OF YOU, TWO YAGARA WILL BE SUFFICIENT.
SCRAPE
GASP!!
OKAY. GRILL 'EM UP NICELY!
WHAT A WEIRD CONVER-SATION!

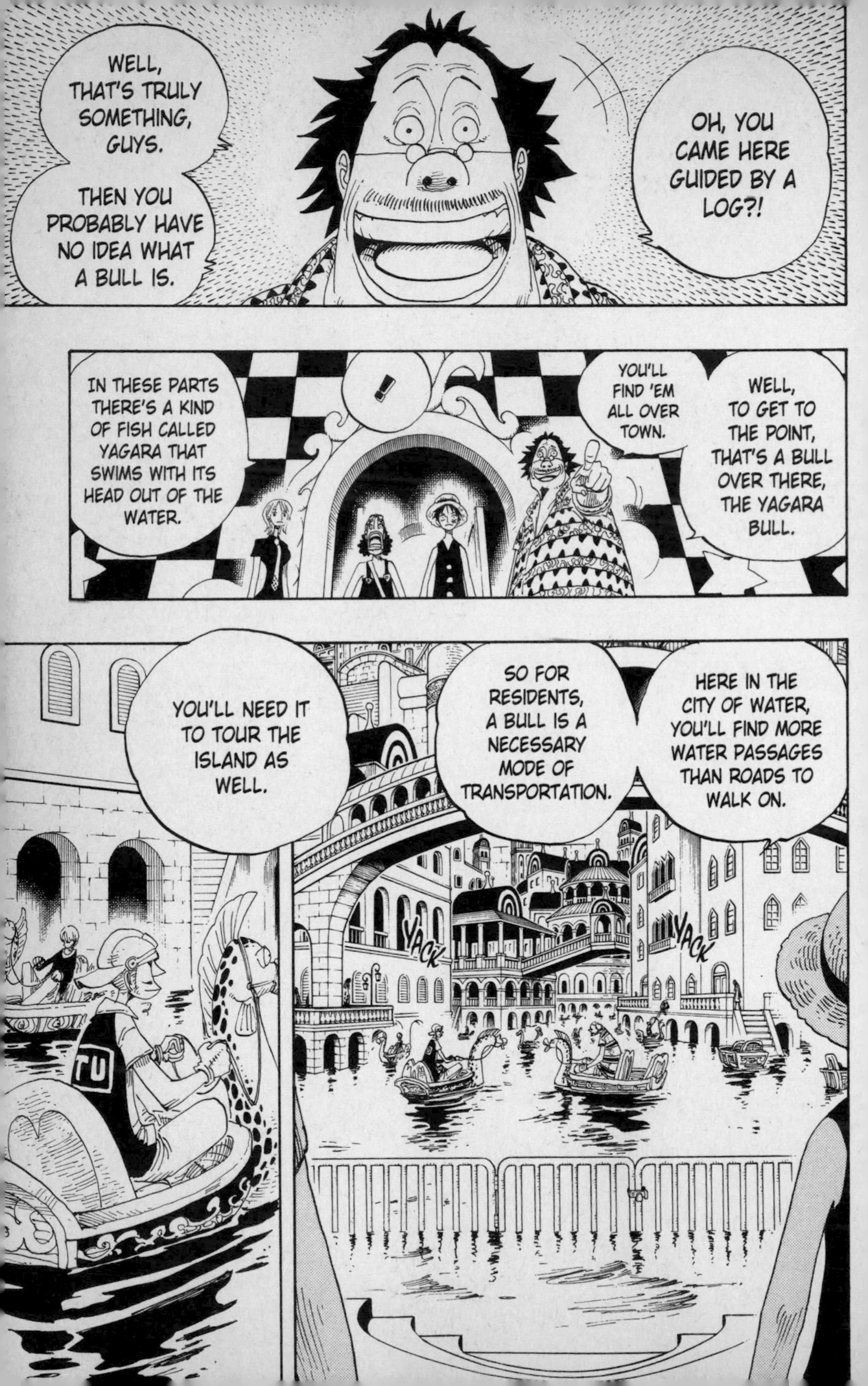
OH, YOU CAME HERE GUIDED BY A LOG?!
WELL, THAT'S TRULY SOMETHING, GUYS.
THEN YOU PROBABLY HAVE NO IDEA WHAT A BULL IS.
WELL, TO GET TO THE POINT, THAT'S A BULL OVER THERE, THE YAGARA BULL.
YOU'LL FIND 'EM ALL OVER TOWN.
!
IN THESE PARTS THERE'S A KIND OF FISH CALLED YAGARA THAT SWIMS WITH ITS HEAD OUT OF THE WATER.
HERE IN THE CITY OF WATER, YOU'LL FIND MORE WATER PASSAGES THAN ROADS TO WALK ON.
SO FOR RESIDENTS, A BULL IS A NECESSARY MODE OF TRANSPORTATION.
YACK
YACK
YOU'LL NEED IT TO TOUR THE ISLAND AS WELL.
TU

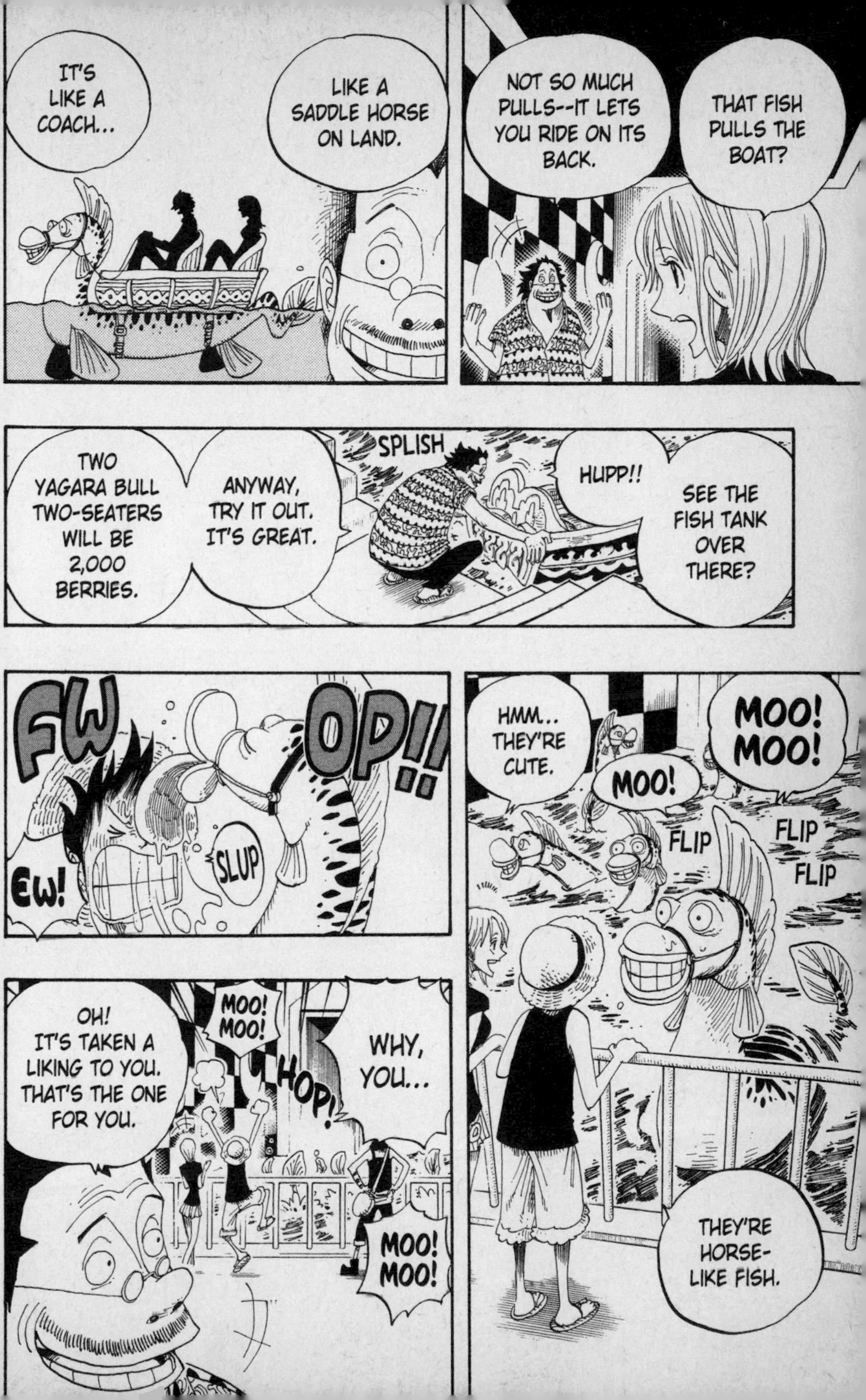
THAT FISH PULLS THE BOAT?
NOT SO MUCH PULLS--IT LETS YOU RIDE ON ITS BACK.
LIKE A SADDLE HORSE ON LAND.
IT'S LIKE A COACH...
SEE THE FISH TANK OVER THERE?
HUPP!!
SPLISH
ANYWAY, TRY IT OUT. IT'S GREAT.
TWO YAGARA BULL TWO-SEATERS WILL BE 2,000 BERRIES.
MOO! MOO!
HMM... THEY'RE CUTE.
MOO!
FLIP
FLIP
FLIP
THEY'RE HORSE-LIKE FISH.
FWOP!!
SLUP
EW!
MOO! MOO!
WHY, YOU...
HOP!
MOO! MOO!
OH! IT'S TAKEN A LIKING TO YOU. THAT'S THE ONE FOR YOU.

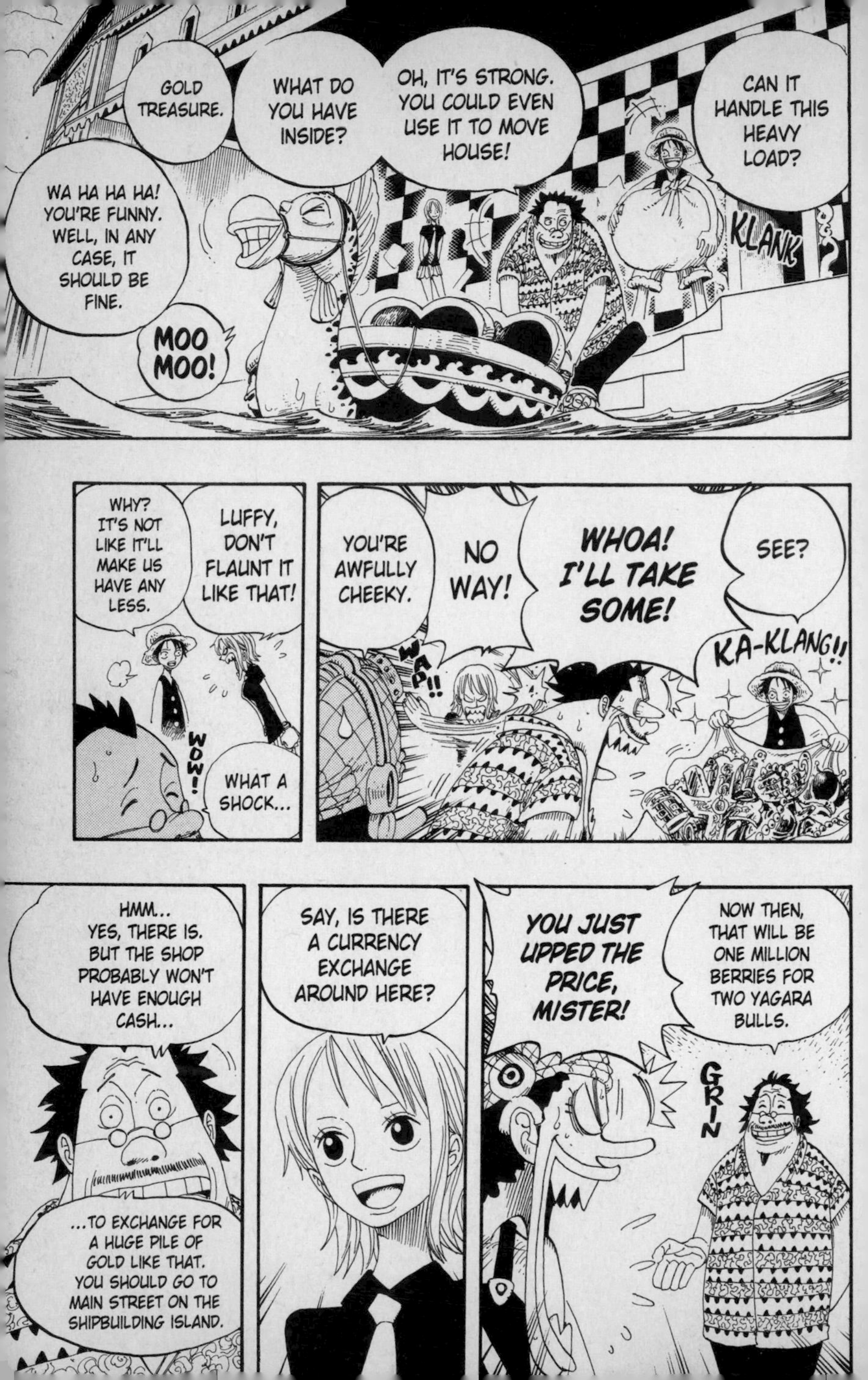
CAN IT HANDLE THIS HEAVY LOAD?
KLANK
OH, IT'S STRONG. YOU COULD EVEN USE IT TO MOVE HOUSE!
WHAT DO YOU HAVE INSIDE?
GOLD TREASURE.
WA HA HA HA! YOU'RE FUNNY. WELL, IN ANY CASE, IT SHOULD BE FINE.
MOO MOO!
SEE?
KA-KLANG!!
WHOA! I'LL TAKE SOME!
NO WAY!
YOU'RE AWFULLY CHEEKY.
WAP!!
LUFFY, DON'T FLAUNT IT LIKE THAT!
WHY? IT'S NOT LIKE IT'LL MAKE US HAVE ANY LESS.
WOW!
WHAT A SHOCK...
NOW THEN, THAT WILL BE ONE MILLION BERRIES FOR TWO YAGARA BULLS.
GRIN
YOU JUST UPPED THE PRICE, MISTER!
SAY, IS THERE A CURRENCY EXCHANGE AROUND HERE?
HMM... YES, THERE IS. BUT THE SHOP PROBABLY WON'T HAVE ENOUGH CASH...
...TO EXCHANGE FOR A HUGE PILE OF GOLD LIKE THAT. YOU SHOULD GO TO MAIN STREET ON THE SHIPBUILDING ISLAND.

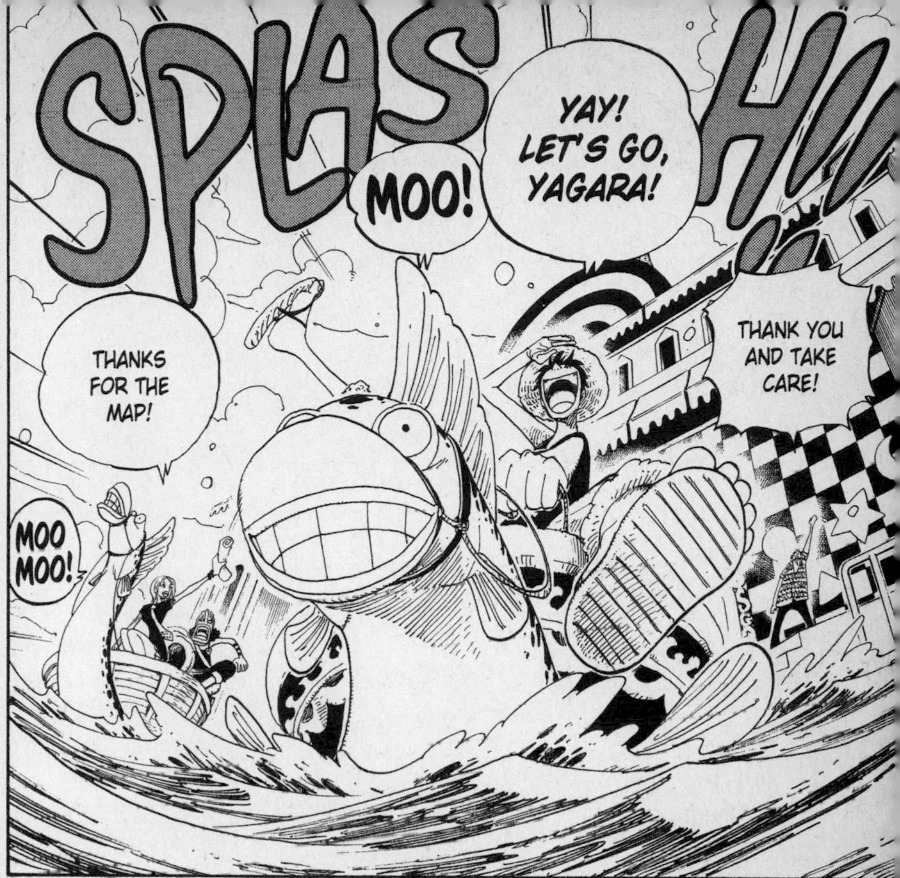
SPLASH
YAY! LET'S GO, YAGARA!
MOO!
THANK YOU AND TAKE CARE!
THANKS FOR THE MAP!
MOO MOO!

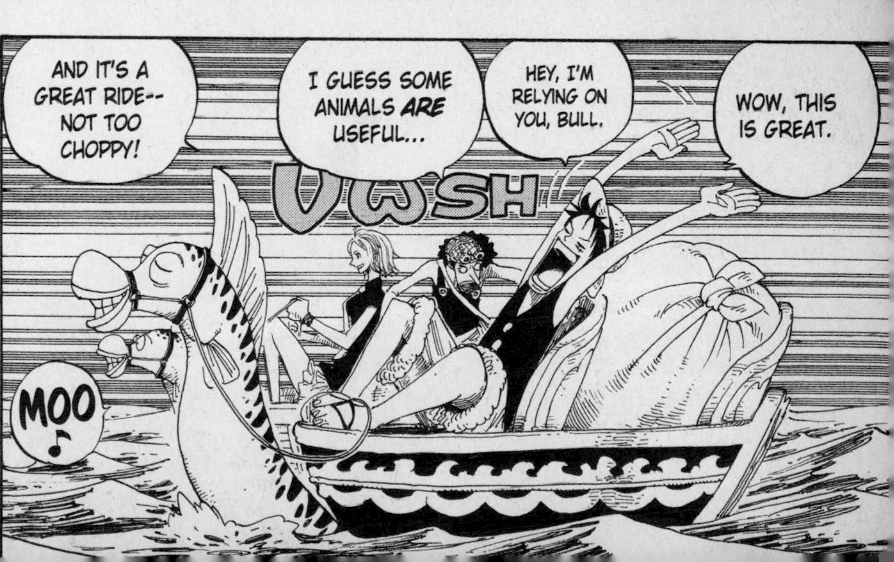
WOW, THIS IS GREAT.
HEY, I'M RELYING ON YOU, BULL.
I GUESS SOME ANIMALS *ARE* USEFUL...
AND IT'S A GREAT RIDE--NOT TOO CHOPPY!
VWSH
MOO ♪

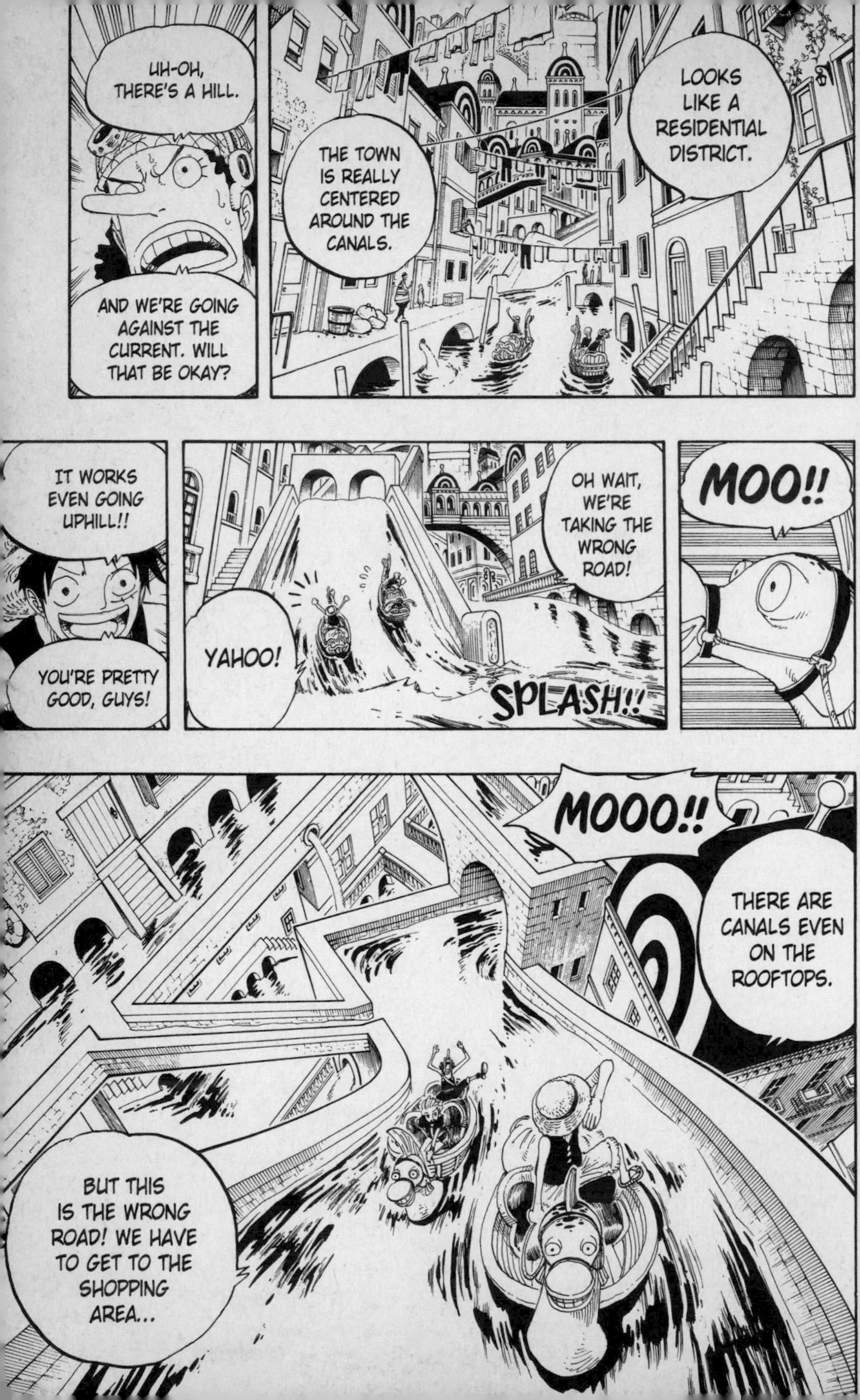
LOOKS LIKE A RESIDENTIAL DISTRICT.
THE TOWN IS REALLY CENTERED AROUND THE CANALS.
UH-OH, THERE'S A HILL.
AND WE'RE GOING AGAINST THE CURRENT. WILL THAT BE OKAY?
MOO!!
OH WAIT, WE'RE TAKING THE WRONG ROAD!
SPLASH!!
YAHOO!
IT WORKS EVEN GOING UPHILL!!
YOU'RE PRETTY GOOD, GUYS!
MOOO!!
THERE ARE CANALS EVEN ON THE ROOFTOPS.
BUT THIS IS THE WRONG ROAD! WE HAVE TO GET TO THE SHOPPING AREA...

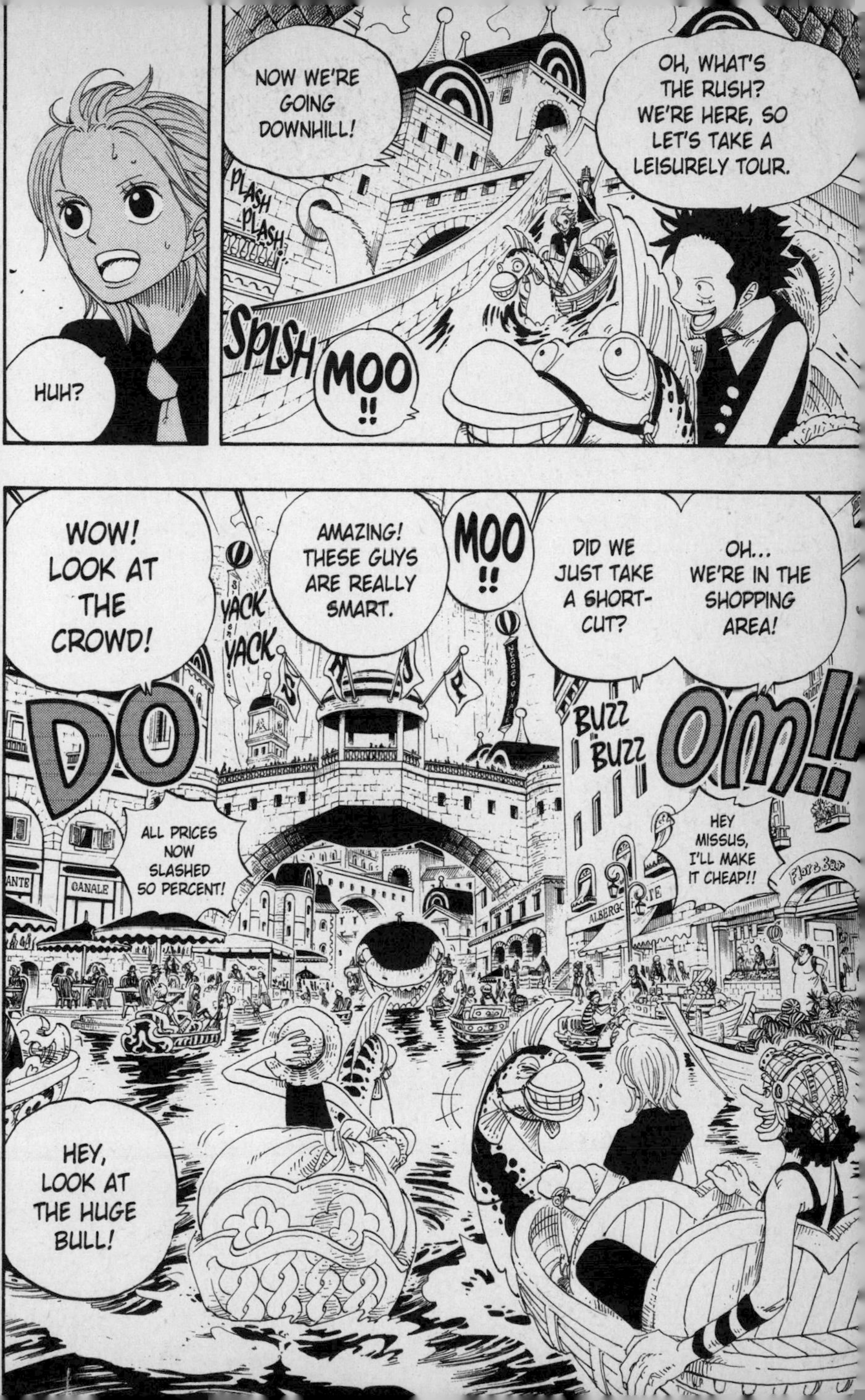
OH, WHAT'S THE RUSH? WE'RE HERE, SO LET'S TAKE A LEISURELY TOUR.
NOW WE'RE GOING DOWNHILL!
PLASH PLASH
SPLSH
MOO!!
HUH?
OH... WE'RE IN THE SHOPPING AREA!
DID WE JUST TAKE A SHORT-CUT?
MOO!!
AMAZING! THESE GUYS ARE REALLY SMART.
WOW! LOOK AT THE CROWD!
YACK YACK
DOOM!!
BUZZ BUZZ
HEY MISSUS, I'LL MAKE IT CHEAP!!
ALL PRICES NOW SLASHED 50 PERCENT!
CANALE
HEY, LOOK AT THE HUGE BULL!

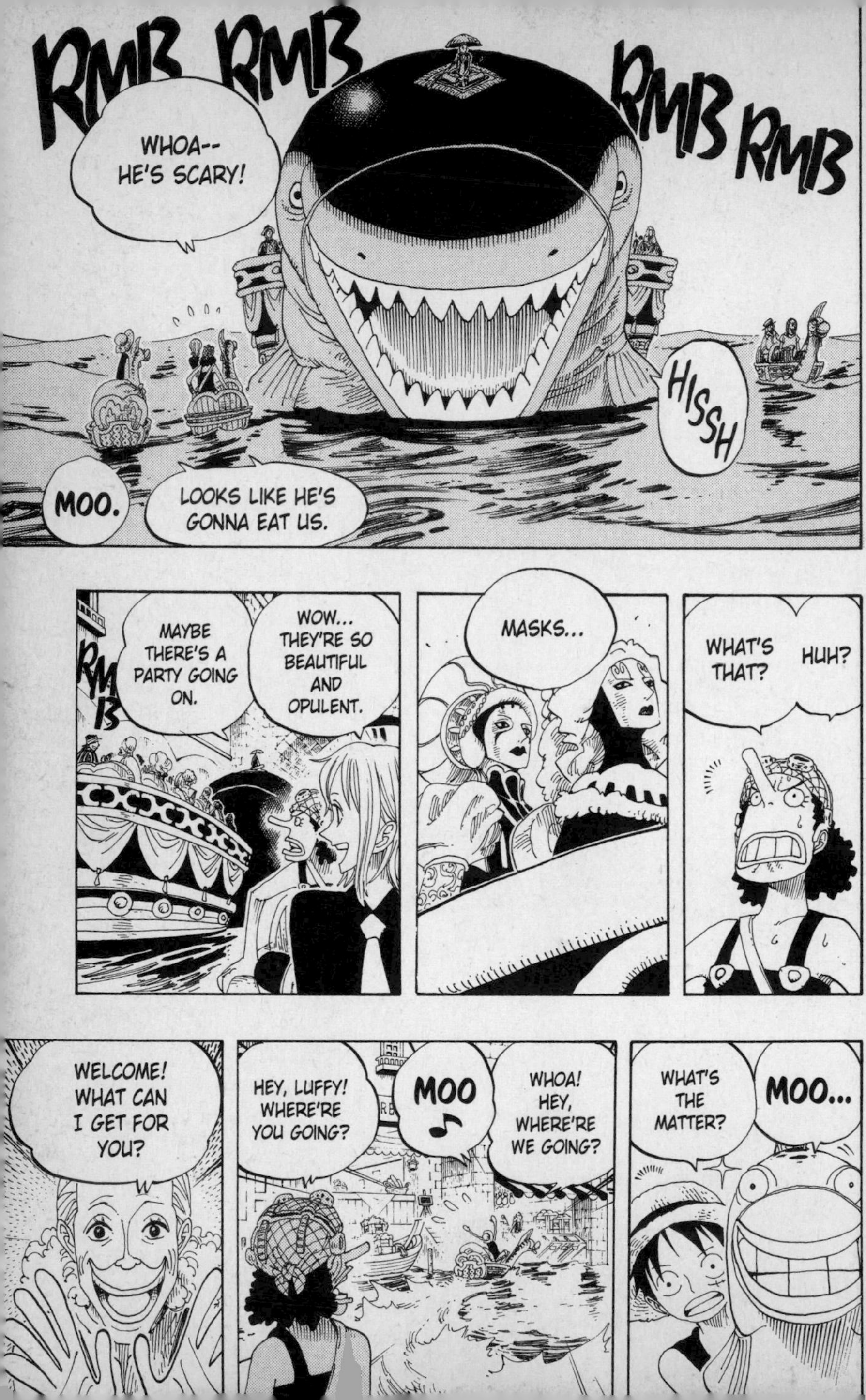
RMB RMB
RMB RMB
WHOA-- HE'S SCARY!
HISSH
LOOKS LIKE HE'S GONNA EAT US.
MOO.
HUH?
WHAT'S THAT?
MASKS...
WOW... THEY'RE SO BEAUTIFUL AND OPULENT.
MAYBE THERE'S A PARTY GOING ON.
RMB
MOO...
WHAT'S THE MATTER?
WHOA! HEY, WHERE'RE WE GOING?
MOO ♪
HEY, LUFFY! WHERE'RE YOU GOING?
WELCOME! WHAT CAN I GET FOR YOU?

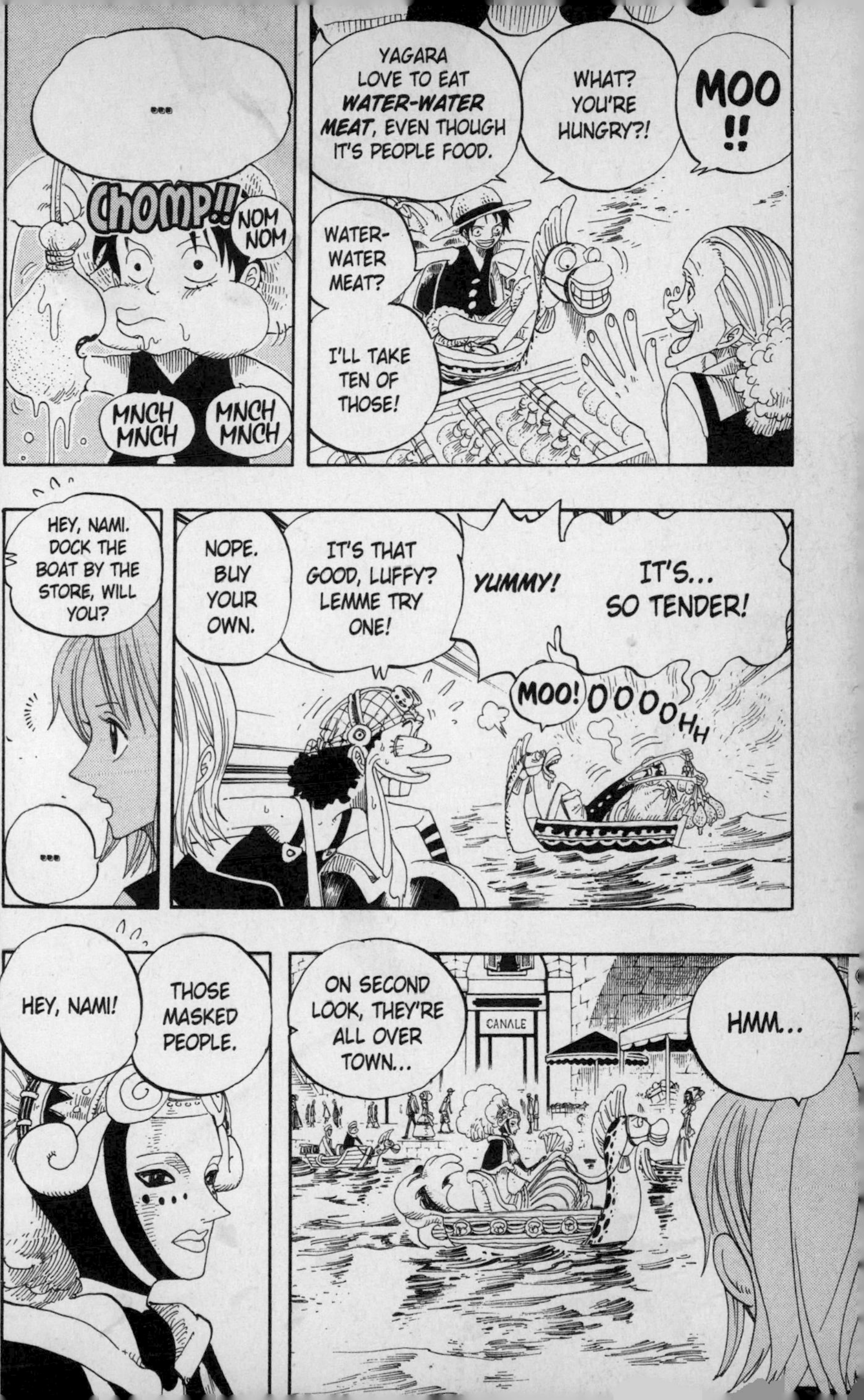
MOO!!
WHAT? YOU'RE HUNGRY?!
YAGARA LOVE TO EAT WATER-WATER MEAT, EVEN THOUGH IT'S PEOPLE FOOD.
WATER-WATER MEAT?
I'LL TAKE TEN OF THOSE!
...
CHOMP!!
NOM NOM
MNCH MNCH
MNCH MNCH
IT'S... SO TENDER!
YUMMY!
IT'S THAT GOOD, LUFFY? LEMME TRY ONE!
NOPE. BUY YOUR OWN.
MOO!
OOOOHH
HEY, NAMI. DOCK THE BOAT BY THE STORE, WILL YOU?
...
HMM..
ON SECOND LOOK, THEY'RE ALL OVER TOWN...
CANALE
THOSE MASKED PEOPLE.
HEY, NAMI!

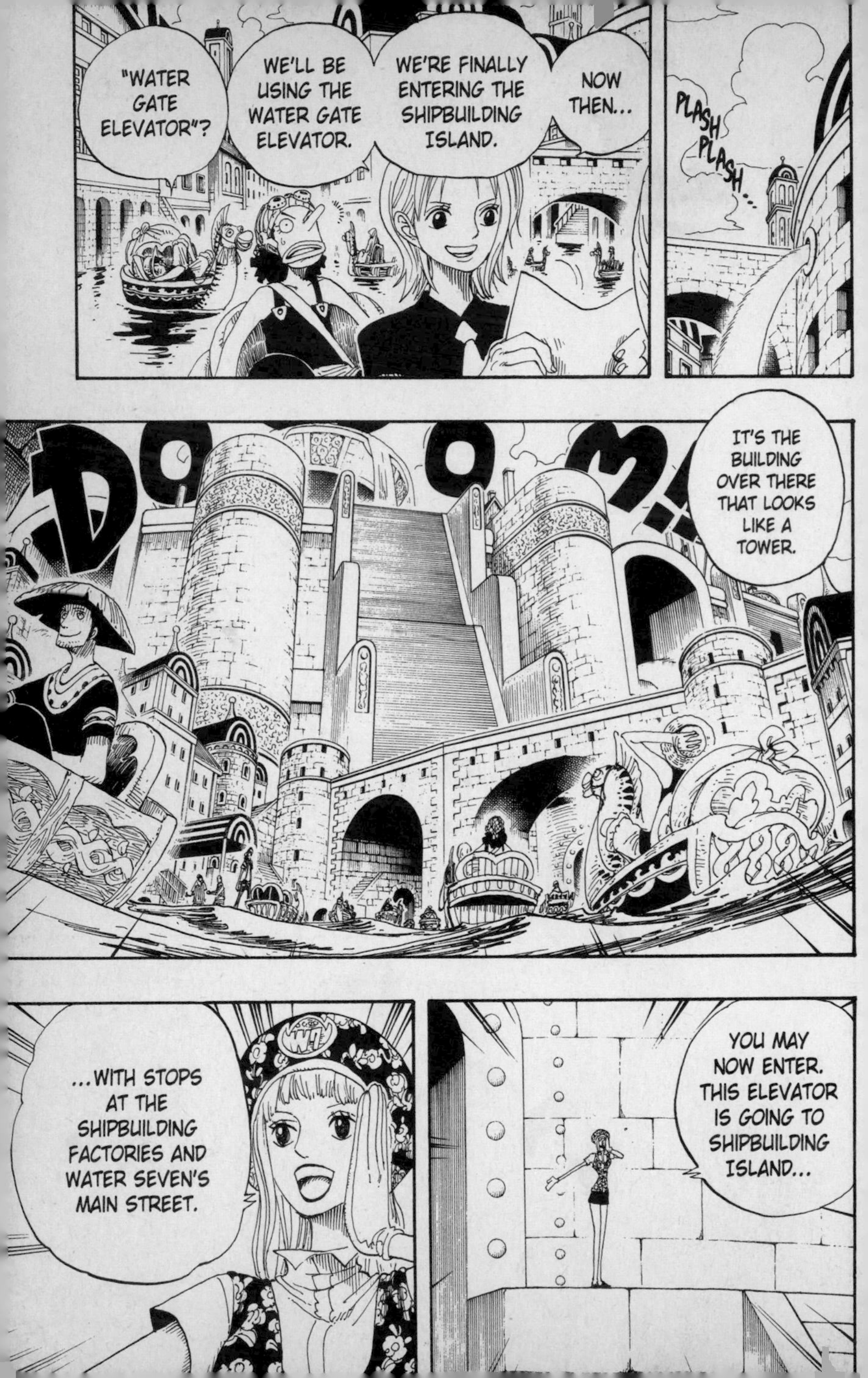
PLASH PLASH...
NOW THEN...
WE'RE FINALLY ENTERING THE SHIPBUILDING ISLAND.
WE'LL BE USING THE WATER GATE ELEVATOR.
"WATER GATE ELEVATOR"?
DOOM!!
IT'S THE BUILDING OVER THERE THAT LOOKS LIKE A TOWER.
YOU MAY NOW ENTER. THIS ELEVATOR IS GOING TO SHIPBUILDING ISLAND...
...WITH STOPS AT THE SHIPBUILDING FACTORIES AND WATER SEVEN'S MAIN STREET.

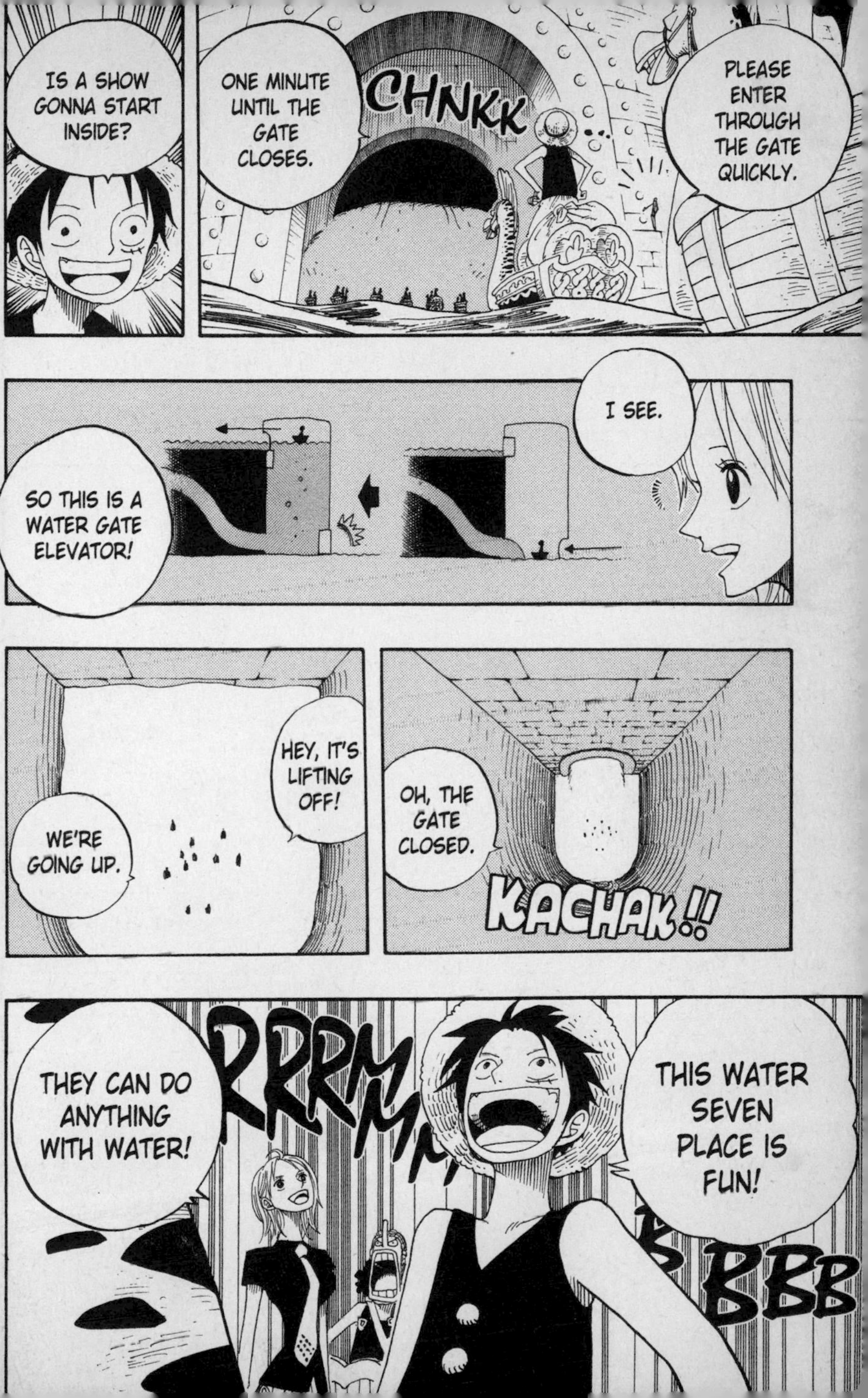
PLEASE ENTER THROUGH THE GATE QUICKLY.
CHNKK
ONE MINUTE UNTIL THE GATE CLOSES.
IS A SHOW GONNA START INSIDE?
I SEE.
SO THIS IS A WATER GATE ELEVATOR!
OH, THE GATE CLOSED.
KACHAK!!
HEY, IT'S LIFTING OFF!
WE'RE GOING UP.
THIS WATER SEVEN PLACE IS FUN!
RRRM
THEY CAN DO ANYTHING WITH WATER!
BBB

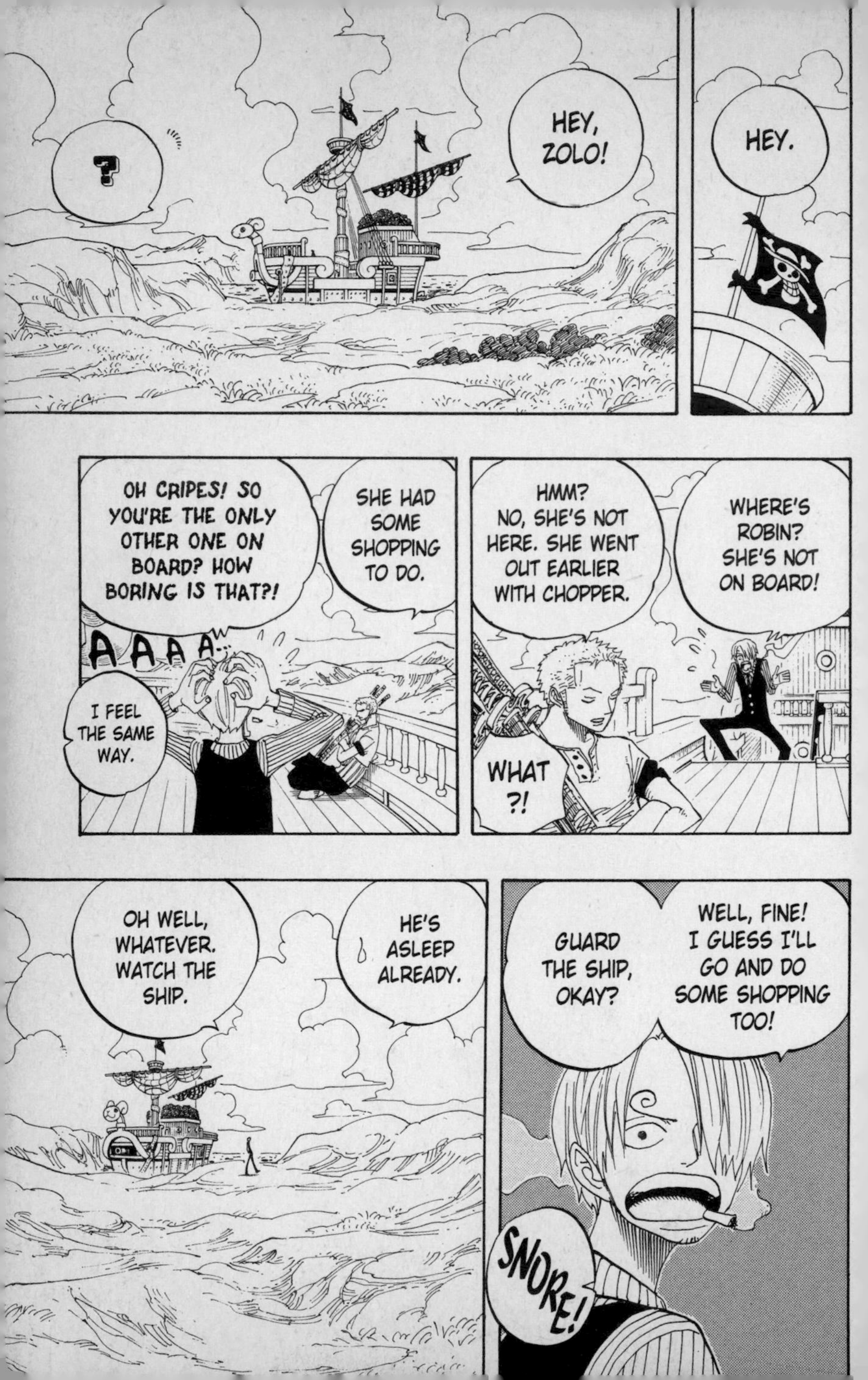
HEY.
HEY, ZOLO!
?
WHERE'S ROBIN? SHE'S NOT ON BOARD!
HMM? NO, SHE'S NOT HERE. SHE WENT OUT EARLIER WITH CHOPPER.
WHAT ?!
SHE HAD SOME SHOPPING TO DO.
OH CRIPES! SO YOU'RE THE ONLY OTHER ONE ON BOARD? HOW BORING IS THAT?!
AAAA...
I FEEL THE SAME WAY.
WELL, FINE! I GUESS I'LL GO AND DO SOME SHOPPING TOO!
GUARD THE SHIP, OKAY?
SNORE!
HE'S ASLEEP ALREADY.
OH WELL, WHATEVER. WATCH THE SHIP.

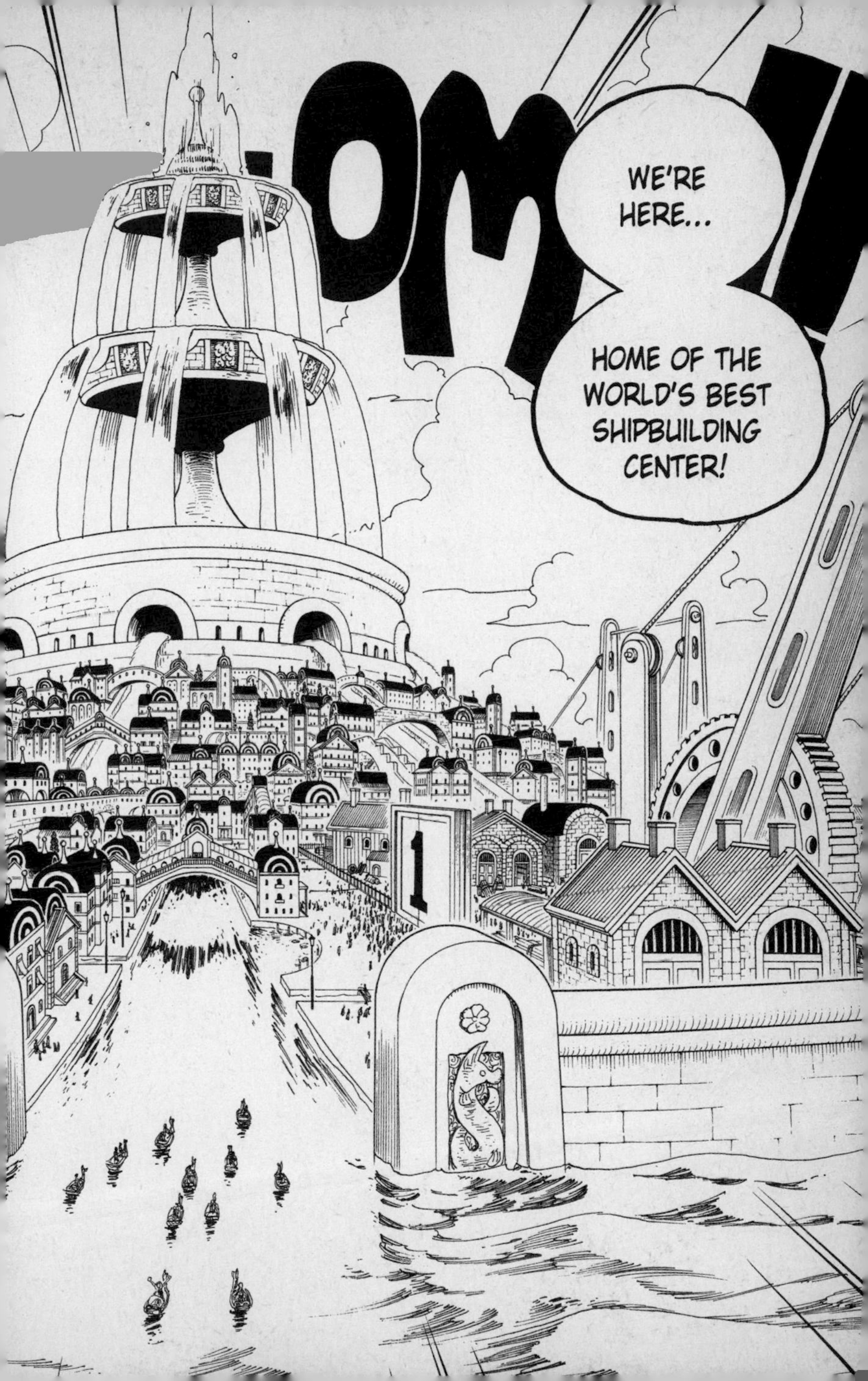
WE'RE HERE...
HOME OF THE WORLD'S BEST SHIPBUILDING CENTER!

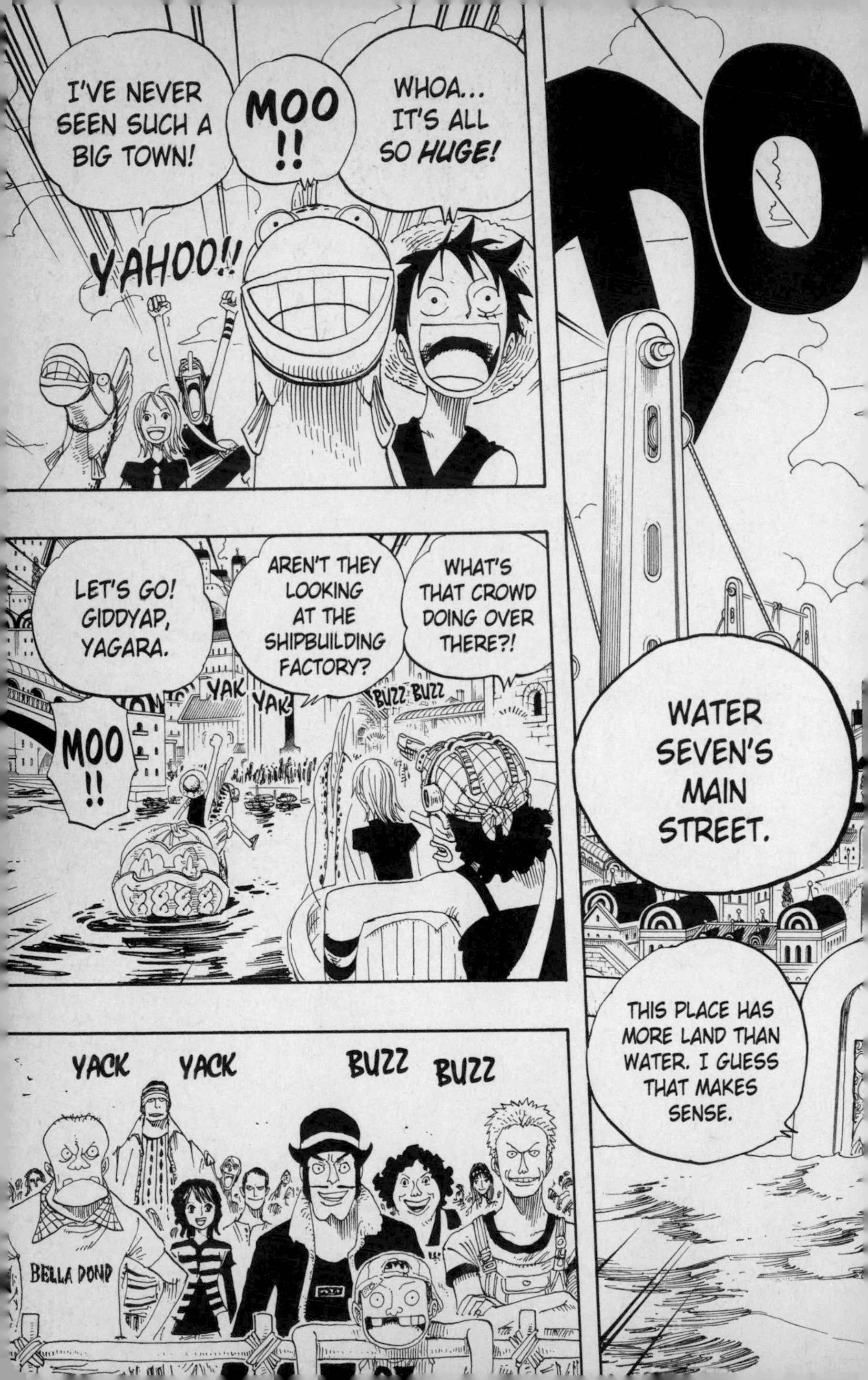
DO
WATER SEVEN'S MAIN STREET.
THIS PLACE HAS MORE LAND THAN WATER. I GUESS THAT MAKES SENSE.
WHOA... IT'S ALL SO HUGE!
MOO !!
I'VE NEVER SEEN SUCH A BIG TOWN!
YAHOO!!
WHAT'S THAT CROWD DOING OVER THERE?!
BUZZ BUZZ
AREN'T THEY LOOKING AT THE SHIPBUILDING FACTORY?
YAK YAK
LET'S GO! GIDDYAP, YAGARA.
MOO !!
BUZZ BUZZ
YACK YACK
BELLA DONP

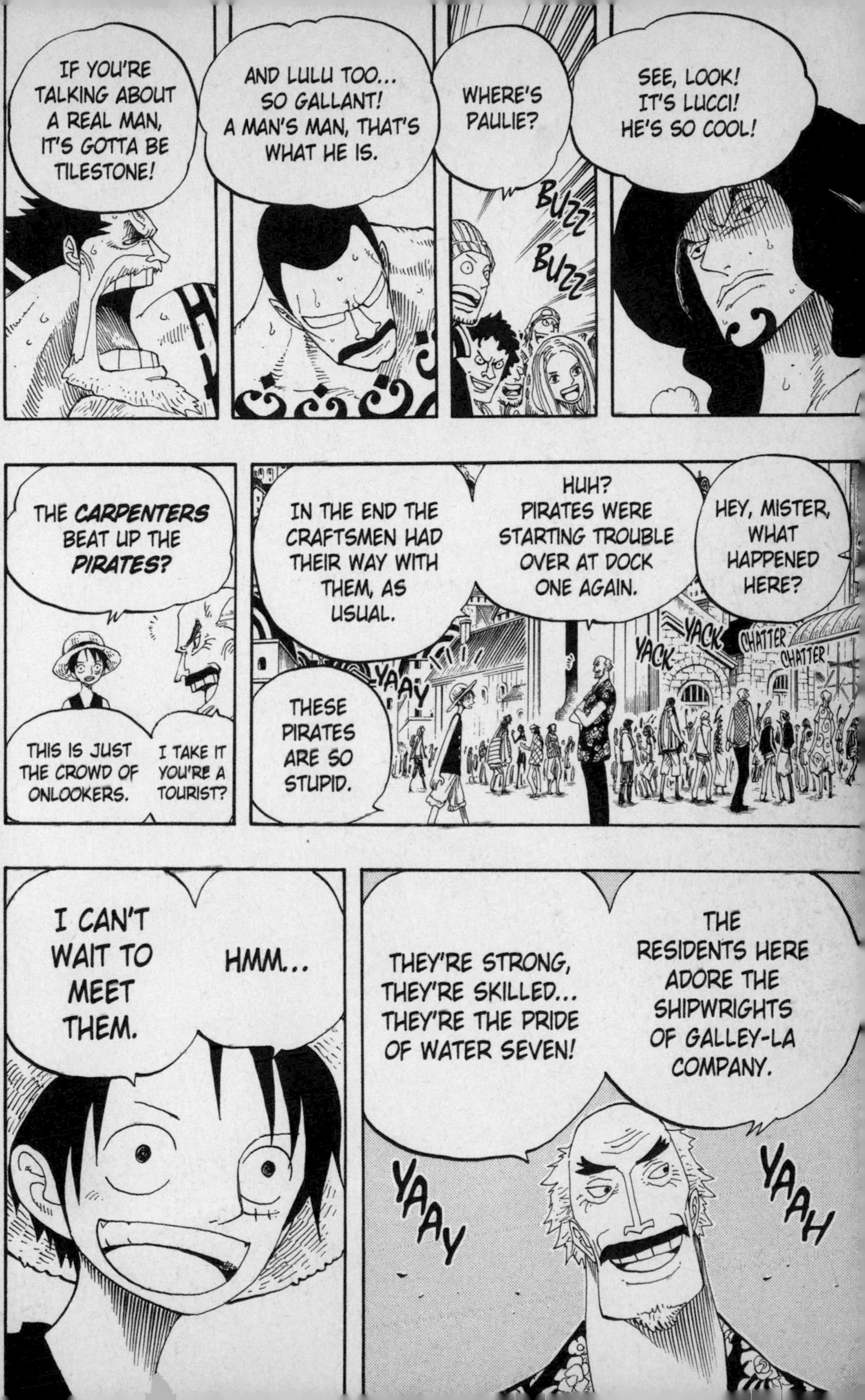
SEE, LOOK! IT'S LUCCI! HE'S SO COOL!
WHERE'S PAULIE?
BUZZ
BUZZ
AND LULU TOO... SO GALLANT! A MAN'S MAN, THAT'S WHAT HE IS.
IF YOU'RE TALKING ABOUT A REAL MAN, IT'S GOTTA BE TILESTONE!
HEY, MISTER, WHAT HAPPENED HERE?
HUH? PIRATES WERE STARTING TROUBLE OVER AT DOCK ONE AGAIN.
CHATTER
CHATTER
YACK
YACK
IN THE END THE CRAFTSMEN HAD THEIR WAY WITH THEM, AS USUAL.
YAAY
THESE PIRATES ARE SO STUPID.
THE *CARPENTERS* BEAT UP THE *PIRATES?*
I TAKE IT YOU'RE A TOURIST?
THIS IS JUST THE CROWD OF ONLOOKERS.
THE RESIDENTS HERE ADORE THE SHIPWRIGHTS OF GALLEY-LA COMPANY.
THEY'RE STRONG, THEY'RE SKILLED... THEY'RE THE PRIDE OF WATER SEVEN!
YAAH
YAAY
HMM...
I CAN'T WAIT TO MEET THEM.

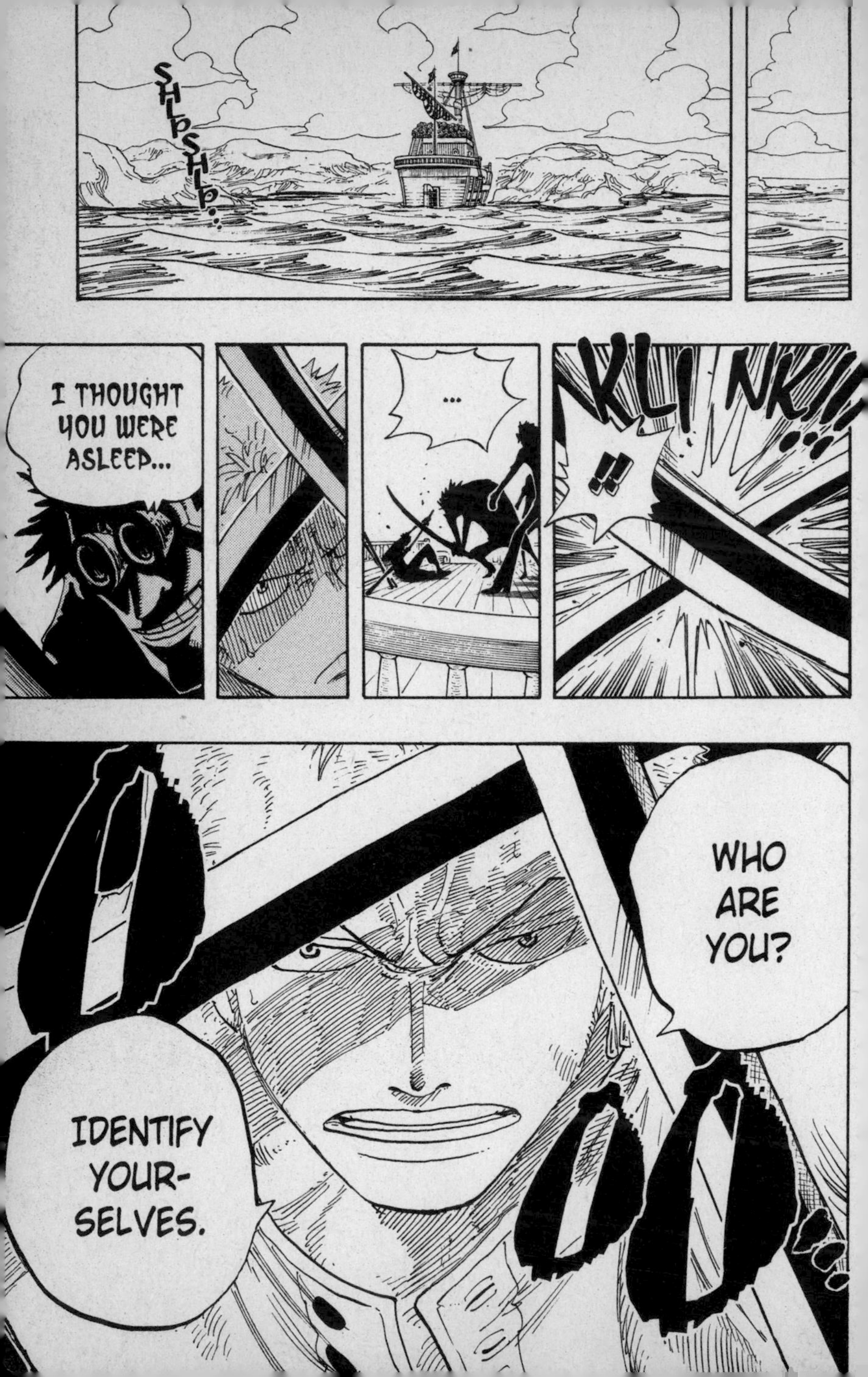
SHLPSHLP...
KLINK!!!
!!
...
I THOUGHT YOU WERE ASLEEP...
WHO ARE YOU?
IDENTIFY YOUR-SELVES.

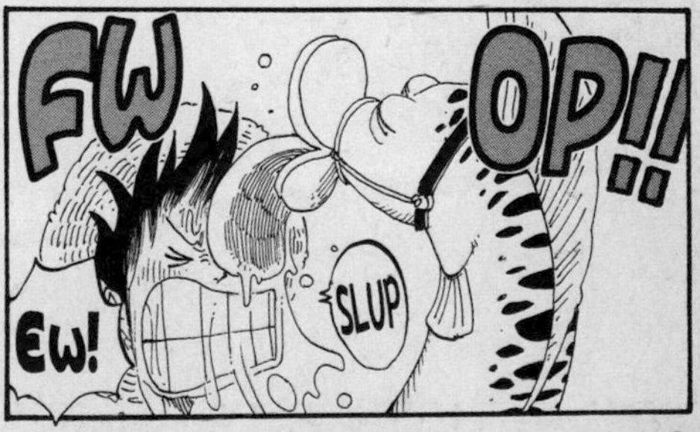
FW OP!!
SLUP
EW!

Chapter 325:

THE FRANKY FAMILY

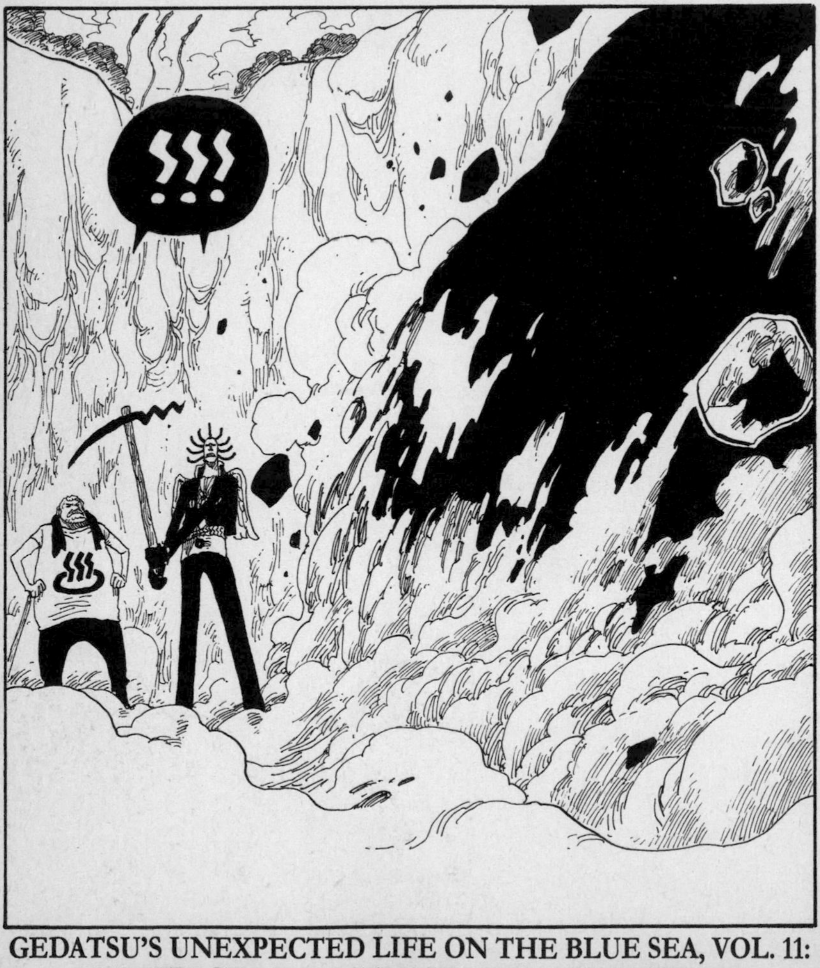

!!!

GEDATSU'S UNEXPECTED LIFE ON THE BLUE SEA, VOL. 11:
"UNEXPECTEDLY, I STRUCK UPON SOMETHING"

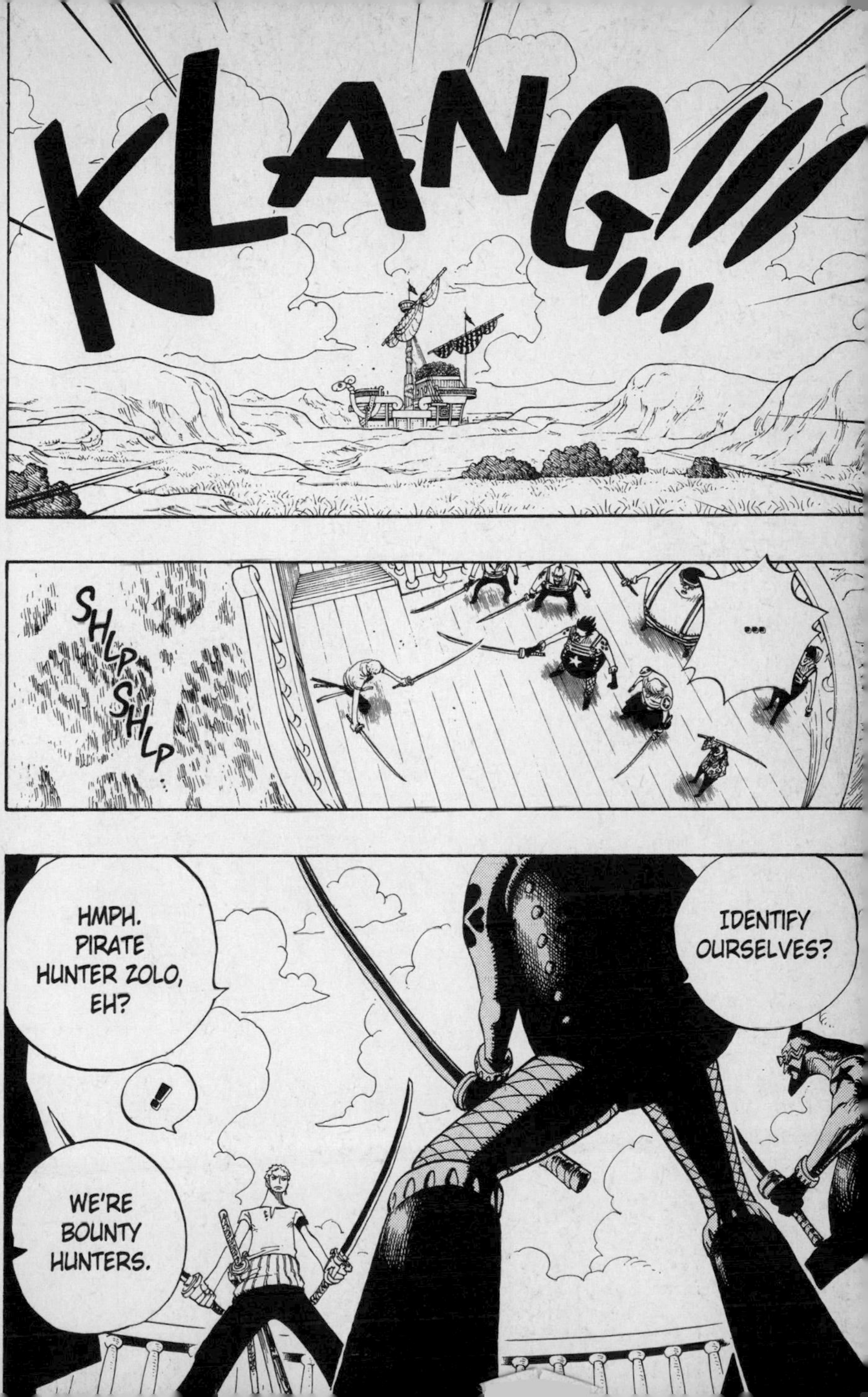
KLANG!!!
...
SHLP SHLP...
IDENTIFY OURSELVES?
HMPH. PIRATE HUNTER ZOLO, EH?
!
WE'RE BOUNTY HUNTERS.

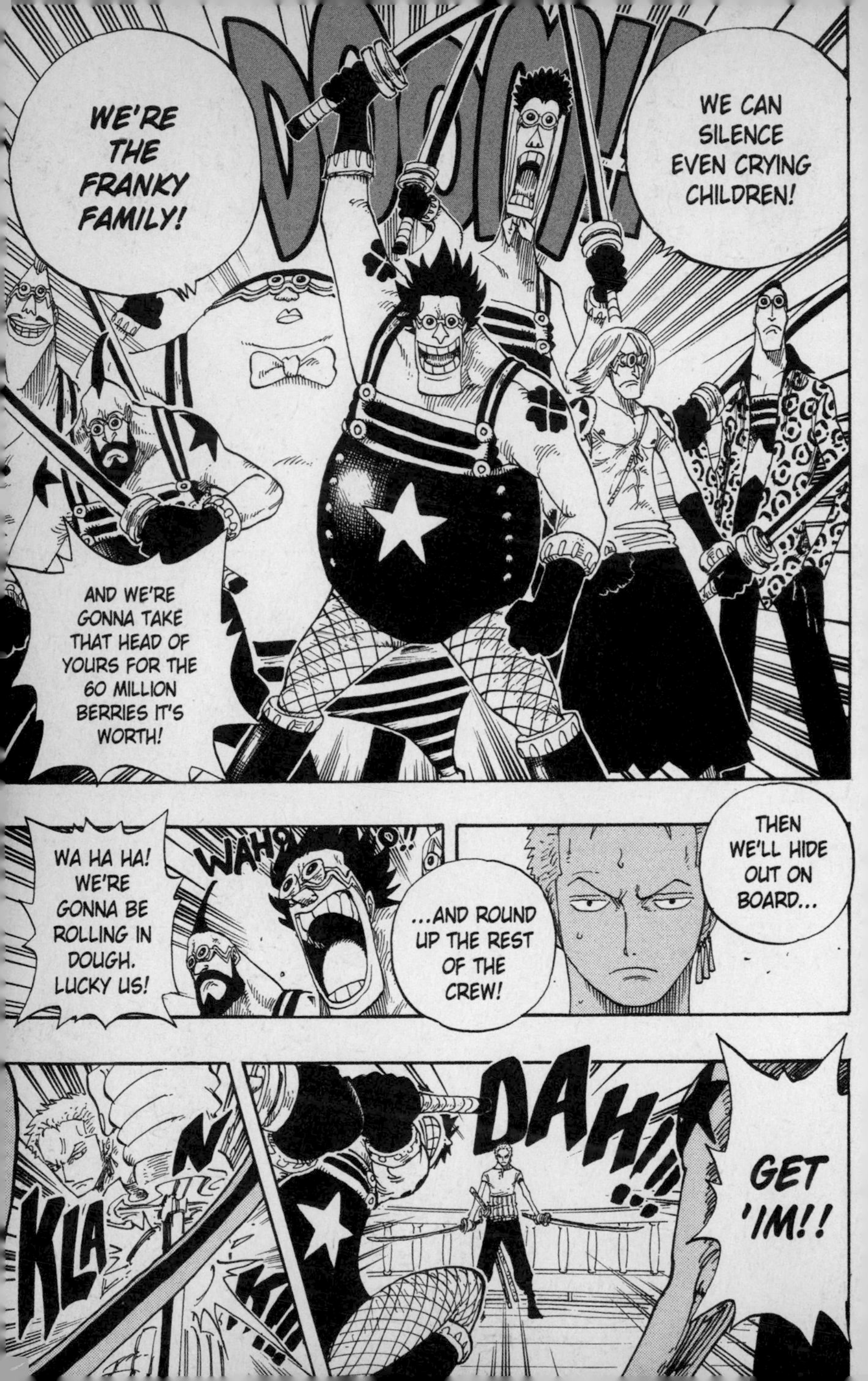
WE CAN SILENCE EVEN CRYING CHILDREN!
DOOOM!
WE'RE THE FRANKY FAMILY!
AND WE'RE GONNA TAKE THAT HEAD OF YOURS FOR THE 60 MILLION BERRIES IT'S WORTH!
THEN WE'LL HIDE OUT ON BOARD...
...AND ROUND UP THE REST OF THE CREW!
WA HA HA! WE'RE GONNA BE ROLLING IN DOUGH. LUCKY US!
GET 'IM!!
DAH!!!
KLANK!!

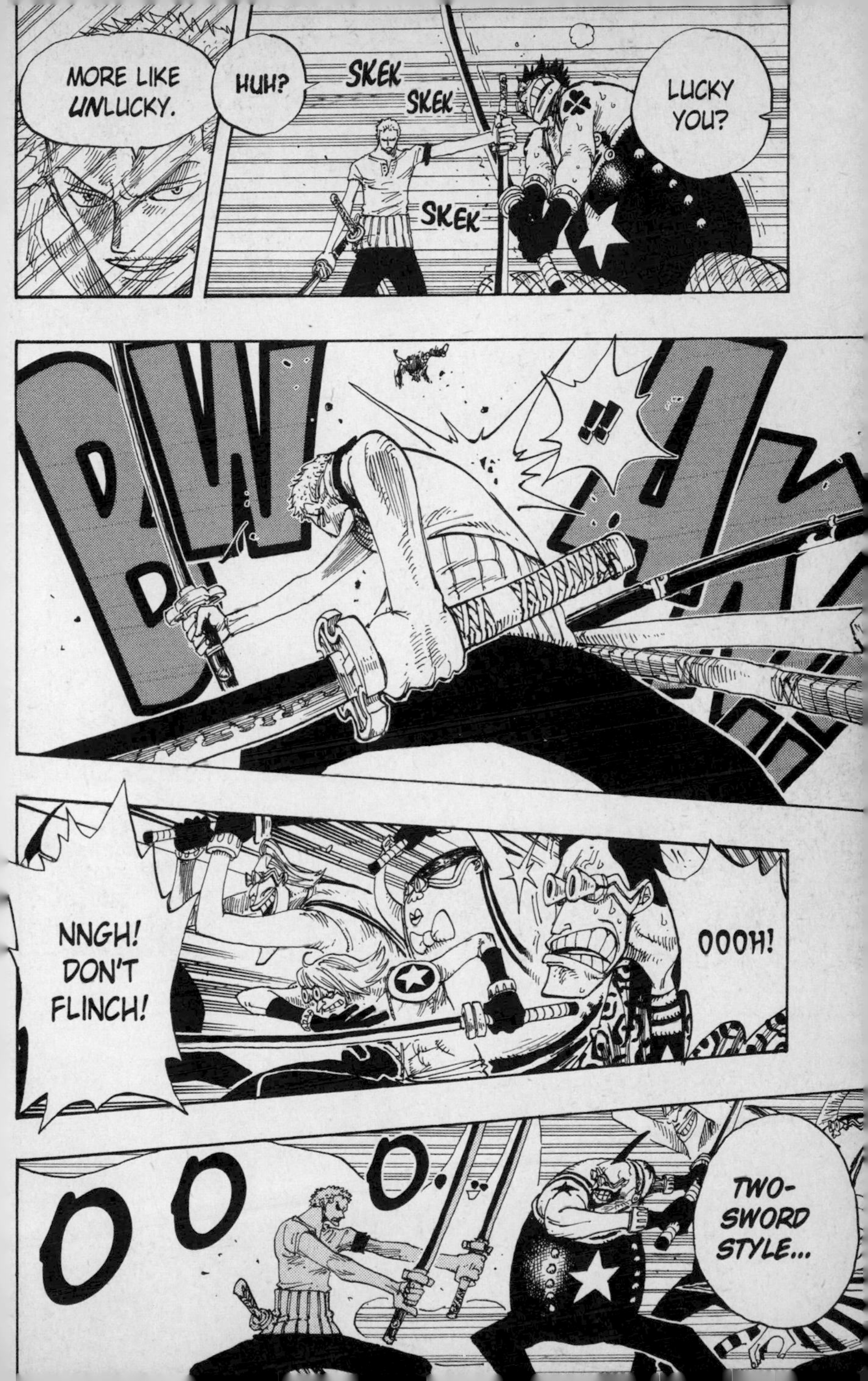
LUCKY YOU?
HUH?
SKEK
SKEK
SKEK
MORE LIKE UNLUCKY.
!!
OOOH!
NNGH! DON'T FLINCH!
TWO-SWORD STYLE...

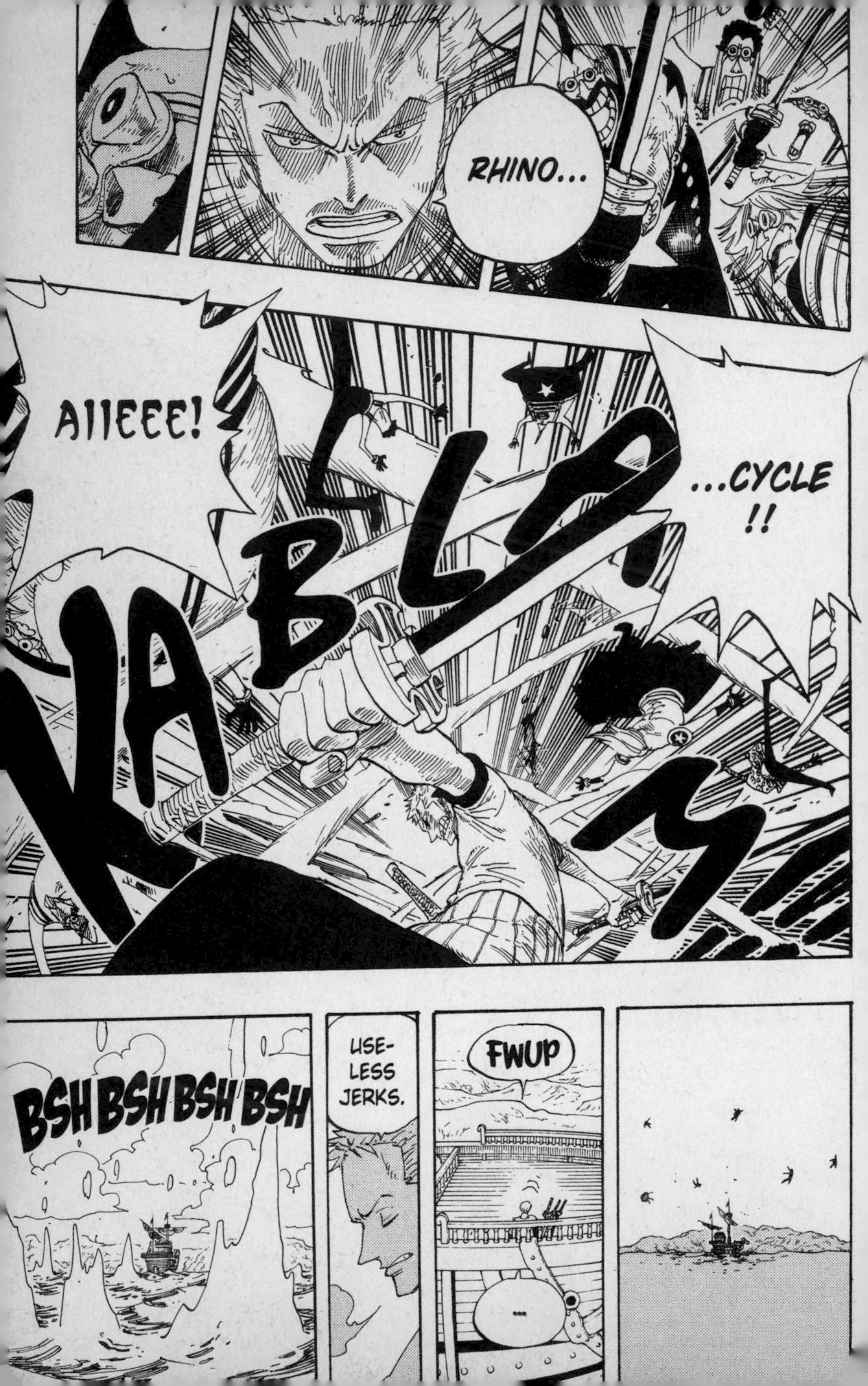
RHINO...
...CYCLE !!
AIIEEE!
KABLAM
FWUP
...
USELESS JERKS.
BSH BSH BSH BSH

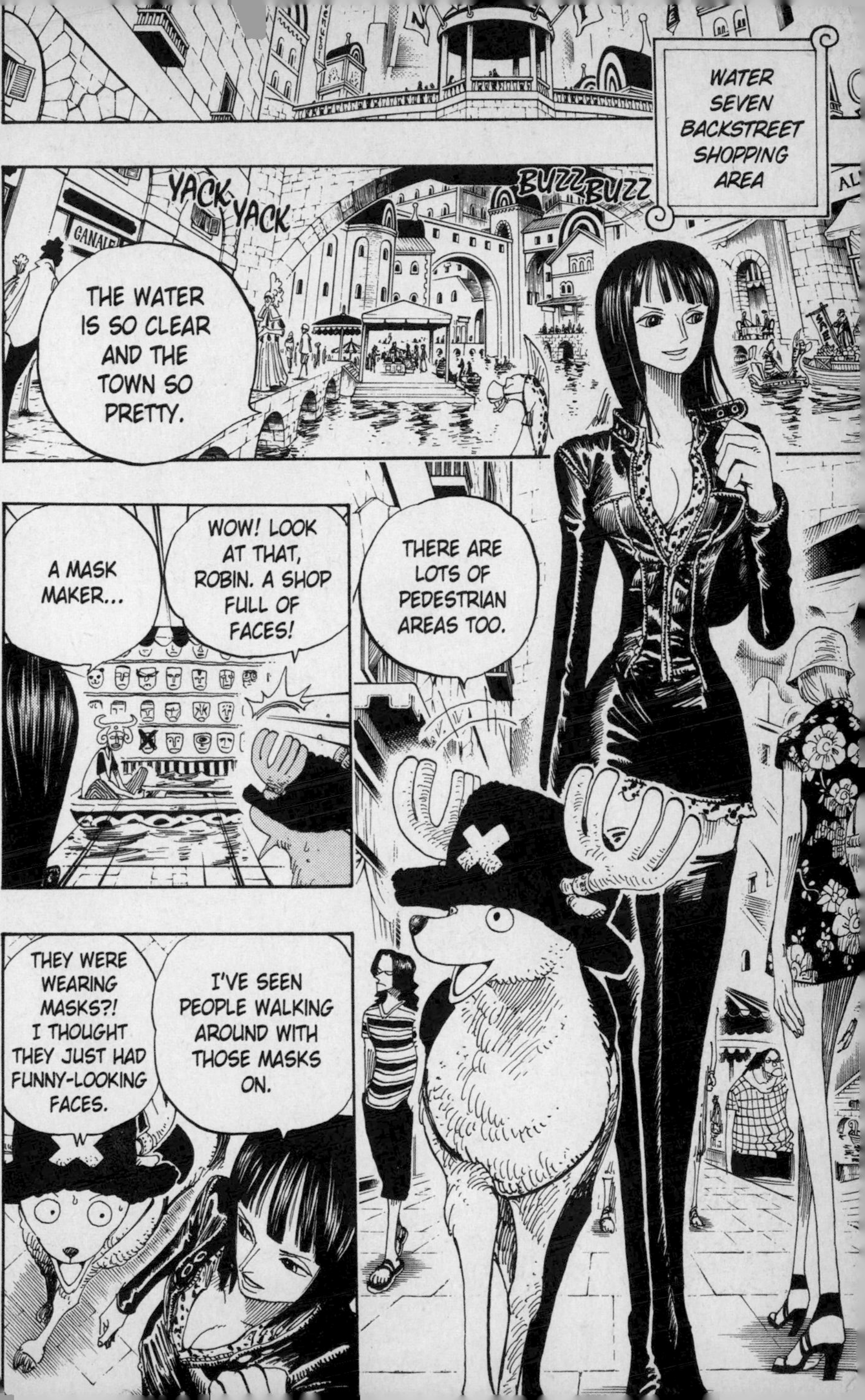
WATER SEVEN BACKSTREET SHOPPING AREA
BUZZ BUZZ
YACK YACK
CANALE
THE WATER IS SO CLEAR AND THE TOWN SO PRETTY.
THERE ARE LOTS OF PEDESTRIAN AREAS TOO.
WOW! LOOK AT THAT, ROBIN. A SHOP FULL OF FACES!
A MASK MAKER...
I'VE SEEN PEOPLE WALKING AROUND WITH THOSE MASKS ON.
THEY WERE WEARING MASKS?! I THOUGHT THEY JUST HAD FUNNY-LOOKING FACES.

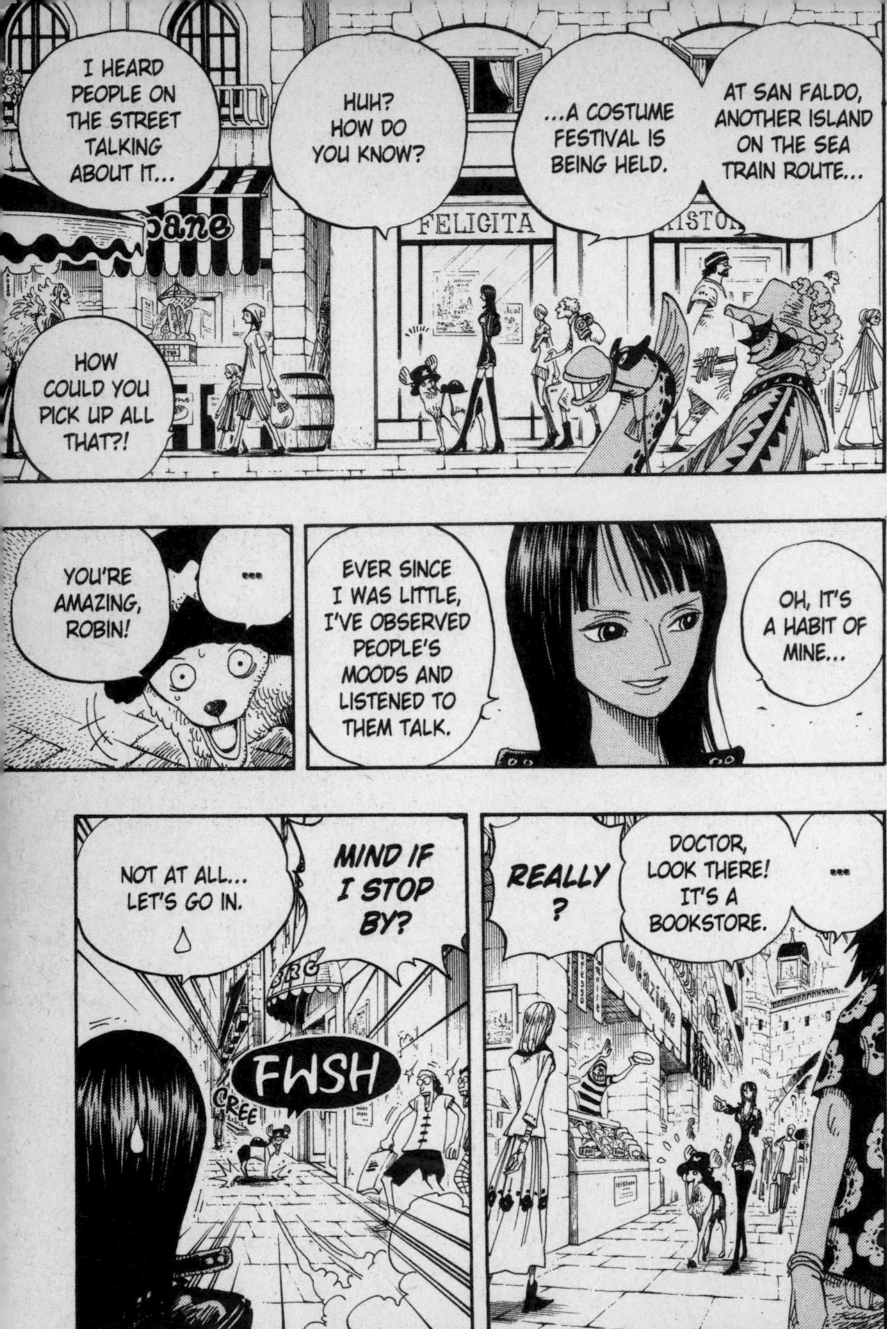
AT SAN FALDO, ANOTHER ISLAND ON THE SEA TRAIN ROUTE...
...A COSTUME FESTIVAL IS BEING HELD.
HUH? HOW DO YOU KNOW?
I HEARD PEOPLE ON THE STREET TALKING ABOUT IT...
HOW COULD YOU PICK UP ALL THAT?!
OH, IT'S A HABIT OF MINE...
EVER SINCE I WAS LITTLE, I'VE OBSERVED PEOPLE'S MOODS AND LISTENED TO THEM TALK.
...
YOU'RE AMAZING, ROBIN!
...
DOCTOR, LOOK THERE! IT'S A BOOKSTORE.
REALLY?
MIND IF I STOP BY?
NOT AT ALL... LET'S GO IN.
FWSH
CREE

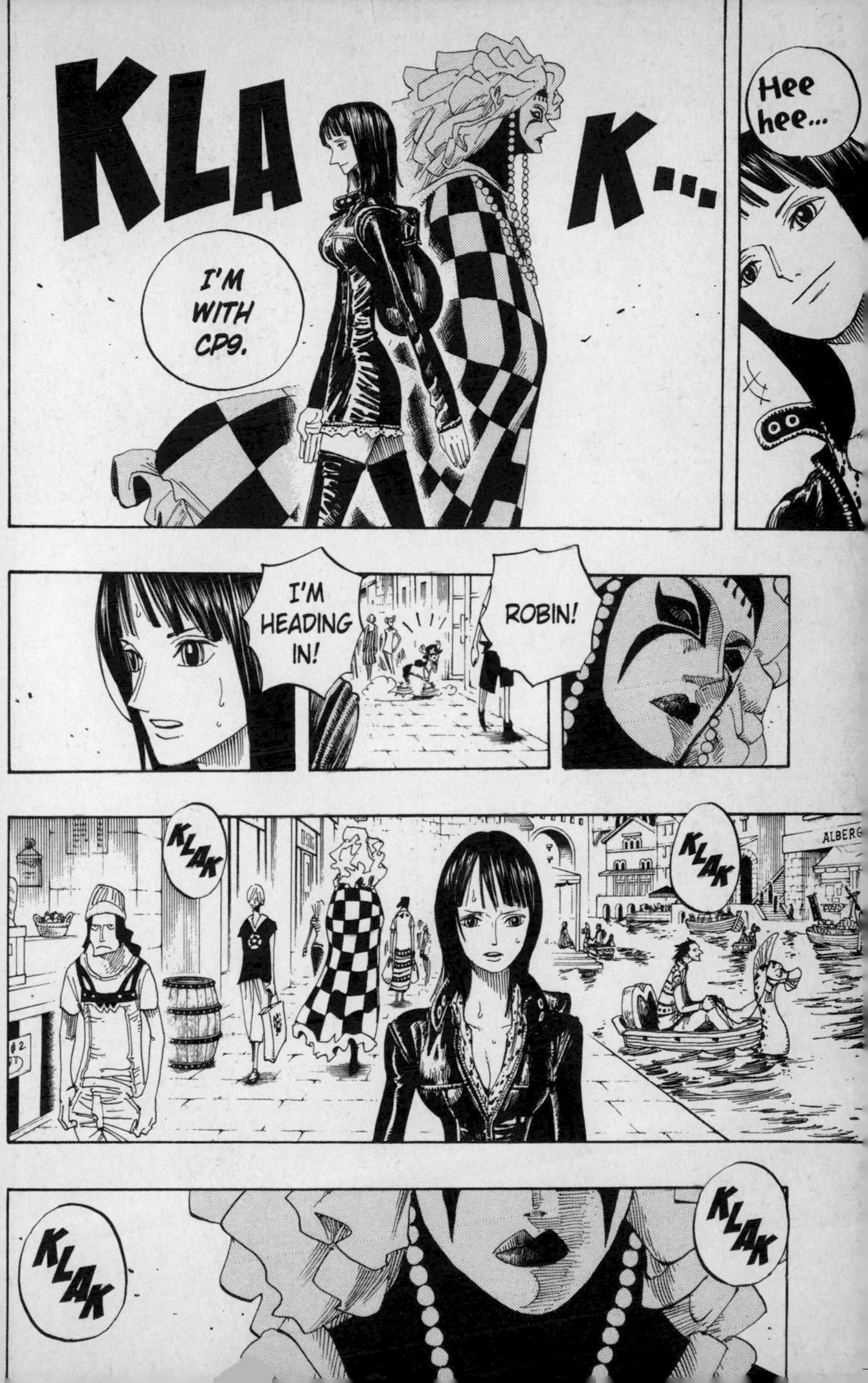
Hee hee...
KLA K...
I'M WITH CP9.
ROBIN!
I'M HEADING IN!
ALBERG
KLAK
KLAK
KLAK
KLAK

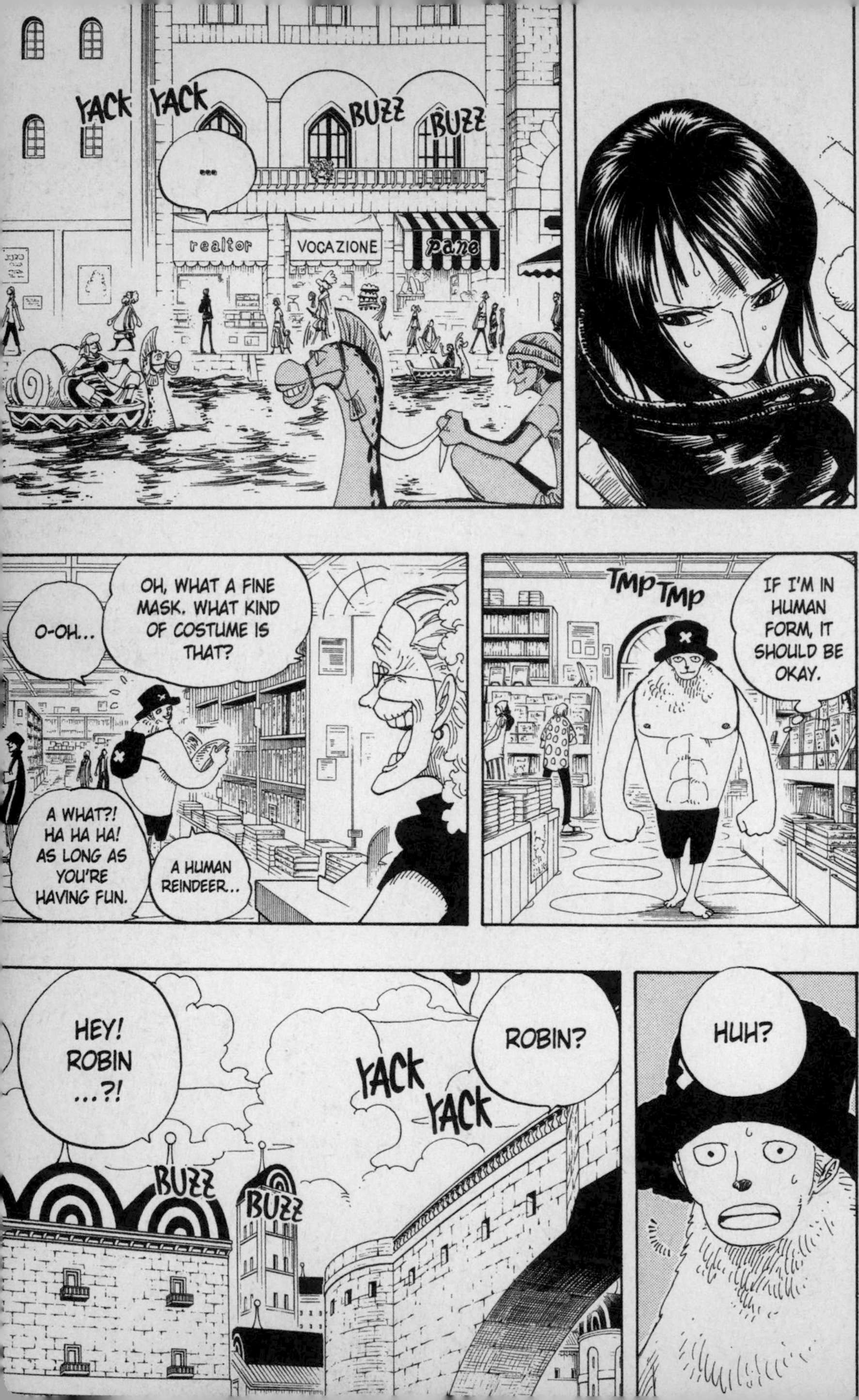
BUZZ BUZZ
YACK YACK
...
pane
VOCAZIONE
realtor
TMP TMP
IF I'M IN HUMAN FORM, IT SHOULD BE OKAY.
OH, WHAT A FINE MASK. WHAT KIND OF COSTUME IS THAT?
O-OH...
A HUMAN REINDEER...
A WHAT?! HA HA HA! AS LONG AS YOU'RE HAVING FUN.
HUH?
ROBIN?
YACK YACK
HEY! ROBIN ...?!
BUZZ BUZZ

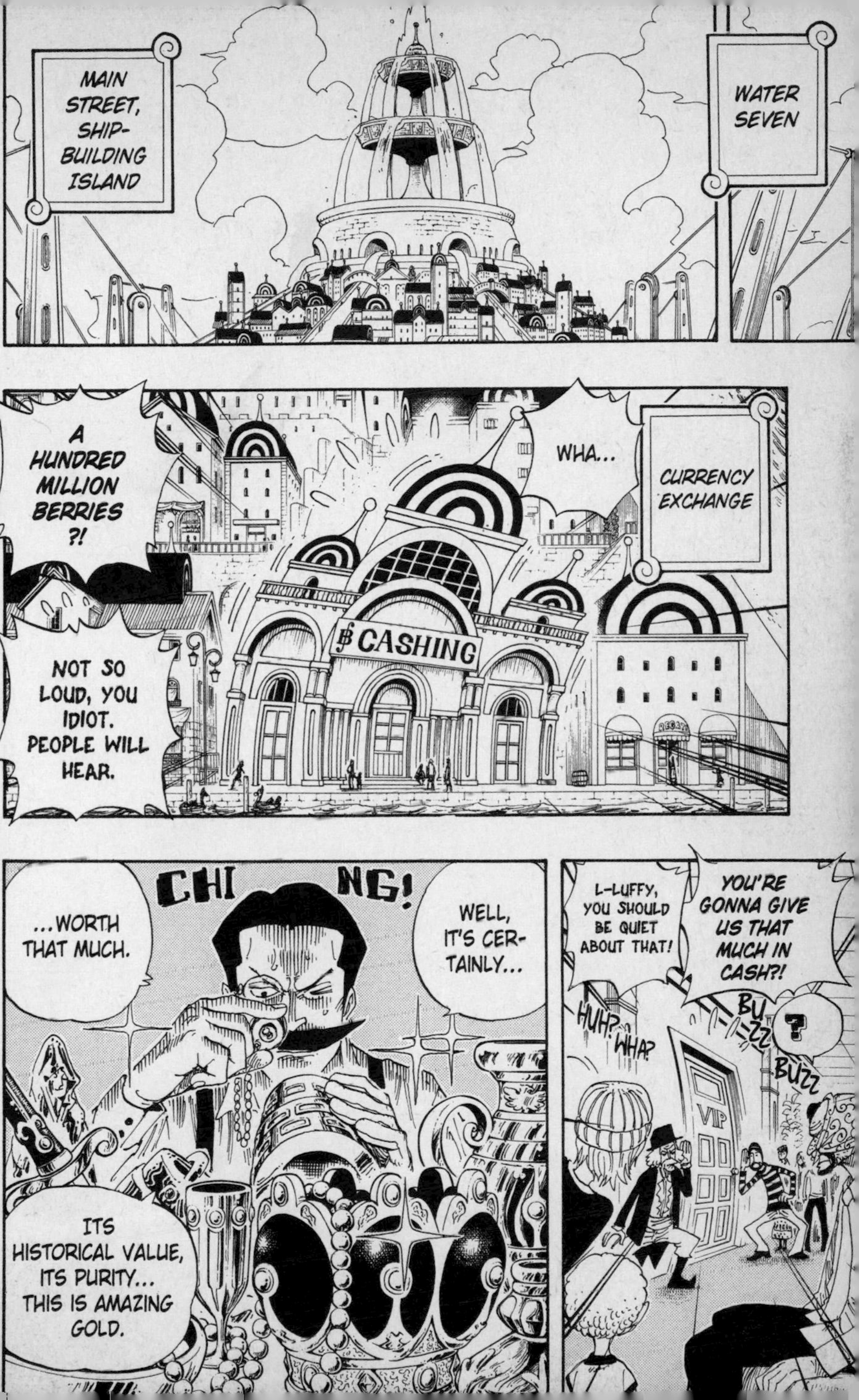
WATER SEVEN
MAIN STREET, SHIP-BUILDING ISLAND
CURRENCY EXCHANGE
WHA...
A HUNDRED MILLION BERRIES?!
฿ CASHING
NOT SO LOUD, YOU IDIOT. PEOPLE WILL HEAR.
YOU'RE GONNA GIVE US THAT MUCH IN CASH?!
L-LUFFY, YOU SHOULD BE QUIET ABOUT THAT!
BUZZ
?
HUH? WHA?
BUZZ
VIP
CHING!
WELL, IT'S CERTAINLY...
...WORTH THAT MUCH.
ITS HISTORICAL VALUE, ITS PURITY... THIS IS AMAZING GOLD.

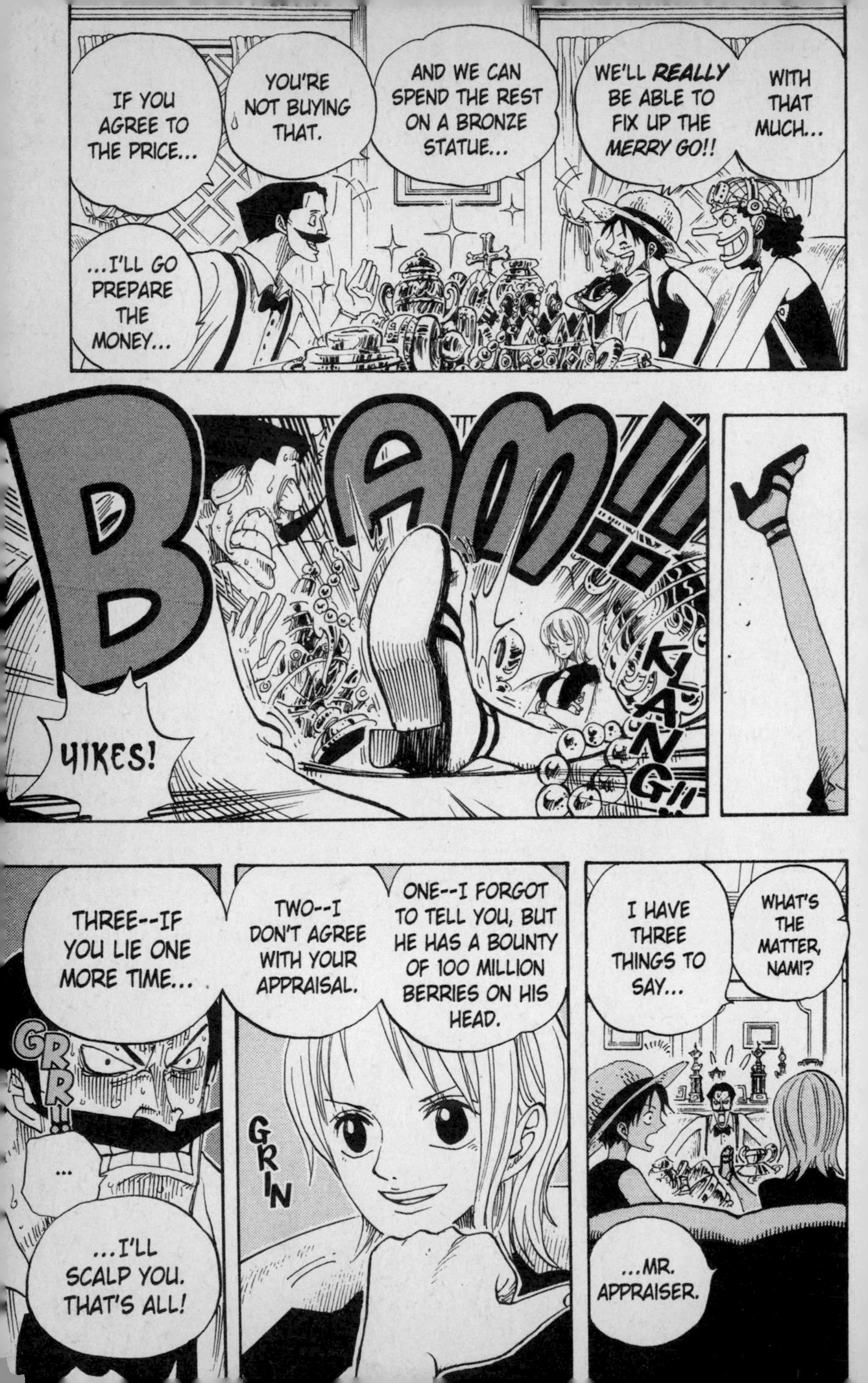
WITH THAT MUCH...
WE'LL *REALLY* BE ABLE TO FIX UP THE *MERRY GO*!!
AND WE CAN SPEND THE REST ON A BRONZE STATUE...
YOU'RE NOT BUYING THAT.
IF YOU AGREE TO THE PRICE...
...I'LL GO PREPARE THE MONEY...
KLANG!!
BAM!!
YIKES!
WHAT'S THE MATTER, NAMI?
I HAVE THREE THINGS TO SAY...
...MR. APPRAISER.
ONE--I FORGOT TO TELL YOU, BUT HE HAS A BOUNTY OF 100 MILLION BERRIES ON HIS HEAD.
TWO--I DON'T AGREE WITH YOUR APPRAISAL.
GRIN
THREE--IF YOU LIE ONE MORE TIME...
GRR
...
...I'LL SCALP YOU. THAT'S ALL!

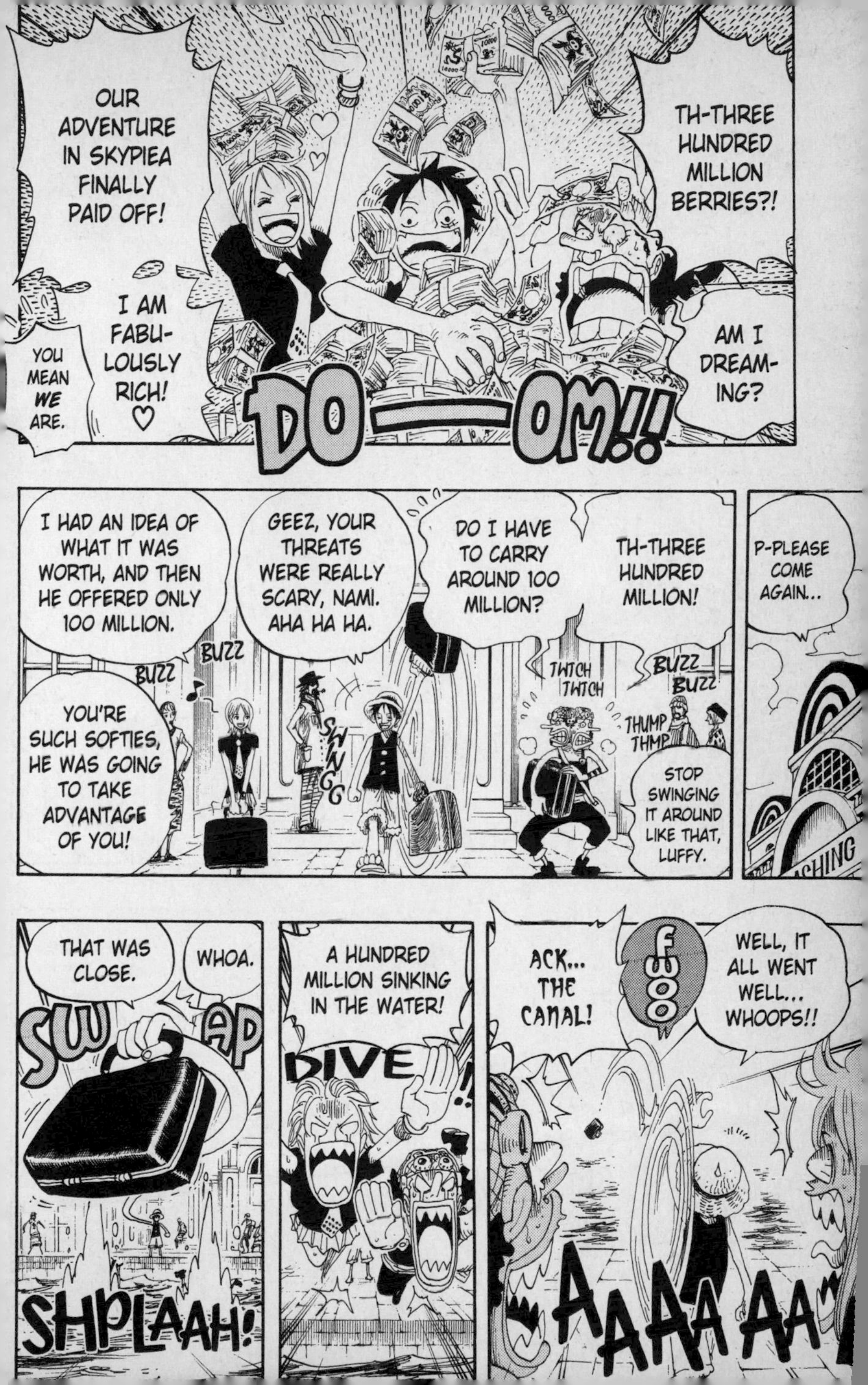
TH-THREE HUNDRED MILLION BERRIES?!
AM I DREAMING?
OUR ADVENTURE IN SKYPIEA FINALLY PAID OFF!
I AM FABULOUSLY RICH! ♡
YOU MEAN WE ARE.
DO—OM!!
P-PLEASE COME AGAIN...
TH-THREE HUNDRED MILLION!
DO I HAVE TO CARRY AROUND 100 MILLION?
GEEZ, YOUR THREATS WERE REALLY SCARY, NAMI. AHA HA HA.
I HAD AN IDEA OF WHAT IT WAS WORTH, AND THEN HE OFFERED ONLY 100 MILLION.
BUZZ BUZZ
TWITCH TWITCH
THUMP THMP
STOP SWINGING IT AROUND LIKE THAT, LUFFY.
SWINGG
BUZZ BUZZ
YOU'RE SUCH SOFTIES, HE WAS GOING TO TAKE ADVANTAGE OF YOU!
WELL, IT ALL WENT WELL... WHOOPS!!
FWOO
ACK... THE CANAL!
AAAAAA
A HUNDRED MILLION SINKING IN THE WATER!
DIVE!!
WHOA.
THAT WAS CLOSE.
SWAP
SHPLAAH!

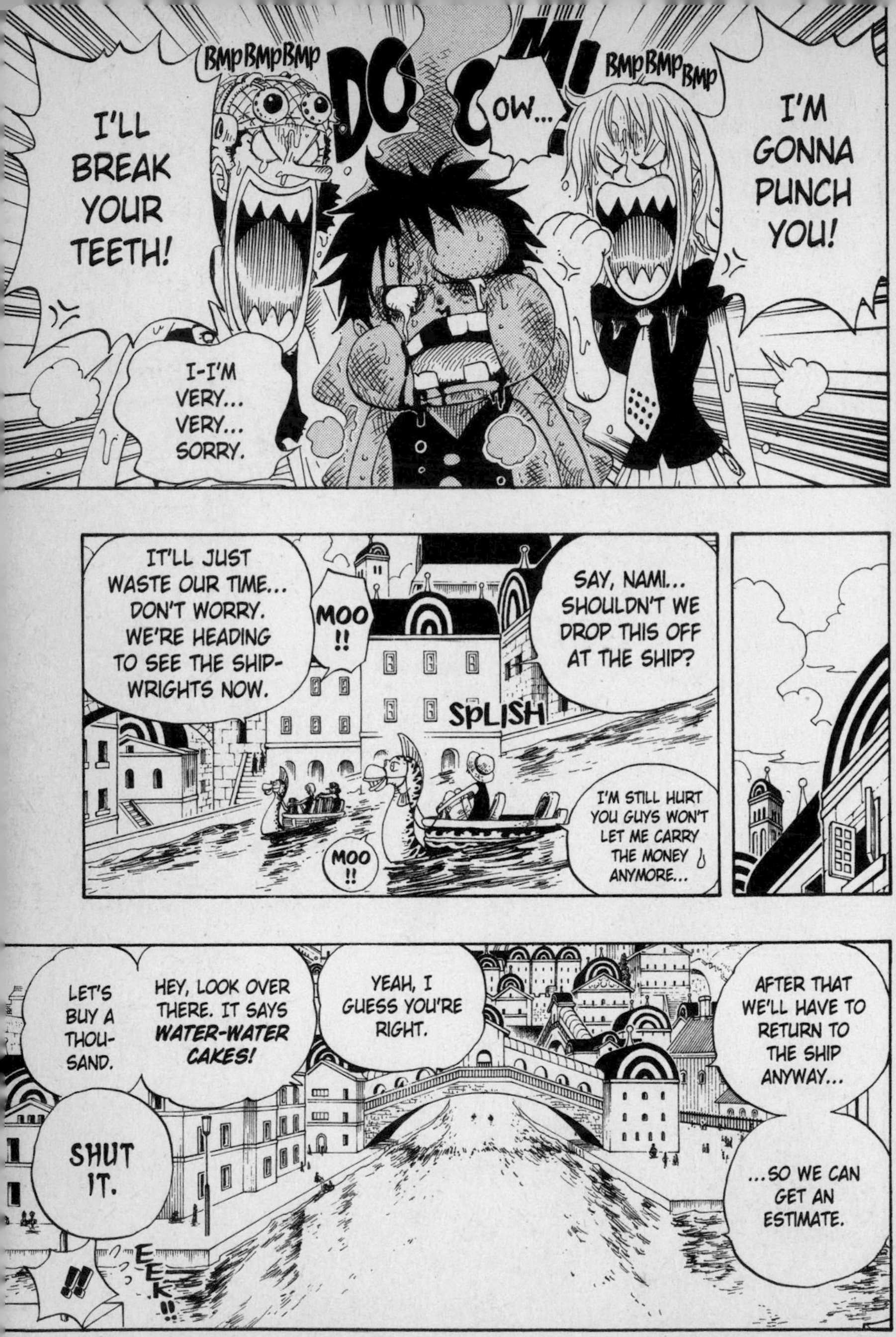
BmpBmpBmp
I'M GONNA PUNCH YOU!
OW...
BmpBmpBmp
I'LL BREAK YOUR TEETH!
I-I'M VERY... VERY... SORRY.
SAY, NAMI... SHOULDN'T WE DROP THIS OFF AT THE SHIP?
MOO!!
IT'LL JUST WASTE OUR TIME... DON'T WORRY. WE'RE HEADING TO SEE THE SHIP-WRIGHTS NOW.
SPLISH
I'M STILL HURT YOU GUYS WON'T LET ME CARRY THE MONEY ANYMORE...
MOO!!
AFTER THAT WE'LL HAVE TO RETURN TO THE SHIP ANYWAY...
...SO WE CAN GET AN ESTIMATE.
YEAH, I GUESS YOU'RE RIGHT.
HEY, LOOK OVER THERE. IT SAYS WATER-WATER CAKES!
LET'S BUY A THOUSAND.
SHUT IT.
!!
EEK!!

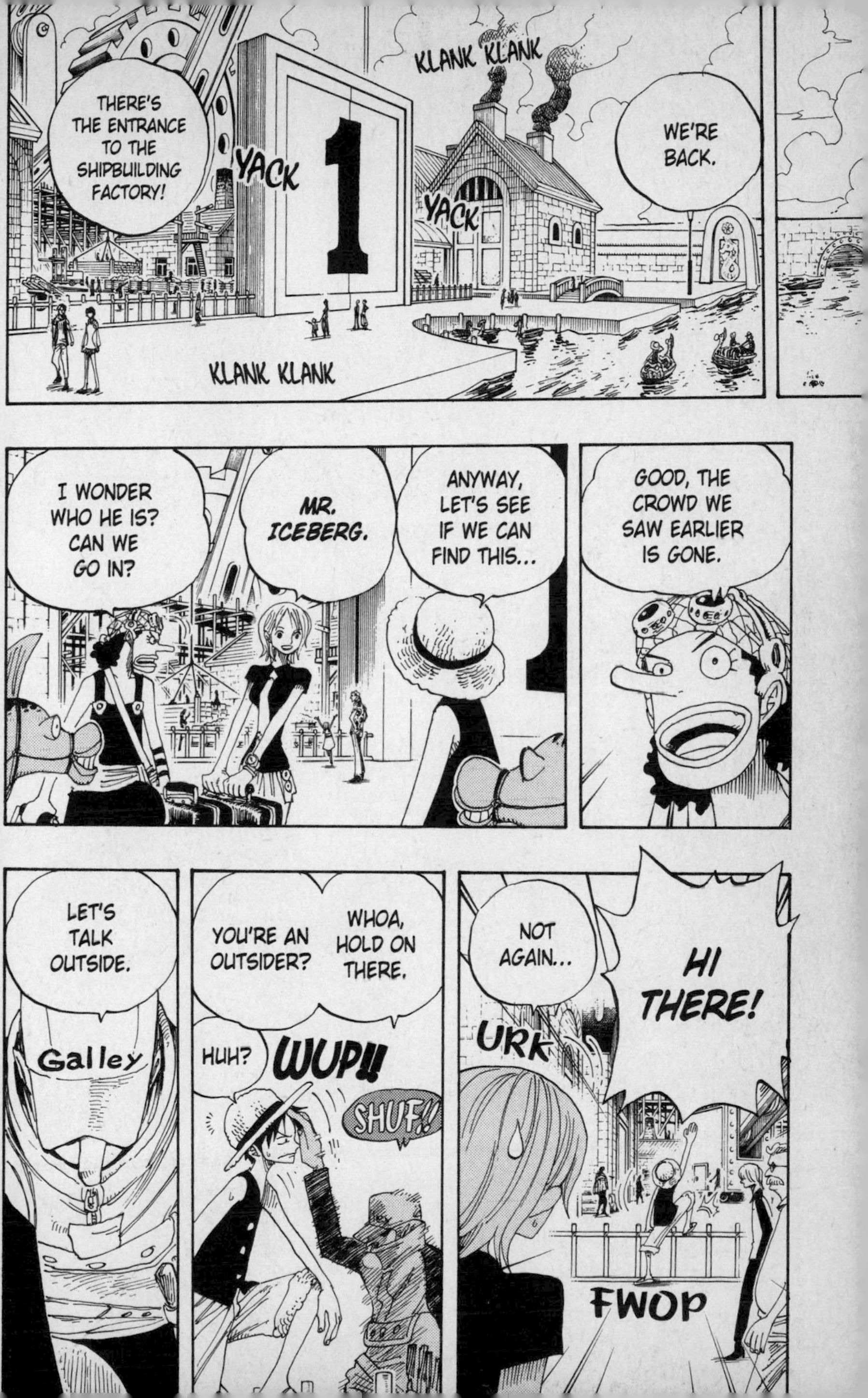
WE'RE BACK.
KLANK KLANK
THERE'S THE ENTRANCE TO THE SHIPBUILDING FACTORY!
YACK
YACK
KLANK KLANK
GOOD, THE CROWD WE SAW EARLIER IS GONE.
ANYWAY, LET'S SEE IF WE CAN FIND THIS...
MR. ICEBERG.
I WONDER WHO HE IS? CAN WE GO IN?
HI THERE!
NOT AGAIN...
URK
FWOP
WHOA, HOLD ON THERE.
YOU'RE AN OUTSIDER?
WUP!!
HUH?
SHUF!!
LET'S TALK OUTSIDE.
Galley

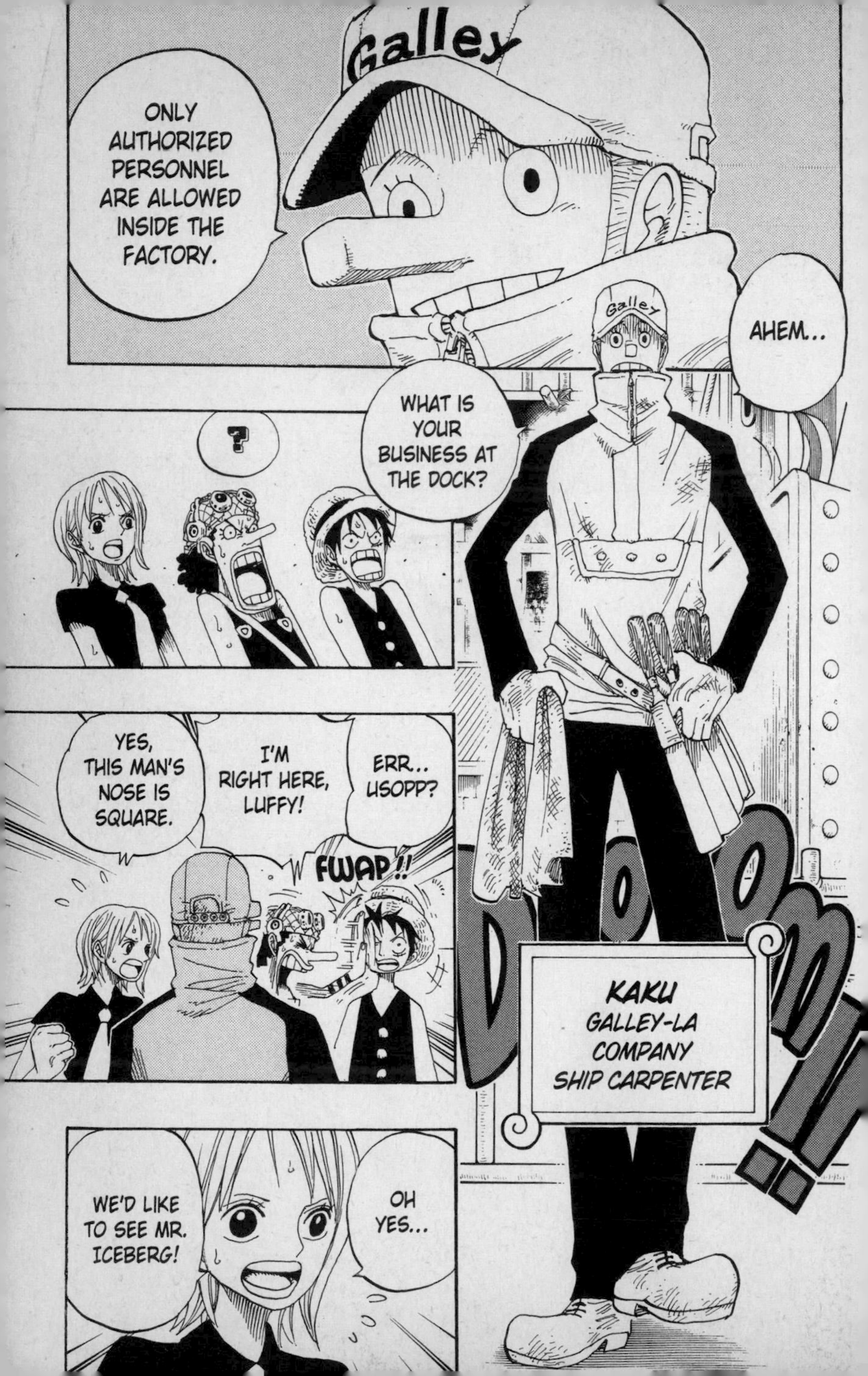

AHEM...
ONLY AUTHORIZED PERSONNEL ARE ALLOWED INSIDE THE FACTORY.
WHAT IS YOUR BUSINESS AT THE DOCK?
?
KAKU GALLEY-LA COMPANY SHIP CARPENTER
ERR.. USOPP?
I'M RIGHT HERE, LUFFY!
FWAP!!
YES, THIS MAN'S NOSE IS SQUARE.
OH YES...
WE'D LIKE TO SEE MR. ICEBERG!

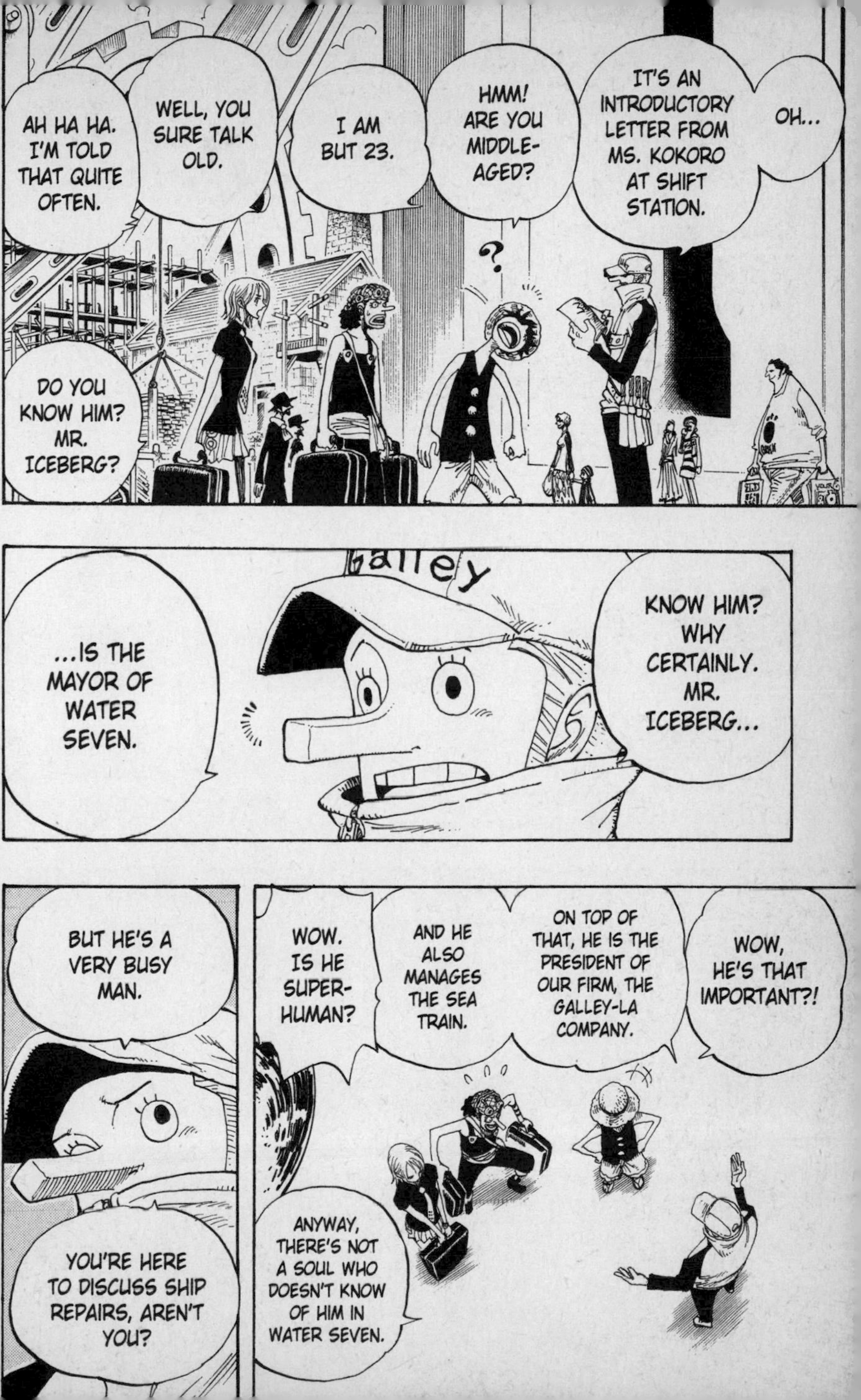
OH...
IT'S AN INTRODUCTORY LETTER FROM MS. KOKORO AT SHIFT STATION.
HMM! ARE YOU MIDDLE-AGED?
I AM BUT 23.
WELL, YOU SURE TALK OLD.
AH HA HA. I'M TOLD THAT QUITE OFTEN.
DO YOU KNOW HIM? MR. ICEBERG?
KNOW HIM? WHY CERTAINLY. MR. ICEBERG...
...IS THE MAYOR OF WATER SEVEN.
WOW, HE'S THAT IMPORTANT?!
ON TOP OF THAT, HE IS THE PRESIDENT OF OUR FIRM, THE GALLEY-LA COMPANY.
AND HE ALSO MANAGES THE SEA TRAIN.
WOW. IS HE SUPER-HUMAN?
ANYWAY, THERE'S NOT A SOUL WHO DOESN'T KNOW OF HIM IN WATER SEVEN.
BUT HE'S A VERY BUSY MAN.
YOU'RE HERE TO DISCUSS SHIP REPAIRS, AREN'T YOU?

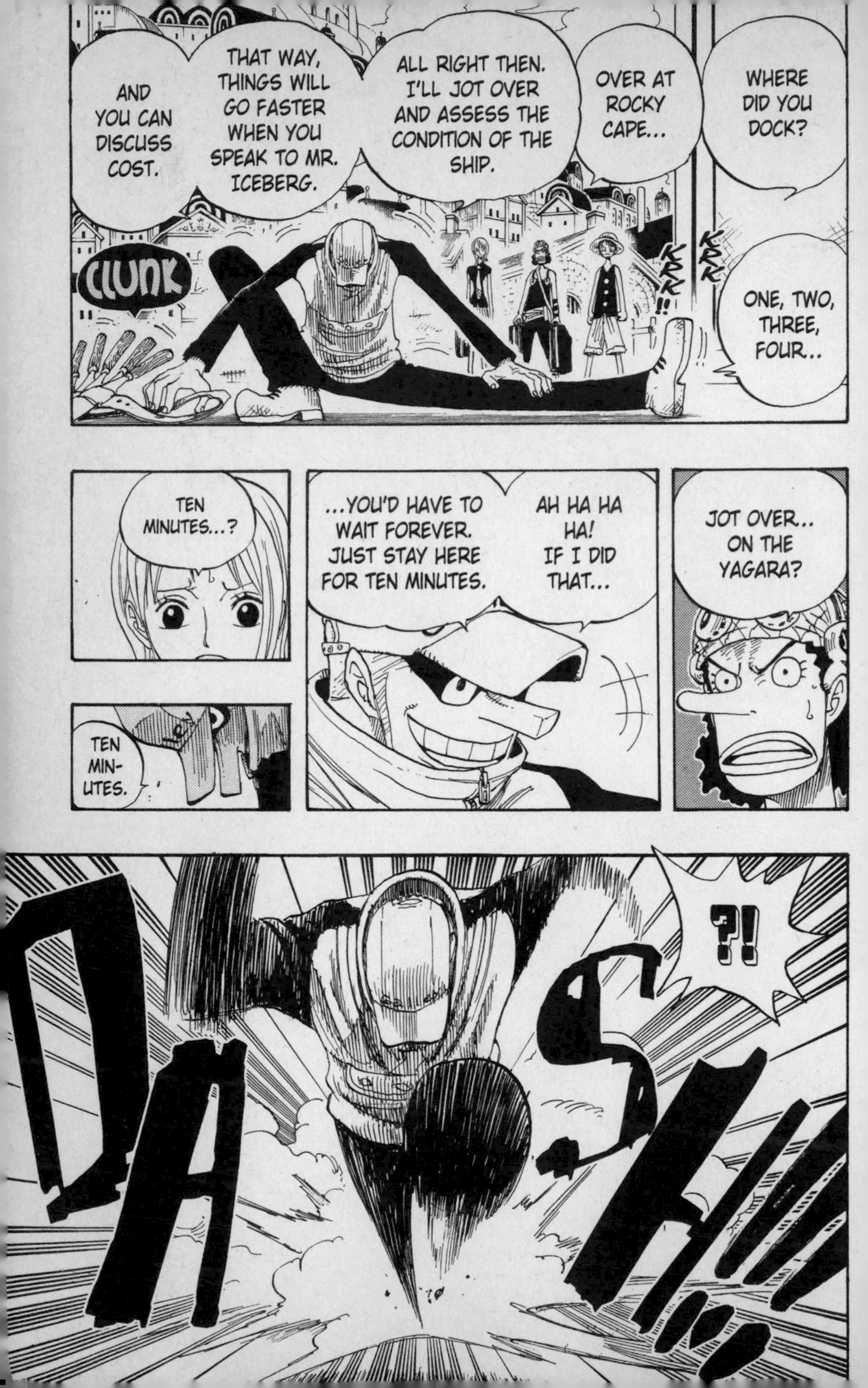
WHERE DID YOU DOCK?
OVER AT ROCKY CAPE...
ALL RIGHT THEN. I'LL JOT OVER AND ASSESS THE CONDITION OF THE SHIP.
THAT WAY, THINGS WILL GO FASTER WHEN YOU SPEAK TO MR. ICEBERG.
AND YOU CAN DISCUSS COST.
KRK
KRK!!
ONE, TWO, THREE, FOUR...
CLUNK
JOT OVER... ON THE YAGARA?
AH HA HA HA! IF I DID THAT...
...YOU'D HAVE TO WAIT FOREVER. JUST STAY HERE FOR TEN MINUTES.
TEN MINUTES...?
TEN MIN-UTES.
?!
DASH!!

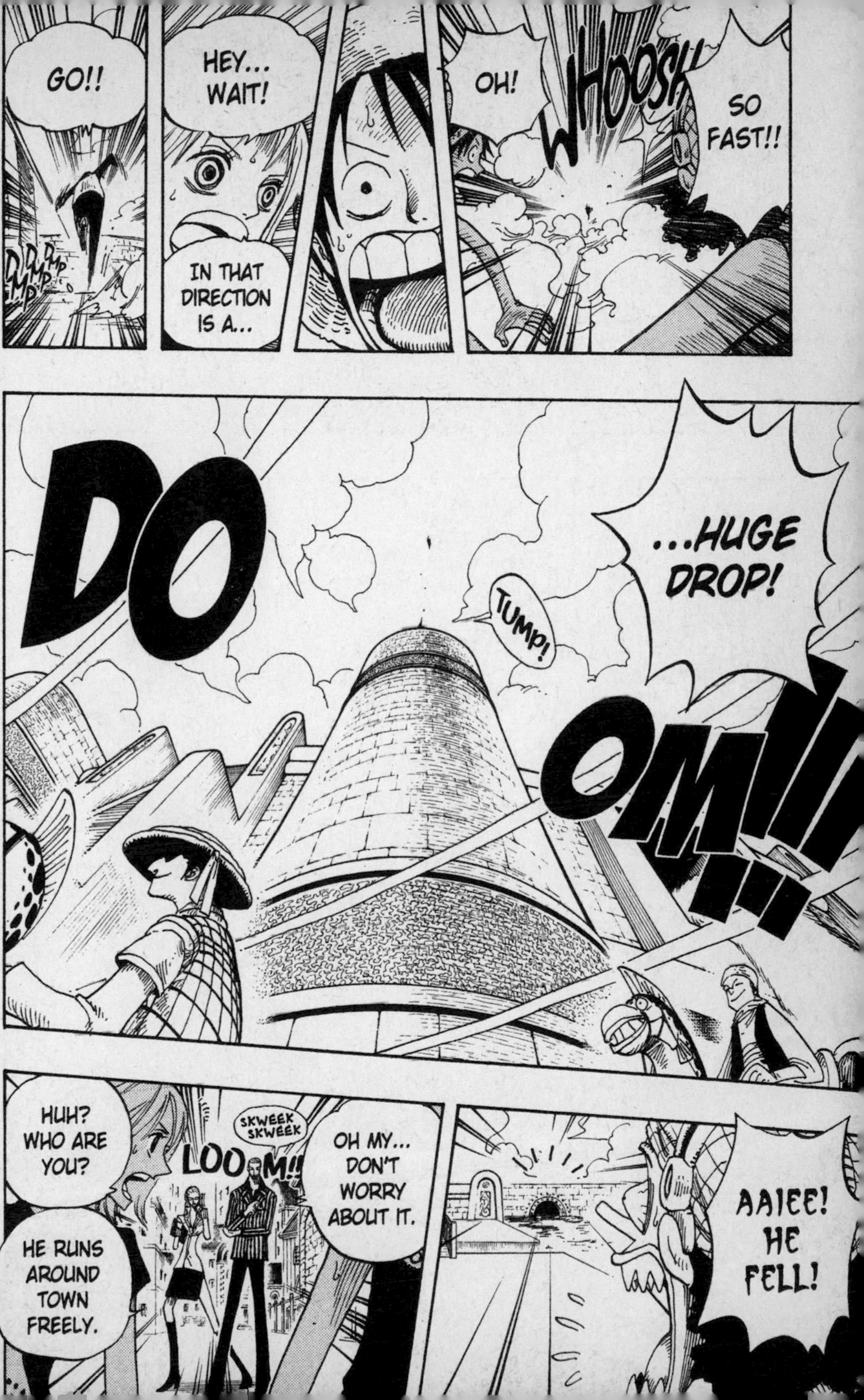
SO FAST!!
WHOOSH
OH!
HEY... WAIT!
IN THAT DIRECTION IS A...
GO!!
DMP DMP DMP
...HUGE DROP!
TUMP!
DOOM!!!
AAIEE! HE FELL!
OH MY... DON'T WORRY ABOUT IT.
SKWEEK SKWEEK
LOOM!!
HUH? WHO ARE YOU?
HE RUNS AROUND TOWN FREELY.

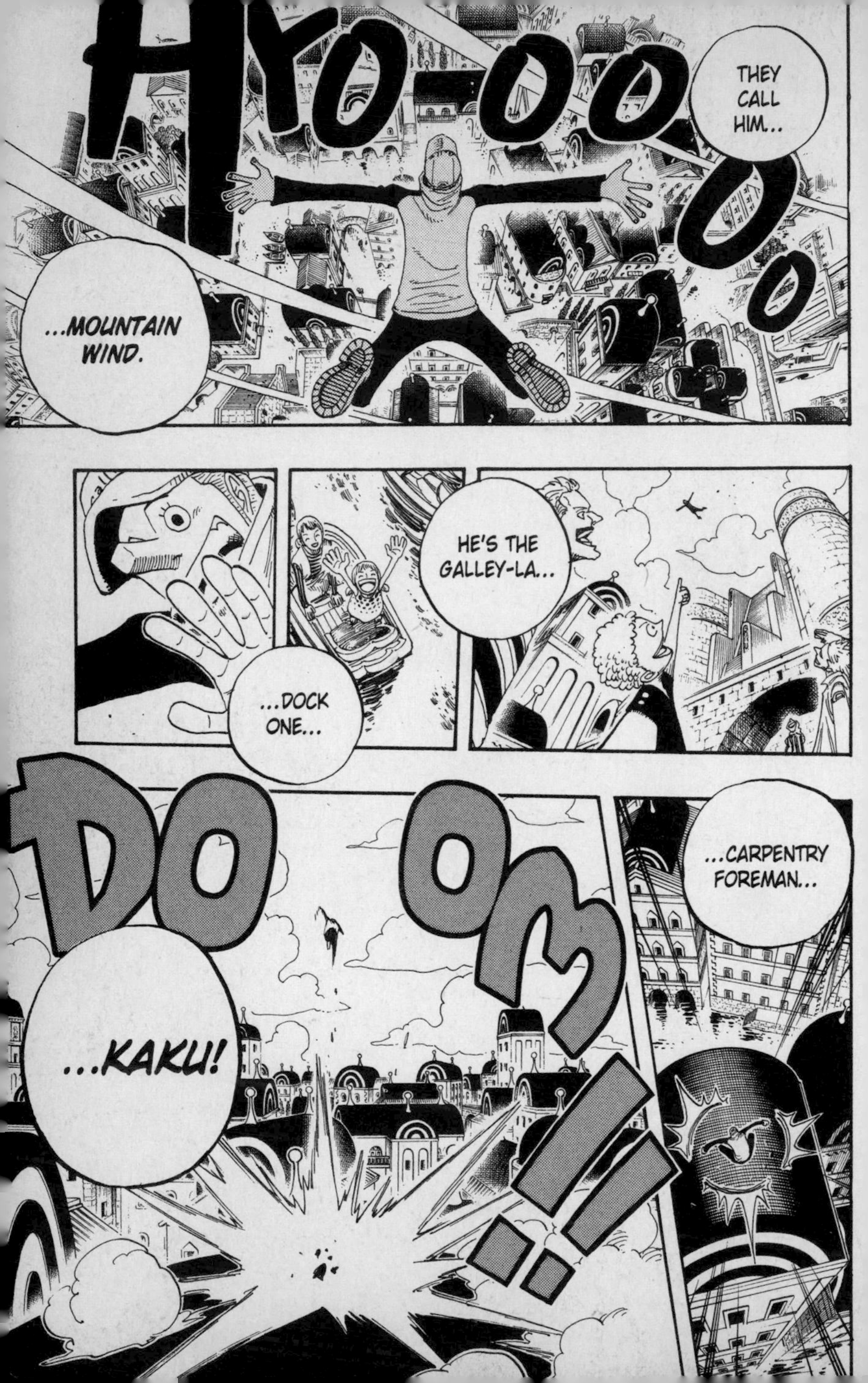
HYO-OOOOOO
THEY CALL HIM...
...MOUNTAIN WIND.
HE'S THE GALLEY-LA...
...DOCK ONE...
...CARPENTRY FOREMAN...
DOOM!!
...KAKU!

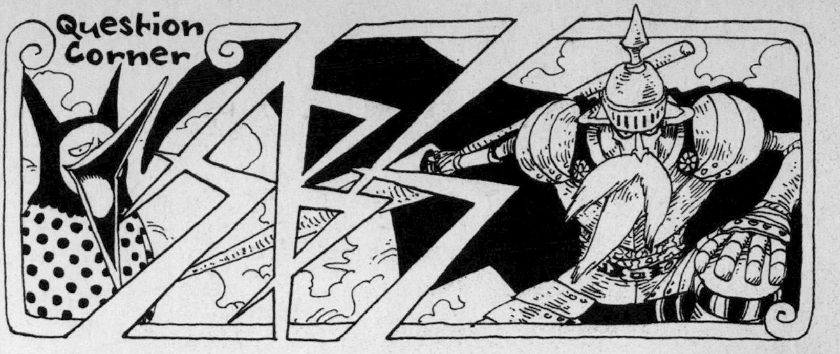
Question Corner

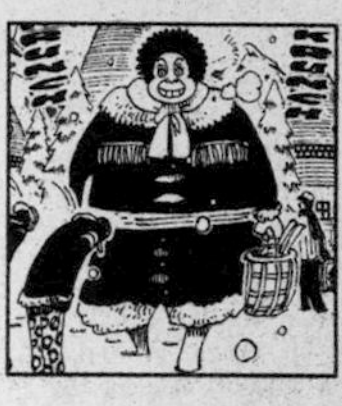

Q: How about some yummy onion cake?
--Onionbear Maria

A: Wow, onion cake, huh? I can have some? Sure thing! Nom nom! Mmm, yes, the indescribable harmony of onions and cream...! Mnch mnch crunch crunch nom nom slurp gulp!
Wee-oo Wee-oo!

Q: Hello, Odacchi! Something is bothering me. In volume 30, chapter 277, Luffy's trying to find a way out of the giant serpent and lifts up its eyelid. But how can he lift it when he's inside the eye? Go ask Luffy!!
--Miinyan

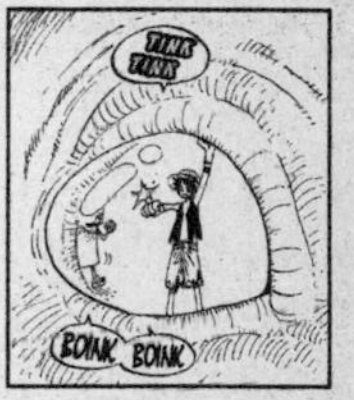
TINK TINK
BOINK BOINK

A: Yes, yes, that's strange, isn't it? Luffy! Come on out!

Luffy: What is it? What's the problem? There's nothing strange about that.

Oda: Sure there is! How can you lift the eyelid from inside the eyeball? Not only that, but how did you get inside the eyeball in the first place?!

Luffy: Who cares? Never mind about that. It was interesting, wasn't it?

Oda: Yeah, as long as it was fun! Anything works.

Luffy: Yeah, yeah. Ah ha ha ha.

Oda: Ah ha ha ha...

Q: Oda Sensei, hello. I know this is out of the blue, but please say Nami's technique, "Tornado Tempo," with a "chi" instead of "te." The Question Corner cannot end until you say it.
--Pon

A: Tornado Chimpo, eh? Tornado Chimpo! All right! See you in the next volume!! Oh, wait. Was this...sexual harrasment? Tell me... Was it sexual harrasment?

[Note: chinpo = slang for male parts]

Chapter 326:
MR. ICEBERG

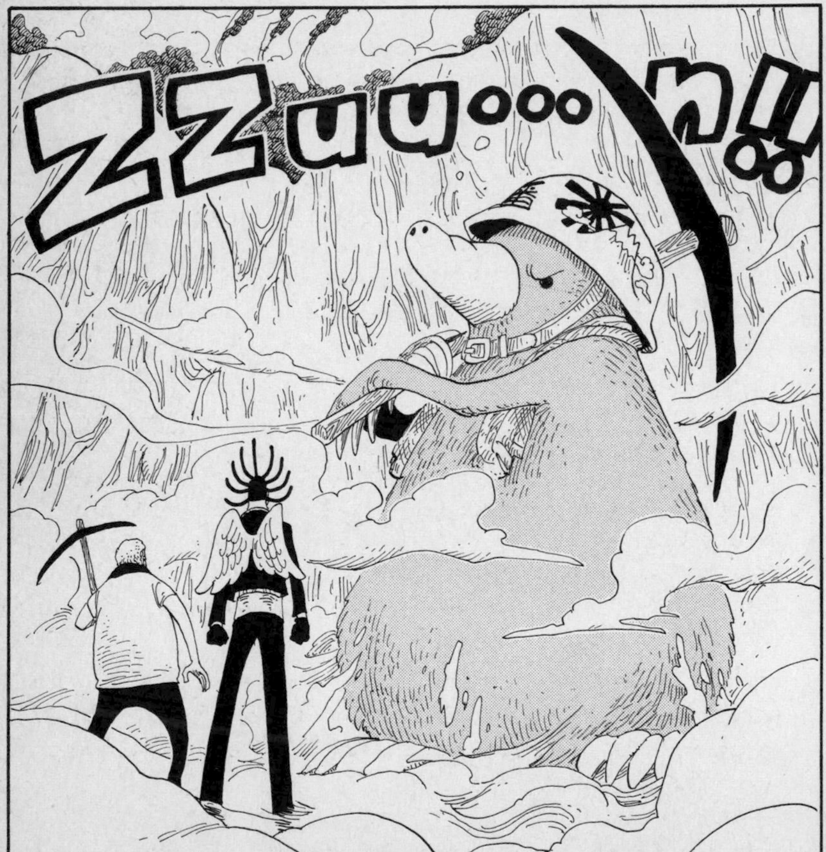
ZZuuu...n!!

GEDATSU'S UNEXPECTED LIFE ON THE BLUE SEA, VOL. 12: "I UNEXPECTEDLY AWAKENED THE LEGENDARY BOSS OF THE EARTH"

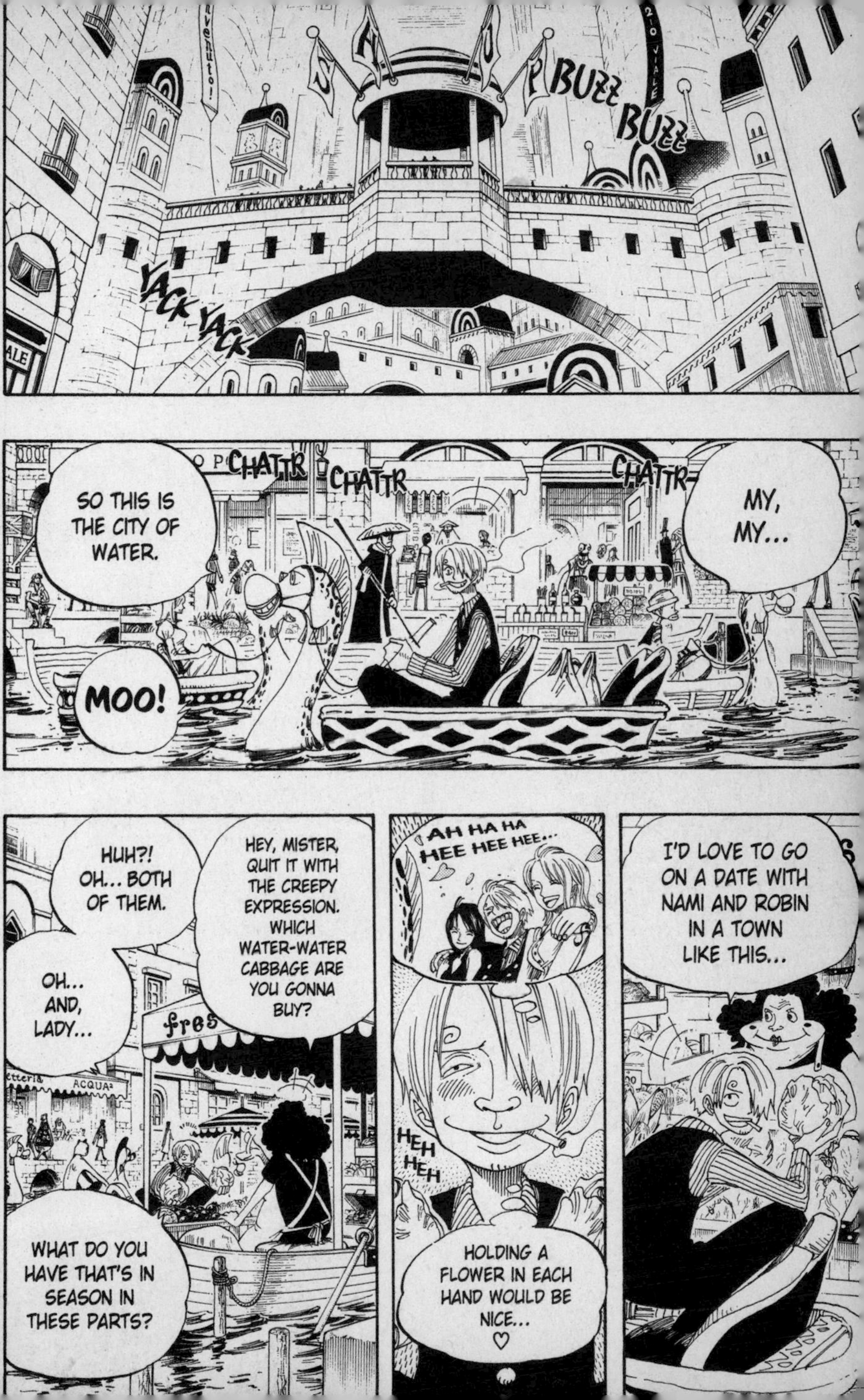
BUZZ BUZZ
YACK YACK
MY, MY...
CHATTR
CHATTR
CHATTR
SO THIS IS THE CITY OF WATER.
MOO!
I'D LOVE TO GO ON A DATE WITH NAMI AND ROBIN IN A TOWN LIKE THIS...
AH HA HA HEE HEE HEE...
HEH HEH
HOLDING A FLOWER IN EACH HAND WOULD BE NICE... ♡
HEY, MISTER, QUIT IT WITH THE CREEPY EXPRESSION. WHICH WATER-WATER CABBAGE ARE YOU GONNA BUY?
HUH?! OH... BOTH OF THEM.
OH... AND, LADY...
WHAT DO YOU HAVE THAT'S IN SEASON IN THESE PARTS?

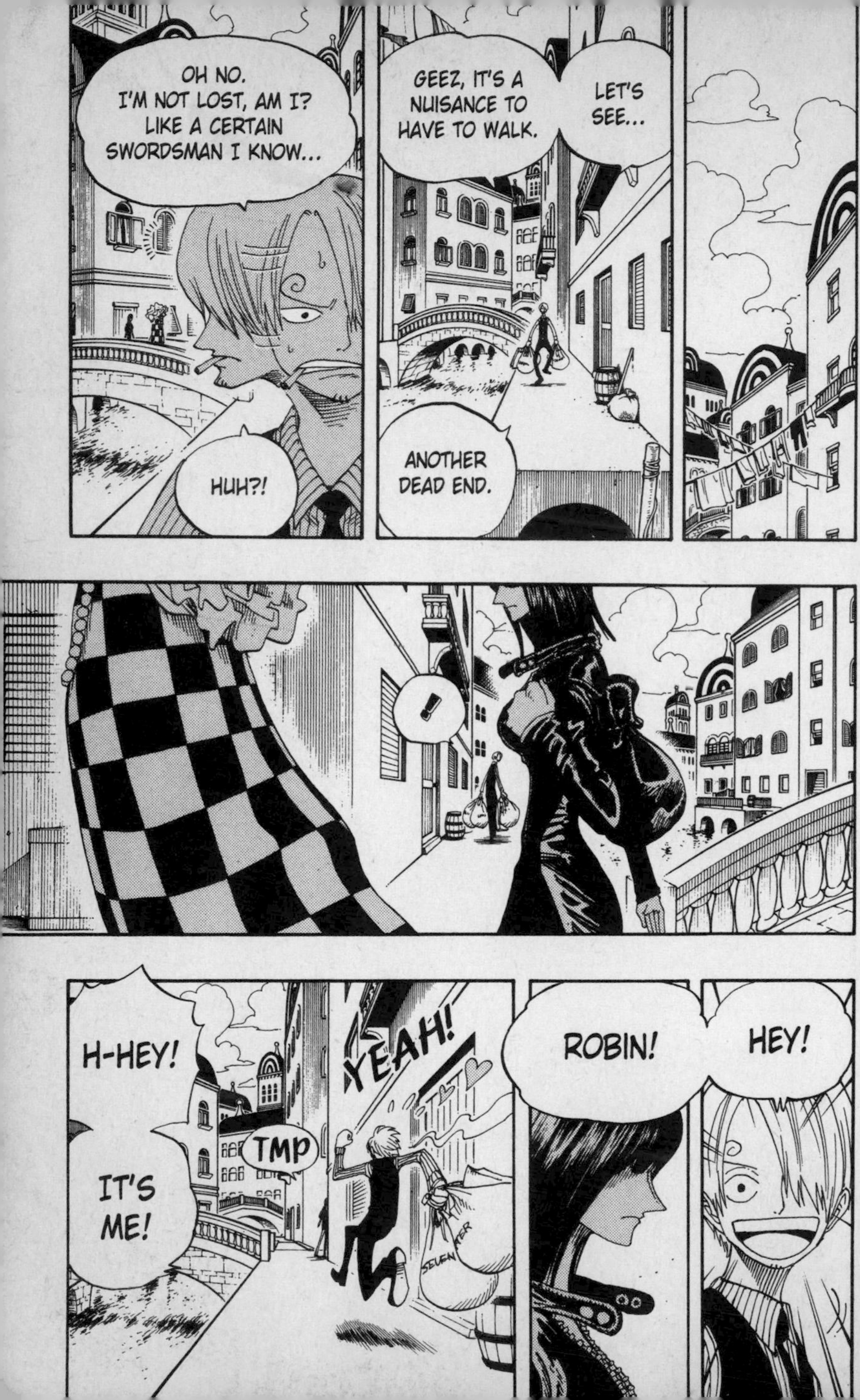
LET'S SEE...
GEEZ, IT'S A NUISANCE TO HAVE TO WALK.
ANOTHER DEAD END.
OH NO. I'M NOT LOST, AM I? LIKE A CERTAIN SWORDSMAN I KNOW...
HUH?!
!
HEY!
ROBIN!
YEAH!
H-HEY!
TMP
IT'S ME!

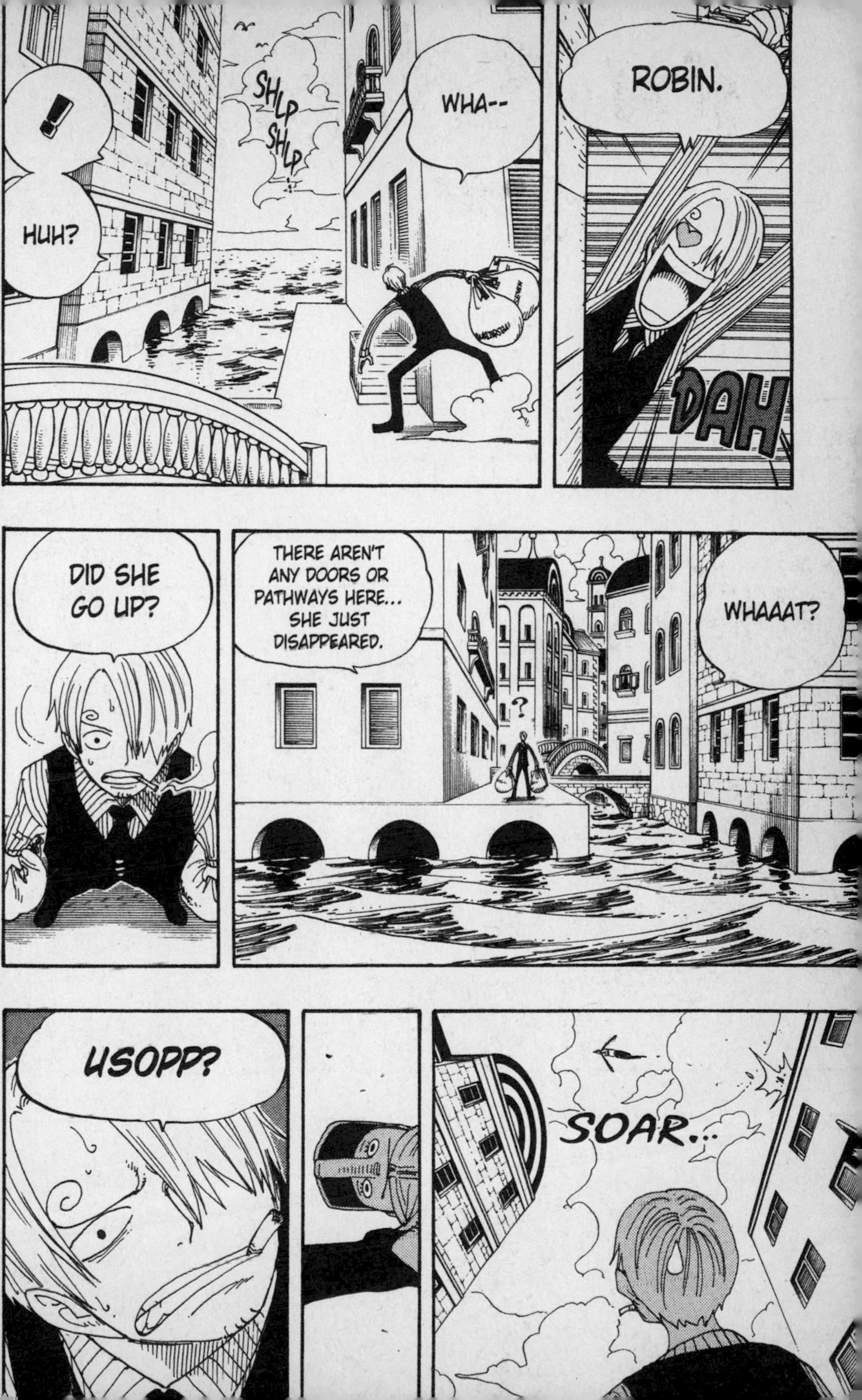
ROBIN.
DAH
WHA--
SHLP
SHLP
!
HUH?
WHAAAT?
THERE AREN'T ANY DOORS OR PATHWAYS HERE... SHE JUST DISAPPEARED.
DID SHE GO UP?
SOAR...
USOPP?

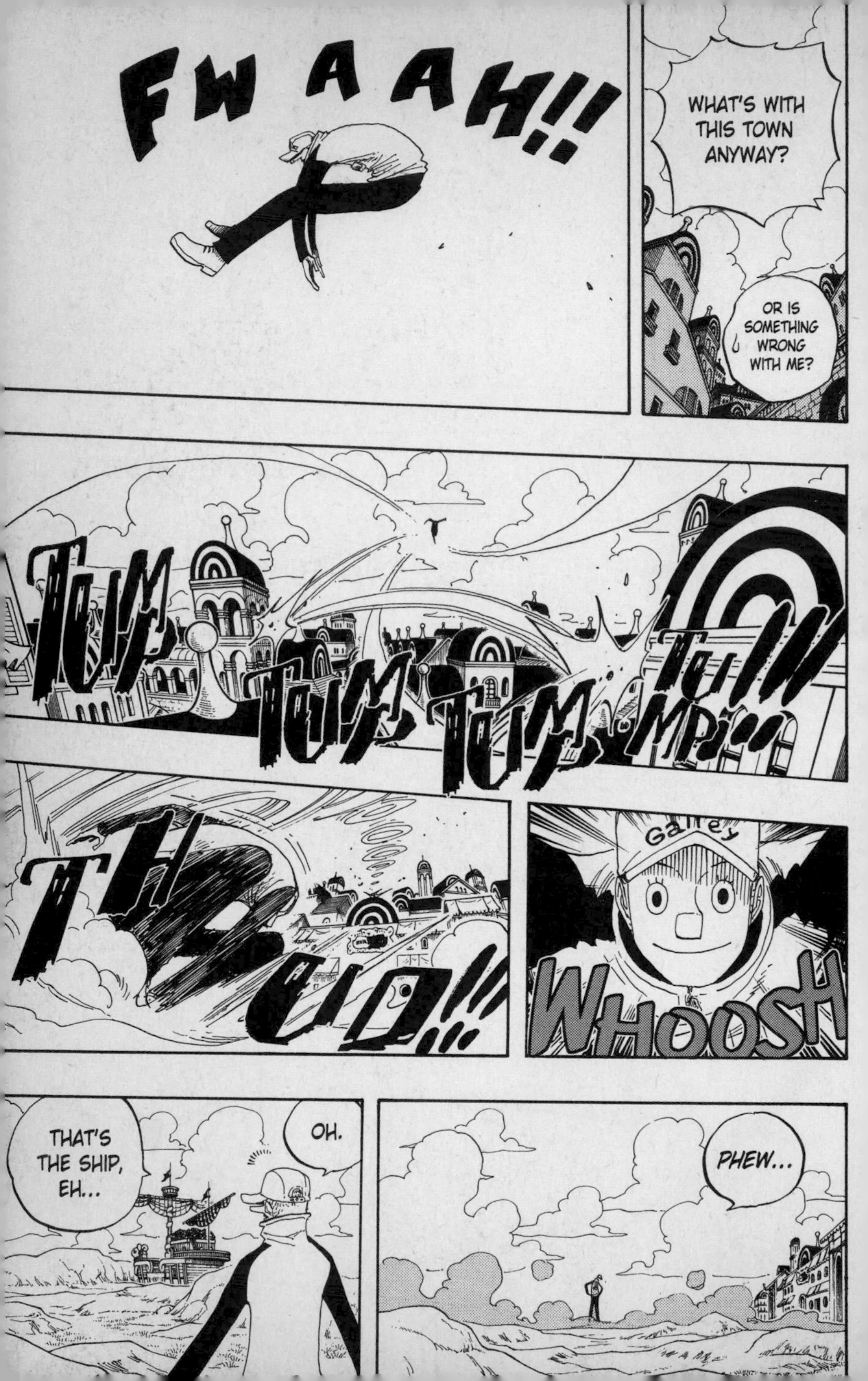
WHAT'S WITH THIS TOWN ANYWAY?
OR IS SOMETHING WRONG WITH ME?
FWAAAH!!
THUMP!!!
TUMP
TUMP
TUMP
Galley
WHOOSH
THUD!!!
PHEW...
OH.
THAT'S THE SHIP, EH...

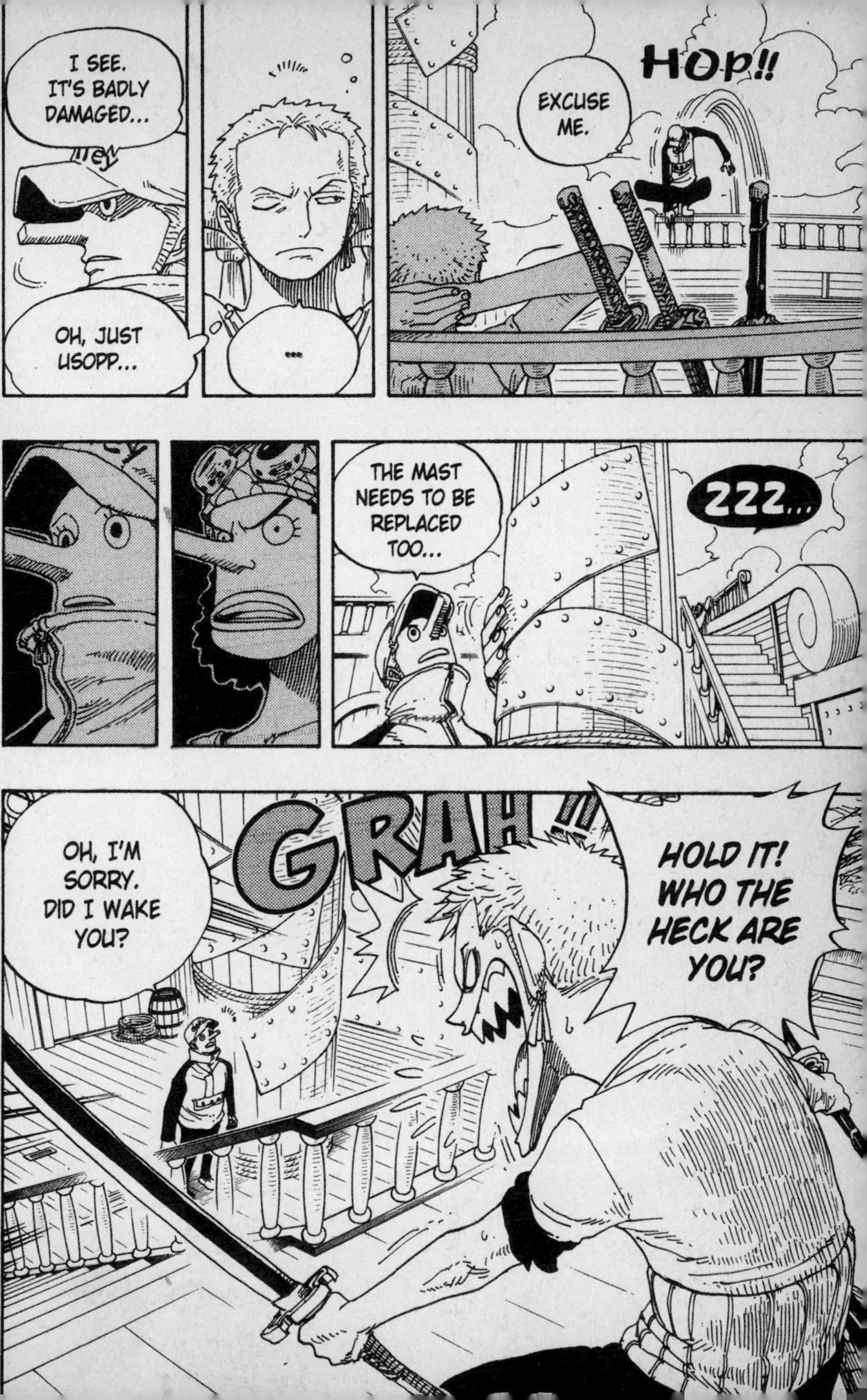
HOP!!
EXCUSE ME.
...
I SEE. IT'S BADLY DAMAGED...
OH, JUST USOPP...
ZZZ...
THE MAST NEEDS TO BE REPLACED TOO...
HOLD IT! WHO THE HECK ARE YOU?
GRAH!!
OH, I'M SORRY. DID I WAKE YOU?

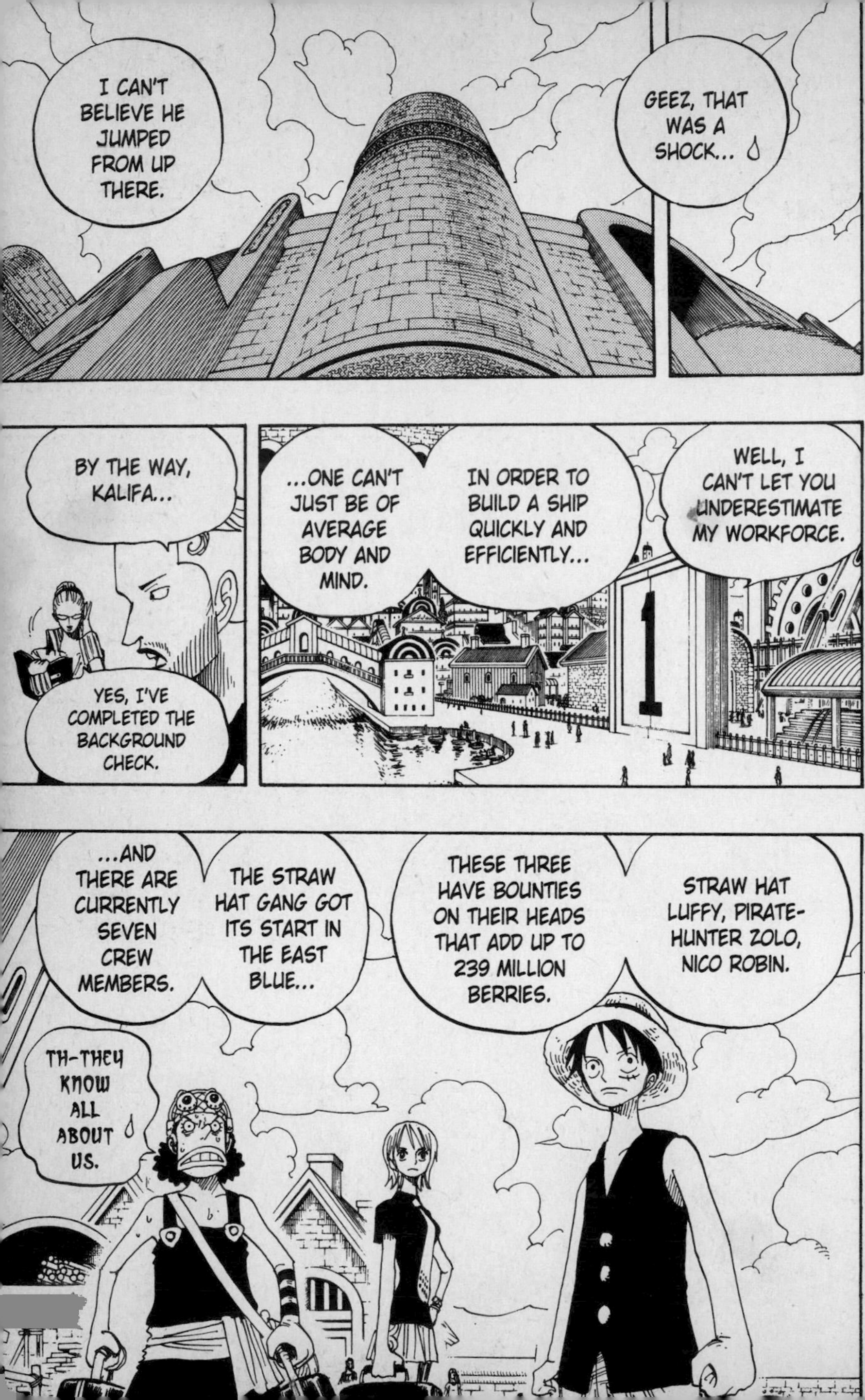
GEEZ, THAT WAS A SHOCK...
I CAN'T BELIEVE HE JUMPED FROM UP THERE.
WELL, I CAN'T LET YOU UNDERESTIMATE MY WORKFORCE.
IN ORDER TO BUILD A SHIP QUICKLY AND EFFICIENTLY...
...ONE CAN'T JUST BE OF AVERAGE BODY AND MIND.
BY THE WAY, KALIFA...
YES, I'VE COMPLETED THE BACKGROUND CHECK.
STRAW HAT LUFFY, PIRATE-HUNTER ZOLO, NICO ROBIN.
THESE THREE HAVE BOUNTIES ON THEIR HEADS THAT ADD UP TO 239 MILLION BERRIES.
THE STRAW HAT GANG GOT ITS START IN THE EAST BLUE...
...AND THERE ARE CURRENTLY SEVEN CREW MEMBERS.
TH-THEY KNOW ALL ABOUT US.

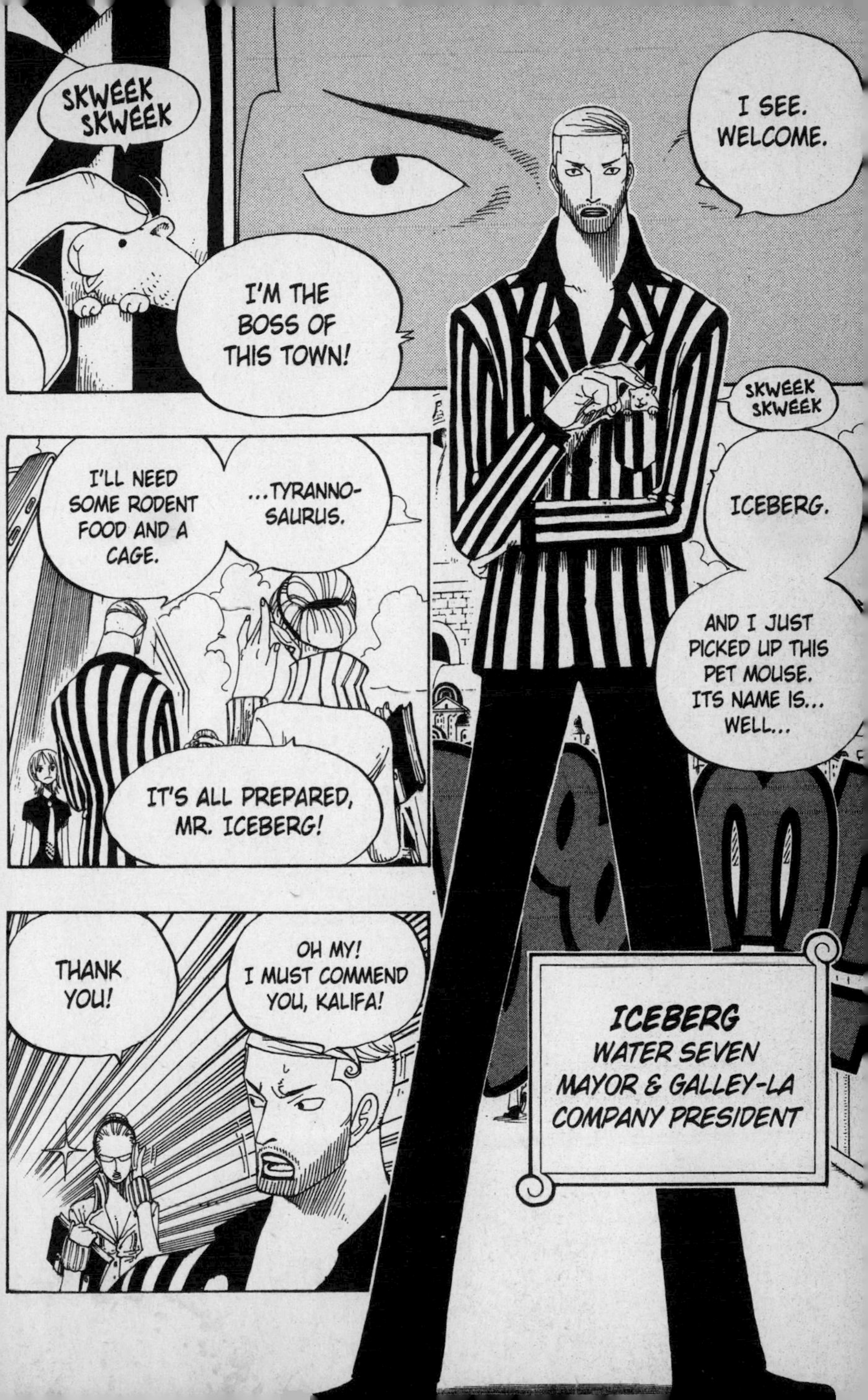
I SEE. WELCOME.
SKWEEK SKWEEK
I'M THE BOSS OF THIS TOWN!
SKWEEK SKWEEK
ICEBERG.
AND I JUST PICKED UP THIS PET MOUSE. ITS NAME IS... WELL...
ICEBERG
WATER SEVEN MAYOR & GALLEY-LA COMPANY PRESIDENT
...TYRANNOSAURUS.
I'LL NEED SOME RODENT FOOD AND A CAGE.
IT'S ALL PREPARED, MR. ICEBERG!
OH MY! I MUST COMMEND YOU, KALIFA!
THANK YOU!

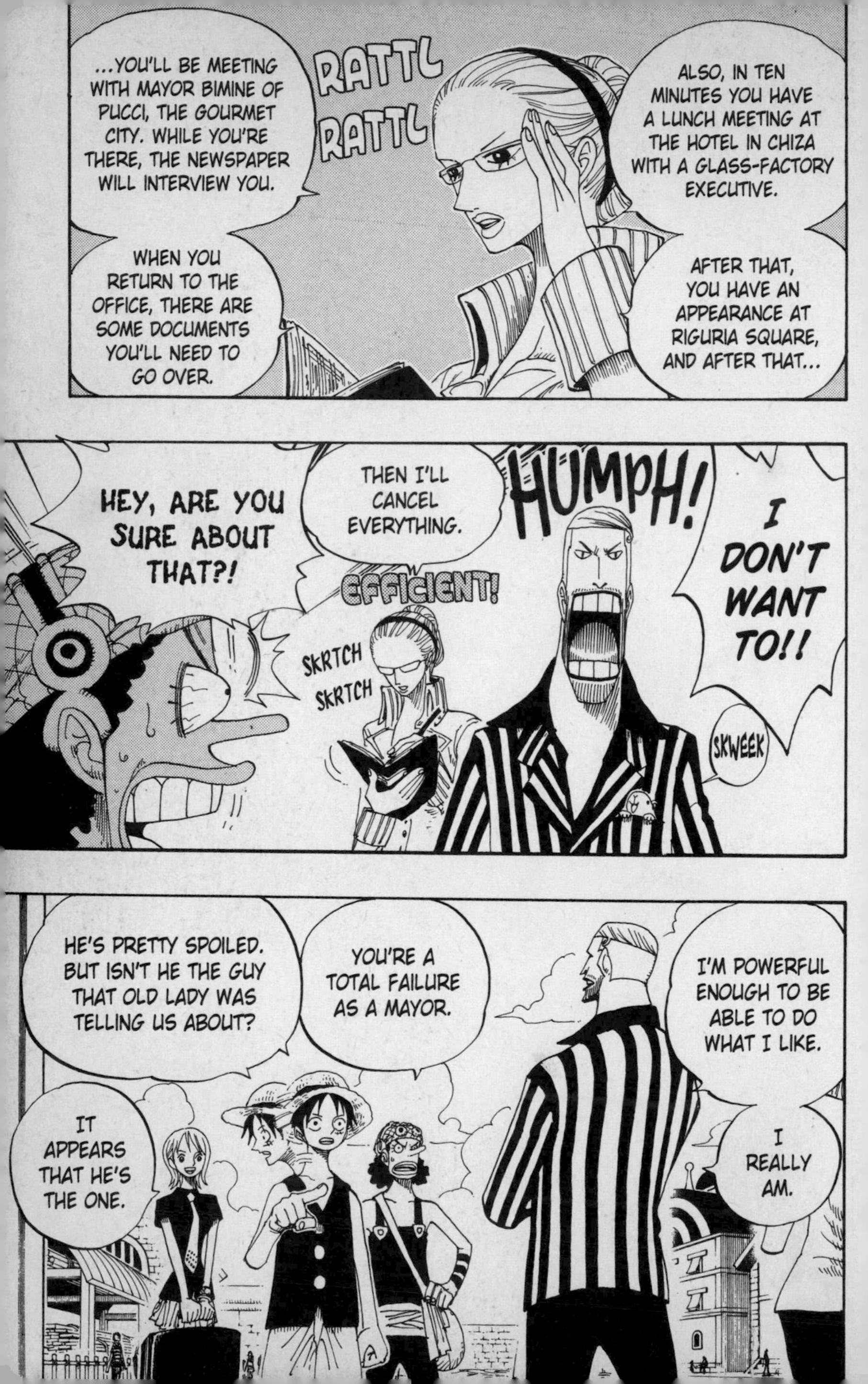
ALSO, IN TEN MINUTES YOU HAVE A LUNCH MEETING AT THE HOTEL IN CHIZA WITH A GLASS-FACTORY EXECUTIVE.
RATTL RATTL
...YOU'LL BE MEETING WITH MAYOR BIMINE OF PUCCI, THE GOURMET CITY. WHILE YOU'RE THERE, THE NEWSPAPER WILL INTERVIEW YOU.
AFTER THAT, YOU HAVE AN APPEARANCE AT RIGURIA SQUARE, AND AFTER THAT...
WHEN YOU RETURN TO THE OFFICE, THERE ARE SOME DOCUMENTS YOU'LL NEED TO GO OVER.
HUMPH!
I DON'T WANT TO!!
SKWEEK
THEN I'LL CANCEL EVERYTHING.
EFFICIENT!
SKRTCH SKRTCH
HEY, ARE YOU SURE ABOUT THAT?!
I'M POWERFUL ENOUGH TO BE ABLE TO DO WHAT I LIKE.
I REALLY AM.
YOU'RE A TOTAL FAILURE AS A MAYOR.
HE'S PRETTY SPOILED. BUT ISN'T HE THE GUY THAT OLD LADY WAS TELLING US ABOUT?
IT APPEARS THAT HE'S THE ONE.

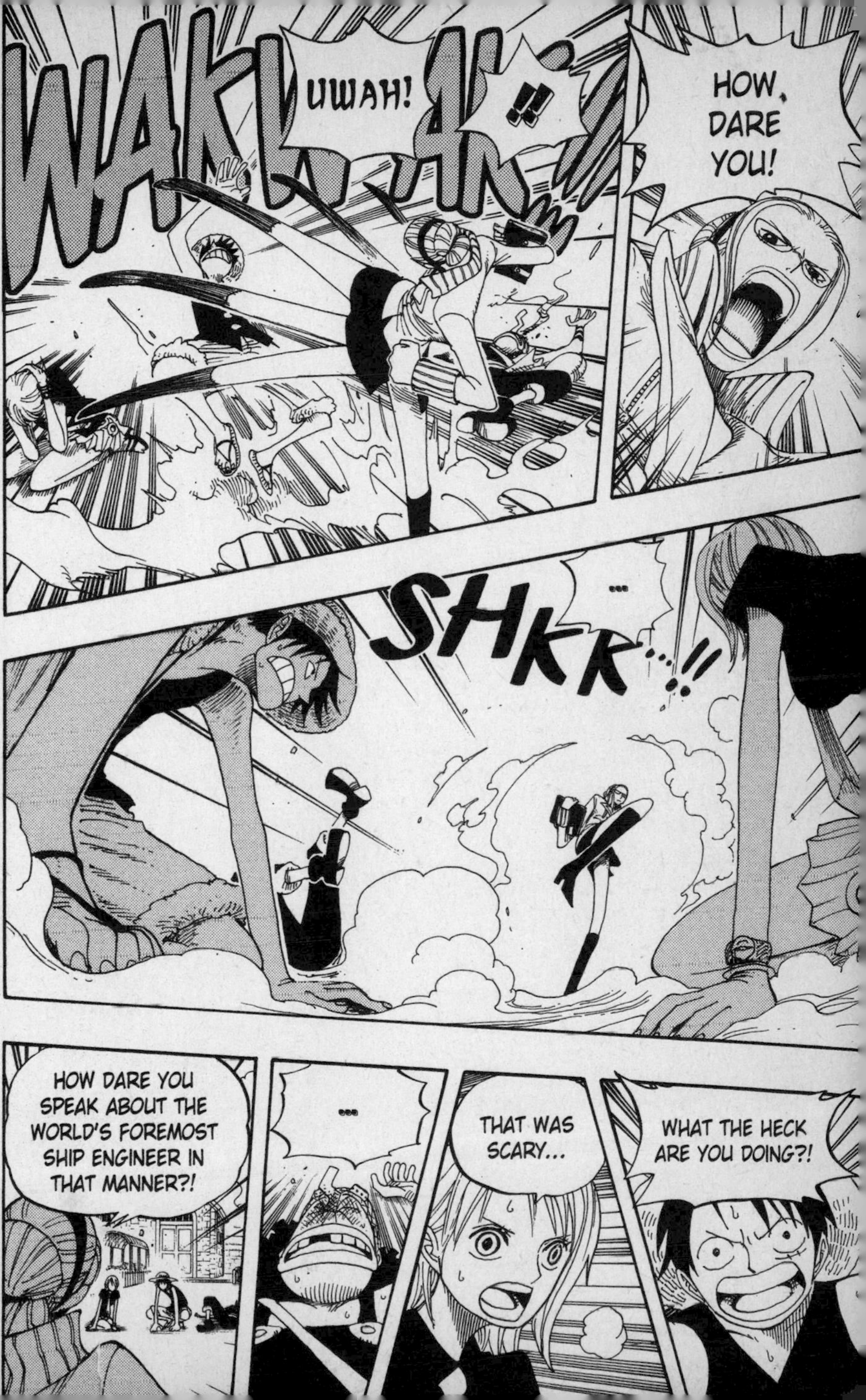
HOW, DARE YOU!
WAK
UWAH!
!!
...
SHKR...!!
WHAT THE HECK ARE YOU DOING?!
THAT WAS SCARY...
...
HOW DARE YOU SPEAK ABOUT THE WORLD'S FOREMOST SHIP ENGINEER IN THAT MANNER?!

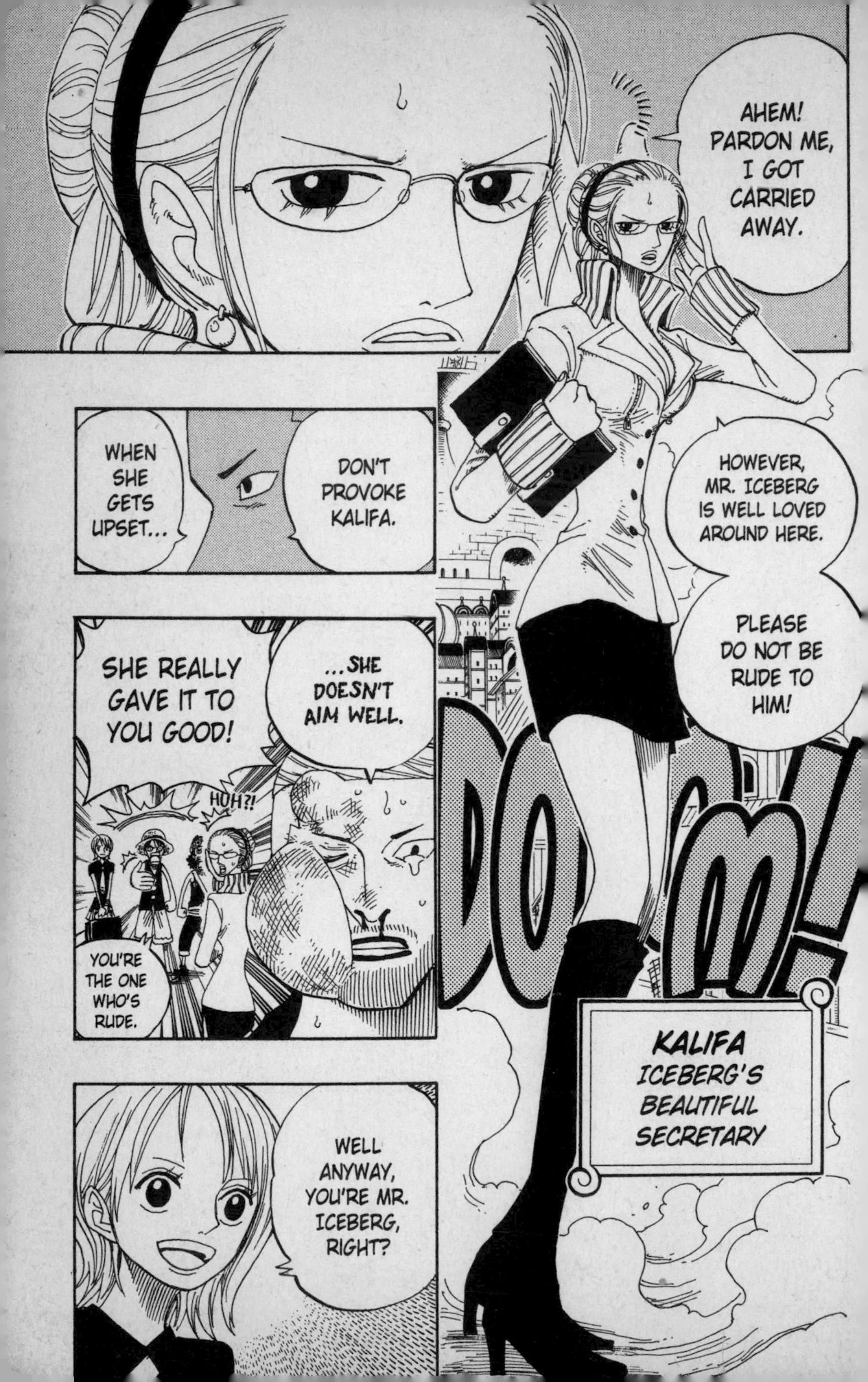
AHEM! PARDON ME, I GOT CARRIED AWAY.
HOWEVER, MR. ICEBERG IS WELL LOVED AROUND HERE.
PLEASE DO NOT BE RUDE TO HIM!
DOOM!
KALIFA
ICEBERG'S BEAUTIFUL SECRETARY
DON'T PROVOKE KALIFA.
WHEN SHE GETS UPSET...
...SHE DOESN'T AIM WELL.
SHE REALLY GAVE IT TO YOU GOOD!
HUH?!
YOU'RE THE ONE WHO'S RUDE.
WELL ANYWAY, YOU'RE MR. ICEBERG, RIGHT?

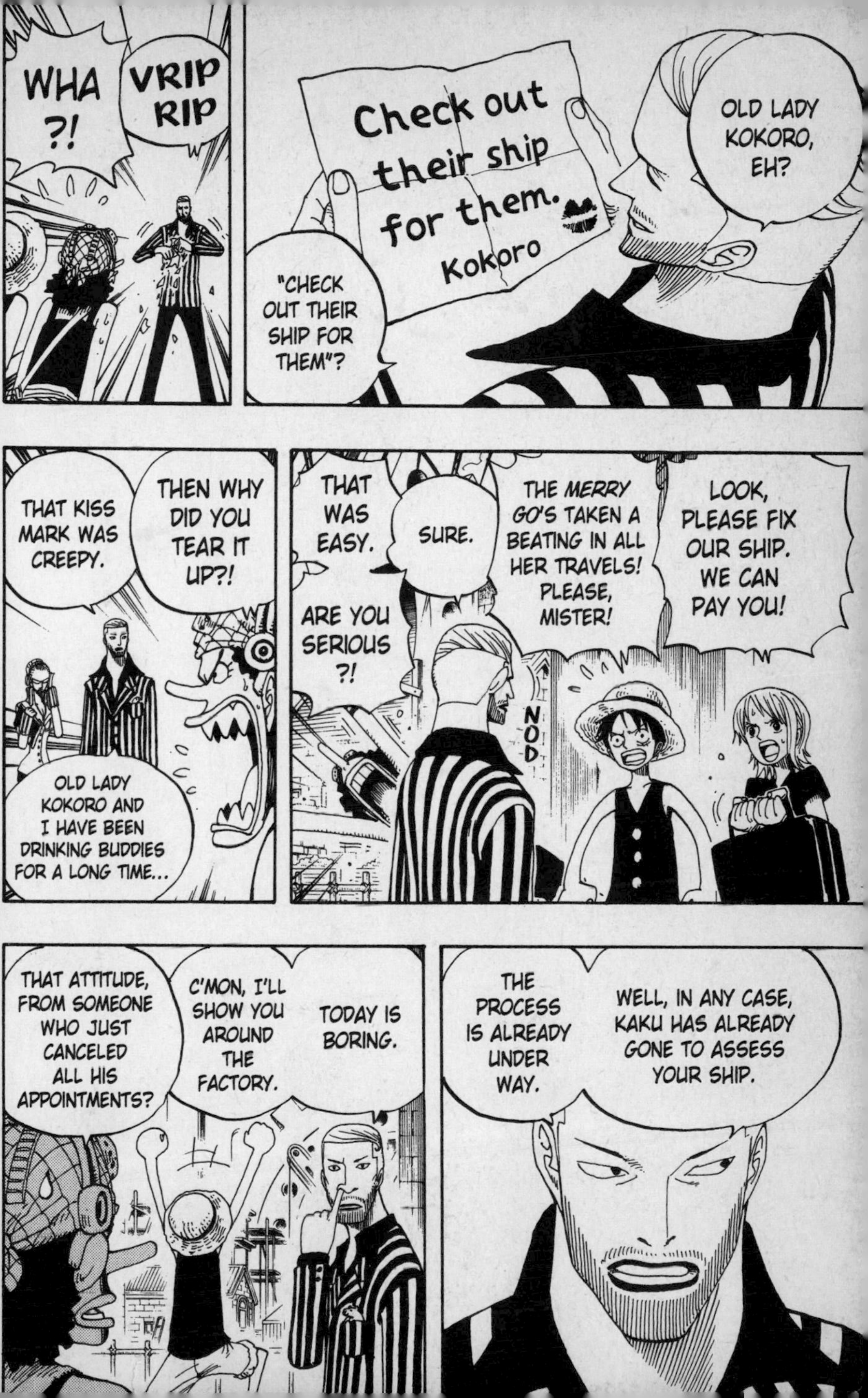
OLD LADY KOKORO, EH?
Check out their ship for them.
Kokoro
"CHECK OUT THEIR SHIP FOR THEM"?
VRIP RIP
WHA ?!
LOOK, PLEASE FIX OUR SHIP. WE CAN PAY YOU!
THE MERRY GO'S TAKEN A BEATING IN ALL HER TRAVELS! PLEASE, MISTER!
SURE.
THAT WAS EASY.
NOD
ARE YOU SERIOUS ?!
THEN WHY DID YOU TEAR IT UP?!
THAT KISS MARK WAS CREEPY.
OLD LADY KOKORO AND I HAVE BEEN DRINKING BUDDIES FOR A LONG TIME...
WELL, IN ANY CASE, KAKU HAS ALREADY GONE TO ASSESS YOUR SHIP.
THE PROCESS IS ALREADY UNDER WAY.
TODAY IS BORING.
C'MON, I'LL SHOW YOU AROUND THE FACTORY.
THAT ATTITUDE, FROM SOMEONE WHO JUST CANCELED ALL HIS APPOINTMENTS?

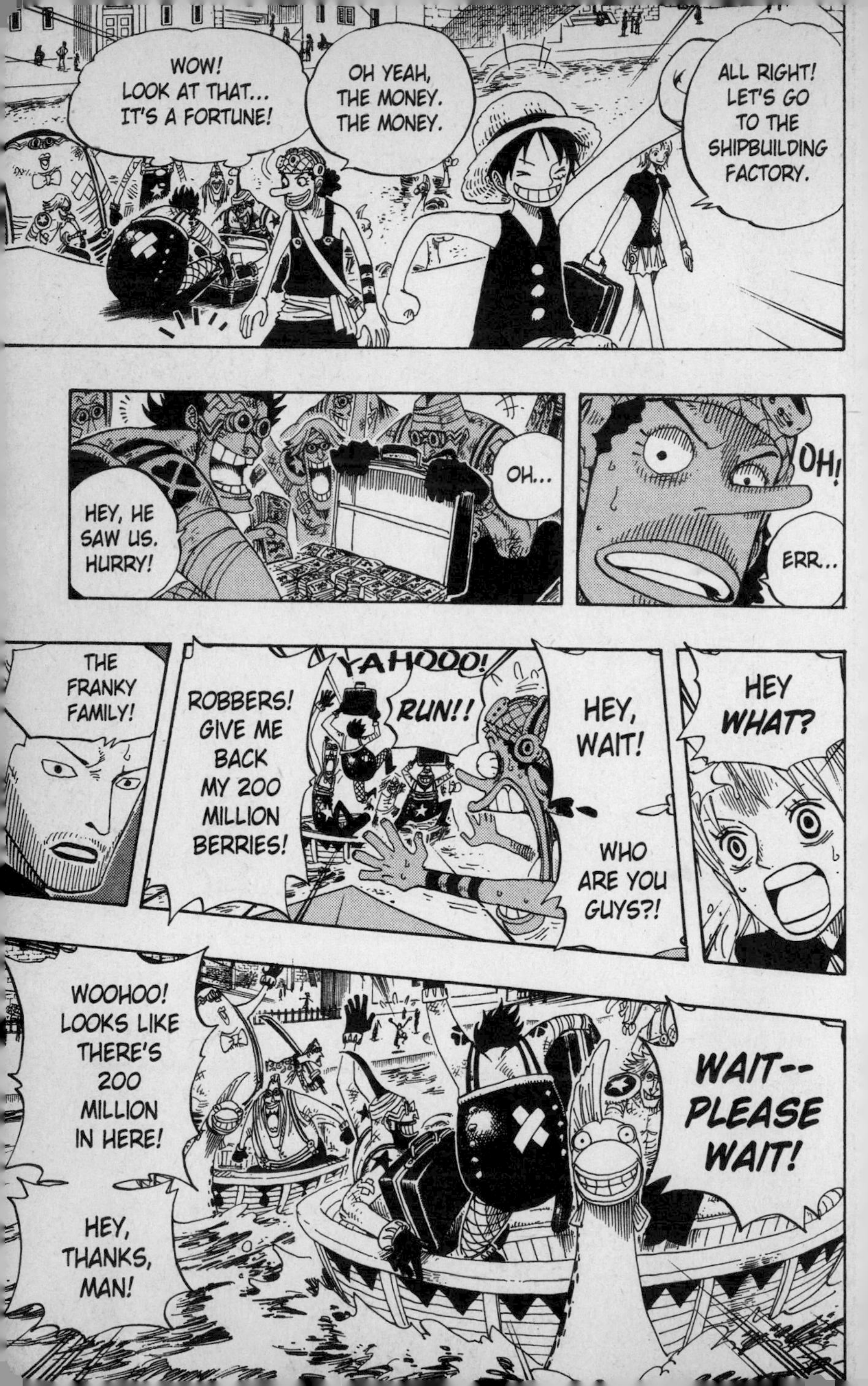
ALL RIGHT! LET'S GO TO THE SHIPBUILDING FACTORY.
OH YEAH, THE MONEY. THE MONEY.
WOW! LOOK AT THAT... IT'S A FORTUNE!
OH!
ERR...
OH...
HEY, HE SAW US. HURRY!
HEY WHAT?
HEY, WAIT!
WHO ARE YOU GUYS?!
YAHOOO!
RUN!!
ROBBERS! GIVE ME BACK MY 200 MILLION BERRIES!
THE FRANKY FAMILY!
WAIT-- PLEASE WAIT!
WOOHOO! LOOKS LIKE THERE'S 200 MILLION IN HERE!
HEY, THANKS, MAN!

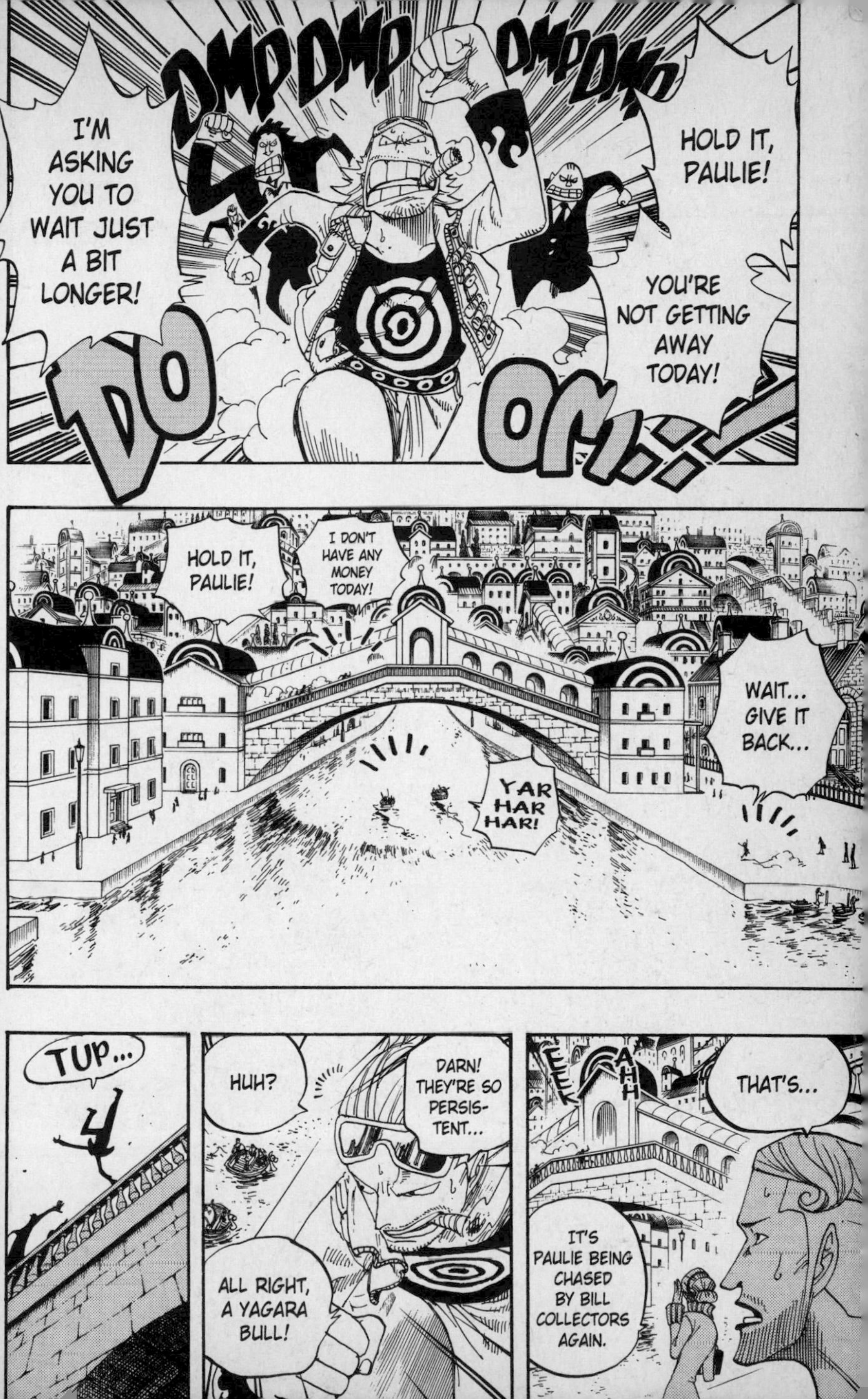
HOLD IT, PAULIE!
YOU'RE NOT GETTING AWAY TODAY!
DMP DMP DMP DMP
I'M ASKING YOU TO WAIT JUST A BIT LONGER!
DO
OM...!
WAIT... GIVE IT BACK...
YAR HAR HAR!
I DON'T HAVE ANY MONEY TODAY!
HOLD IT, PAULIE!
THAT'S...
EEK
AHH
IT'S PAULIE BEING CHASED BY BILL COLLECTORS AGAIN.
DARN! THEY'RE SO PERSIS-TENT...
HUH?
ALL RIGHT, A YAGARA BULL!
TUP...

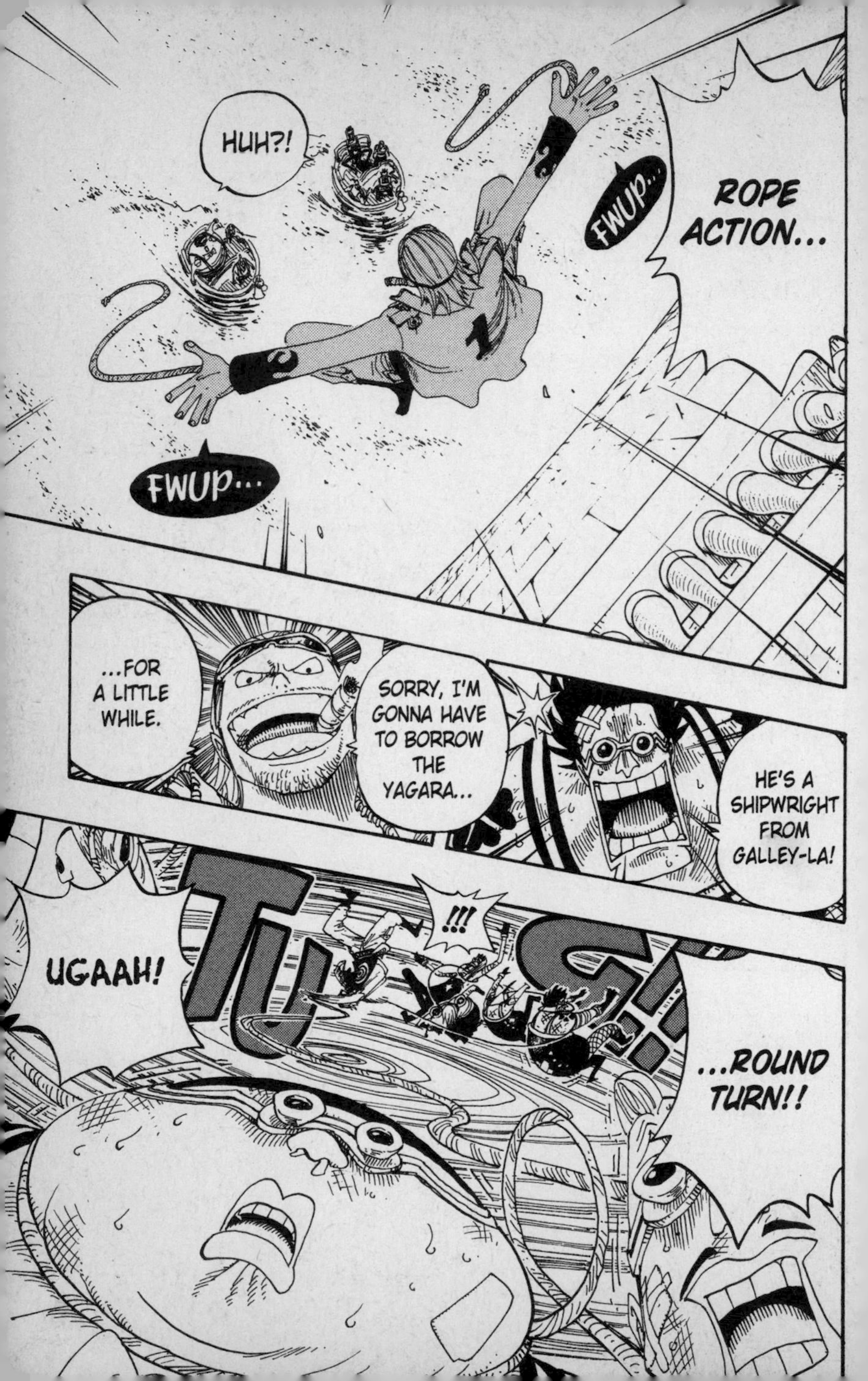
ROPE ACTION...
FWUP...
HUH?!
FWUP...
HE'S A SHIPWRIGHT FROM GALLEY-LA!
SORRY, I'M GONNA HAVE TO BORROW THE YAGARA...
...FOR A LITTLE WHILE.
...ROUND TURN!!
!!!
UGAAH!

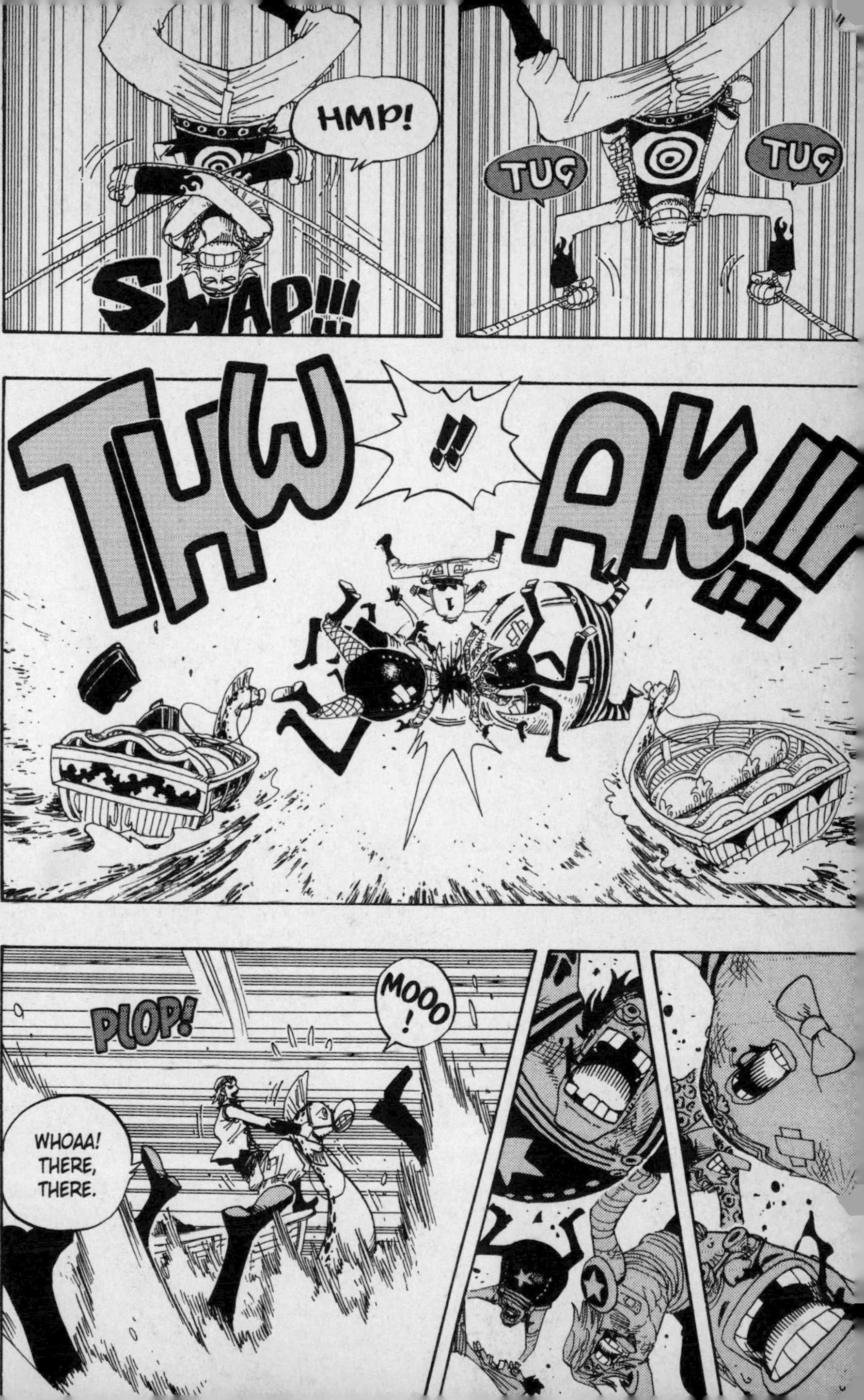
TUG
TUG
HMP!
SNAP!!!
THW
!!
AK!!!
MOOO!
PLOP!
WHOAA! THERE, THERE.

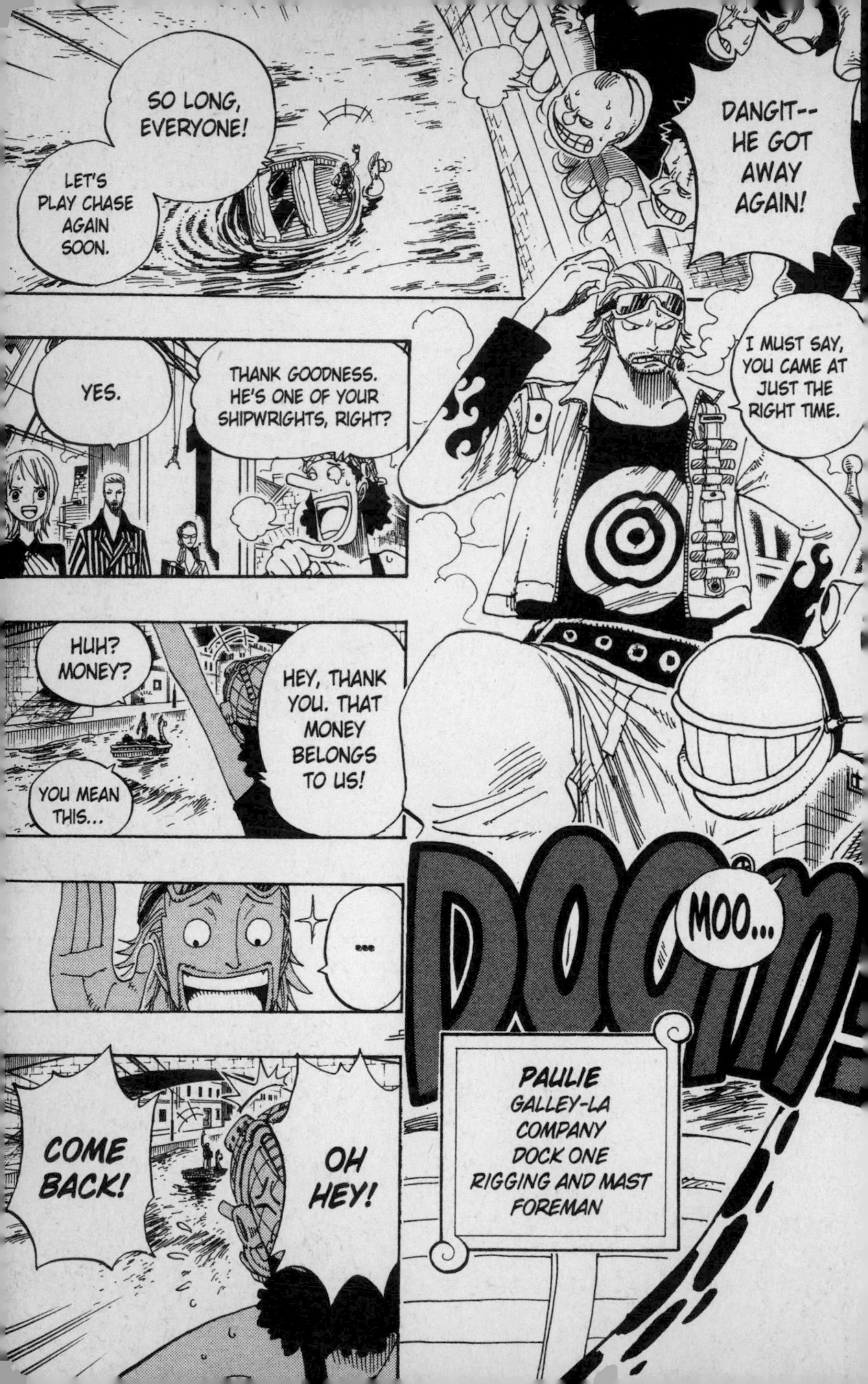
DANGIT-- HE GOT AWAY AGAIN!
I MUST SAY, YOU CAME AT JUST THE RIGHT TIME.
DOOOM
MOO...
PAULIE
GALLEY-LA COMPANY
DOCK ONE
RIGGING AND MAST FOREMAN
SO LONG, EVERYONE!
LET'S PLAY CHASE AGAIN SOON.
THANK GOODNESS. HE'S ONE OF YOUR SHIPWRIGHTS, RIGHT?
YES.
HEY, THANK YOU. THAT MONEY BELONGS TO US!
HUH? MONEY?
YOU MEAN THIS...
...
OH HEY!
COME BACK!

ISLAND, REPAIR DOCK No. 1

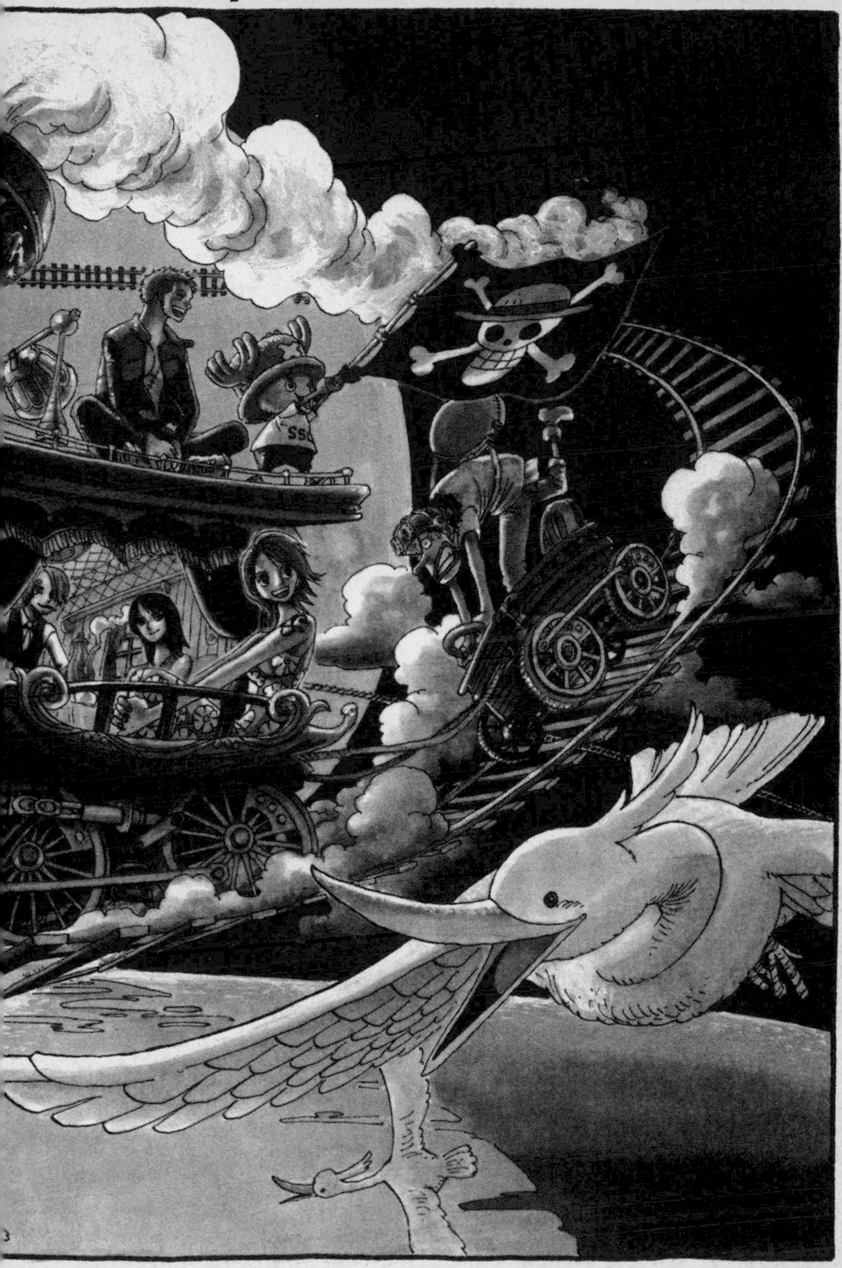

Chapter 327: SHIPBUILDING

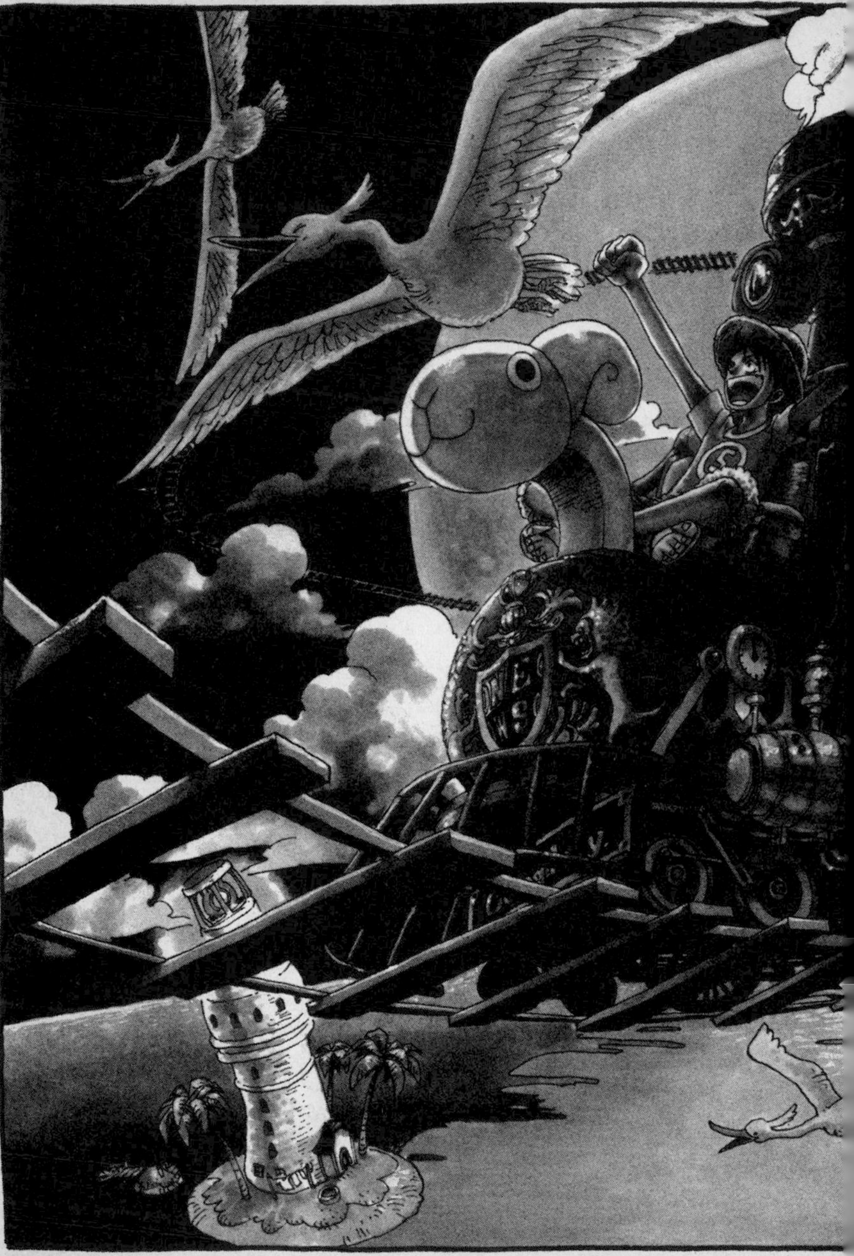

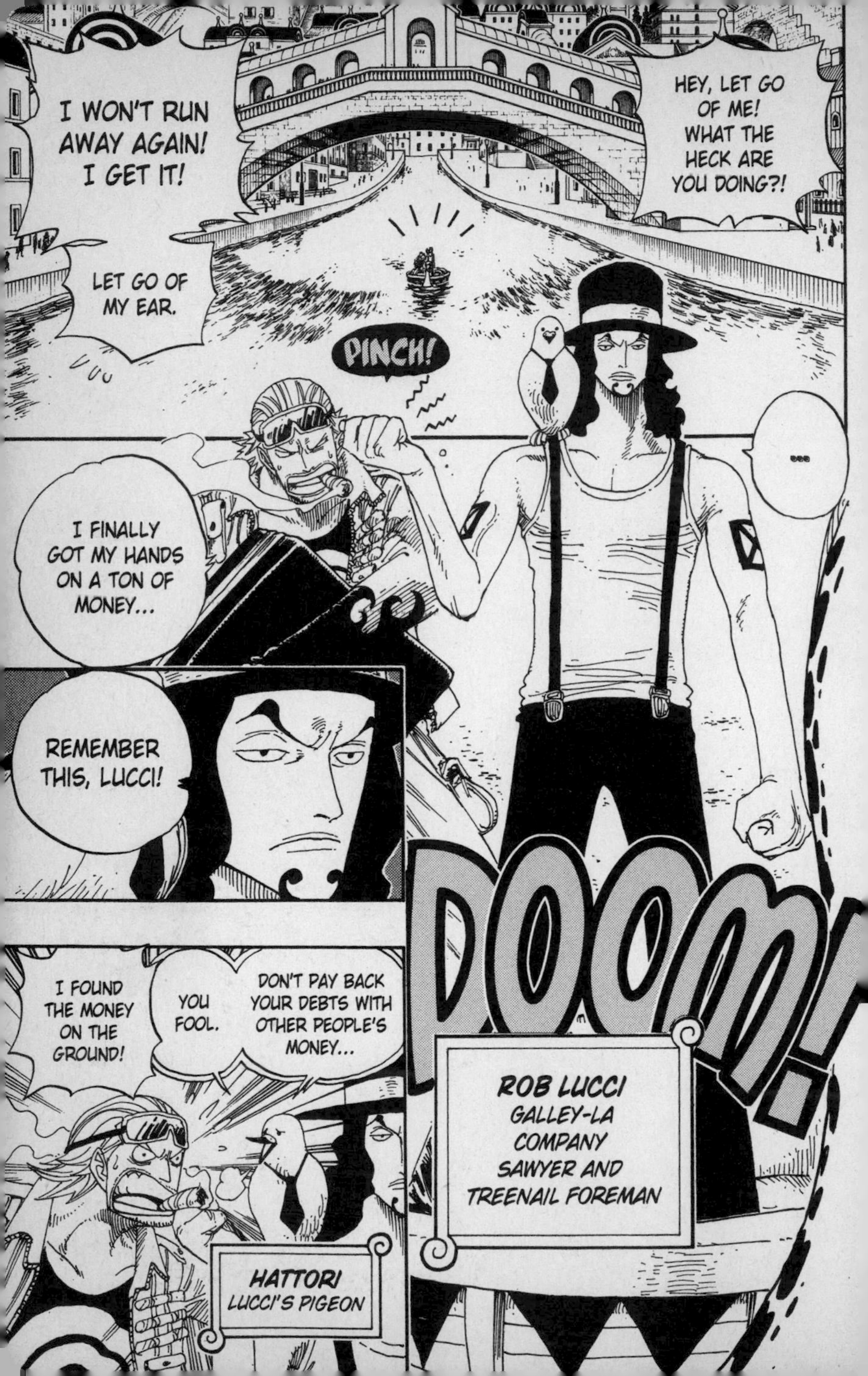
HEY, LET GO OF ME! WHAT THE HECK ARE YOU DOING?!
I WON'T RUN AWAY AGAIN! I GET IT!
LET GO OF MY EAR.
PINCH!
...
DOOM!
ROB LUCCI GALLEY-LA COMPANY SAWYER AND TREENAIL FOREMAN
I FINALLY GOT MY HANDS ON A TON OF MONEY...
REMEMBER THIS, LUCCI!
DON'T PAY BACK YOUR DEBTS WITH OTHER PEOPLE'S MONEY...
YOU FOOL.
I FOUND THE MONEY ON THE GROUND!
HATTORI LUCCI'S PIGEON

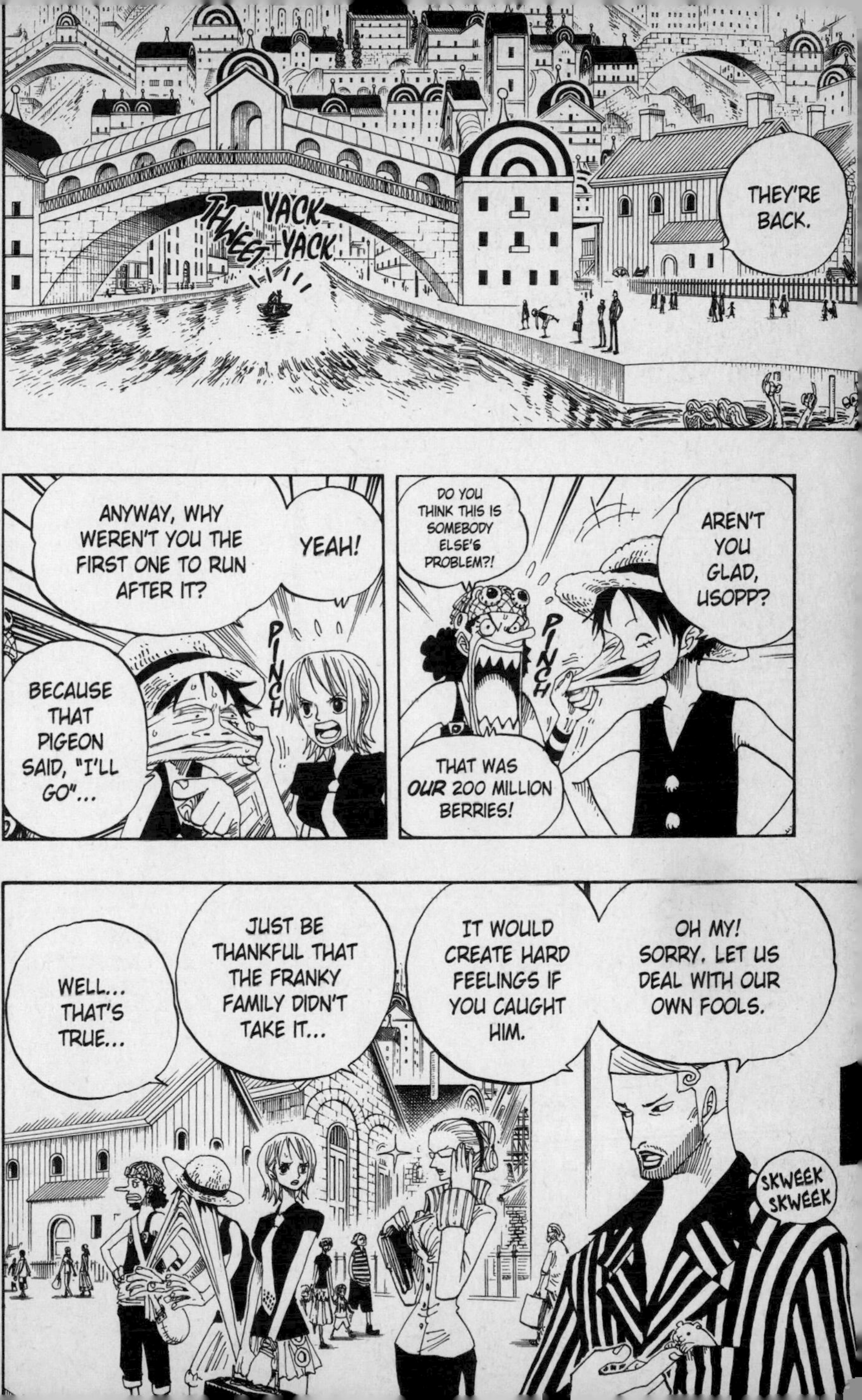
THEY'RE BACK.
YACK YACK
THWEET
AREN'T YOU GLAD, USOPP?
DO YOU THINK THIS IS SOMEBODY ELSE'S PROBLEM?!
PINCH
THAT WAS OUR 200 MILLION BERRIES!
YEAH!
ANYWAY, WHY WEREN'T YOU THE FIRST ONE TO RUN AFTER IT?
PINCH
BECAUSE THAT PIGEON SAID, "I'LL GO"...
OH MY! SORRY. LET US DEAL WITH OUR OWN FOOLS.
IT WOULD CREATE HARD FEELINGS IF YOU CAUGHT HIM.
JUST BE THANKFUL THAT THE FRANKY FAMILY DIDN'T TAKE IT...
WELL... THAT'S TRUE...
SKWEEK SKWEEK

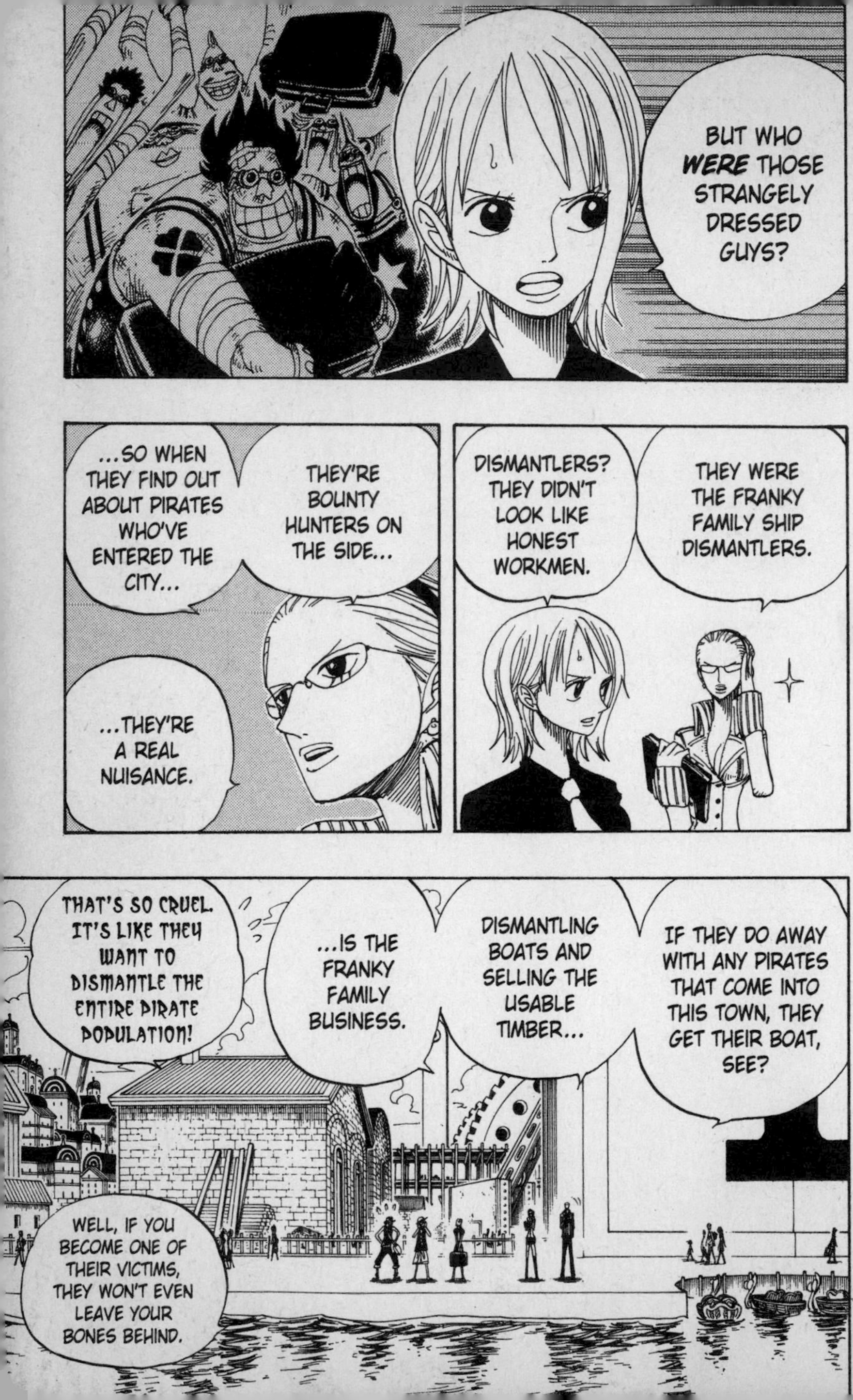
BUT WHO **WERE** THOSE STRANGELY DRESSED GUYS?
THEY WERE THE FRANKY FAMILY SHIP DISMANTLERS.
DISMANTLERS? THEY DIDN'T LOOK LIKE HONEST WORKMEN.
THEY'RE BOUNTY HUNTERS ON THE SIDE...
...SO WHEN THEY FIND OUT ABOUT PIRATES WHO'VE ENTERED THE CITY...
...THEY'RE A REAL NUISANCE.
IF THEY DO AWAY WITH ANY PIRATES THAT COME INTO THIS TOWN, THEY GET THEIR BOAT, SEE?
DISMANTLING BOATS AND SELLING THE USABLE TIMBER...
...IS THE FRANKY FAMILY BUSINESS.
THAT'S SO CRUEL. IT'S LIKE THEY WANT TO DISMANTLE THE ENTIRE PIRATE POPULATION!
WELL, IF YOU BECOME ONE OF THEIR VICTIMS, THEY WON'T EVEN LEAVE YOUR BONES BEHIND.

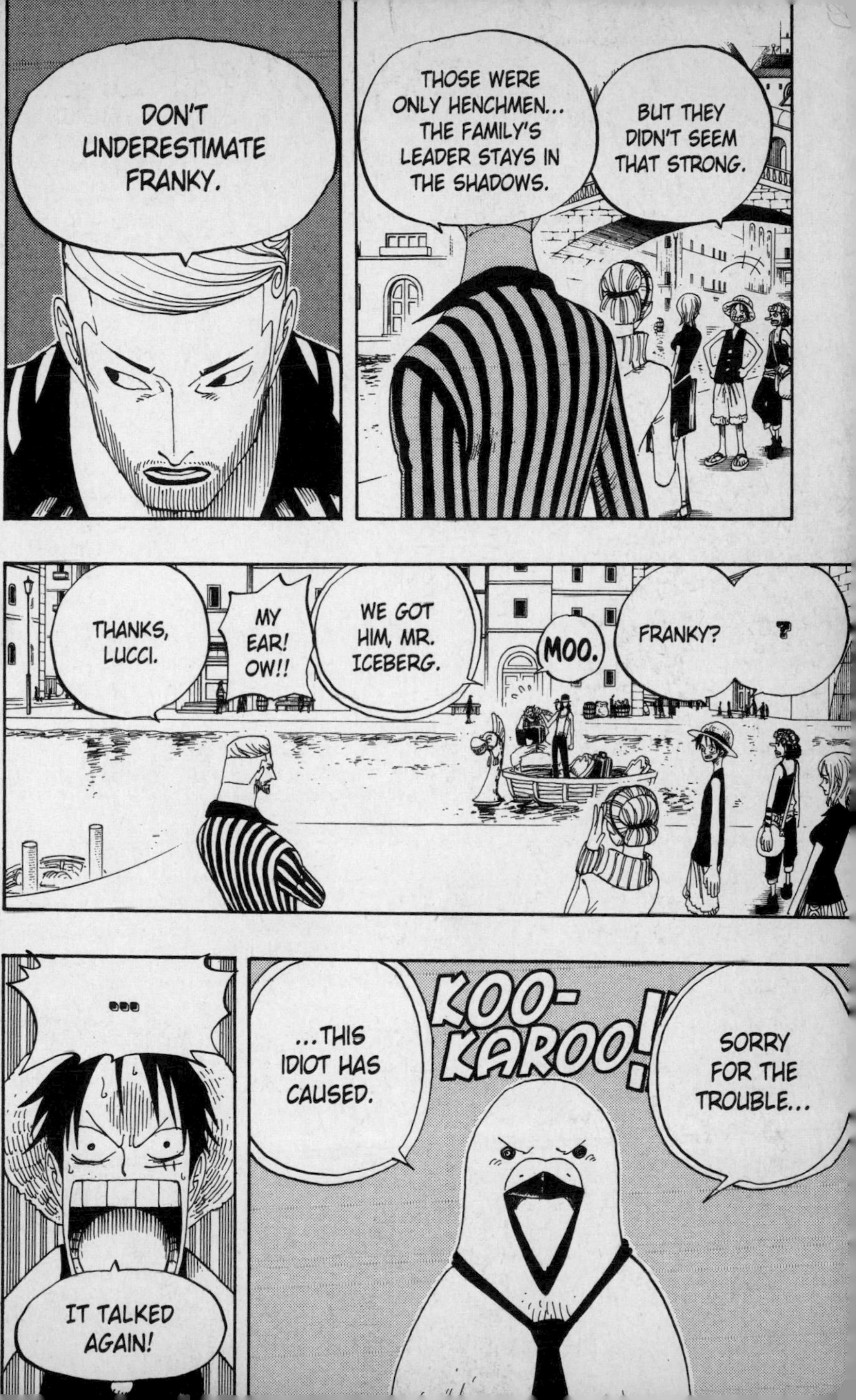
BUT THEY DIDN'T SEEM THAT STRONG.
THOSE WERE ONLY HENCHMEN... THE FAMILY'S LEADER STAYS IN THE SHADOWS.
DON'T UNDERESTIMATE FRANKY.
FRANKY?
?
MOO.
WE GOT HIM, MR. ICEBERG.
MY EAR! OW!!
THANKS, LUCCI.
SORRY FOR THE TROUBLE...
KOO-KAROO!
...THIS IDIOT HAS CAUSED.
...
IT TALKED AGAIN!

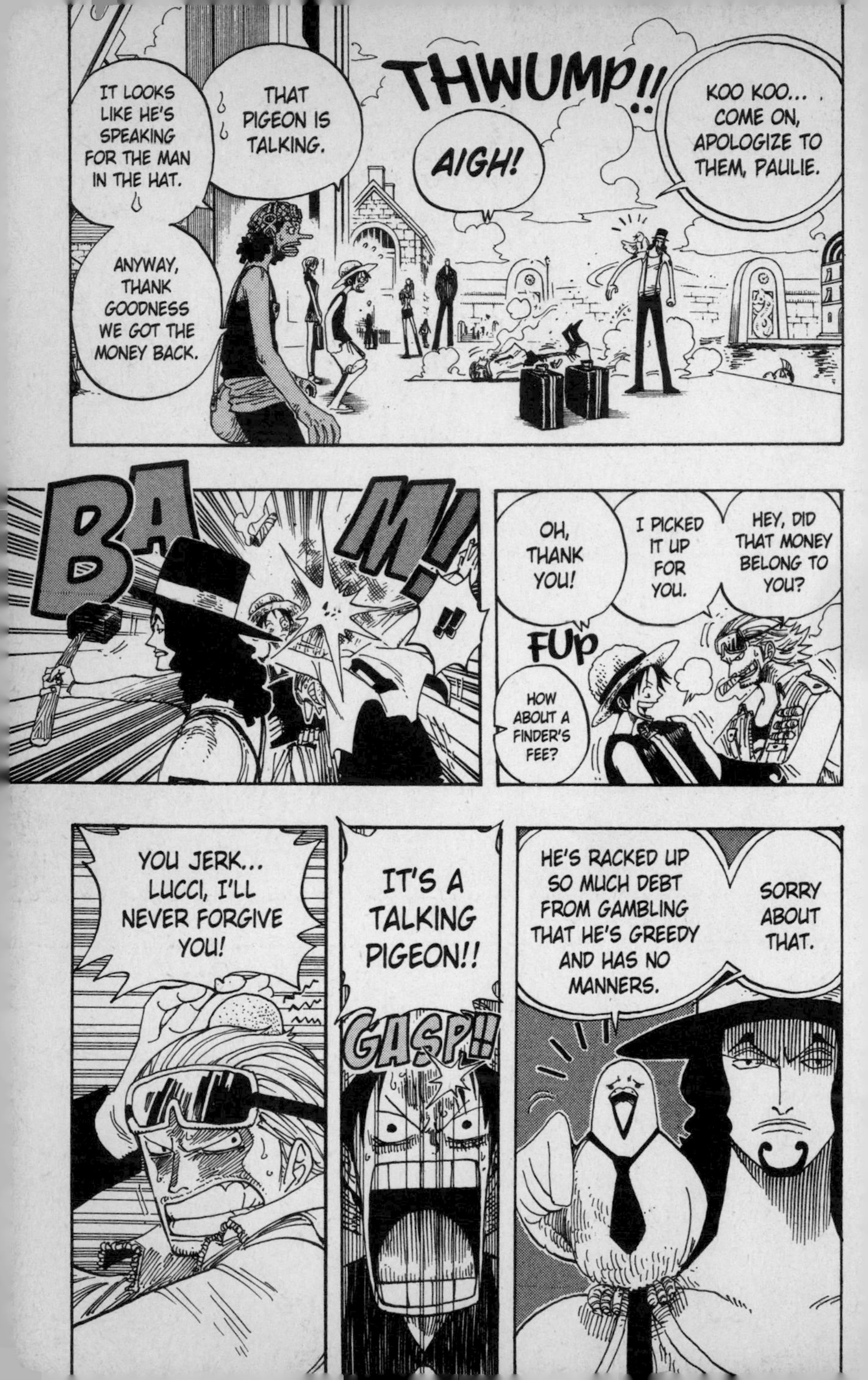
KOO KOO... COME ON, APOLOGIZE TO THEM, PAULIE.
THWUMP!!
AIGH!
THAT PIGEON IS TALKING.
IT LOOKS LIKE HE'S SPEAKING FOR THE MAN IN THE HAT.
ANYWAY, THANK GOODNESS WE GOT THE MONEY BACK.
HEY, DID THAT MONEY BELONG TO YOU?
I PICKED IT UP FOR YOU.
OH, THANK YOU!
FUP
HOW ABOUT A FINDER'S FEE?
BAM!
!!
SORRY ABOUT THAT.
HE'S RACKED UP SO MUCH DEBT FROM GAMBLING THAT HE'S GREEDY AND HAS NO MANNERS.
IT'S A TALKING PIGEON!!
GASP!!
YOU JERK... LUCCI, I'LL NEVER FORGIVE YOU!

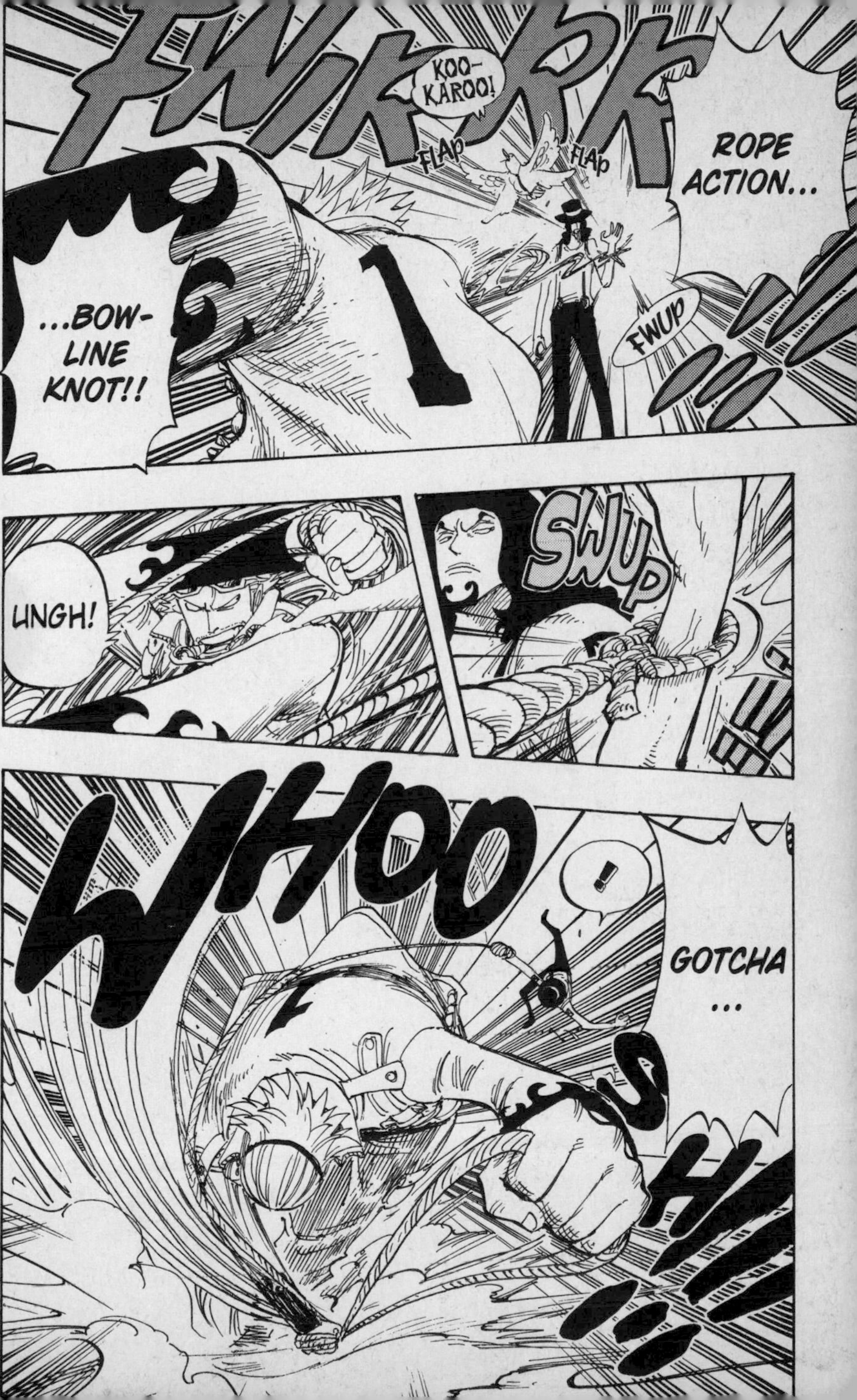
ROPE ACTION...
FWIRRR
KOO-KAROO!
FLAP
FLAP
FWUP
...BOW-LINE KNOT!!
SWUP
UNGH!
!
GOTCHA...
WHOOSH!!

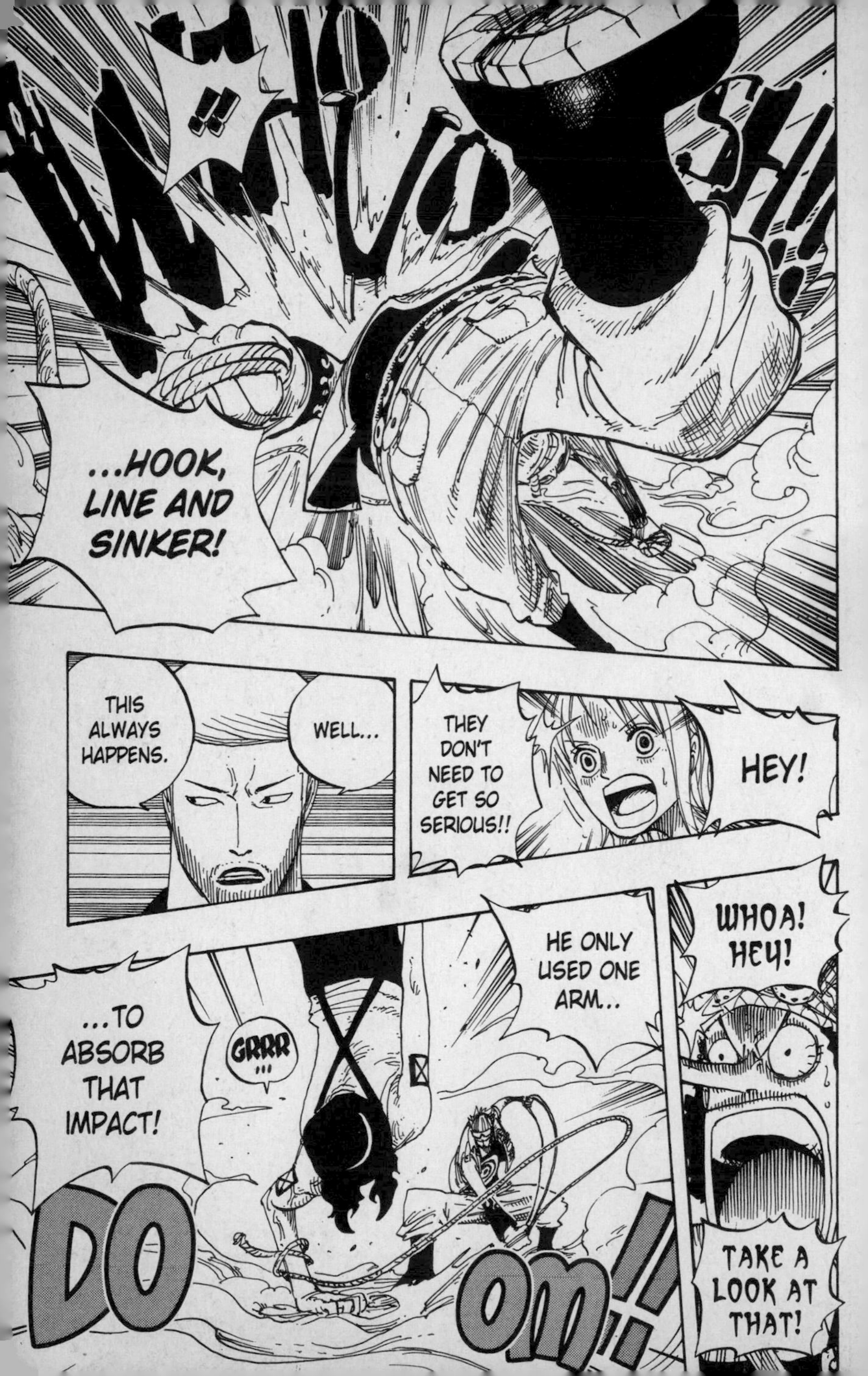
...HOOK, LINE AND SINKER!
HEY!
THEY DON'T NEED TO GET SO SERIOUS!!
WELL...
THIS ALWAYS HAPPENS.
WHOA! HEY!
TAKE A LOOK AT THAT!
HE ONLY USED ONE ARM...
...TO ABSORB THAT IMPACT!
GRRR !!!
DO OM!!

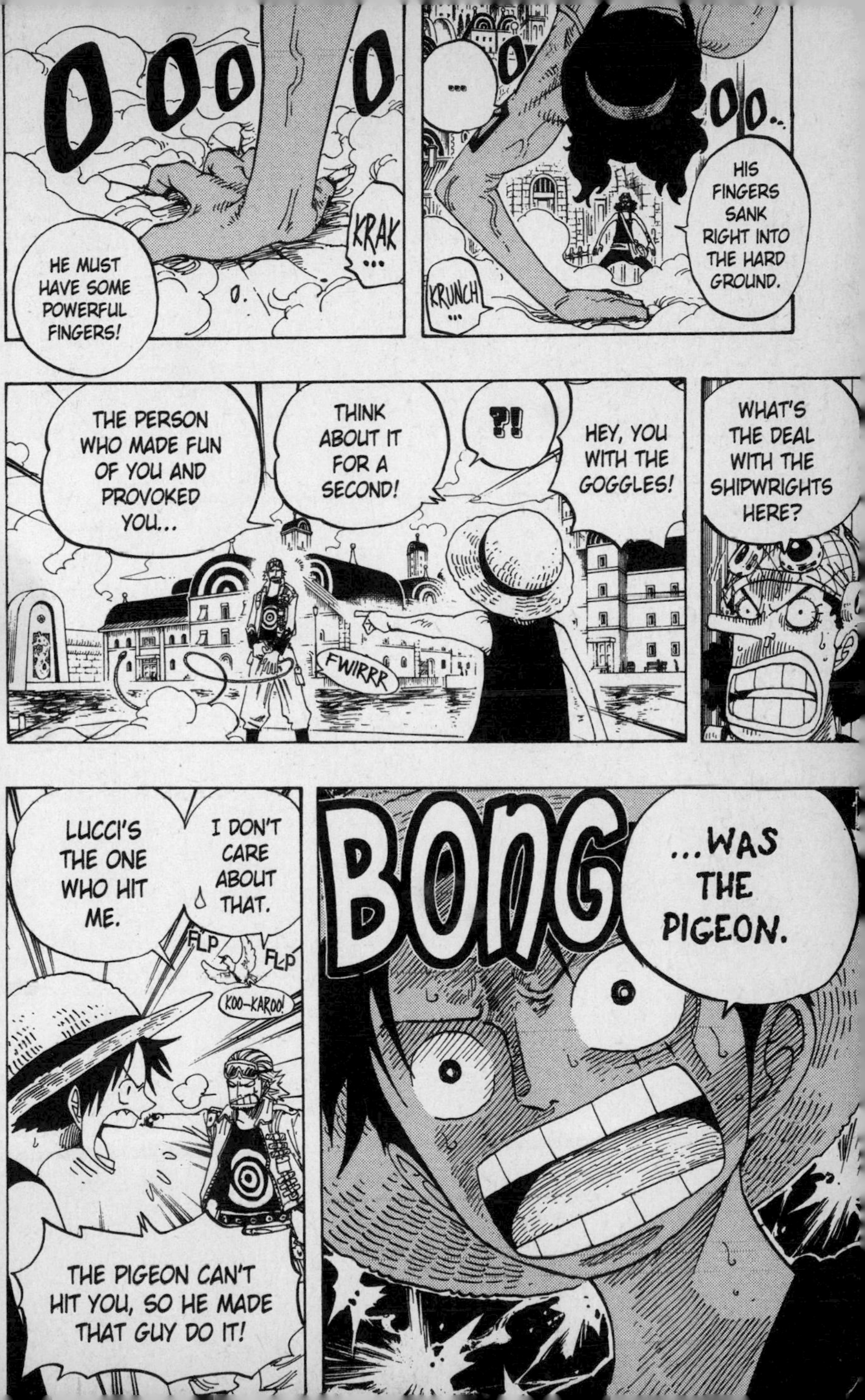
OO..
...
HIS FINGERS SANK RIGHT INTO THE HARD GROUND.
KRUNCH ...
OOOO
KRAK ...
HE MUST HAVE SOME POWERFUL FINGERS!
O.
WHAT'S THE DEAL WITH THE SHIPWRIGHTS HERE?
HEY, YOU WITH THE GOGGLES!
?!
THINK ABOUT IT FOR A SECOND!
THE PERSON WHO MADE FUN OF YOU AND PROVOKED YOU...
FWIRRR
BONG
...WAS THE PIGEON.
I DON'T CARE ABOUT THAT.
LUCCI'S THE ONE WHO HIT ME.
FLP
FLP
KOO-KAROO!
THE PIGEON CAN'T HIT YOU, SO HE MADE THAT GUY DO IT!

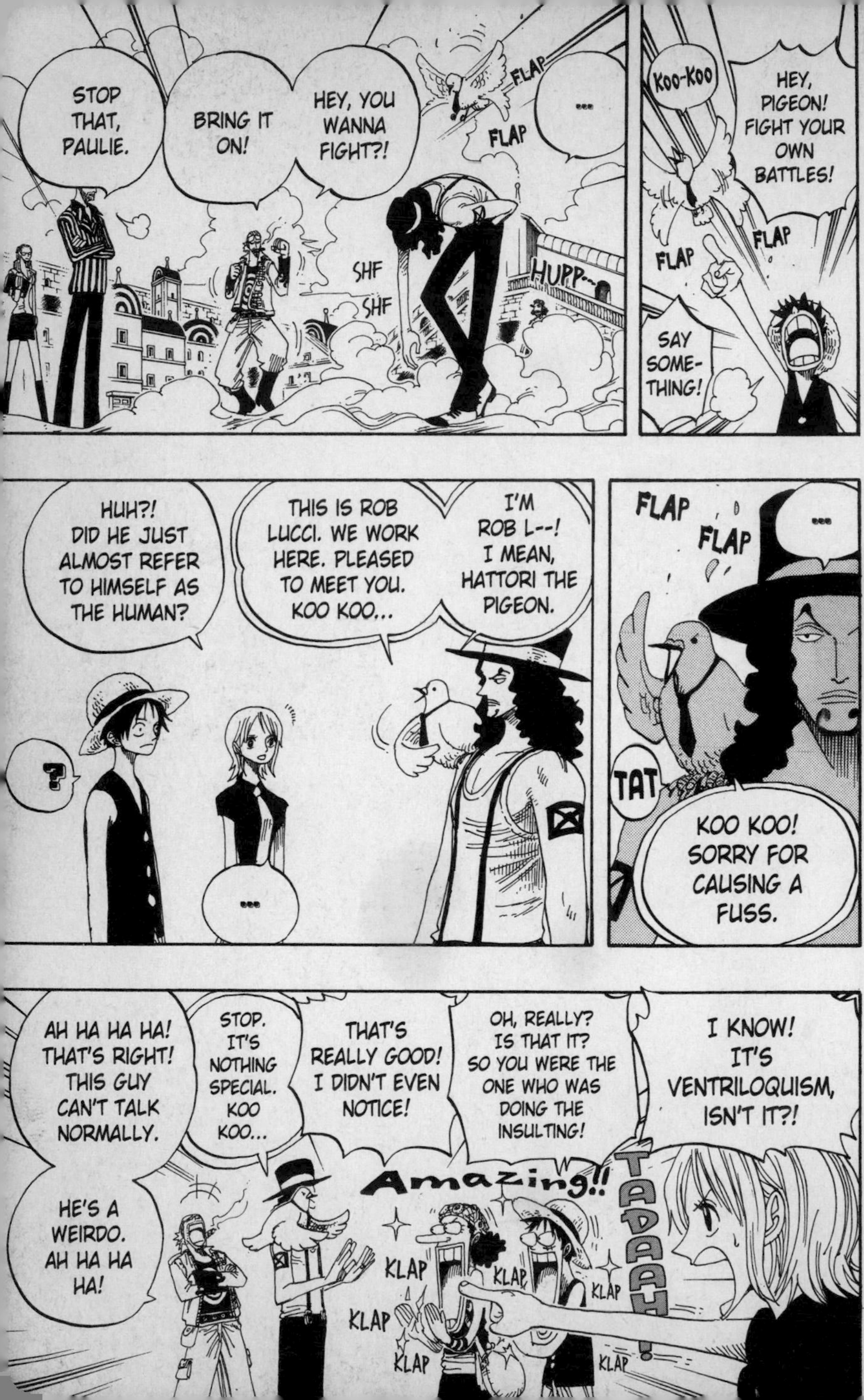
HEY, PIGEON! FIGHT YOUR OWN BATTLES!
KOO-KOO
FLAP
FLAP
SAY SOME-THING!
...
FLAP
FLAP
HEY, YOU WANNA FIGHT?!
BRING IT ON!
STOP THAT, PAULIE.
HUPP...
SHF
SHF
...
FLAP
FLAP
TAT
KOO KOO! SORRY FOR CAUSING A FUSS.
I'M ROB L--! I MEAN, HATTORI THE PIGEON.
THIS IS ROB LUCCI. WE WORK HERE. PLEASED TO MEET YOU. KOO KOO...
HUH?! DID HE JUST ALMOST REFER TO HIMSELF AS THE HUMAN?
?
...
I KNOW! IT'S VENTRILOQUISM, ISN'T IT?!
TADAAH!
OH, REALLY? IS THAT IT? SO YOU WERE THE ONE WHO WAS DOING THE INSULTING!
THAT'S REALLY GOOD! I DIDN'T EVEN NOTICE!
Amazing!!
STOP. IT'S NOTHING SPECIAL. KOO KOO...
AH HA HA HA! THAT'S RIGHT! THIS GUY CAN'T TALK NORMALLY.
HE'S A WEIRDO. AH HA HA HA!
KLAP
KLAP
KLAP
KLAP
KLAP
KLAP

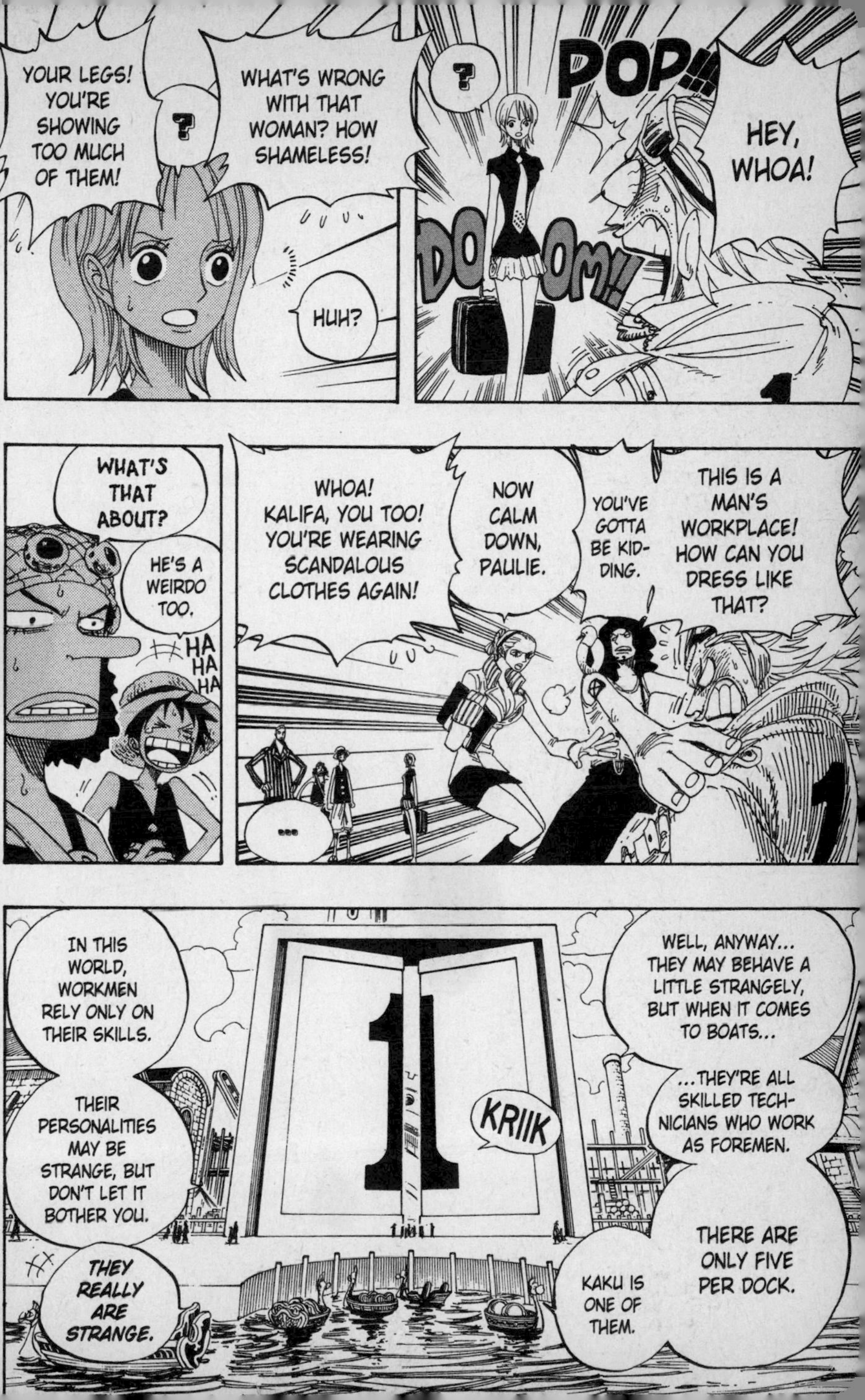
HEY, WHOA!
POP!!
?
DOOM!!
WHAT'S WRONG WITH THAT WOMAN? HOW SHAMELESS!
?
YOUR LEGS! YOU'RE SHOWING TOO MUCH OF THEM!
HUH?
THIS IS A MAN'S WORKPLACE! HOW CAN YOU DRESS LIKE THAT?
YOU'VE GOTTA BE KID-DING.
NOW CALM DOWN, PAULIE.
WHOA! KALIFA, YOU TOO! YOU'RE WEARING SCANDALOUS CLOTHES AGAIN!
!
...
WHAT'S THAT ABOUT?
HE'S A WEIRDO TOO.
HA HA HA
WELL, ANYWAY... THEY MAY BEHAVE A LITTLE STRANGELY, BUT WHEN IT COMES TO BOATS...
...THEY'RE ALL SKILLED TECH-NICIANS WHO WORK AS FOREMEN.
THERE ARE ONLY FIVE PER DOCK.
KAKU IS ONE OF THEM.
KRIIK
IN THIS WORLD, WORKMEN RELY ONLY ON THEIR SKILLS.
THEIR PERSONALITIES MAY BE STRANGE, BUT DON'T LET IT BOTHER YOU.
THEY REALLY ARE STRANGE.

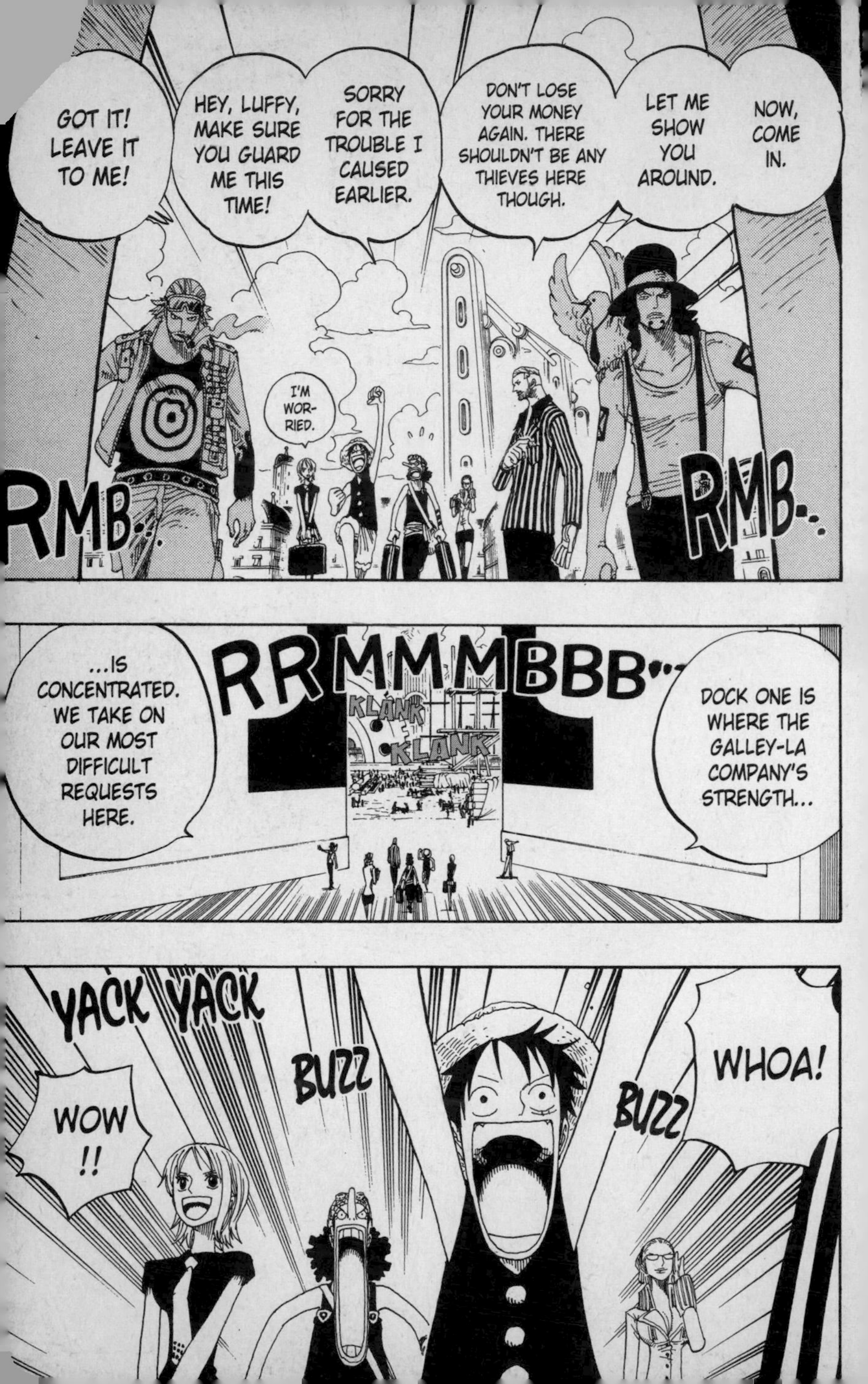
RMB...
NOW, COME IN.
LET ME SHOW YOU AROUND.
DON'T LOSE YOUR MONEY AGAIN. THERE SHOULDN'T BE ANY THIEVES HERE THOUGH.
SORRY FOR THE TROUBLE I CAUSED EARLIER.
HEY, LUFFY, MAKE SURE YOU GUARD ME THIS TIME!
GOT IT! LEAVE IT TO ME!
I'M WOR-RIED.
RMB...
DOCK ONE IS WHERE THE GALLEY-LA COMPANY'S STRENGTH...
RRMMMBBB...
KLANK KLANK
...IS CONCENTRATED. WE TAKE ON OUR MOST DIFFICULT REQUESTS HERE.
WHOA!
BUZZ
BUZZ
WOW!!
YACK YACK

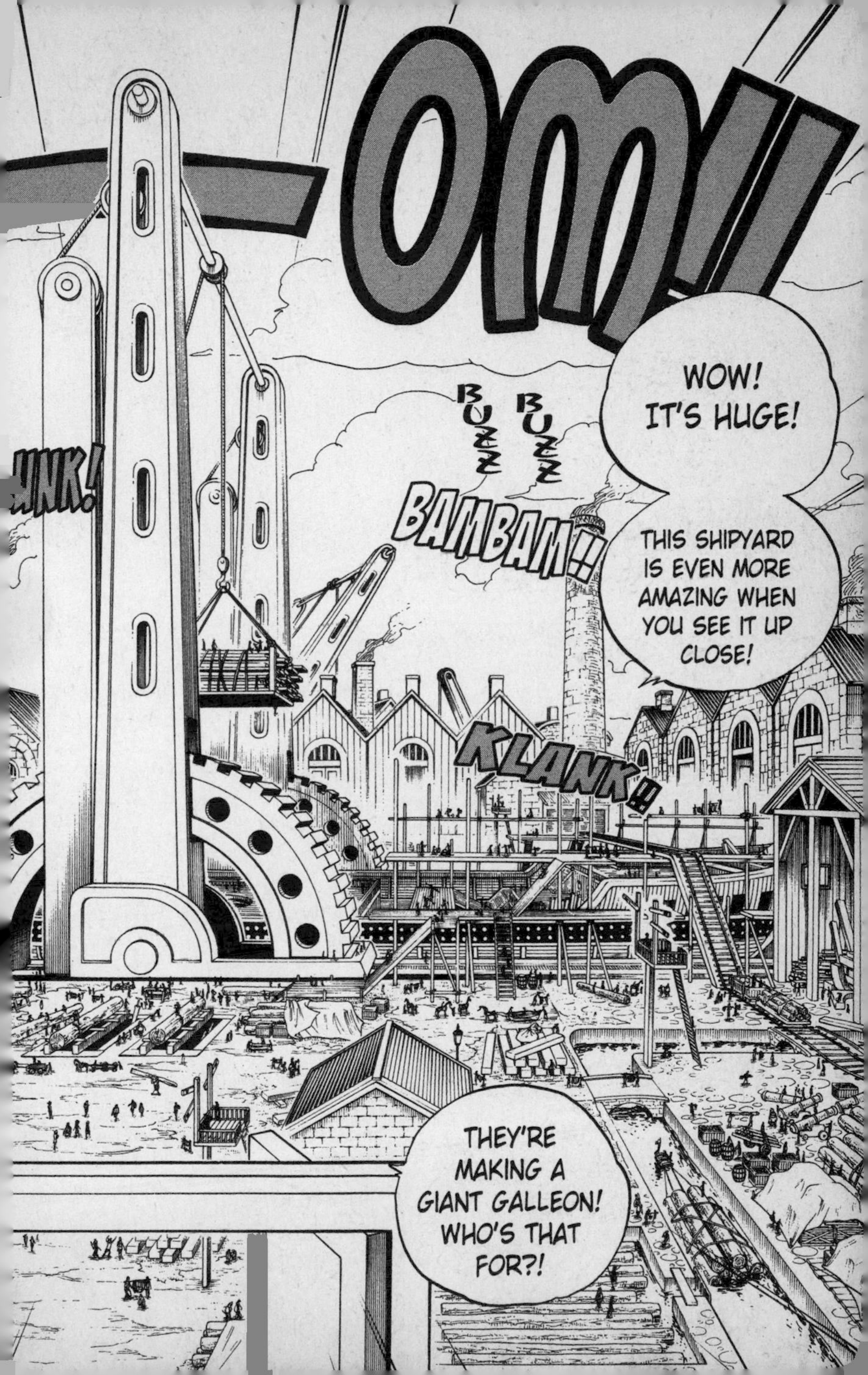
-OOM!!
WOW! IT'S HUGE!
THIS SHIPYARD IS EVEN MORE AMAZING WHEN YOU SEE IT UP CLOSE!
BUZZ BUZZ
BAMBAM!!
KLANK!!
THEY'RE MAKING A GIANT GALLEON! WHO'S THAT FOR?!

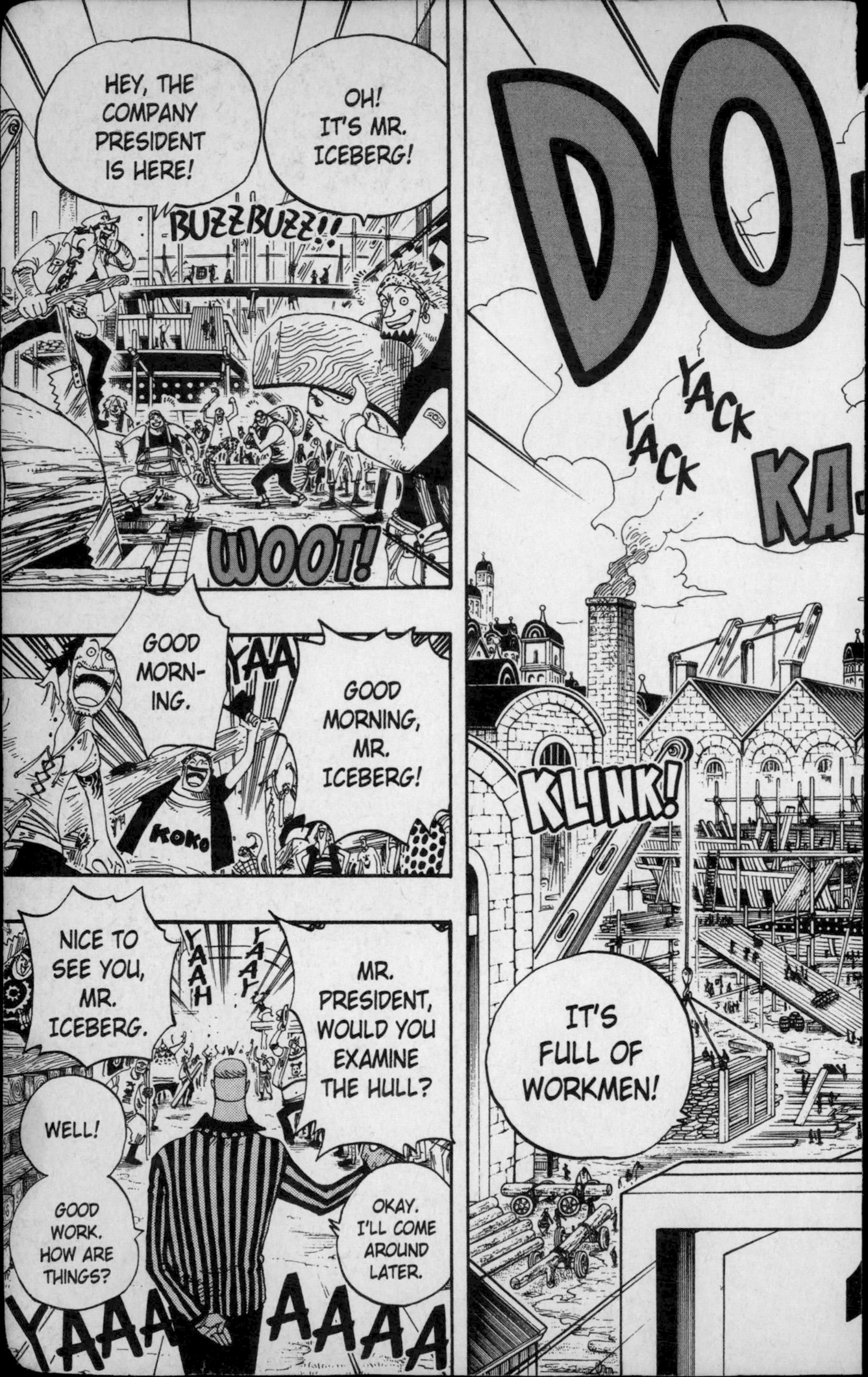
DO-
YACK
YACK
KA-
KLINK!
IT'S FULL OF WORKMEN!
OH! IT'S MR. ICEBERG!
HEY, THE COMPANY PRESIDENT IS HERE!
BUZZBUZZ!!
WOOT!
GOOD MORNING, MR. ICEBERG!
YAAA
GOOD MORN-ING.
KOKO
MR. PRESIDENT, WOULD YOU EXAMINE THE HULL?
YAAY
YAAH
NICE TO SEE YOU, MR. ICEBERG.
WELL!
OKAY. I'LL COME AROUND LATER.
GOOD WORK. HOW ARE THINGS?
YAAAAAAAA

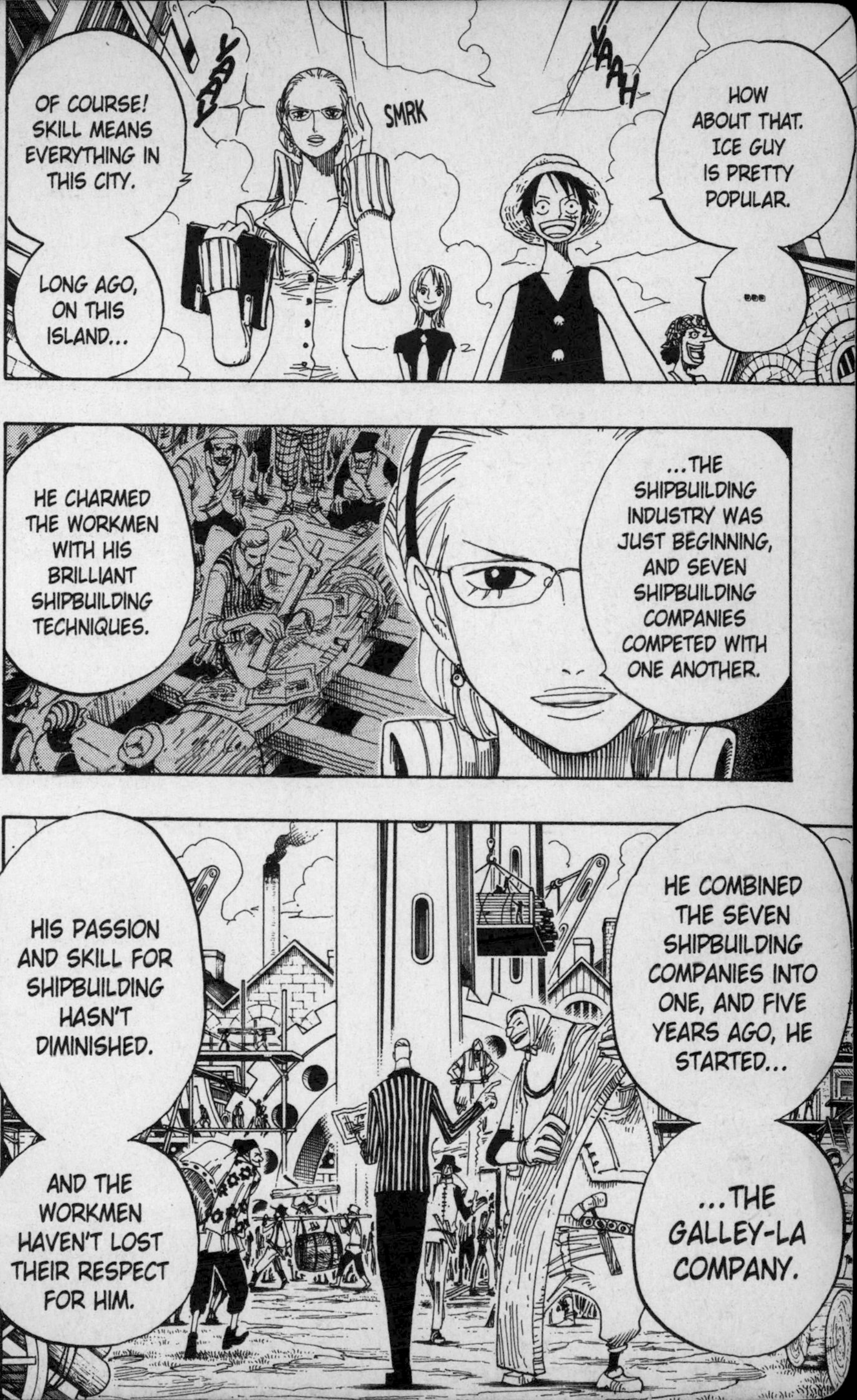
YAAAH
HOW ABOUT THAT. ICE GUY IS PRETTY POPULAR.
...
SMRK
YAAAY
OF COURSE! SKILL MEANS EVERYTHING IN THIS CITY.
LONG AGO, ON THIS ISLAND...
...THE SHIPBUILDING INDUSTRY WAS JUST BEGINNING, AND SEVEN SHIPBUILDING COMPANIES COMPETED WITH ONE ANOTHER.
HE CHARMED THE WORKMEN WITH HIS BRILLIANT SHIPBUILDING TECHNIQUES.
HE COMBINED THE SEVEN SHIPBUILDING COMPANIES INTO ONE, AND FIVE YEARS AGO, HE STARTED...
...THE GALLEY-LA COMPANY.
HIS PASSION AND SKILL FOR SHIPBUILDING HASN'T DIMINISHED.
AND THE WORKMEN HAVEN'T LOST THEIR RESPECT FOR HIM.

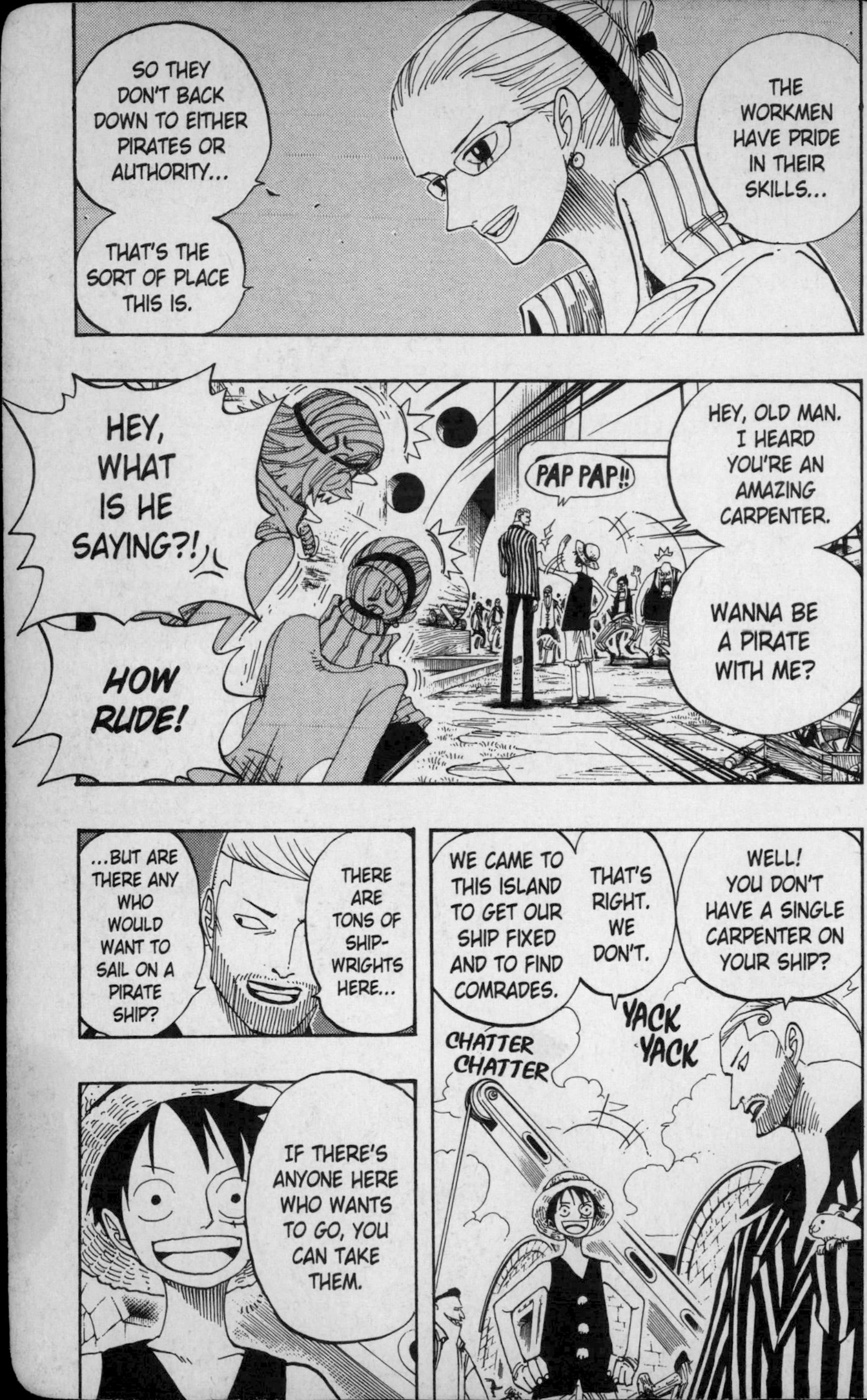
THE WORKMEN HAVE PRIDE IN THEIR SKILLS...
SO THEY DON'T BACK DOWN TO EITHER PIRATES OR AUTHORITY...
THAT'S THE SORT OF PLACE THIS IS.
HEY, OLD MAN. I HEARD YOU'RE AN AMAZING CARPENTER.
WANNA BE A PIRATE WITH ME?
PAP PAP!!
HEY, WHAT IS HE SAYING?!
HOW RUDE!
WELL! YOU DON'T HAVE A SINGLE CARPENTER ON YOUR SHIP?
THAT'S RIGHT. WE DON'T.
WE CAME TO THIS ISLAND TO GET OUR SHIP FIXED AND TO FIND COMRADES.
YACK YACK
CHATTER CHATTER
THERE ARE TONS OF SHIP-WRIGHTS HERE...
...BUT ARE THERE ANY WHO WOULD WANT TO SAIL ON A PIRATE SHIP?
IF THERE'S ANYONE HERE WHO WANTS TO GO, YOU CAN TAKE THEM.

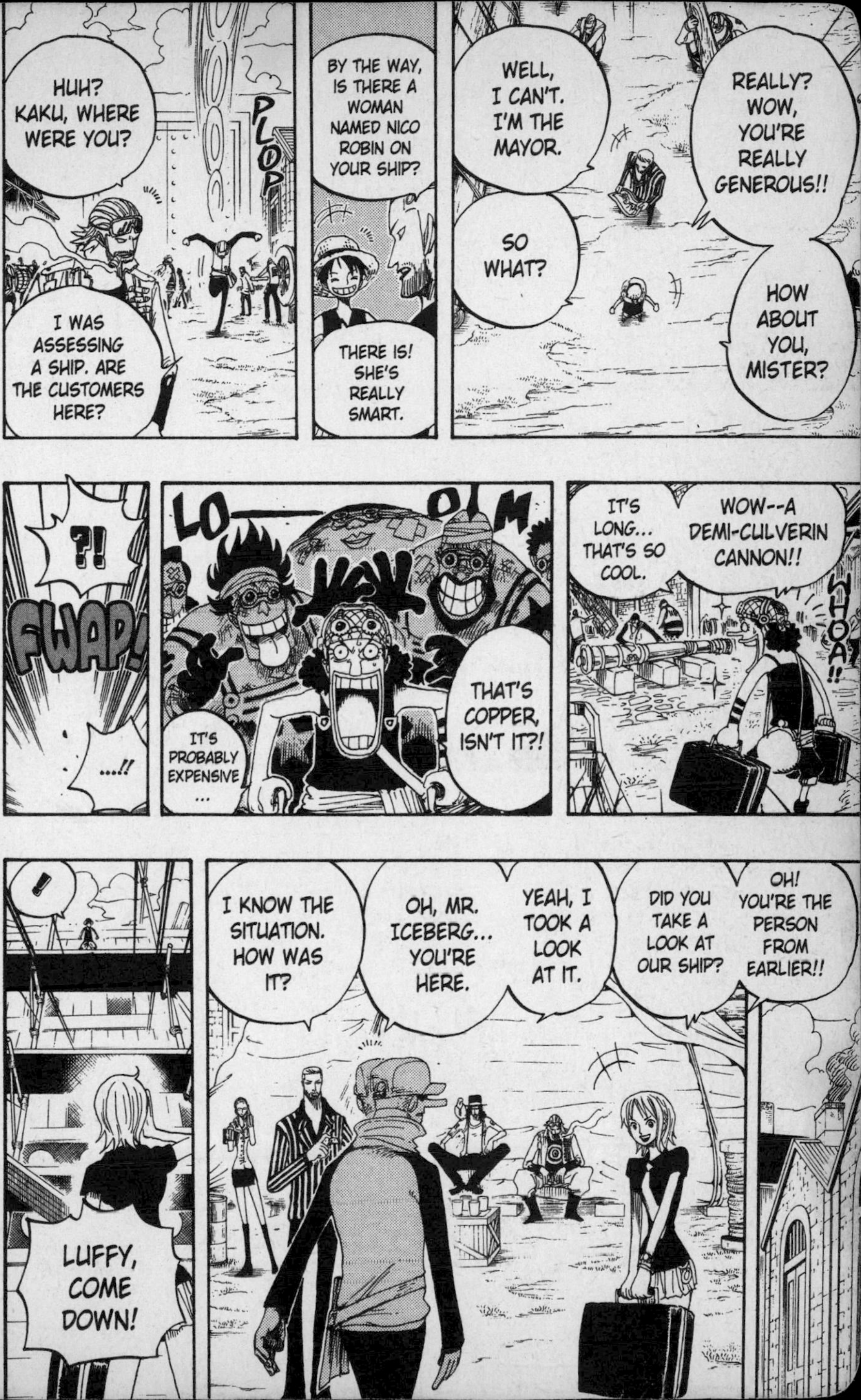
REALLY? WOW, YOU'RE REALLY GENEROUS!!
WELL, I CAN'T. I'M THE MAYOR.
HOW ABOUT YOU, MISTER?
SO WHAT?
BY THE WAY, IS THERE A WOMAN NAMED NICO ROBIN ON YOUR SHIP?
THERE IS! SHE'S REALLY SMART.
PLOP
HUH? KAKU, WHERE WERE YOU?
I WAS ASSESSING A SHIP. ARE THE CUSTOMERS HERE?
WOW--A DEMI-CULVERIN CANNON!!
IT'S LONG... THAT'S SO COOL.
WHOA!!
LO—OM
THAT'S COPPER, ISN'T IT?!
IT'S PROBABLY EXPENSIVE ...
?!
FWAP!
...!!
OH! YOU'RE THE PERSON FROM EARLIER!!
DID YOU TAKE A LOOK AT OUR SHIP?
YEAH, I TOOK A LOOK AT IT.
OH, MR. ICEBERG... YOU'RE HERE.
I KNOW THE SITUATION. HOW WAS IT?
!
LUFFY, COME DOWN!

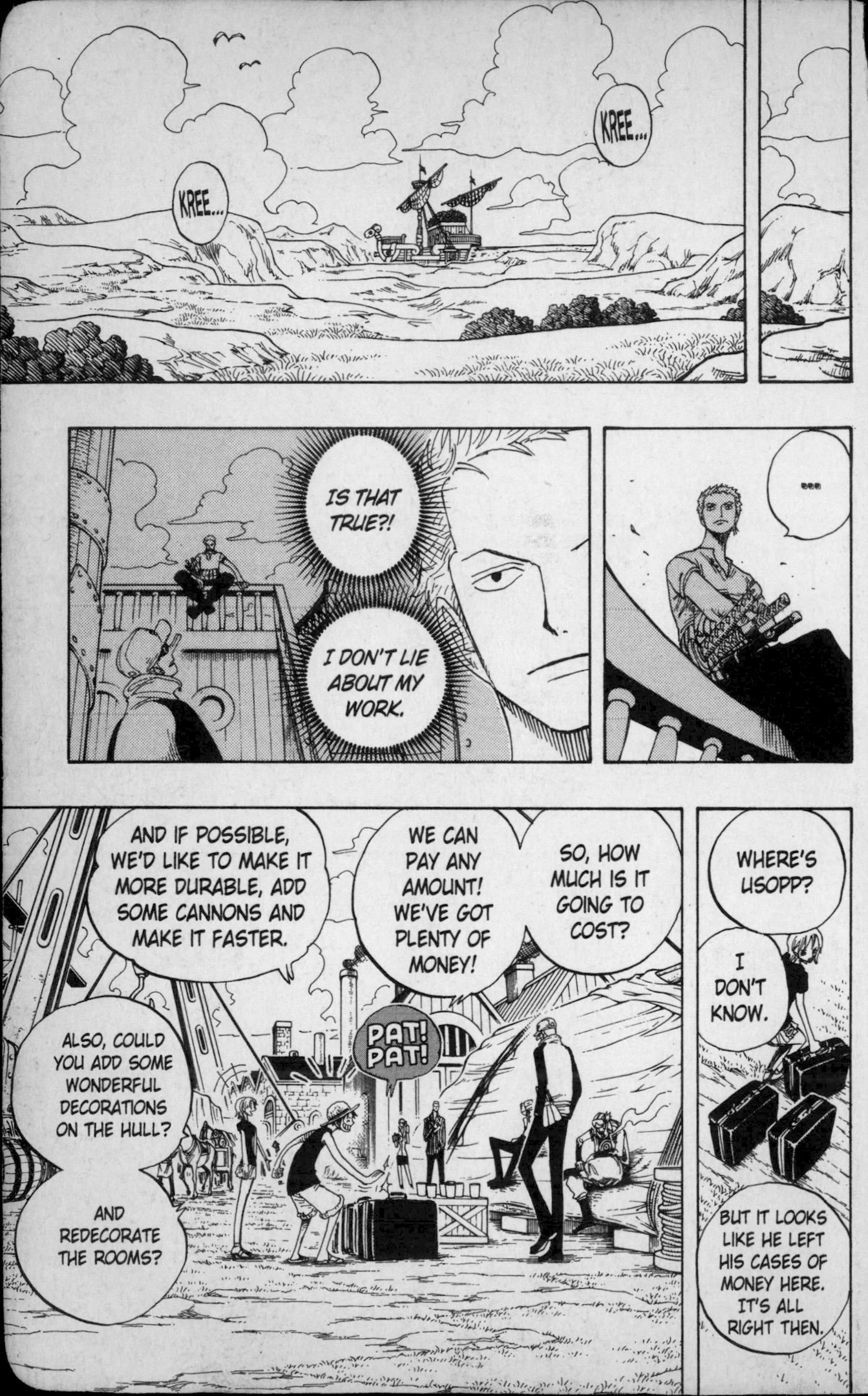

KREE...
KREE...
...
IS THAT TRUE?!
I DON'T LIE ABOUT MY WORK.
WHERE'S USOPP?
I DON'T KNOW.
BUT IT LOOKS LIKE HE LEFT HIS CASES OF MONEY HERE. IT'S ALL RIGHT THEN.
SO, HOW MUCH IS IT GOING TO COST?
WE CAN PAY ANY AMOUNT! WE'VE GOT PLENTY OF MONEY!
AND IF POSSIBLE, WE'D LIKE TO MAKE IT MORE DURABLE, ADD SOME CANNONS AND MAKE IT FASTER.
PAT! PAT!
ALSO, COULD YOU ADD SOME WONDERFUL DECORATIONS ON THE HULL?
AND REDECORATE THE ROOMS?

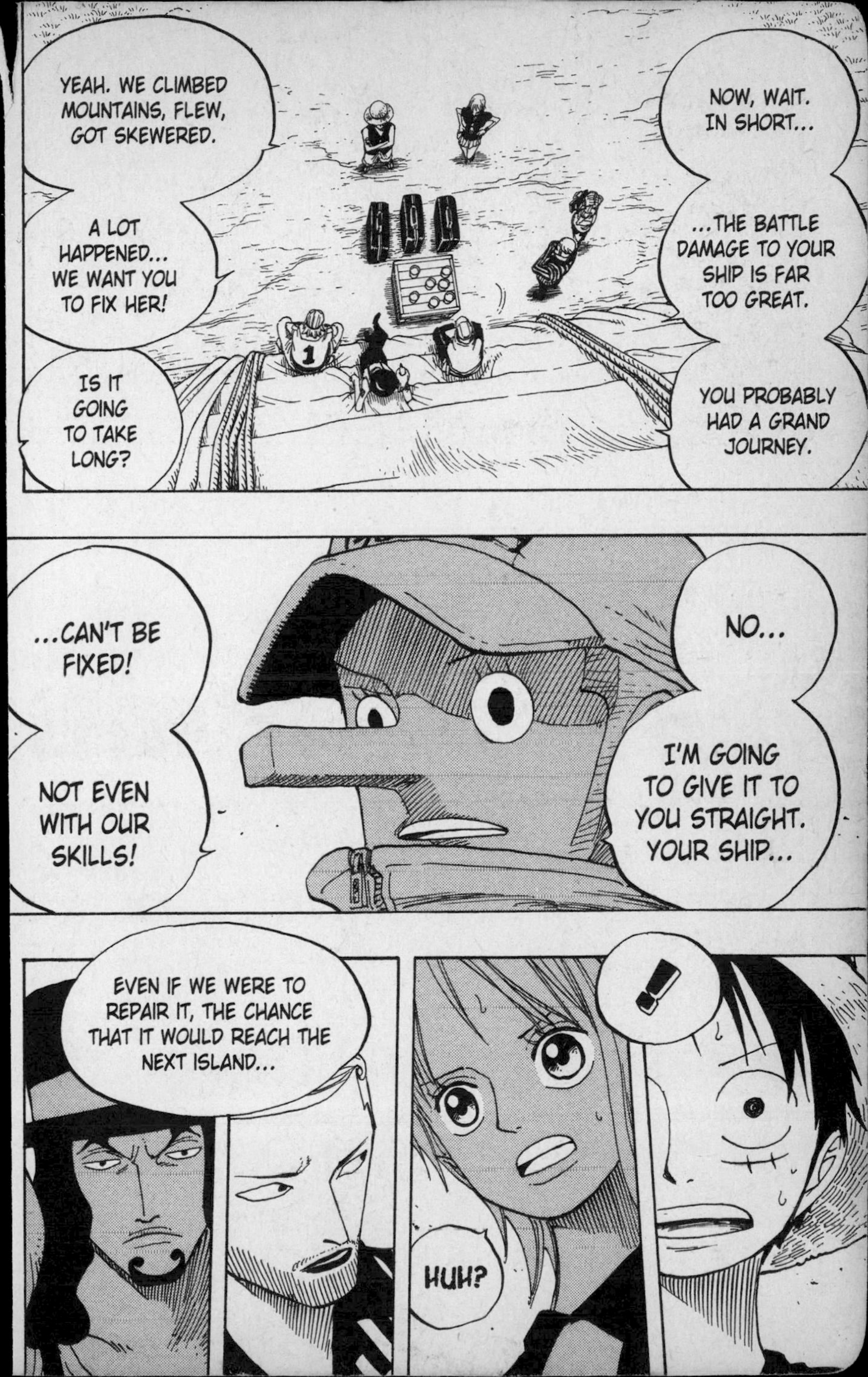
NOW, WAIT. IN SHORT...
...THE BATTLE DAMAGE TO YOUR SHIP IS FAR TOO GREAT.
YOU PROBABLY HAD A GRAND JOURNEY.
YEAH. WE CLIMBED MOUNTAINS, FLEW, GOT SKEWERED.
A LOT HAPPENED... WE WANT YOU TO FIX HER!
IS IT GOING TO TAKE LONG?
NO...
I'M GOING TO GIVE IT TO YOU STRAIGHT. YOUR SHIP...
...CAN'T BE FIXED!
NOT EVEN WITH OUR SKILLS!
!
HUH?
EVEN IF WE WERE TO REPAIR IT, THE CHANCE THAT IT WOULD REACH THE NEXT ISLAND...

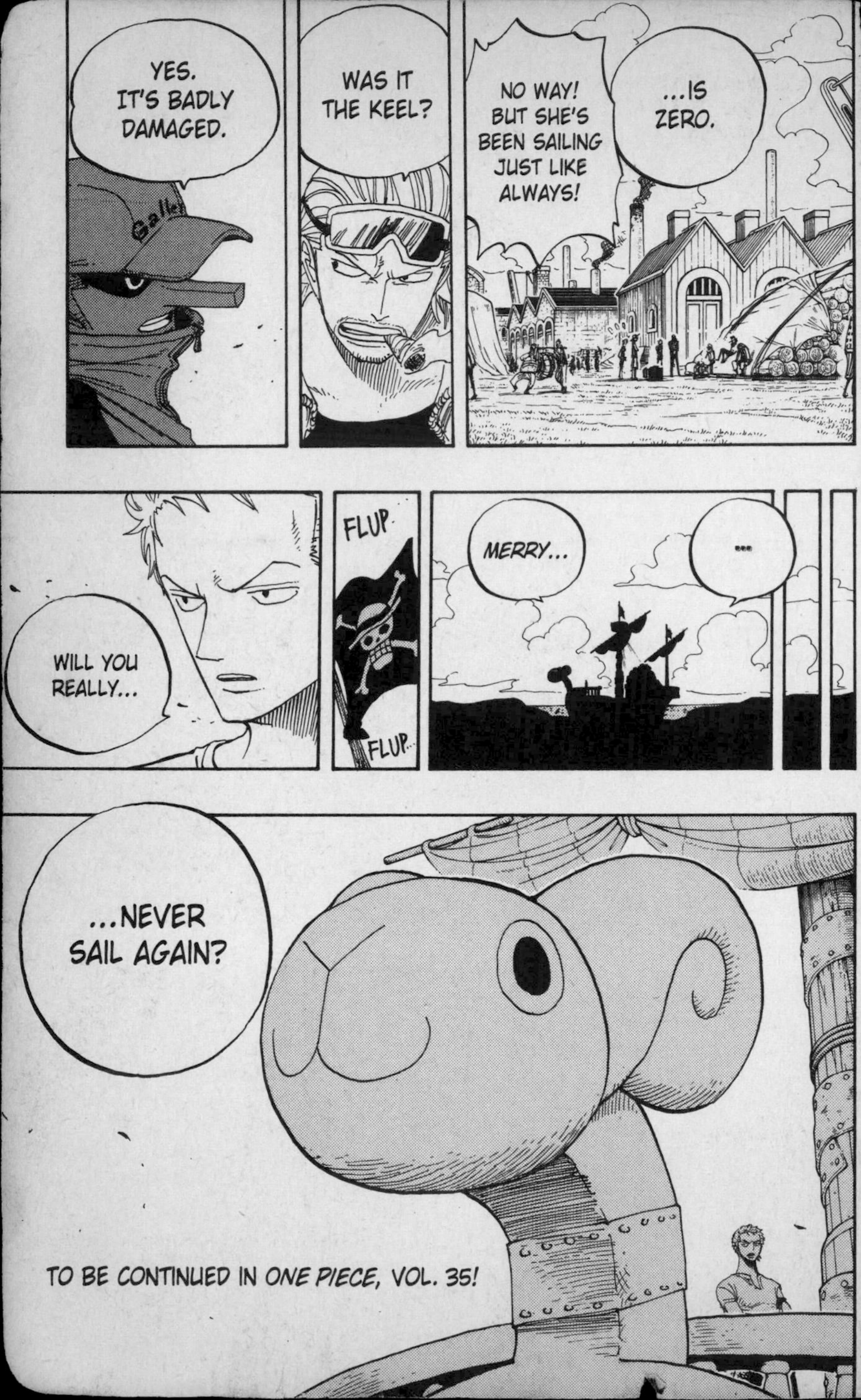
...IS ZERO.
NO WAY! BUT SHE'S BEEN SAILING JUST LIKE ALWAYS!
WAS IT THE KEEL?
YES. IT'S BADLY DAMAGED.
...
MERRY...
FLUP
FLUP...
WILL YOU REALLY...
...NEVER SAIL AGAIN?
TO BE CONTINUED IN ONE PIECE, VOL. 35!

COMING NEXT VOLUME:

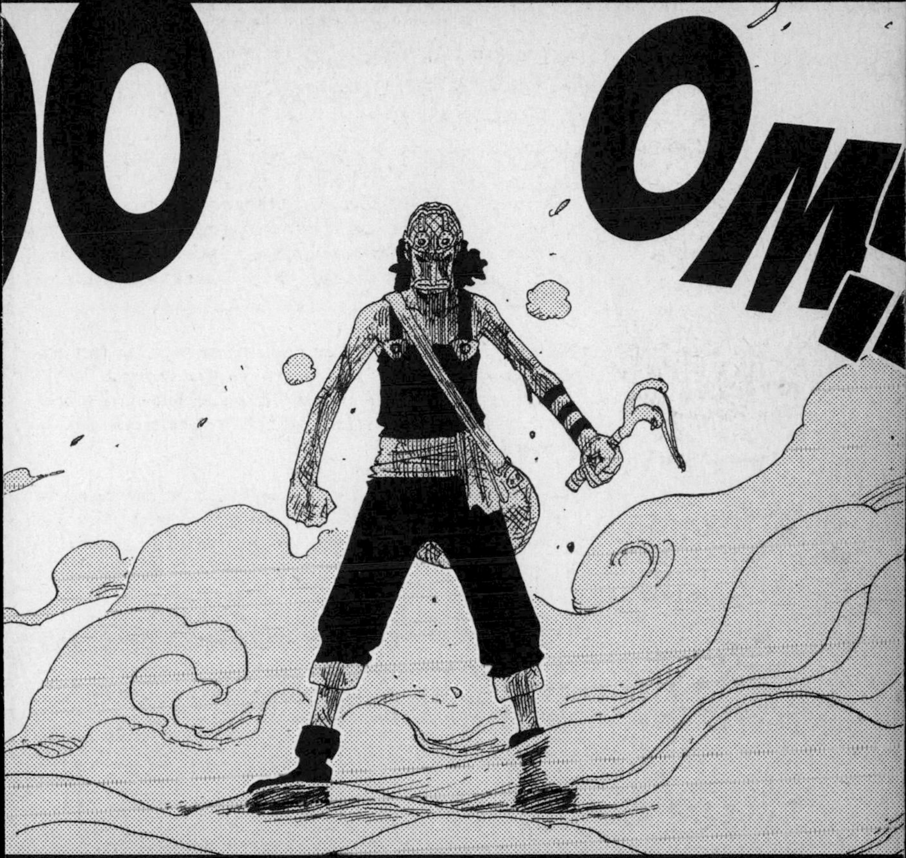

Luffy and Usopp try to find a way to repair the *Merry Go*, but after Usopp is attacked and the money they had saved to repair the ship is stolen, Luffy must make the most difficult decision as captain yet. What will become of their beloved ship? And where did Nico Robin go?

AVAILABLE NOW!

Set Sail with

Read all about **MONKEY D. LUFFY**'s adventures as he sails around the world assembling a motley crew to join him on his search for the legendary treasure **"ONE PIECE."** For more information, check out **onepiece.viz.com.**

EAST BLUE
(Vols. 1-12)
Available now!

See where it all began! One man, a dinghy and a dream. Or rather… a rubber man who can't swim, setting out in a tiny boat on the vast seas without any navigational skills. What are the odds that his dream of becoming King of the Pirates will ever come true?

BAROQUE WORKS
(Vols. 12-24)
Available now!

Friend or foe? Ms. Wednesday is part of a group of bounty hunters—or isn't she? The Straw Hats get caught up in a civil war when they find a princess in their midst. But can they help her stop the revolution in her home country before the evil Crocodile gets his way?!

SKYPIEA
(Vols. 24-32)
Available now!

Luffy's quest to become King of the Pirates and find the elusive treasure known as "One Piece" continues…in the sky! The Straw Hats sail to Skypiea, an airborne island in the midst of a territorial war and ruled by a short-fused megalomaniac!

WATER SEVEN
(Vols. 32-46)
Available from February 2010!

The *Merry Go* has been a stalwart for the Straw Hats since the beginning, but countless battles have taken their toll on the ship. Luckily, their next stop is Water Seven, where a rough-and-tumble crew of shipwrights awaits their arrival!

THRILLER BARK
(Vols. 46-50)
Available from May 2010!

Luffy and crew get more than they bargained for when their ship is drawn toward haunted Thriller Bark. When Gecko Moria, one of the Warlords of the Sea, steals the crew's shadows, they'll have to get them back before the sun rises or else they'll all turn into zombies!

SABAODY
(Vols. 50-54)
Available from June 2010!

On the way to Fish-Man Island, the Straw Hats disembark on the Sabaody archipelago to get soaped up for their undersea adventure! But it's not too long before they get caught up in trouble! Luffy's made an enemy of an exalted World Noble when he saves Camie the mermaid from being sold on the slave market, and now he's got the Navy after him too!

IMPEL DOWN
(from Vol. 54)
Available from July 2010!

Luffy's brother Ace is about to be executed! Held in the Navy's maximum security prison Impel Down, Luffy needs to find a way to break in to help Ace escape. But with murderous fiends for guards inside, the notorious prisoners start to seem not so bad. Some are even friendly enough to give Luffy a helping hand!

Tell us what you

SHONEN JUM

Our survey is now available online.
Go to: www.SHONENJUMP.com/mangasurvey

Help us make our product offering better!

THE REAL ACTION STARTS IN...

SHONEN JUMP
THE WORLD'S MOST POPULAR MANGA
www.shonenjump.com